THE PROLETARIANIZING

OF THE FONCTIONNAIRES

THE PROLETARIANIZING
OF THE FONCTIONNAIRES

Civil Service Workers and the Labor Movement

Under the Third Republic

JUDITH WISHNIA

LOUISIANA STATE UNIVERSITY PRESS

Baton Rouge and London

Copyright © 1990 by Louisiana State University Press
All rights reserved
Manufactured in the United States of America
First printing
99 98 97 96 95 94 93 92 91 90   5 4 3 2 1

Designer: Laura Roubique Gleason
Typeface: Bembo
Typesetter: G&S Typesetters, Inc.
Printer and binder: Thomson-Shore, Inc.

LIBRARY OF CONGRESS CATALOGING-IN-PUBLICATION DATA

Wishnia, Judith.
   The proletarianizing of the fonctionnaires : civil service workers and the labor
movement under the Third Republic / Judith Wishnia.
      p.   cm.
   Includes bibliographical references and index.
   ISBN 0-8071-1590-8 (alk. paper) ISBN 0-8071-1659-9 (pbk.: alk. paper)
      1. Trade-unions—Government employees—France—History.
   2. France—Politics and government—1870–1940.   I. Title.
   HD8005.2.F7W57   1990
   331.88'1135444—dc20
                                                          90-6064
                                                          CIP

The paper in this book meets the guidelines for permanence and durability of the Committee
on Production Guidelines for Book Longevity of the Council on Library Resources. ∞

Aux Camarades des PTT

Contents

Acknowledgments

Although the long hours of research and writing must necessarily be done by the lone scholar, any work of scholarship is a communal activity based not only on the work of those who have gone before but on the interchange of ideas with friends and associates. I would like to express my gratitude to the community of family, friends, and colleagues who gave me their intellectual and personal support.

I thank my husband, Arnold, for his devoted support and belief in my intellectual abilities and independence. I never cease to be amazed at his wide knowledge in fields other than his own beloved science. He did not type this manuscript, but he burned many a midnight candle rescuing me from computer errors. I thank my sons, Steven, David, and Kenneth, for the love and respect they gave, for the thousands of dishes washed, for proving, as they grew to be intelligent, sensitive, and creative men, that it was all worthwhile. I thank them also for bringing into my life Carol and Mercy and, of course, my wonderful grandchildren, Ian, Karen Ann, Leah Victoria, and Jeremy.

Among my colleagues and friends, Herman (Gene) Lebovics always asked the right questions and gave the right answers; Richard F. Kuisel provided careful criticism that made me tighten, justify, and clarify my thinking and writing; Robert O. Paxton first kindled my interest in French history, and his historical breadth of vision has served as a role model for me; Konrad F. Bieber gave warm friendship and scholarly guidance and helped me develop a love for and understanding of French civilization; Judith Stone read my writing and provided valuable and intelligent comments; and the late Sanford Elwitt, whose groundbreaking books on the Third Republic will serve generations of French historians, gave a most careful and perceptive reading of my manuscript.

My university, the State University of New York at Stony Brook, has been most supportive. I am grateful for a summer research grant and for a wonderful library staff, especially the people in interlibrary loan who saved me several trips to distant libraries by graciously and efficiently getting me obscure books and articles. I would also like to thank Joel Rosenthal and Eli Seifman for their encouragement and support.

A grant from the American Council of Learned Societies enabled me to do the research for the last three chapters of the book; I thank the council.

I would like to thank the following people for helping my research in France: Professor Marcel Piquemal of the University of Dijon for enlightening discussion based on his own research and for his invaluable aid in introducing me to most of the leading syndicalists of the fonctionnaire movement; the late professor Jean Maitron, for the hours he took from his own work to discuss my research with enthusiasm and for his permission to use the archives at the Syndicalist Library; to Colette Chambelland of the Musée Social and the librarians and archivists at the Archives Nationales and the Institut Français d'Histoire Social.

To all the activists of the syndicats where I did my research, to the Fédération des Fonctionnaires, the Finance Workers, and those of the PTT I express gratitude: MM. Georges Frischmann, François Mercier, René Crenier, Louis Viannet, Albert Le Guern, and, of course, dozens of others, the dactylos, *les retraités,* and other syndicalists. The long hours we spent, often in cafés, discussing politics and history, not only helped me understand fonctionnaire consciousness more than any archival material could, but it gave me lasting friendships.

Finally, I would like to thank my late father. We often disagreed about politics, but it was his fierce pride in being a worker and his devotion to his own organization, the International Typographical Union, that helped forge my social conscience. I like to think he would have been proud of this effort.

Abbreviations

Note on Italicization of French Terms

To avoid confusion and inexact translations, the following French terms are used throughout the text. Their American approximations are also given.

Fonctionnaires—civil service workers
Syndicat—union
Le droit syndical—the legal right to unionize

These and other frequently used French terms are italicized in their first usage only. Less frequently used French words or phrases are italicized throughout the text.

THE PROLETARIANIZING
OF THE FONCTIONNAIRES

Introduction

The birth of the Third Republic was prolonged and difficult. But by 1884, when legislation permitting the unionization of workers in industry and agriculture was passed, the crucial first stage in the formation of a republic based on a "stable bourgeois social order" was over.[1] In the following years, while public attention was captured by the flamboyant affairs of Dreyfus and Boulanger and the Panama scandal, the basic patterns of the new conservative Republic were set. It was in this period that the forms of bourgeois democracy were forged and its influence extended, political parties and alliances developed, church and state separated, and social reform begun, albeit slowly and belatedly. It was also a period when the continued growth of industry drew more and more workers into the mines and mills of France.

With the growth of political democracy and the expansion of industry, two more developments occurred. One was the organization of the blue-collar working class through the founding and growth of the Confédération Générale du Travail (CGT), the spread of revolutionary syndicalism, and the growing militancy and strikes that marked the domestic scene of Third Republic France. Although the bourgeoisie and some sections of agriculture had a tenuous economic and political alliance, a major problem remained—how to respond to increasing working-class demands for economic and political change. The crucial problem of the young Third Republic was not the resolution of the church-state controversy but the nature of working-class participation in the political system. This issue was to dominate domestic politics until the fall of the Republic in 1940. Although it maintained a strong attachment to the re-

1. For an excellent analysis of this period, see Sanford Elwitt, *The Making of the Third Republic: Class and Politics in France, 1868–1884* (Baton Rouge, 1975).

publican form of government, the working-class movement, theoretically revolutionary syndicalist in the years before World War I, was at
first alienated from the state and the political parties. As the unions, the
syndicats, developed, there was a fierce struggle between the syndicats
and the state, marked by the strikes and violence of the pre–World War I
era. But as the syndicalists grew in number, they also grew more reformist, allying themselves with political parties and giving up the ideology of the revolutionary general strike. This does not mean that there
ceased to be a struggle between the state and the working class; the
struggle had become more systematized, more institutionalized.

The second new development was the growth and spread of state service, *la fonction publique,* and the ensuing increase in the number of civil
service workers, *les fonctionnaires.* The Third Republic, committed to
serving the growing needs of an urbanizing and industrializing nation
and heir to the highly centralized state of the two Napoleons, expanded
government monopolies and public service, and hence government employment, at a breathtaking pace. The extension of such traditional state
functions as finance, taxation, and postal service was combined with the
establishment of state control over such new services as telephone and
telegraph. The separation of church and state and the commitment of
the young Republic to secular education brought thousands more into
the state-run school system. Many of these new fonctionnaires were
women. Urbanization fostered rapid growth of the police forces and of
the new systems of transportation and utilities, adding even more workers to the public sector. The nationalization of part of the railroads before World War I began a process of industrial nationalization that was to
add even more workers to the state's domain. Inheriting a bureaucracy
of approximately two hundred thousand, the Republic had quintupled
that number by the first decade of the new century. In little over a generation, the state had emerged as the most formidable of employers.

The subject of this book is the fonctionnaires and the development of
their class consciousness and organization, their struggle for the right to
unionize, to form syndicats, their search for a political identity and
ideology, their eventual alliance with the blue-collar working class,
and their emergence as a major force within the CGT and in national
politics.

The extent of the state's involvement in public service and employment and the fonctionnaires' demands for economic and social justice opened for public debate the question of whether fonctionnaires—citizens and employees of the state at the same time—would be permitted to organize so as to challenge collectively the authority of the state. The state's answer to the question of organization was a resounding no; fonctionnaires would not be permitted the use of the 1884 law which allowed workers to unionize. Fonctionnaires were to be denied the right to form syndicats, the *droit syndical,* until 1946.

Despite these restrictions, the French fonctionnaires were the first state workers in a modern industrial nation to organize, unionize, and strike. French fonctionnaires were the first state workers to abandon the ideology that they were servants of the people and to view themselves as hired workers of the state. They were the first to recognize that the state was an employer, and like other employers the *Etat-Patron* (employer-state) exploited its workers. Denied the droit syndical, the fonctionnaires at first used the 1901 Law of Associations to form legal associations. First in a trickle and then in a flood, hundreds of thousands of fonctionnaires organized to defend their professional and economic interests. In contrast to the militant but largely unorganized blue-collar workers, by 1914 the majority of fonctionnaires were organized, mainly in legal associations and *amicales* (friendly societies). But their drive for the droit syndical, the right to use the blue-collar organizational form, the syndicat, was growing.

State employees in the nineteenth century were clearly different from their blue-collar counterparts because of their superior education, better working conditions, and higher social status. But as state services expanded, these advantages were gradually eroded. Although state workers continued to be separated from blue-collar workers by the nature of their work, by hiring and recruitment policies, by the right to living allowances and pensions, and by that most important benefit to all workers—job security—the attachment of the fonctionnaires to the blue-collar organizational form and to the blue-collar organization, the CGT, continued to develop. The movement that began with a handful of militant teachers and postal workers forming illegal syndicats gained momentum in the last years before the Great War with the growth in the fonctionnaires' dissatisfaction and the intensification of blue-collar militancy.

The fonctionnaires' attachment to the blue-collar organizational form was strengthened during the war, when inflation lowered the standard of living of all workers in the public sector. The difficult inflationary period 1919–1926 further intensified this "proletarianization." As the fonctionnaires moved closer to the working-class organizations, the CGT abandoned its prewar ideology of revolutionary syndicalism and moved closer to the fonctionnaires. In the years immediately following the war, the fonctionnaires transformed their associations into syndicats or created new syndicats; most joined the CGT, forging an alliance of fonctionnaires and blue-collar workers that was to withstand the ideological and political schism of the interwar years. Moreover, because of their position as employees of the state and their awareness of the importance of the government's executive and legislative power, the fonctionnaires moved quickly into the arena of national politics, actively supporting candidates and parties that were responsive to their demands.

After a period of relative calm in the wake of Raymond Poincaré's currency reforms and salary increases granted to employees in the public sector, militancy reached a peak in the early 1930s, when the twin specters of economic crisis and fascism pushed the fonctionnaires into demonstrations and strikes to protect their jobs and their standard of living and aroused them to enormous efforts to unify the CGT. The powerful, well-organized, and politically astute fonctionnaires, with more than one-third of the membership, played a major role within the CGT, helping to maintain it as a bastion of reformism and pushing it into open support of the Popular Front. By the end of the Third Republic, the fonctionnaires were a powerful force within the labor movement and in national politics.

This study concentrates on lower-level state workers—the postal service employees, the teachers, the clerks in the finance offices, the police—the millions of civil service workers who fall under the rubric *les petits fonctionnaires.* Upper-level fonctionnaires, *les hauts fonctionnaires,* the graduates of the Grandes Ecoles, as well as municipal workers and blue-collar workers employed in state manufacturing monopolies such as tobacco and armaments, and railroad and other blue-collar workers of the nationalized transportation systems, will be mentioned only in passing and for comparison. These workers are indeed important, but to tell a coherent story, I have chosen to focus on those who perform the traditional bureaucratic functions that keep the state machinery operating.[2]

But even within this more limited group of lower-level fonction-naires, there are wide differences in work and consciousness. Some of these fonctionnaires would be categorized as professionals: teachers, sur-veyers, public nurses. Others have traditional white-collar jobs: the sec-retaries in the various offices of the ministries, the clerks in the finance offices, and still others such as the mail sorters and line repairers of the postal and telecommunications services are closer to blue-collar workers. All these fonctionnaires, however, have the same employer, the state.

We should not expect that these state employees, who performed so many different tasks—and indeed even those who did similar work—to share the same consciousness, the same attitudes toward unionization, toward alliances with the working-class organizations, and toward po-litical involvement with the left-wing parties. Indeed, as I will show, there were always those who hesitated to identify with the working class, and throughout the period of developing consciousness, there were constant struggles among the fonctionnaires over their political and professional roles. But eventually, most did accept this identifica-tion. A crucial question we must ask is why a majority of fonction-naires, separated as they were from the traditional blue-collar working class by life-style and culture, by special fringe benefits and by job secu-rity, would gradually come to identify themselves with the blue-collar working-class organizations, to see themselves, though different from blue-collar workers, as part of the working class.

The evolution of fonctionnaires' class consciousness and organization was first a response to developments on two levels: at the workplace, that is, the changing nature of the fonctionnaires themselves and the work they do, and in the larger economic and political structure, that is, the changing nature of modern industrial society and the increased func-tions of the state in that society. In addition, the fonctionnaires' con-sciousness was affected by a third determinant, their unique position as employees of a powerful and highly centralized state, a position that dis-tinguishes them not only from blue-collar workers but from white-collar workers in the private sector as well.

The enormous growth in the size, concentration, and complexity of

2. For a study of hauts fonctionnaires, see the work of the political scientist Ezra N. Su-leiman, *Politics, Power and Bureaucracy in France* (Princeton, 1974).

industrial enterprise, coupled with the increased use of sophisticated and costly technology, has drastically changed the process of industrial production and, necessarily, the nature of the working class. Even though production has expanded, the increase in workers' productivity engendered by these technological and organizational changes has resulted in a decrease in the need for manual workers—the blue-collar working class. But as the need for workers directly involved in the productive process has receded, the new technology, bringing new complexities of production and marketing, has created a need for other workers, what the French social scientists call *la nouvelle classe ouvrière,* the new working class.[3] As the proportion of production workers has decreased, the number of these support workers (many of them women) has increased dramatically. These workers do not always produce a commodity, but if one accepts that production is indeed a process and that these workers are vital to that process, it would follow that these support workers are also part of the working class, that the working class has not decreased with the relative decline of blue-collar work but has merely changed. The working class has never been a given body of people or group of occupations; the working class is constantly changing, constantly evolving. The vast army of miners and railroad workers has been replaced by the typists, the computer programmers, and even the janitors. The working class thus has not decreased in size; it has, if *la nouvelle classe ouvrière* is included, increased in size.

As industry grew in size and complexity, it created a need for state intervention. The growth of state services was interrelated with modern industry.[4] States have always existed to preserve internal order, to provide the infrastructure required by the level of economic development, and to carry out foreign policy. Late nineteenth-century capitalist society called forth increased state intervention in the running of the economic system and a massive expansion of state services to supply needs the private sector could not provide. It is difficult to conceive of modern industry (or commerce) running without postal service or without government-owned or subsidized roads and transportation. Where

3. See, for example, Serge Mallet, *La Nouvelle classe ouvrière* (Paris, 1969), and Pierre Belleville, *Une Nouvelle classe ouvrière* (Paris, 1963).
4. For a convincing analysis of this phenomenon, see James O'Connor, *The Fiscal Crisis of the State* (New York, 1973).

would the new working class receive its training if not in state-sponsored schools? In more recent years, it has also fallen on the state to provide social services that had previously been ignored or tended by private charities. Social security, unemployment insurance, and welfare payments made by the state enable industrial enterprise to hire and fire, to expand and contract, without having to deal with any of the social problems of its work force. Since many state services became so tied to the maintenance of industrial production and the economy in general, it would follow that employees of the state, the fonctionnaires, also became integrally tied to the capitalist economic system and to the productive process.

In France, the significant expansion of state services and state employment began in the three decades before World War I. The number of state workers increased as well because of the expansion of free public schools. Established primarily for political reasons, to bind the allegiance of the children of peasants and workers to the Republic rather than to the church, the free school system simultaneously trained these children to become literate, orderly, modern workers of use to the new technological society and the state. These republican schools reached into every town and village; some of their pupils would go to the factories, others, usually from the less industrialized areas, would become the teachers, the postal workers, the tax receivers, the fonctionnaires of the Third Republic. Although fonctionnaires in the nineteenth century enjoyed a certain status (in the Weberian sense), which gave state workers a relative middle-class orientation, the thousands of peasant, working-class, and artisan children who entered public service in the decades before the Great War became fonctionnaires at precisely the time they could not move up to middle-class status. It was imperative to taxpayers and to those in industry and government who accepted the expansion of public service that the cost of these services be kept at a minimum. Liberal economists were agreed that the state must not draw too much money from industrial and individual taxpayers; it must not hinder the accumulation of capital. Consequently, as public service expanded, the state resisted increases in the salaries, pensions, and other remunerations fonctionnaires received.

It was not only the standard of living that was debased. Precisely at the time this new group of fonctionnaires arrived on the scene, the expansion of state services engendered routinization, impersonalization, and the deskilling of work. Following the ground-breaking work of Harry Braverman, numerous scholars have argued that the labor process in modern industrial society, for blue-collar and white-collar workers alike, has become increasingly routine and fragmented, requiring little skill and allowing little or no worker control.[5] Even in jobs that require skills, they are easily learned and the worker is easily replaced. The entrance of large numbers of women into white-collar employment has intensified this deskilling or debasement of work. Women's work is not only undervalued, that is, paid less, but women are more frequently put into routine, bottom-of-the-ladder positions. As state services expanded in France, the offices became larger, the tasks more routinized, and the source of control more removed. A few might advance, but the majority of the men and almost all the women remained at the same level. The work of the fonctionnaires had become more proletarianized.

Thus I suggest that the fonctionnaires became part of the working class on two levels. On one level, they were attached to the industrial working class because the services they provided became necessary for the maintenance of production; on the other level, they were attached to the working class because their social origins, their milieu of work, and their salary scales became more like those of the industrial proletariat.

But there is yet another crucial factor. The proletarianization of the workplace has been experienced by white-collar workers in the private sector as well. Yet these white-collar workers did not organize as early or as strongly as state workers. Indeed, even today, compared to the strength of civil service unions in the industrialized nations, white-collar unions, with few exceptions, are either nonexistent or feeble.[6] Fonction-

5. Harry Braverman, *Labor and Monopoly Capital* (New York, 1974). See also Rosemary Crompton and Gareth Jones, *White Collar Proletariat: Deskilling and Gender in Clerical Work* (Philadelphia, 1984), and Evelyn Nakano Glenn and Roslyn Feldberg, "Degraded and Deskilled: The Proletarianization of Clerical Work," *Social Problems,* XXV (October, 1977), 52–64, and "Proletarianizing Clerical Work: Technology and Organizational Control in the Office," in Andrew Zimbalist (ed.), *Case Studies on the Labor Process* (New York, 1979), 51–72.

6. For information on white-collar unions, see Jürgen Kocka, *White Collar Workers in America, 1890–1940* (London, 1980); Pierre Delon, *Les Employés* (Paris, 1969); George Sayers Bain, *The Growth of White Collar Unionism* (Oxford, 1970); Martin Oppenheimer, *White Collar Politics* (New York, 1985); Michel Crozier, *The World of the Office Worker* (Chicago, 1971); Clive Jenkins and Barrel Sherman, *White Collar Unionism: The Rebellious Salariat* (London, 1979); and Roger Lumley, *White Collar Unionism in Britain* (London, 1973).

naires, by contrast, no matter how separated they may have been geographically or professionally, have had as an employer, the centralized state, the employer-state. Teachers, postmen, tax assessors, all were employees of the state; conditions of employment—salaries, advancement, and work load—were determined for all employees by this one employer. In addition, most state employees entered state service at a young age, and no matter where they might be transferred, they remained in the same service, serving the same state. This continuity and unity of employment helped the fonctionnaires develop an identity, a consciousness of themselves as fonctionnaires. And it did not take long for them to learn that the state was a boss like any other. When fonctionnaires turned to the state for economic justice, for salary increases, and for the right to organize, the employer-state, like any other employer attempting to maintain its authority and restrain its expenditures, refused these demands. With all the power of the government—the courts, the army, the legislative system—behind it, the state proved to be an even more formidable employer than those in the private sector. The recalcitrance of the state to accede to fonctionnaires' demands for improvements in working conditions and in salaries intensified the alienation of the fonctionnaires from the employer-state. Repelled by the state in their quest for economic and social justice, fonctionnaires began to organize, gradually moving toward the specific organizational form of the working class, the syndicat, the union.

That the fonctionnaires became conscious of their proletarianization in the state apparatus and in the industrial process is borne out by the rapid and nearly total unionization of fonctionnaires and by their attachment to working-class organizations and activity. But does unionization prove the class consciousness of fonctionnaires? Clearly there are differences among fonctionnaires. Without regional studies and studies of specific occupations, it would be difficult to determine the class consciousness of all fonctionnaires. There is evidence that the provincial fonctionnaires were less militant than the state workers of Paris or Marseilles, but the most militant teachers' organizations—revolutionary syndicalist and feminist groups—emerged not in the industrial and commercial centers but in the small towns and villages. It appears that although postal workers were more militant than white-collar finance workers, teachers made the most articulate and strongest statements of fonctionnaire-worker solidarity. But even without this information and with the recognition that one can never fully determine the consciousness or political ideology of any group, the unionization of fonctionnaires and their alliance with the major blue-collar working-class organization, the CGT, is significant.

One might ask how we know that these organizations and their activities reflected the true feelings of the rank-and-file fonctionnaires rather than the feelings and rhetoric of a few militants. Some of our main sources are the speeches and writings of the leaders and other activists of the associations and syndicats. What about the thousands of inarticulate fonctionnaires? Were fonctionnaire organizations made up of leaders without followers? A number of historians have made this charge about the pre–World War I CGT.[7] It would appear from the evidence in this study that this is not the case. First, there is evidence of extensive organization. Fonctionnaires were more organized than blue-collar workers; almost all fonctionnaires, even before World War I, were in some sort of association or syndicat. Second, after the war, almost all fonctionnaires chose the working-class organizational form, the syndicat. The syndicat was illegal, and it was difficult to maintain an illegal organization. It would have been much simpler for the fonctionnaires to remain in associations. The syndicat was chosen precisely because it was the organizational form of the working class, intended for *la lutte,* for battle. And chosen it was, not by the leadership but by all fonctionnaires. At hundreds of meetings, at annual congresses, over and over again, the syndicat was supported by rank-and-file fonctionnaires. Third, there is the significance of CGT membership, the conscious alliance with the organized working class, a decision ratified by rank-and-file members at meetings and congresses. Fourth, there is evidence of wide support of syndicat activity, attendance at meetings and participation in demonstrations, work stoppages, and even strikes. Finally, there is evidence that fonctionnaires and their organizations have traditionally allied themselves with the parties of the Left—first the Radical party and then the Socialist and Communist parties.[8] In contrast to the German civil service

7. See, for example, Peter Stearns, *Revolutionary Syndicalism and French Labor* (New Brunswick, 1971).

8. In the left-wing victory in the 1981 legislative elections, for example, the largest bloc of seats—140—belonged not to lawyers or businessmen but to teachers; most of them were Socialists and members of the teachers' union.

workers, who openly supported or quietly acquiesced to fascism in the
1930s, French fonctionnaires were largely anti-fascist and were instrumental in the election of the Popular Front government of 1936.

What historical developments occurred in France to make French
fonctionnaires the first to organize? What events encouraged the attachment of the fonctionnaires to the blue-collar working class? France has
had a long tradition of centralized government and bureaucracy, which
was fortified by the enormous administrative changes of the French
Revolution and the Empire. The Third Republic continued this development by expanding state service and establishing a unified school system. State employment, the concept of the employer-state, has had a
long historical tradition, which helped French fonctionnaires develop a
consciousness of themselves as state employees. The civil service itself,
though highly centralized and bureaucratic, was nonetheless largely the
product of the French Revolution, infused with the democratic ideology
of *liberté* and *égalité*. Although French fonctionnaires complained bitterly about authoritarianism and favoritism, there was a good deal of
egalitarianism within the government services. The educational system,
the examination system, and the democratic ideals of republicanism all
contributed to a recruitment and advancement system that allowed open
access to all who were qualified. Most critical is that the fonctionnaires
recruited by the Third Republic were hired precisely because of their republican beliefs. Thus French fonctionnaires automatically entered state
service on the left of the political spectrum. These fonctionnaires were
not only attached to the Republic, they were attached to the more radical
aspects of the Republic, those that stressed economic justice and equality. The failure of the bourgeois Republic to develop the hoped-for
république sociale, coupled with the refusal of the state to accede to
fonctionnaires' demands for improvements in working conditions, intensified the alienation of the fonctionnaires from the bourgeois state.
When the fonctionnaires organized, they turned to the working class.
Whether revolutionary syndicalist or not, the French blue-collar working class and its syndicats have had a militant political tradition, often
going beyond bread-and-butter issues, committing themselves to political activity aimed at social change. When fonctionnaires organized, it
was to this tradition they adhered. The violent reaction of the state to
the merging of fonctionnaire and blue-collar organizations, the failure to
grant the droit syndical or the right to strike, and the harassment of syn-

dicalist fonctionnaires only served to fortify the alliance, which had been forged by the economic and social experiences of the fonctionnaires.

Although French fonctionnaires developed their attachment to the working class for specific historical reasons, this is not unique to France. As more industrialized nations have expanded and centralized state functions, and as recruitment has been democratized and the nature of their work proletarianized, state workers in other countries have and are now traveling the same path. I would urge more historians of working-class history, as well as other social scientists, to continue the study of state workers so that we can better understand the role of the state, the changing relationships of the working class to the state as the state takes over more and more functions, the role of the working class in politics, and the changing nature of the working class itself in an advanced technological society.

I

La Bourgeoisie au Pouvoir, 1884–1901

After nearly a century of struggle, in political clubs, in the corridors of the National Assembly, and on the barricades, the bourgeoisie, under the Third Republic, finally attained complete political control of France. From the lowest municipal councils to the highest ministries, the bourgeoisie dominated every aspect of the state and thus the lives of the French people. The Third Republic was, as many historians have noted, *la bourgeoisie au pouvoir,* and the nature of its power was conservative. Once the right-wing monarchists had been defeated in their bid to control the young Republic, once the "Republic of Dukes" was ended, the aim of the bourgeois republicans, whether they called themselves moderates, opportunists, or radicals, was to build and conserve their power.

To maintain their control of the state apparatus, the bourgeois republicans had to win over or eliminate the political strength of three other segments of French society: the rightist group consisting of what remained of the landed gentry, the military elite, and the higher bureaucracy, who supported the monarchical tendencies of the previous seventy years; the leftist group, mostly working class, who supported the socialist or anarchist organizations; and the peasantry, some left, some right, most noncommitted. Because the bourgeois Republic was conservative, it was able to win over or neutralize both the right wing and the peasantry. Because the bourgeois Republic was conservative, it could not win over the working class. The prorepublican sympathies of the workers were based on a longtime allegiance to a republican form of government and on expectations of a république sociale, a republic of social and economic justice. The failure of the bourgeois leaders to fulfill these hopes for social and economic reforms alienated many workers. The struggle between the bourgeois state and the working class was to be the center of the domestic political scene until the fall of the Third Republic in 1940.

Throughout the nineteenth century, the average French wage earner was more an artisan than a proletarian; even those who hired out their labor to factory owners were more likely to work in small shops than in large industrial plants. It was these artisans, living precariously in a changing society, who had been the backbone of the *émeutes* and revolutions from 1789 to the Commune. But the French economy was changing, and an industrial proletariat was growing. Under the benevolence, even largesse, of the Second Empire, large textile mills replaced smaller domestic establishments in the north, thousands of miles of railroads were built, millions of tons of coal and iron ore mined, and the foundations of the heavy industries of steel and machinery laid. Industrialization was to continue at a swifter pace under the Third Republic. Although French industrial growth was more gradual and on a smaller scale than in Great Britain, Germany, and the United States, the French economy expanded and industrialized, and this expansion brought a rapidly growing and changing working class. Miners, railroad workers, textile workers, foundry workers, and factory workers filled the industrial towns and suburbs of France. The young Republic, anxious to placate the peasants and neutralize the notables, tried to ignore the working class. In disarray after the events of the Commune, workers made only small and hesitant attempts to organize themselves and to present their demands to the bourgeoisie in the early days of the Republic. But organize they did eventually, and some government leaders were forced to recognize the growth of workers' syndicats. As a contemporary observer noted, "Between employers who fought against worker organization and workers who organized, between reactionary employers and revolutionary workers, republicans, opportunists and radicals searched for a combination which might forge a reconciliation between the two sides."[1] But attempts at class collaboration such as Léon Gambetta's 1875 call for an alliance of workers and the bourgeoisie against the monarchy and the church fell on the deaf ears of both workers and bourgeoisie.

The period 1880 to 1890 was marked by violent strikes, notably of miners at Anzin in 1884 and the lengthy strike at Décazeville which lasted from January to June, 1886. The prophetic underground rumblings of Emile Zola's *Germinal* were heard; the working class could no

1. Maxime Leroy, *Syndicats et services publics* (Paris, 1909), 114.

longer be ignored. Recognizing the fait accompli and anxious to have some government control over the syndicats, which were mushrooming illegally, on March 21, 1884, the parliament passed a law, proposed by Pierre Waldeck-Rousseau, ending the prohibition of the Le Chapelier Law of 1791; at last, workers were allowed to organize in syndicats. Significantly, the Chambre des Syndicats, the syndicat federation, meeting in congress at Lyons in October, 1886, condemned the law. Despite the arguments of the delegates from the Bouches-du-Rhône, who attested to the success of the law and pointed to the protection it afforded militants of the syndicats, the delegates rejected the law as an opportunist fabrication, "which is no more than a trap for workers."[2] That the workers had reason to mistrust the bourgeoisie and its state can be understood when one considers the violence with which the workers' activity was met. The infamous *journée* of Fourmies of May 1, 1891, when troops fired on workers, who, against the wishes of the factory owners, were celebrating May Day with the traditional floral offerings, is but one terrible example.

Open warfare was to erupt again and again in the period before World War I, exacerbating mutual antagonism and mistrust. Most workers, especially those who were organized, had proven their devotion to the Republic many times when called upon to defend *la République en danger,* the Republic in danger, from its enemies. But when the working class looked for social reform from the government it had defended and supported, it faced vacillation and inaction. Despite the efforts of the more progressive Radicals and other reformers, little of any consequence was done.[3] A child labor law and provisions for a weekly day off were won only after years of agitation and pressure. The first workman's compensation law was passed in 1898, eighteen years after it was introduced, and the first retirement legislation was not enacted until 1910, and the law was weak and ineffectual. It was considered "at least a defeat if not a fiasco." When Joseph Caillaux, the Radical deputy who was to be finance minister for numerous Third Republic cabinets, told the socialist leader, Jean Jaurès, in a parliamentary debate in 1905, "It is the Council

2. Edouard Dolléans, *Histoire du mouvement ouvrier* (3 vols.; Paris, 1968), II, 26.
3. For a full discussion of the politics of social reform, see Judith Stone, *The Search for Social Peace: Reform Legislation in France, 1890–1914* (Albany, 1985).

of State which will make the social revolution," it was meant more as a threat than a promise. Even the much heralded reform-minded Clemenceau government of 1906 accomplished very little. As Henri Hatzfeld has noted, on the eve of World War I, the French had to recognize that socially they were backward.[4]

Comparing the slowness with which the government enacted social legislation to the speed with which it sent troops to put down strikes, it is no wonder that much of the French working class was antagonistic toward the bourgeois state and its leaders. It was to feel special antagonism toward those leaders who had been considered more progressive but who served the bourgeoisie as well as the more openly reactionary. René Viviani and Aristide Briand had begun their careers as socialists, Georges Clemenceau as a republican of the Left. All three were vilified by the orators and writers of the working class, and Clemenceau earned the title of *briseur de grèves*, the strikebreaker.

It was in this milieu that the consciousness and organization of thousands of fonctionnaires was to be forged.

When the republicans took power, they inherited a highly centralized and hierarchical state. The centralization that had begun with the ministerial decrees of Louis XIV and continued with the reorganization of the country into departments during the Revolution culminated with the laws of Napoleon I. Governments rose and fell, laws were passed, but the basic Napoleonic system of centralized hierarchy was never really changed. One of the problems the new Republic would have to face was how to reconcile the new democracy of universal male suffrage with the intense hierarchy and favoritism that dominated the government bureaucracy. This bureaucracy was controlled by elites whose appointments often depended on family, school, or business connections to ministers, prefects, or deputies. Under the elites, there were thousands of others—tax auditors, finance clerks, postal clerks, customs collectors—the fonctionnaires, who keep the public services operating. It is these fonctionnaires who are of prime concern in this study.

4. Henri Hatzfeld, *Du Paupérisme à la securité sociale, 1850–1940* (Paris, 1971), 34; Dolléans, *Mouvement ouvrier*, II, 8.

If one thinks of the typical fonctionnaire of the nineteenth century, the picture that comes immediately to mind is that of the stupid, plodding, work-avoiding caricature in Georges Courteline's *Messieurs les ronds de cuir*. In fact, there is practically no literature on the subject of fonctionnaires of the nineteenth century. Present-day sociologists examine and reexamine the attitudes, life-styles, organizations, and frustrations of thousands of contemporary petits fonctionnaires but have left the government workers of the nineteenth century largely untouched. Guy Thuillier has published a short impressionistic account of daily life in the ministerial offices and a longer study largely about various famous fonctionnaires and the administrative press, but a real history of the nineteenth-century fonctionnaires is yet to be written.[5]

From literature, memoirs, and other sources, it would appear that though some nineteenth-century fonctionnaires were indeed *ronds de cuir,* or petty tyrants who plagued the countryside, most were capable and devoted civil servants. Because of the nature of their work and the educational advantages they possessed compared to the rest of the population, these government employees enjoyed a certain amount of prestige. In addition, most fonctionnaires had their jobs for as long as they wanted, and under the law of June 9, 1853, they were the first French employees to receive retirement pensions. Public service often meant hard work, but it was frequently compensated by security and prestige within the community. Despite the hierarchical nature of the bureaucracy, the lower fonctionnaires were often left to their own devices and in many cases were able to make individual decisions about their work.

But all was not sweetness and light. Offices were frequently dusty and unsanitary, and salaries, especially for lower fonctionnaires, were barely high enough to maintain a standard of living that would enable

5. Guy Thuillier, *La Vie quotidienne dans les ministères au XIXème siècle* (Paris, 1976); Thuillier, *Bureaucratie et bureaucrates en France au XIXème siècle* (Geneva, 1980). The fourth section of the Ecole Pratique des Hautes Etudes and the Institut Français des Sciences Administratives have recently sponsored numerous seminars and publications devoted to the history of government administration. See, for example, *Histoire de l'administration français depuis 1800* (Geneva, 1975); *Les Directeurs de ministère en France* (Geneva, 1976); *Paris et son administration, 1800–1978* (Geneva, 1979), all published by the fourth section, and *Histoire de l'administration,* published in 1972 by the Institut Français des Sciences Administratives. Thuillier's *Bureaucratie et bureaucrates* is part of this series.

them to educate their children properly. In 1860, *Le Siècle* published the budget of a father of three, whose earnings of two thousand francs per year left him an annual debt of seven hundred francs.[6]

The complaints and frustrations that must have been long smoldering among the fonctionnaires erupted during the Revolution of 1848. Between February and June, a host of clubs and newspapers appeared from out of nowhere demanding an end to favoritism, despotism, nepotism, and arbitrariness. Although some economic demands were made, notably for job security and higher pay for the lowest echelon of workers, administrative reform was most frequently and passionately urged. A call was issued for fixed standards for admission and advancement and an end to favoritism for *enfants de famille,* the children of privilege. "The reign of favors, of injustice, of despotism is over." The isolation of fonctionnaires was deplored, and hundreds of them flocked to meetings calling for unity. "For too long, pariahs of bureaucracy . . . they have suffered injustice and arbitrariness in silence." Not only was unity urged, but one can discern in these short-lived organizations and newspapers the first stirrings of feelings of exploitation and identification with other workers. In a brochure aimed at administrative workers, one reads, "You poor fonctionnaires of the state, are you anything else but hard workers, always crushed and exploited by an office bureaucracy all the more stupid and unbearable as they are arrogant and vain. . . . Gentlemen, unite, you are the common people." And from the heady days of April, "In one word, the clerk is the worker of the pen. Worker through his manual work, man of letters through his thoughts, he is at the same time an artisan and an artist."[7]

But the coming of Louis Napoleon, first as president and then as emperor, ended this brief flurry of open debate. Gradually the newspapers and organizations disappeared or became instruments for organizing outings and printing lists of promotions. Even the tiny group of teachers who dared to form the Société des Instituteurs et Institutrices Primaires in 1831 and those who welcomed and read the "democratic re-

6. Cited by Thuillier, *La Vie quotidienne,* 54.

7. Guy Thuillier, "Aux Origines du syndicalisme des fonctionnaires: La presse administrative en 1848–9," *Revue Administrative,* XXII (July–August, 1969), 432–44; *Moniteur des Postes,* cited *ibid.;* brochure written by G. François, cited *ibid.;* Thuillier, "Aux Origines du syndicalisme fonctionnaire," *Revue Administrative,* XXII (October, 1969), 576–88.

publican" paper *L'Echo des Instituteurs* could not survive after 1850. Arsène Meunier, the editor of *L'Echo,* was tried in 1850. The tiny association that formed under the influence of the paper, as well as a second group started by the socialists Pauline Roland, Gustave LeFrançais, and Jeanne Deroin were scattered after the coup. Some went to prison or into exile. The rest of the teachers were put under the direction of the prefects until 1852 to prevent any further trouble from these precocious fonctionnaires who called for social equality, professional dignity, and freedom from clerical influence.[8]

The few attempts at organizing fonctionnaires in the twilight days of the Empire (the postal organization had a mere two thousand members in Paris) were swept away by the war and the Commune. But as with the blue-collar workers, tentative organizational steps were taken in the 1870s and 1880s, mostly in the form of amicales, mutualist professional societies, such as the Association Amicale des PTT in 1879, and societies of the *anciens élèves* (alumni) among teachers. By 1882, the Association Générale des Répetiteurs was holding open meetings. With the passage of the law of 1884, the question of fonctionnaire organization arose as an important issue.

The Magna Carta of the French syndicats, the law of March 21, 1884, allowed the organization of syndicats or associations for the defense of economic, industrial, commercial, and agricultural interests. Article three reads, "The professional syndicats have as an exclusive aim the study and defense of economic, industrial, commercial, and agricultural interests," and Article five says, "Legally constituted according to the stipulations of the present law, professional syndicats can freely work together for the study and defense of their economic, industrial, commercial, and agricultural interests."[9] No specific mention is made of the liberal professions, of state, departmental, or communal workers, or of fonctionnaires. Immediately, there was an attempt to clarify the law to extend it to these groups. Some of the legislators, including the leading sponsor of the law, Pierre Waldeck-Rousseau, agreed to this liberal interpretation. Henri-Louis Tolain, another sponsor, stated that "every person engaged in a profession can secure the right to make use of the

8. Max Ferré, *Histoire du mouvement syndicaliste révolutionnaire chez les instituteurs* (Paris, 1955), 9–10.
9. Marcel Piquemal, *Le Droit syndical en France* (Paris, 1962), 36–37.

new legislation." But the government and its juridical arm clearly wished to restrict the use of the law to prevent the organization of state employees. As early as June, 1885, an *arrêt* of the Cour de Cassation (the highest French court) upheld the strict interpretation that the law did not extend beyond industrial, agricultural, and commercial employees. The court was to hand down similar decisions in February, 1902, and May, 1908.[10]

The fonctionnaires, however, continued to try to use the 1884 law, employing three basic organizational forms: the amicale, the association, and the syndicat. The amicale was of nineteenth-century origin. Similar to the English "friendly society," amicales had begun as mutual aid societies or professional organizations whose members gathered to discuss professional issues and to hear speakers. At the end of the nineteenth century and especially in the early years of the twentieth century, the amicales became more concerned with the issues of wages, working conditions, and retirement, as well as political developments. The primary school teachers and the police used the amicale form until they became syndicats after World War I. Most other fonctionnaires formed associations. Legalized in 1901, the associations, though technically similar to other cultural or religious associations, almost immediately concerned themselves with issues of wages and working conditions. Before World War I, the blue-collar form of organization, the syndicat, equivalent to the English or American union, though illegal for fonctionnaires, was used by a militant minority.

In March, 1887, the first teachers' syndicat, the Syndicat des Membres de l'Enseignement pour l'Organisation des Congrès, was formed, mostly for professional reasons. They joined with a Parisian group created at the same time to form the Union Nationale des Instituteurs de France and, claiming the right to have a syndicat under the 1884 law, met in congress on September 20, 1887. On the same day, the prefects of France received a circular from the minister of education, Eugène Spuller, denying teachers any benefit of the law of 1884. This now famous circular argued that "public service is not a profession," that a fonctionnaire's *traitement* (salary) was not the same as a *salaire* (wage). A

10. AN, F7 13724; Musée Social, *Le Droit d'association des fonctionnaires* (Paris, 1912), 21.

worker had to bargain with his boss for his wages and the terms of his contract and so needed not only the right to join with other workers for negotiation but governmental protection of this right as well. The *insti-tuteur* could not, on one hand, claim the rights of the 1884 law meant for workers and, on the other, accept the security, pensions, and regulated *traitement* that were his due as an employee of the state.[11] The syndicalist group was small; most instituteurs remained in the tamer and more so-cial amicales. The Spuller memorandum had its desired result; the tiny syndicalist movement among teachers was arrested.

Even the liberal professions had trouble with the government over the interpretation of the law. The medical syndicat was declared illegal in 1885, but Waldeck-Rousseau repudiated this interpretation, and in 1892 a special law was passed allowing syndicats for doctors, except those who worked for the state. But the generosity shown the doctors was not extended to the fonctionnaires or to blue-collar workers employed by the state.

The state employed, in the manufacturing plants of its monopolies of tobacco, matches, armaments, and porcelain, thousands of workers whose jobs and contractual arrangements were similar to those of work-ers in private industry performing similar functions. In addition, sewer workers, road workers, street cleaners, and construction workers worked under state, departmental, and communal command. In the wake of the law of 1884, many of these workers, emulating blue-collar workers in private industry, organized in syndicats. The *égoutiers* (sewer workers) of Paris, who organized in 1887; the *allumettiers* (match workers) of Mar-seilles, who formed their syndicat in 1890; the Ouvriers de la Manufac-ture d'Armes de Chatellerault, the Magasins Centraux de la Guerre de Paris (armaments workers), and the workers of Monnaies et Médailles (workers in the Mint) are just a few of the many state workers who or-ganized syndicats at this time. The *ouvriers des PTT* (line workers, equipment manufacturers) organized a syndicat in Paris in 1899 which had two thousand members a mere six weeks after its birth. A small group of seventy-five *ouvriers des appareils télégraphiques* had already ex-

11. The Spuller memorandum is in the appendix of Jules Jeanneney, *Associations et syndicats des fonctionnaires* (Paris, 1908), 24-25.

hibited militancy as early as 1881, when they struck the privately owned plant of Postel-Venax. After six weeks, the strike was lost, as were the jobs of all the strikers.[12]

In 1893, the prefectural administration of the department of the Seine outlawed the syndicat of the *cantonniers* (road workers), and in 1894, the issue of the organization of blue-collar state workers came to a head in the Chamber of Deputies when Charles Jonnart, the minister of public works, tried to outlaw the syndicat of railroad workers on lines belonging to the state. If the 1884 law allowed syndicats for commerce and industry, what would happen when the state owned a commercial or industrial enterprise? The Chamber, on May 22, 1894, repudiated Jonnart, an act that led to the fall of the Casimir-Périer cabinet, by passing an order of the day (not a law) calling on the government to permit workers to form syndicats. "The Chamber, considering that the 1884 law applies to workers and clerks of state enterprises as well as to those of private industry, asks the government to respect the law and to facilitate its execution."[13]

A rash of organizing followed. By 1901, the syndicats of blue-collar workers united into the Fédération des Travailleurs de l'Etat, which affiliated with the CGT a few years later. If such organization was more or less tolerated by the government, occasionally, depending on the political situation and on who was in office, some of these workers' syndicats found themselves outside the law again. In 1903, a Seine tribunal surprisingly refused to recognize the *égoutier* syndicat, and later that year the already existing *cantonnier* syndicat was outlawed.

For the fonctionnaires, the government's inconsistency was in the opposite direction. From time to time, an occasional fonctionnaire organization would be allowed, but in general the leaders of the state and its courts followed a hard line, refusing recognition not only to syndicats but to those who organized themselves into associations as well. Using the 1885 Cour de Cassation decision and the 1894 Chamber order of the day, the ministers Emile Combes, Léon Bourgeois, Briand, and others, followed the spirit and language of the Spuller memorandum over and over again to prevent the organization of teachers. Directors of the PTT

12. AP, BA 181.
13. AN, F7 13724.

refused to recognize the various postal syndicats and associations, and employees of the Ministry of Finance met with similar opposition. The minister of commerce and industry, Jules Roche, summarized the arguments: "State employees do not face private interests but a general interest, the highest of all, that of the state itself. If they unionize, they would be organizing a struggle against the nation itself, against the general interest of the country, against the national sovereignty."[14]

After the elections of 1898, the situation eased and associations were tolerated, although no federations or annual congresses were allowed. When Alexandre Millerand entered the government as minister of commerce, he persuaded the prime minister, Waldeck-Rousseau, to allow the *sous-agents* of the PTT to have an association. On July 1, 1901, the Law of Associations was passed. Meant primarily for religious and cultural organizations, it also allowed fonctionnaires to organize into associations, as long as they were not "based on an illicit cause or aim" and did not have "as an aim the injury to the integrity of the territory and the republican form of government." For the first time, it was legal for fonctionnaires to join together in organizations to defend their professional and economic interests. In the ensuing years, almost every state occupation, from customs collectors to college professors, formed a professional organization. Jules Jeanneney estimated from the records of the *Journal Officiel* that between 1901 and 1907, at least 515 associations made declarations of their bylaws and officers as was required by law; 20 of these were in the PTT alone.[15]

But the droit syndical still eluded the fonctionnaires. The government would allow its employees to form organizations but not syndicats. Although the majority of organized fonctionnaires used the 1901 law and formed associations, a number of syndicats were established even though they were illegal and their existence precarious. One cannot help but ask why a small group of militants, facing opposition, dissolution, censure, and occasional arrest for illegal activity, continued to press for the right to form syndicats. The law of 1884 seemed more desirable to some fonctionnaires than the Law of Associations because there was a difference in the intention of the two laws. The stated purpose of the syndicat was the

14. *Ibid.*
15. Jeanneney, *Associations*, 48, 52.

advocacy and defense of professional interests; the association was legally no different from nonprofessional associations. Whereas Article five of the 1884 law gave members the right to study and defend their professional interests and allowed the syndicat to represent employees in negotiations with employers, the 1901 law says simply, "The members may permanently pool information and activities for purposes *other than* sharing benefits."[16] The 1901 law is not explicit enough; it leaves too much to the arbitrary whims of individual politicians. One minister might change what another had allowed. Syndicats could not easily be dissolved. Furthermore, syndicats, unlike associations, could join together to form occupational federations, and, most important, their members were allowed to belong to the larger organizations of blue-collar workers, the Bourses du Travail and the newly formed Confédération Générale du Travail. In short, the syndicat was meant to aid workers in defense of their economic and professional interests; the association was an organization like any other. Still, in practice, the associations could and did perform many of the same functions as the syndicats; some were even more militant than the syndicats. Yet the demand for the droit syndical continued as more and more fonctionnaires organized. That demand was to grow.

Many fonctionnaires wanted the right to organize into syndicats, not only because of the wider legal freedom allowed by the 1884 law but because it allowed workers to make demands and to negotiate these demands. In addition, many fonctionnaires preferred the syndicat because it was the form of organization used by blue-collar workers. And it is for these reasons that the government denied the droit syndical to fonctionnaires and was to deny that right throughout the life of the Third Republic.

The French syndicat and its movement, syndicalism, is roughly equivalent to the English union and unionism. In the two decades before World War I, however, the French syndicalist movement might more accurately be designated revolutionary syndicalism. Most workers in the industrialized nations of Great Britain, Germany, and the United States joined trade unions to present their economic demands and joined various socialist parties to express their political demands. A minority in Great Britain followed the revolutionary syndicalist form under Tom

16. AN, F7 13724; italics added.

Mann, Ben Tillett, and James Larkin. The American syndicalist organization the Industrial Workers of the World (IWW) was to have a short, persecuted life, organizing primarily miners in the western United States. Only in the south of Europe, in Italy, in Spain, and primarily in France, was the revolutionary syndicalist movement to dominate the organized working class.

Although the French movement was influenced by the early nineteenth-century theories of Pierre Joseph Proudhon and Auguste Blanqui, as well as by later anarchist and Marxist socialist theorists, revolutionary syndicalism was more a movement than an ideology; the theories unfolded as the movement developed. In the 1880s and 1890s, the organized French labor movement was dominated by two national groups, the loose conglomeration of labor exchanges, the Bourses du Travail, founded by the anarchist Fernand Pelloutier, and the more centralized Fédération des Chambres Syndicales, which was under the control of the Marxist followers of Jules Guesde from 1886 to 1894. At the Marseilles congress of the federations in 1892, the then anarchist Aristide Briand introduced a resolution in support of the *grève générale,* the general strike, as the method of social revolution. Despite the opposition of the Guesdists, the next congress in 1894 at Nantes not only endorsed the concept of the general strike but made provisions to join with the Bourses du Travail in forming a large federation of workers' organizations. The Guesdist minority split off in opposition. In 1895, the CGT was officially launched.

Despite its early numerical weakness, the CGT dominated the labor scene from 1900 to 1914, a period during which there were thousands of strikes and hundreds killed and wounded in violent confrontations between workers and employers backed by government authority. As the number of strikes increased, as the violence intensified, as the government dragged its feet on the question of social reform, and as the socialist parties, newly unified as the Section Française de l'Internationale Ouvrière (SFIO), argued the merits of reformism over revolution, the CGT and its revolutionary syndicalist leadership became more antistate, more antiparty, and more determined that workers would bring about a social revolution with their unique weapon, the general strike. The concept of direct action and general strike did not necessarily involve violence. The CGT leaders, Victor Griffuehles and later Léon

Jouhaux, often emphasized the peaceful nature of the movement. They believed that the massiveness of the strike movement would assure its orderliness and success.

In October, 1906, the CGT congress was held at Amiens, and after days of debate, the ideological "charter" defining the beliefs and goals of the CGT was issued. The months before the congress had been filled with heightening antagonism. A catastrophe at Courrières on March 10 had resulted in the death of 1,100 miners and precipitated a prolonged miners' strike. Ten thousand troops were sent to control the strikers. As the spring progressed so did the strike movement; 150,000 workers in the printing industry and 50,000 metallurgists went on strike in the Paris area. Using the miners' strike as an excuse, the government invaded CGT headquarters and arrested its leaders. The Charte d'Amiens re-affirmed the political independence of the CGT, eschewing formal connections with any of the political parties of the Left. It reaffirmed its dedication to the fight against capitalism and to the general strike as the ultimate weapon that would bring about the fall of the bourgeois government and capitalism itself.

It is difficult to determine just how influential the CGT and revolutionary syndicalism were in the period before World War I. Certainly the CGT could count only a minority of workers in its ranks, and its strength varied from occupation to occupation. At the 1901 congress in Lyons, it was estimated that 60 percent of miners were in syndicats, but only 9 percent of textile workers were.[17] (Within a few years, representation of textile workers increased in the CGT.) By 1906, of the nearly 1 million workers in syndicats, about one-third affiliated with the CGT.[18] Moreover, it is clear that while the leadership of the CGT talked revolution, the local syndicats were often more interested in bread-and-butter issues. Still, the role played by the CGT and the revolutionary syndicalists must not be denigrated. Membership figures can be misleading. The Amiens charter spoke for more workers than those who were members of the CGT. The CGT publications, *La Vie Ouvrière, Le Mouvement Social, Père Peinard,* and others, were widely read; *La Bataille Syndicaliste,* the daily newspaper started in 1911 by militant revolution-

17. Dolléans, *Mouvement ouvrier,* II, 53.
18. Jean Bron, *Histoire du mouvement ouvrier français* (2 vols.; Paris, 1968–70), II, 80.

ary syndicalists from several federations within the CGT, distributed twenty-five thousand copies per day and probably had a wider circulation.[19] Thousands attended meetings and demonstrations, and on the first of May, workers all over France, rallying to the CGT's call, demanded the eight-hour day. The CGT was very strong in certain critical trades such as railroads, printing, and building. Its very existence and its attack on capitalism terrorized the bourgeoisie and its state apparatus. Between 1906 and 1911, as the number of strikes increased and the violence of their repression intensified, the class struggle described by Karl Marx seemed to have become a reality. To the government, the idea that the fonctionnaires, as cautious as they may have been, might adopt the syndicalist form and join with blue-collar workers in the CGT was much too threatening to be tolerated. The fonctionnaires were to be kept out of the syndicalist movement.

19. Roger Picard, *Le Mouvement syndical durant la guerre* (Paris, 1927), 20.

2

The Fonctionnaires Organize, 1901–1906

Vague and limited as it was, the Law of Associations of 1901 still enabled fonctionnaires to have legal organizations for the first time, and the cautious fonctionnaires used the law to advantage. First in a trickle, then in a flood, hundreds of thousands of employees in public service organized themselves, largely in amicales and associations but also in illegal syndicats. By 1914, almost all fonctionnaires were organized.

Among the first to organize were the employees of the Ministère des Postes, Télégraphes, et Téléphones (PTT). In 1878, the postal and telegraph services had been unified, and in 1881 the Caisse d'Epargne (postal savings) was added. Telephone service, begun in 1881, was, like the railroads, partially state-run and partially private, but in 1889 all telephone service became the monopoly of the state. By 1896, the PTT had grown to an impressive seventy-three thousand employees. Following the lead of the *ouvriers des lignes* (line installers and repairmen), the *sous-agents* (postmen) of Lyons attempted to form a syndicat in 1884, but it dissolved under administrative pressure. Four years later, distressed by the limitations placed on advancement by the administration (one of the new provisions stated that women had to get the permission not of their parents but of their administrative superiors if they wished to marry), the sous-agents held meetings in Paris which drew at one gathering at the Salle Wagram three thousand men and, for the first time, women. The administration answered by transferring twenty militants out of Paris, and the infant movement died. Further attempts to organize were made in Marseilles in 1891 and in Paris in 1891 and 1892. There was particular ferment among the sous-agents; lower ranked and lower paid than the full agents, they were, as an editorial in the socialist paper *L'Egalité* described, the pariahs of the administration: "The powerful syndicalist movement which is growing at this time has given the sous-agents the notion of forming a strong organization so that they also can face the administration when the need occurs." Indeed, a minority of postal workers went even further, declaring in a May Day petition of 1892 that their interests were "identical with those of the workers" and that they "gave their assistance to defenders of socialism."[1] But all of these attempts at organization were aborted.

At four o'clock in the morning of May 18, 1899, about thirteen hundred sous-agents who did the *tri* (sorting) and distribution of mail from the Recette Principale in Paris declared themselves on strike.[2] The administration was astounded by this sudden and spectacular event, the first strike of fonctionnaires. The *facteur*'s (postman) day began at four in the morning and often ended at nine in the evening. Except for the afternoon of July 14, when they enjoyed twelve hours off, there was no paid vacation. For this work, they received one thousand francs per year as a minimum and seventeen hundred francs as a maximum. Most other state workers started at twelve hundred francs, and the Chamber had authorized a raise for the sous-agents. On the day before the strike, the Senate, supporting the actions of the under secretary of state, Léon Mougeot, had rejected the raise. The strike action was spontaneous and seemed leaderless, yet by the time the sun came up, the entire staff was out in the street and an appeal was made to the public. A poster found on the wall of the urinal at the Central Post Office on rue du Louvre explained their position:

> The postmen . . . distribute each day . . . one of the most precious tools of the intellectual life of the nation . . . the mail. For fulfilling this function, they are paid the preposterous sum of 2.78 francs a day—1,000 francs a year. This is how the public powers reward its servants for unceasing toil and trustworthiness.

1. Georges Frischmann, *Histoire de la fédération CGT des PTT* (Paris, 1967), 82, 84–85; *L'Egalité*, June 16, 1891; *La Revue des Postes*, May 4, 1892, quoted in Susan Dimlich Bachrach, "The Feminization of the French Postal Service, 1750–1914" (Ph.D. dissertation, University of Wisconsin, 1981), 176. Bachrach's dissertation was published as "Dames Employées: The Feminization of Postal Workers in Nineteenth Century France," *Women and History*, No. 8 (Winter, 1983).

2. The number of strikers is hard to determine. Frischmann says twelve hundred (*Histoire PTT*, 94); the Police of Paris reported thirteen hundred (AP, BA 1393); and a report of the Musée Social issued ten years after the strike put the number at three thousand (*Le Droit d'association des fonctionnaires* [Paris, 1912], 129).

With an eye on the imminent elections, the Chamber of Deputies by 423 votes, approved a raise of 100–200 francs a year for these simple workers. Yesterday by 350 votes, these same deputies reversed themselves by giving a vote of confidence to Minister MOUGEOT, who betrayed them in front of the Senate.

The poster went on to ask all citizens to answer this injustice by refusing to accept mail from anyone other than their usual postman. By this action, the public would help justice triumph and "show that above public power, there is another power, that of the people, that is, the national will."[3]

Six hundred women of the Caisse d'Epargne et de la Comptabilité were brought in to do the sorting, and under the hissing and booing of the sous-agents in the street, five hundred Gardes Républicains and seven hundred infantrymen began to distribute the mail. By afternoon, twenty-seven *grévistes* (strikers) were fired, and the Senate gave Mougeot a vote of confidence for his strong measures. Within twenty-four hours, the facteurs were back at work. On June 22, when the new Waldeck-Rousseau government was formed, on the advice of Millerand the fired facteurs were reinstated and some changes were made in the salary structure; they had achieved a victory of sorts. The strike was unorganized and of short duration, but the implications were clear. Every newspaper covered the event and asked whether the government service might be interrupted by strikes again.[4]

By the end of the year, the blue-collar line workers formed a syndicat, and despite the mild language of some of its leaders—"the syndicat is not a threat to our leaders, we will involve ourselves in politics as little as possible"—the syndicat affiliated with the CGT.[5] These workers realized that to achieve their goal of better working and living conditions affiliation with the working class was necessary and the PTT workers *might* have to join in a general strike. Applause greeted a declaration announcing the possibility of joining a general strike in the near future "if that eventuality occurred." Between February and May, 1900, nearly two thousand men and women attended meetings to call for an eight-hour day, a minimum salary of five francs per day, two paid days of rest

3. AP, BA 1393.
4. *La Patrie,* May 20, 1899.
5. AP, BA 1436, February 9, 1900.

per month, and, an issue of importance to workers in the ateliers, the
end of leasing work to private industry. Although affiliation with the
blue-collar working class was recognized and solidarity was often
shown by collecting money for the miners at Montceau-les-Mines, for
example, most of the activity of the syndicat centered around these
bread-and-butter issues.[6]

As the line workers were organizing their syndicat, some of the sous-
agents who had participated in the 1899 strike met at the Bourse du Travail in September, 1900, to form the Syndicat National des Sous-Agents
des PTT. Told by Millerand that they were illegal, they became an association early in 1901 and within a few years could count forty-three
thousand of the fifty-five thousand sous-agents of France as members.[7]
Between its inception and 1905, the Association Générale des Sous-
Agents played a cautious role, abandoning the aggressiveness that had
characterized the strike of 1899. But a militant group remained within
the association, and in 1905 these "syndicalists" came once again to
dominate the sous-agents.

The agents (commis and clerks of the post offices, railroad station
offices, "flying squad," and telegraph and telephone services) formed
their own organization, the Association Générale des Agents des PTT,
in October, 1900. Within three years they numbered sixteen thousand
members in eighty departments, published a newspaper, Bulletin Officiel
de l'Association Générale, and played a continuous and active role in pressing for improvements in working conditions.[8] A major campaign for the
repos hebdomadaire, the weekly day off, was launched, but demands for
shorter working hours, improved pay for women, sick leave, improved
advancement procedures, paid vacations, and improved functioning of
the postal service in general were made constantly in the early years of
the association's existence.[9] The Association Générale, though vigorous
in its demands, avoided the rhetoric and activities such as work stoppages that characterized the blue-collar workers' revolutionary syndicalist movement. The agents regularly sent delegates to present their

6. Ibid.
7. Musée Social, Le Droit d'association, 131.
8. Frischmann, Histoire PTT, 103.
9. Bulletin Officiel de l'Association Générale, 1901-1905 (hereafter cited as Bulletin de
l'AG).

demands to various deputies and ministers in the government, and their meetings were often addressed by socialists and deputies. The Association Générale des Agents was firm in its demands for economic and social improvements, but it clearly wished to work within the system. An order of the day from a 1903 meeting reads, "The agents and sous-agents . . . after having heard their valiant and legitimate defenders, Sembat and Allemane[10] enlarge upon their corporative interests, renew their deep attachment to the government of republican action, express their profound gratitude to the members of parliament who ceaselessly defend their just demands."[11] Still, as with the sous-agents, a more militant group was gradually increasing its strength within the association.

The years of the liberal Waldeck-Rousseau government brought some welcome improvements in the working conditions of postal employees. Salaries for blue-collar workers and for facteurs were raised in 1902, as was the special allowance for housing. The ordinary facteur in cities was placed on a salary scale of a minimum of 1,100 francs and a maximum of 1,600 francs; rural or local facteurs received 700 to 1,150 francs per year. The salary for *facteur sous-chef* and *facteur-chef* could go as high as 1,800 and 2,000 francs per year. For agents in Paris, the housing allowance went up to 250 francs, for the sous-agents to 200 francs, and for those in the department of the Seine outside of Paris, 50 francs less. Most blue-collar workers in the PTT now benefited from the eight-hour day in Paris, and the *repos hebdomadaire* was beginning to be instituted.

Despite these small advances, discontent continued to grow. Salaries were still low, the weekly day off was not granted by many departmental administrations, and the advancement procedure was still arbitrary. A brochure, meant as an open letter to senators and deputies, published in 1902 or 1903, *L'Arrivisme dans l'Administration des PTT depuis 1896,* listed a large number of exceptional advancements made without regard to seniority or merit. To the fonctionnaires of the PTT these actions were demoralizing.

Salaries, advancement, and the *repos hebdomadaire* were of prime concern to the Association Générale, but yet another issue was to be debated and discussed at meetings and congresses over the years—the position of

---

10. Both were socialist deputies.
11. *Bulletin de l'AG,* October, 1903.

women in the postal services. Both the PTT and the Ministry of Education employed a large number of women. As the PTT grew, like many other private and public establishments it hired more and more women. Women had been employed in the postal service since the *ancien régime,* and by the middle of the nineteenth century one-half of the white-collar personnel was female, employed almost exclusively in small, one-person rural post offices.[12] By the last decade of the century, when postal and telegraph usage was expanding rapidly and the government was anxious to get the best-educated workers at the lowest possible wage, a well-thought-out decision was made in 1892 to begin the "feminization" of the post offices in larger cities and their suburbs. Although a few women replaced men in some clerical positions, female employees were used mostly to fill positions created by the new services of the PTT. Women did some work in the telegraph services, they were the *receveuses,* the clerks who dealt with money orders and postal savings, and also in 1892, when the government, again anxious to lower costs, feminized the telephone service, *les demoiselles du téléphone* dominated that branch of the PTT. Although women were paid less than men and placed mostly in dead-end jobs without hope for advancement, the lack of other employment opportunities for educated women made the postal service jobs very desirable, and the pool of qualified (and overqualified) applicants was large. The *dames-employées* were to become a significant segment of the postal services, especially after 1914.

The attitude of male workers toward their female counterparts was ambivalent and underwent many changes over the years. Although fonctionnaires were not as hostile to women workers as were some blue-collar workers, who still followed the Proudhonist view that there were two types of women—housewives and harlots—and that workers should be paid enough to keep their wives *au foyer,* in the home, the postal workers nevertheless worried about the government's use of women to replace men and to undercut the general wage level. Their concerns were somewhat assuaged because women were used in the newer services and rarely competed with men for advancement, but they still viewed women as a group apart from the mainstream of postal worker life. Gradually, though, the women began to take their place in

12. For a full analysis of women postal workers, see Bachrach, "Dames Employées."

the associations, which, with much backtracking, began to see their shared interests.

At the first general assembly of the Association Générale des Agents, a description of the crowded meeting began with the gentlemanly words, "Several women with ravishing outfits occupied the first row of the platform and their presence made the general scene most agreeable," but before the congress was over, a vigorous exchange occurred over the question of asking for equal pay for women. A male speaker who complained that there were no women members was told that the Section Bordelaise alone had seventy female members in its first few months of existence.[13] That same year, the women in the telephone service complained when the government began to replace them with men at the Passy central office. They said the service was going from bad to worse because men did not have "our patience, nor our resignation."[14] The following year, a delegation from the agents was sent to the minister with a host of demands, including a special request for increases in the wages of women workers. In September, the association issued a special report on women's wages and the difficulties they encountered in advancement, which stated that women of the postal services had been waiting since 1877 for a raise in their maximum salaries.[15]

In July, 1900, the first issue of *L'Union des Dames de la PTT* appeared. It had some connections to the feminist movement—the editor, Renée Rambaud, wrote for Marguerite Durand's *La Fronde*—and it urged women to join the Association Générale but also to maintain their independence.[16] In October, 1902, the *dames téléphonistes* at the Paris centers of Gutenberg, Rive Droite, and Rive Gauche formed a "group" within the association.[17] The second general assembly of the Association Générale des Agents was addressed by a woman militant, Mlle Kuntz, who, while remarking that there had been tremendous improvement in the representation of women—seventeen female delegates as compared to two the first year—told the agents that this progress had not been sufficient. She castigated the men; too many wanted benefits for men only

13. *Bulletin de l'AG,* April, 1901.
14. Frischmann, *Histoire PTT,* 109.
15. *Bulletin de l'AG,* September, 1902.
16. Bachrach, "Feminization," 320–21.
17. *Bulletin de l'AG,* October, 1902.

and at the expense of female workers. An appeal was made for a real spirit of fraternity and solidarity.[18] Later that year, in a report on the budget, the deputy Marcel Sembat told the Association Générale that it must deal with women's problems and fight for them because the women themselves had no suffrage.[19] Apparently the remarks of Mlle Kuntz and Sembat touched home because the question of women's wages and advancement became a regular part of the demands of the Association Générale.

Still, antagonisms between the men and the lower-paid women remained. Although a large number of women were active in the organizations of the PTT and played a major role in the strike of 1909, many women, burdened by the double demands of work and family or discouraged by the attitudes of male workers, were not active in the association. These women were told by a sister activist that they must join the fight for their dignity and eventual emancipation. Recognizing "that their duties were heavier than those of men, that they had more responsibilities to carry, while their rights were limited," she urged her sisters to join the association, asserting "that by no longer detaching themselves from the struggle for a living wage, their dignity would be raised and their emancipation would thus be realized."[20] When the Association Générale voted against the existence of separate groups and Mme Chambin, one of the two female members of the national council, was expelled, she formed the Association des Dames Employées. Considering itself more elitist, it remained a small group compared to the nearly two thousand women in the Association Générale. It was important mostly for its defense of women's rights.[21] Although these divisions between male and female workers, common to blue-collar workers and fonctionnaires alike, continued, the PTT fonctionnaires, who at first linked female raises to male raises, began to fight for and eventually won equal pay for women workers.

As the Association Générale des Agents increased its numerical strength, it began to experience internal factional struggles that mirrored the ideological differences of many fonctionnaires. The Associa-

18. *Ibid.*, May, 1903.
19. *Ibid.*, September, 1903.
20. *Ibid.*, January, 1907.
21. Bachrach, "Feminization," 330–31, and "Dames Employées," 90–97.

tion Générale, though strong in its demands for improved working conditions for its members, was, compared to blue-collar syndicats, fairly conservative and reformist. Its actions consisted mostly of sending delegations and petitions to ask favors from the administration or from some of the more sympathetic deputies. This policy began to erode at the 1903 congress, when an attempt was made to eliminate leaders of the association who were too beholden to the administration. The association statutes were modified to exclude all *cadres supérieurs* from the administration of the Association Générale. A further decision was made to avoid the pitfalls of separating into crafts and to remain an organization of all agents. This latter decision provoked some of the more professionally oriented, who wanted each profession to chart its own course. By the end of the year, a number of *receveurs* and *receveuses* had separated from the Association Générale. The next year, they joined with other dissidents to form the Fédération des Associations Professionnelles des PTT, claiming this right under the law of 1901.[22] This group, consisting of the more conservative commis, receveurs, telephone, telegraph, stenographic, and central administration workers, claimed membership almost equal to that of the Association Générale. But the Association Générale was able to rebuild its strength in the following years as the fight for improved wages and working conditions intensified. At the end of 1904, after a preliminary agreement was worked out between the Association Générales of the agents, sous-agents, and the fonctionnaires of the Ministry of Ponts et Chaussées (bridges and roads), the agents became part of the Fédération Générale des Associations Professionnelles des Employés Civils de l'Etat, the first federation of fonctionnaires.[23]

With the more conservative wing of the Association Générale now in professionally oriented organizations, the strength of the militant mi-

---

22. Frischmann, *Histoire PTT,* 110–11.

23. The federation consisted of the following organizations: Association des Personnels des Travaux Publics, Association Générale des Agents des PTT, Association Générale des Sous-Agents des PTT, Société des Commis des Ponts et Chaussées, Union Générale des Agents des Contributions Indirectes, Fédération des Amicales des Instituteurs et Institutrices Laïques, Société Amicale des Commissaires de Surveillance Administrative des Chemins de Fer, Association Professionnelle des Huissiers, Gardiens de Bureau, Fédération des Associations Professionnelles des Ministères, and Fédération Générale des Cantonniers et Agents de la Navigation.

nority, who found the moderate policies of the Association Générale insufficient, increased. This vocal and active group, led by Clavier and
Frédéric Subra in the secretariat, began to press for the transformation of
the association into a true syndicat. By 1905, the syndicalists within the
Association Générale des Agents had made the question of such a transformation a critical issue, and it was discussed vigorously in the newspapers and meetings of the association. Both the congresses of 1905 and
1906 reflected the dichotomy of the membership. If the moderate "hat-
in-hand" policies were not meeting the needs of the postal employees,
the question was how to change the organization and action to become
more effective.

For many agents, it was evident that fonctionnaires could achieve
nothing if they remained isolated from the working class. The postal
proletariat must use the organization of the working class, the syndicat,
to join other workers in the CGT to struggle for the emancipation of the
working class as a whole. The state, by denying the 1884 law to fonctionnaires, was attempting to create a false chasm between workers of
the state and those of private industry. The association's newspaper, the
Bulletin, made its position clear: "Our association is a weapon of study.
The syndicat is a weapon of struggle."[24] Jaurès addressed the 1905 congress: "Do you suppose that the freedom that you are using tonight belongs to you, that you have won it all alone? Indeed, it required the
struggles, the strikes of other factory workers, it required the universal
affirmation of proletarians facing the all-powerful employers of private
industry in order to make that grand collective employer, the state hierarchy, aware of your rights and the strength of your demands."[25]

A syndicalist organization was formed, the Comité de Propagande
d'Action Syndicale des Agents des PTT, which acted as a subgroup
within the Association Générale. Its principles were clearly revolutionary syndicalist, and though the number of adherents is uncertain, its
existence indicates that there was sympathy among some fonctionnaires
for the revolutionary syndicalism of the working class in the period before 1914. Sections of a brochure issued by the Comité indicate how
strong this ideological attachment was:

24. *Bulletin de l'AG,* No. 60.
25. *Ibid.,* June, 1905.

Considering that the proletariat must organize itself economically as a class party, that it must have as a goal the socialization of the means of production and exchange, that is, the transformation of capitalist society into a collective or communist society. . . .

Considering that in order to reach this goal, that of all forms of organization, the syndicat is the best, inasmuch as it is an interest group uniting the exploited against the common enemy: THE CAPITALIST.[26]

Others in the Association Générale may have thought the syndicat form was desirable but hesitated to attach themselves to the revolutionary blue-collar movement, an attachment that was, of course, still illegal for state employees. Subra, the secretary general of the Association Générale, told the 1905 congress, "Far from being a machine of war against the state, our Association Générale is a great democratic force placed in the service of the nation."[27] The administrative council equivocated, desirous of the syndicat form but fearful of taking the ultimate step: "The council, favoring in principle the transformation of the Association Générale into a syndicat, but recognizing that this transformation does not seem to be possible while things are in their present state, thinks it better to continue the orientation of the Association Générale in the direction of the syndicalist path."[28]

The issue was hotly debated at the congress of 1906. A leader of the Parisian syndicalist sympathizers, Clavier, had already called for the organization of a syndicat, linking the emancipation of the agents to the union with other workers.[29] But many delegates worried about government repression and preferred to stay with the organization that had been successful in approaching the government. Others were concerned that the entire membership was not ready for this step toward alliance with the working class. One of the more militant syndicalists attacked their "petit-bourgeois concerns": "When you seek to improve your personal situation you are less attractive than the wine or cheese merchant who seeks to raise his profits." An order of the day was proposed to have the administrative council transform the association into a syndicat,

26. Quilici Papers, Centre de Recherches d'Histoire des Mouvements Sociaux et du Syndicalisme, Paris. I was granted permission to see these papers by Professor Jean Maitron.

27. *Bulletin de l'AG,* June, 1905.

28. *Ibid.,* May, 1905.

29. *La Petite République,* January 8, 1906.

but in the voting immediate action was rejected by a vote of 9,655 to 1,540. It was clear, however, that the idea of transformation was accepted, and the delegates voted to have the council begin the formalities that would enable the Association Générale to become a syndicat, "in order that this transformation become an actuality and that relations of the new syndicat be rapidly established with the organized proletariat."[30] Thus the Association Générale represents a common anomaly of the fonctionnaire movement before 1914. It supported the syndicalist movement but retained the association form.

While the agents were debating their course of action, the sous-agents were making important decisions. The Association Générale des Sous-Agents, the largest of the PTT organizations with thirty-five thousand members in 1905, was under attack from those syndicalist members who were intensely dissatisfied with policies that were even more conservative and hesitant than those of the Association Générale des Agents. In late 1904, this militant group launched a newspaper, La Pile (the Battery) which called for the droit syndical and for the transformation of the association into a syndicat. On September 11, 1905, after a year of intense activity, the Parisian section held a congress at which the sous-agents voted to become a syndicat: "The sous-agents recognize that the syndicat is the only form which will allow them to obtain the moral and material improvements which they have the right to claim."[31] The influential Ligue des Droits de l'Homme voiced its support for the syndicat.[32]

But if the Parisian sous-agents were ready to adopt the syndicalist organization, the more cautious provincial postiers were not; when the national congress met, the order for immediate transformation was voted down, two to one. The syndicalists left the congress, calling a meeting which was attended by forty-five hundred sous-agents, and the Syndicat National des Sous-Agents became a reality. Smaller in size than the Association Générale des Sous-Agents—it claimed a membership of fourteen thousand of the thirty-five thousand organized sous-agents[33]—the Syndicat National, under the leadership of the facteur Henri Grangier,

30. AP, BA 1437.
31. Frischmann, Histoire PTT, 113.
32. L'Humanité, October 30, 1905.
33. La Petite République, November 29, 1905.

nevertheless gained in influence and members as the Association Générale disintegrated into a half-dozen impotent groups.

The year 1906 is an important one in French labor history. It was the
year when Clemenceau's government, which had promised much social
reform, was to find itself locked in bitter struggle with hundreds of
thousands of miners, metallurgists, and other workers, whose strike
movement was to intensify in the period 1906–1911. It was a year when
fonctionnaires began a concerted effort for the droit syndical, and it was
the year the lowly sous-agents of Paris went out on strike.

The Syndicat des Sous-Agents, only a year old, had been under constant attack from the government. But each threat only seemed to draw
more support for the syndicat from the sous-agents; even those who
were not members supported its demands: "The syndicat represented,
moreover, even for those who lacked consciousness, great hope, because it had established as its first task, the raising of starting salaries."[34]
The hope for improved starting salaries was dashed in 1906, when the
Chamber, in debating the budget, neglected to add even the slightest
raise for the especially low-paid *facteurs d'imprimés* (those who delivered
printed matter or second-class mail). But the Senate agreed to review the
budget, and hope revived. After all, the Radicals and other politicians
had promised to improve their meager wages. During the Senate discussion, the syndicat leaders, sensing disaster, hurried to ask the members
of the left bloc in the Chamber to help present their case to the government. A delegation consisting of Louis Codet, Ferdinand Buisson,
Camille Pelletan, Théodore Steeg, Victor Dejéante, and Marcel Sembat,
deputies who had often spoken to and for the fonctionnaires, went to
the head of the Conseil d'Etat, Jean Sarrien, to ask the government to
hear the sous-agents and to intercede on their behalf with the legislature.
The government, speaking through Sarrien, refused. It did not wish
to "trouble" existing syndicats (they would not be disbanded), but it
would not enter into communications with any organization bearing the
name *syndicat*. The budget was closed, and the sous-agents were ignored. Sembat transmitted this news on the evening of April 10. Immediately notices were posted calling for a big meeting the next day

34. Victor Monbruneaud, "La Grève des Postes et Télégraphes," *Le Mouvement Socialiste,*
Nos. 174–75 (May 15–June 15, 1906), 150.

"against the position of the public powers who conspired to avoid dealing with the legitimate demands of the sous-agents."[35] At eleven o'clock on the morning of the eleventh, twelve hundred sous-agents, meeting at Tivoli-Vaux Hall, "considering that the only weapon left to them is the strike," voted for a strike, demanding a salary increase of six hundred francs with a two-hundred-franc increase every six years for second-class facteurs and a four-hundred-franc increase with one hundred francs every six years for third-class facteurs, the end of advancement *au choix* (selection by superiors), the droit syndical, and no punishment for strikers.[36] The strike began in Paris and in the provinces at Lyons, Marseilles, and Bordeaux as the sous-agents, instead of going to work, stayed at what was to become a prolonged meeting, hearing Sembat promise his support even though he disapproved of the strike (it would only confirm the Radicals' worst fears—that to give the droit syndical would mean strikes of government services workers). By the afternoon, as word spread, two thousand people were on hand to hear Griffuehles of the CGT support their cause, and by evening, the secretary of the Syndicat des Sous-Agents, Grangier, spoke to a crowd of twenty-five hundred. Even after midnight, over one thousand sous-agents remained in the hall, setting up committees and issuing declarations.[37]

At first, the minister of public works and the PTT, Louis Barthou, when approached by the SFIO deputies Sembat, Dejéante, and Steeg, expressed his shock at the strike, assuring the socialists that he never refused to see individuals and telling them he would inform the minister of finance about the low wages of the sous-agents, but as soon as the strike was a reality, Barthou threatened the strikers with *révocation* (dismissal).[38] Immediately, the question of what the agents would do was of critical importance. The Association Générale des Agents issued a solidarity statement declaring that it would go on strike if the facteurs were fired; its secretary-general, Subra, expressed the hope that the separation of agents and sous-agents would soon end. The syndicats of teachers, meeting at their first national congress, sent a message giving "their comrades, the postal workers, now striking for the triumph of their de-

35. AP, BA 1390.
36. *Le Temps*, April 12, 1906.
37. AP, BA 1390.
38. *La Petite République*, April 12, 1906.

mands, the assurance of working-class solidarity and the fraternal greetings of the primary school proletariat."[39]

Between the twelfth and the thirteenth, more than three hundred strikers, chosen for reasons known only to the government, received letters of révocation. Despite Subra's request for an immediate strike, the agents sent only verbal support. Still, the strike grew. Most letter carriers, the elite of the sous-agents, those who had seniority and hence the most to lose, had not gone out on strike the first day. But now about four hundred of them were engulfed by the enormity of the movement and followed the younger and more militant strikers. The press was horrified. Most agreed that the demands of the sous-agents were justified but the syndicat and the strike were not. *La Patrie* called the sous-agents "our servants" and cautioned that the strike was the beginning of anarchy. *Le Temps* called them *démissionnaires,* who had broken their contracts. *Le Figaro* declared the strike absurd, the most unpopular strike ever in Paris. Only the newspapers of the Left, *La Lanterne, La Petite République,* and, of course, *L'Humanité,* disapproved of the government's handling of the strike.[40]

By the thirteenth, about twelve hundred sous-agents were on strike. The Tivoli-Vaux Hall, filled with several thousand strikers and sympathizers, cheered the facteurs, who proudly displayed their letters of dismissal in their lapels or wore hand-painted signs, RÉVOQUÉ, in their caps. The military and the police were handling the mail, but the strikers declared that they were not afraid of being fired or of the police; they issued their order of the day, "Vive l'émancipation du prolétariat administratif! Vive la Grève! Vive le syndicat des Sous-Agents!" By the evening of the thirteenth, between five and six thousand people, many of them wives and children of the strikers or sympathizers from other syndicats, filled the hall, and a thousand more milled in the street. Subra of the agents hailed the strike as a prelude to a general strike, and when Albert Lévy of the CGT told them that the government was opposed to the syndicats of fonctionnaires because it was opposed to the CGT and that the proletariat of the fonctionnaires and the proletariat of industry must unite to bring about the general strike, which even the police

39. Frischmann, *Histoire PTT,* 126.
40. Newspapers of April 13 and 14.

would join, the sous-agents greeted this declaration with great enthusiasm. The red flag was flown.

On the fourteenth, the strike was still holding and another crowd of twenty-five hundred pledged to "go to the end" even though Clemenceau had told a reporter the previous evening that the government had decided to be as harsh as possible with the strikers even if their numbers reached considerable proportions: "If there are two thousand, then we will fire two thousand." On the fifteenth, the hostile press was told it was no longer welcome at the huge open meetings. Almost from the beginning, even as thousands rallied to the strike and mail piled up at the central post office, newspapers had said that the strike was crumbling.

Although most workers' organizations suffered from infinitesmal treasuries, some money began to arrive at strike headquarters. The agents, through Subra, had sent seven thousand francs. Although the press insisted that the CGT was underwriting the strike, the poor CGT could send only a pittance; its contribution was added to those of the match workers and the marine, arsenal, and tobacco workers and came to three thousand francs. The treasury of the sous-agents held ten thousand francs. But despite the donations and the vigorous speeches of support, only the sous-agents were on strike and only they carried the letter of révocation. The agents had held a meeting at which a strike vote, supported by the rank and file, was avoided by the leadership. By the sixteenth, the meetings of the sous-agents were getting smaller, and in the next few days strikers began to trickle back to work. Without solidarity, the strike could not last. The strikers, mostly young, had depended on their own *facteurs des lettres,* but they had not come out in force, nor had any others in the postal service.

The speeches remained brave. Grangier claimed that twenty-five hundred workers were on strike, but in truth no one knew the real figure. A representative of the match workers told the sous-agents that the government was in trouble and their strike must continue. On the eighteenth, with more strikers returning to work, the CGT issued a call for help: "All workers will understand that a victory of postiers over the bourgeois government will be like a salutory prelude to the coming of the Social Revolution." Pressure mounted. The police attacked the peaceful marchers of sous-agents and their families. On the twentieth, Grangier was forced to lead a delegation to Sarrien to ask for reintegration of all strikers; the minister refused to see the "fonctionnaires in re-volt." The strike was ended with 380 sous-agents dismissed from ser-vice, among them Grangier, Louis Simonnet, who had led the *jeunes facteurs* out of the Association Générale, and a thirteen-year-old tele-graph boy.[41]

The defeat of the strike, which had begun with so much confidence in the justice of its cause and so much hope for its triumph, serves to em-phasize some of the weaknesses that characterized the fonctionnaires' or-ganizations. The strike was begun by the lowest-ranking and poorest-paid of the fonctionnaires. To be a sous-agent, it was not necessary in 1906 to take an examination, and the pay was low for much hard work, sorting and carrying bundles of mail. It was as close as one could get to being a blue-collar worker and still retain the title *fonctionnaire*. This closeness to the blue-collar workers was intensified as large numbers of facteurs, especially the younger, lower-paid ones, chose the syndicat and the strike as ways to fight for their demands. But to fight the state, which was most willing to fire strikers and bring in troops to keep ser-vices going, more was needed than the small if enthusiastic group who went out on strike. Within their own occupation, the older facteurs, fearful of losing their jobs and pension benefits, refused to join them en masse, and, of course, the agents equivocated. Not even the line work-ers, a blue-collar group, were able to bolster the strength of the poor sous-agents. When the leadership of the line workers was criticized for not supporting the strike of the sous-agents, for being "moral accom-plices of the government," the administrative council answered that only four hundred workers would have followed a strike call and that they would have suffered for doing so but would not have changed the outcome of the strike.[42] The higher-paid fonctionnaires were simply not

41. All the information on the 1906 strike comes from AP, BA 1390. While going through the Archives of the Prefecture of the Police of Paris, I found a box with three folders on the strike of 1906. The first folder contained letters, clippings, and police reports in which the leaders of the syndicat complained that they were being followed and harassed by the police. The second folder was filled with similar letters and clippings in which the police denied that they were following the syndicalists, insisting that they never did such things. The third folder contained the police reports turned in by the agents who had followed about seventeen or eighteen of the strike leaders, which indicates that these militants had been followed every minute of the day through-out the strike.

42. AP, BA 1436.

willing to take the fateful step and join a syndicat in an illegal strike against the employer-state. The blue-collar movement, for all its rhetoric about the general strike and the solidarity of the working class, still could not muster enough strength to reach that goal.

Although the plight of the fired workers, most of whom had no savings to fall back on until they were reinstated, was pitiful, the strike results were not all negative. Indeed, on a general political level, it might be considered a victory. Within a few months, the wages of the sousagents were raised, not as much as demanded but enough to make the strike worthwhile. The campaign for financial support for the *révoqués* and for their reintegration rallied a large number of postal employees to the cause of the syndicat. Syndicats and associations all over France called for the reintegration of the strikers. Membership in the Syndicat National des Sous-Agents grew. By fall, almost all of the révoqués had been reinstated. The actions of the government also heightened the realization among fonctionnaires that the state was a boss like any other and that perhaps the only way to achieve their goals was through the syndicat and the working-class movement. For syndicalists and socialists, the strike was an indication that even the fonctionnaires, who had always been so meek and peaceful, were joining the attack on the bourgeoisie and its state.[43]

By the crucial year 1906, the postiers, who six years before had lacked organization and direction, were joined together, voicing their demands for wage increases and paid vacations as well as changes in advancement and hierarchy. Moreover, though the majority were in associations, the push for syndicalism was growing stronger.

The Spuller memorandum of 1887 had effectively destroyed the organization of teachers for over a decade. Armand Fallières, the minister of education in 1889, reaffirmed the government's hostility to associations and syndicats with another prohibitive circular, and when a handful of teachers in the Vaucluse attempted to hold a congress in 1892, their meeting was forbidden, first by the prefect and then by the minister, Léon Bourgeois. The government's position was to remain constant

43. Gabriel Beaubois, "L'Etat, les partis et le syndicalisme," *Le Mouvement Socialiste,* Nos. 189–90 (August 15–September 15, 1907), 121.

throughout the 1890s: only mutual aid societies and pedagogic study groups were allowed.[44]

But with the political and intellectual ferment caused by the Dreyfus affair, many teachers, caught up in the debate and activity in defense of the democratic republic, began once again to think of forming more meaningful professional groups. As the century drew to a close, several amicales, largely devoted to discussing pedagogy, had been formed. In August, 1899, a group of teachers, meeting at Laon to dedicate a memorial to three instituteurs shot by the Germans in 1870, decided to organize a congress the next year in an attempt to create a federation of amicales. Representatives of fifty-two amicales, *unions pédagogiques,* and mutual aid societies met to plan the congress, which was to be held in Paris in 1900. The government, anxious for the support of teachers in its struggle against the ultranationals, allowed the congress to be held. Minister Georges Leygues stated: "What is good for one category of citizens is good for all the others and you do not lose this attribute when you become a teacher."[45]

The statement of principles issued by the congress was a declaration not only in defense of the profession but also of the secular school system, which was still under attack from the supporters of clerical education. "The Amicale is a society of pedagogic improvement and of defense of the professional and material interests of its members. . . . It is also a group of resistance and of struggle created for the defense of the secular school system."[46]

Another congress was held in 1901, but in 1902, Waldeck-Rousseau, worried about all the activity among the fonctionnaires, prohibited the congress. In 1903, however, the government not only gave its consent but sent the head of the State Council, Emile Combes, a frequent spokesman for the government against the fonctionnaires' organizations, to give its blessings to the Fédération des Amicales, now firmly established under the 1901 law. Within a few years, 90,000 of the 111,000 instituteurs and

44. Suzanne Baudard, *Le Mouvement syndicaliste dans le corps des instituteurs* (Thèse pour le doctorat, Faculté de Droit de Dijon, Paris, 1920), 27–28.

45. *Ibid.,* 30.

46. Max Ferré, *Histoire du mouvement syndicaliste révolutionnaire chez les instituteurs* (Paris, 1955), 28.

institutrices of France were part of the 117 amicales and associations participating in the federation.[47]

The amicales, ostensibly formed to discuss pedagogy, almost immediately turned to questions of working conditions and wages. Although not all teachers lived in the penury described by Antonin Lavergne in the popular novel of 1901 *Jean Coste ou l'instituteur au village,* most teachers were forced to attempt a bourgeois life-style. They were expected to wear suits, for example, despite their inadequate salaries. In 1901, a *stagiaire,* a nontenured teacher, received a mere seventy francs a month and after fourteen years might earn only one hundred francs a month. Moreover, until advancement was regulated by law in 1900, some teachers remained as *stagiaires* for twenty or thirty years.[48] Jacques Ozouf estimates that in 1901, in an average village, pension at an inn cost seventy-five francs per month, a dozen eggs cost one franc, a kilo of lard, one franc sixty, and a suit of clothes, between fifty and sixty francs. In the same village, an agricultural day worker earned three francs fifty per day, and in Paris, the more skilled workers in the printing and metallurgy industries earned twice as much.[49]

The finance laws of March 31, 1903, and April 22, 1905, which raised the salary range to a one-thousand-franc minimum and a twenty-two-hundred maximum, made life a bit more bearable for the instituteurs. The institutrices were on a separate salary schedule and received two hundred francs less on most levels.[50] Teachers remembered their penurious lives during the Belle Epoque:

> Immediately after my marriage (1909) for economy's sake, I decided: 1) not to smoke; 2) not to set foot into a café; 3) to write to *L'Humanité* that I could no longer pay for my subscription, and almost at the same time, I left freemasonry. The membership fee was 2 francs 50 a month and attending a meeting cost me 15 francs for the trip.
>
> My beginnings in the extreme northeast of the department of Bouches-du-Rhône were extremely rough. In the local café restaurant, room and board was 75 francs a month: my monthly salary decreased by pension deductions

47. Musée Social, *Le Droit d'association,* 143.
48. M. T. Laurin, *Les Instituteurs et le syndicalisme, Amicales et syndicats d'instituteurs* (Paris, 1908), 113.
49. Jacques Ozouf, *Nous les maîtres d'école* (Paris, 1967), 113.
50. Laurin, *Les Instituteurs,* 13.

amounted to 71 francs 15. My parents gave me a bed, a table, a few kitchen utensils.

I remember my beginning salary as a probationer in 1910. I believe I received 86 francs 95 per month, a deduction having been taken for the retirement fund and for unemployment . . . 86 francs 95! . . . I did my own cooking; it wasn't possible to take room and board (that cost 75 francs) and I gave 10 francs (appropriated from my 86 francs 95) to my old mother. At 13 miles from the station I could not afford the 2 francs for the coach when I went on vacation to my mother's house. When I arrived at the station, even a glass of beer was too expensive for me. At that time, I personified literally "Jean Coste" as I personified the "petit chose."[51]

The wage demands of the teachers were not too different from those of the postiers and other fonctionnaires; the amicales were relatively successful in pressing for the increases that were granted in 1903 and 1905. But there were other problems which some instituteurs considered even more important than the question of wages. Teachers were deeply distressed by the arbitrary and often dictatorial behavior of the director, whose decisions, often detrimental to the professional integrity of the instituteurs, had to be obeyed without question. Moreover, the behavior, curriculum, and job security of instituteurs were often called into question by local notables. Under the unsatisfactory advancement system, nepotism was the rule in small villages as well as in high circles. "Municipal councillors, mayors, administrative delegates, cantonal delegates, important electors, ward and regional councillors, deputies, senators, all took for themselves the prerogative to transfer the teacher when it suited them, whether he was unable to satisfy their fantasies or above all if he had the bad taste to resist them."[52] Teachers who displayed the wrong politics, were too strongly anticlerical in a clerical village, or talked of organizing syndicats were the prime victims, but all were affected by the atmosphere. Gabrielle Bouët, later a leader of the teachers' syndicat, was suspended for refusing to lead her pupils in prayer as was demanded by the *directrice*. Another future leader of the syndicat, Marie Mayoux, was reprimanded because she went to class without a hat, and her husband was reprimanded for wearing *sabots* in the street.

51. Ozouf, *Nous les maîtres*, 117–20.
52. Laurin, *Les Instituteurs*, 14.

A director in the Ain was transferred from his office because he absented himself for three Sundays without authorization to attend conferences and the socialist congress at Bellegarde. Two teachers who openly sided with him suffered the same fate. Another spoke at an open meeting against war and actively campaigned against Sarrien. A professor of philosophy at the *lycée* of Roanne spoke at an open meeting without telling his superiors what his subject would be. Yet another professor was accused of using unsuitable language in articles he had written. All suffered professional punishment.

Two cases in particular became causes célèbres among the teachers and the population at large. Both are evidence not only of the arbitrary behavior of local officials but also of the gap between official anticlericalism on the national level and the difficulties faced by anticlerical teachers on the local level. One case involved a professor at the prestigious Lycée Charlemagne in Paris, named Thalamas, who was transferred to another school for "lack of tact and restraint." A student had written a paper on Joan of Arc defending the thesis "Joan is a religious heroine and not a pagan goddess of patriotism." Thalamas had given the student a good grade but added the note, "It isn't possible to introduce miracles in history" and suggested that the supposed celestial voices were hallucinations. Two teachers who were considered instrumental in having a motion passed by the amicale of Nancy which declared that Thalamas had the right as a professor to interpret the facts of history according to historical and critical methods were also removed from their positions.[53]

The second case, the affair of an Inspector Guéry, was instrumental in undermining whatever confidence teachers might have had in Briand, the minister of education in 1906. Guéry, a professor of merit, recognized even by Briand, was named *inspecteur d'académie* of the Côtes-du-Nord and, contrary to local wishes, set about emphasizing the secular nature of the schools under his jurisdiction. "We are a school without God . . . we make no use of God to justify our morality. Using a purely human basis, we try to create the aware and fraternal man of the future society." He had already incurred the displeasure of the local notables

53. Charles Fourrier, *La Liberté d'opinion du fonctionnaire* (Paris, 1957), 266–67.

with this anticlerical attitude and further antagonized them when he refused to make a number of political appointments. Finally, the local deputy arranged to have him fired. The teachers of the department protested vigorously. Briand was questioned in the Chamber, and though he agreed that the prefect had been a bit too hasty, he defended the firing, ending his statement with a declaration that shocked many supporters of the liberal republican government: "The teachers want to make use of their civil rights. It is not I who ever thought of restraining them from the use of this right. But I have always told them that their situation was especially delicate and I want to repeat it: teachers are not primarily political men. They are primarily educators." [54]

Although teaching opened up a vast area of employment for women, and thousands of young institutrices, armed with their diplomas and certificates, enthusiastically went off to the girls' schools and the écoles maternelles (nursery schools) of thousands of towns and villages, life was particularly hard for the institutrices who were charged with the education of the "future mothers of the Republic." During the nineteenth century, lay teachers had gradually replaced many of the religious orders in the boys' schools but most girls remained in the hands of nuns. The ideologues of the Third Republic wanted to remove the religious influence of the nuns but nevertheless wished to make sure that girls would still receive a moral education to ensure that these future mothers would be republican in sympathy, while remaining chaste, hardworking, and obedient. Linda Clark's study of primary school textbooks notes that through the famous morale lessons and the popular Suzette series of readers, girls learned early that their education prepared them to be good and uncomplaining wives and mothers. [55]

Female teachers, hired to replace nuns, were expected to behave like secular nuns, to live celibate, devoted, and, of course, poverty-stricken lives. If penury was the expected lot of male teachers, it was even more severe for the young institutrices. Women were paid less than men, and opportunities such as being the secretary to the mayor or the town council that traditionally allowed male teachers to earn extra money were not

54. M. L. Laurin, "Le Syndicalisme et les instituteurs," Le Mouvement Socialiste, No. 185 (April 1, 1907), 302–303.
55. Linda Clark, Schooling the Daughters of Marianne (Albany, 1984), 46.

open to them. It was explained that, of course, women's expenses were lower than those of men. After all, didn't women eat less? Could they not do their own cooking, laundry, and mending? Nor did they smoke or drink. Much to the chagrin of the women, many male colleagues, fearful of the feminization of the boys' and mixed (coeducational) schools, agreed with the administration.

But it was not just the poverty that made life so difficult, it was the way these women were expected to live as teachers. The training of "lay nuns" began in the normal schools, where a uniform of black skirts and dresses was required, dormitories were spartan, and life was regulated by the chiming of the bells. If France was not a convent, said Camille Sée, the normal school remained one.[56] In the small towns and villages, particularly where the beloved nuns had been unwillingly abandoned, the teachers' behavior was scrutinized carefully. To walk at night, to be without hat or gloves, as noted by Marie Mayoux, to talk too much or not enough, or to be too religious or not religious enough—all was noted. In some cases, there was outright harassment with pious merchants refusing to sell supplies to the corrupters of the town's daughters. Even in Paris, the municipal council was asked in 1897 to answer the question, "Can an institutrice ride a bicycle?"[57] It was also expected that women teachers would teach only girls or nursery school children of both sexes. Women were particularly suited to teaching the young—to be a teacher was to be a mother. La Mère institutrice (the mother/teacher) was the title of a series of pedagogic pamphlets for women. A primary school inspector described the role of a nursery school teacher to an 1889 international congress called to discuss the role of women teachers: "Among the little children whom she encourages with a smile, with a caress, whom she consoles with a kiss, she is truly the mother of the family. There she is and there she will stay."[58] Presumably he was considered a progressive for defending the right of women to teach young boys and girls.

56. Danielle Delhome, Nicole Gault, and Josiane Gonthier, *Les Premières institutrices laïques* (Paris, 1980), 33.

57. Leslie Page Moch, "Government Policy and Women's Experience: The Case of Teachers in France," *Feminist Studies,* XIV (Summer, 1988), 310.

58. Memoire of M. LeGouge, quoted in Delhome, Gault, and Gonthier, *Les Premières institutrices,* 49.

Isolation was also a major concern. The need for secular girls' schools was strongest in the smaller villages and hamlets, and it was there that the institutrices were sent. One could request an assignment in her native department, but institutrices were usually sent where there was need. Even in a home department, the twenty or thirty miles between the school and the parental village could be a difficult and lengthy journey. Moreover, within the town or village to which the teacher was assigned, there was little social life for the institutrices. They were separated from both the peasantry and the bourgeoisie by their unique status as educated but low-level fonctionnaires, and their only companions were other teachers, if there were any. Celibacy was desired, but it was also enforced by the lack of suitable male companions. Those who did marry frequently chose the local postman or another teacher as their life's companion. Indeed, to encourage teachers to remain in the small towns and villages, starting in the 1890s the government began to foster marriage between teachers. Educational administrators pointed out the advantages of shared housing, shared intellectual companionship, and, of course, shared salaries. Married couples were promised joint assignments. Despite this encouragement, by 1911, 72 percent of male teachers were married but 62 percent of females were single.[59]

For most female teachers then, life was only lonely. "Misery, with its hopelessness, always new faces, to be a stranger everywhere, without protection, without affection: the drowning solitude everywhere, always! Always moving in the same circle. It will soon be twenty-two years I have stood this. It is perpetual agony. I am forty-six years old; tomorrow, old age. Oh, how afraid I am of the final hopelessness."[60]

Isolated and harassed but determined to persevere, the women teachers turned to each other for comfort and intellectual companionship. In 1903, Marie Guillot, a teacher from Lorraine, founded the first Groupe Féministe Universitaire "to struggle against laws, mores and poor education which have for centuries kept women in a state of dependence and inferiority."[61] She called on women teachers to place themselves in the

59. For a full discussion of the government's marriage policy, see Moch, "Government Policy."
60. Letter from a female teacher, quoted in Delhome, Gault, and Gonthier, Les Premières institutrices, 94.
61. Ibid., 214.

vanguard of feminism. Although they never involved more than 4 or 5 percent of the women teachers, these feminist groups spread throughout the country (at one point there were about fifty groups) and emerged as a formidable center of political activity within the teachers' organizations and in the community at large. Their influence was far greater than their numbers might indicate. The aim of the Groupe Féministe was feminist action, but the special strength of the organizations in the more isolated provincial areas indicates that it also served as a center of intellectual and social support for the young and isolated teachers.

For some of the instituteurs and institutrices, the only way to fight for higher wages and against the arbitrariness of the administrators and politicians was through the syndicat. The syndicalist Emile Glay wrote, "Favoritism and corruption play a role in our profession that is extremely abnormal. How can worthy teachers not be discouraged in the face of these scandalous nominations or when seeing undeserved rapid promotion. We think that the syndicalist organization will bring order to this administrative anarchy." [62]

Most instituteurs, devoted republicans and suspicious of the anarchism and revolutionary ideology of the CGT, supported the amicales as their professional organization. The amicales had been successful in 1902 in eliminating advancement by percentage, an intensely disliked procedure in which the government decided what percentage of teachers would advance. But a small group of militants, many of them socialists and anarchists, continued to see the syndicat as the only organization that could alleviate their working conditions and make the Republic truly democratic. Slowly these syndicalists began to organize. In 1903, a group of teachers formed a new organization, l'Emancipation de l'Instituteur, which was more radical than any of the amicales. Their ideology was expressed in a periodical with the same name as the organization. The Emancipation group was most interested in establishing independence for teachers both in and out of the classroom. In a period when nationalism and clericalism were issues of major political importance, the group vigorously defended the secular schools and pacifism. A small group of teachers entered the Bourses du Travail in 1903, and in 1905 a host of tiny groups all over France began to call themselves syn-

62. *Le Temps,* November 29, 1905.

dicats. The first amicale to become a syndicat was the one in the department of the Var in February, 1905. Groups were soon organized in Morbihan, Pyrénées Orientales, Cher, and Côtes-du-Nord, and in 1906, after the parliamentary debate on the issue, in Bouches-du-Rhône, Maine-et-Loire, Deux Sevres, and several other departments. There were fifteen groups by 1906. At a banquet at the Bourse du Travail held by the amicale of the Sarthe, the local president of the syndicat spoke: "Manual workers, intellectual workers, we are working together in a common task, which to be fruitful requires our complete agreement. We will not fail to do our part."[63] Even the amicales began to be affected by the developing attachment to the working class. The president of the amicale of the Somme wrote in January, 1905: "Let us not appear to be aloof toward our friends of the factory and of the workshop. We are the friends of their children. Let us also be theirs."[64] In July, 1905, the group in the Bourses du Travail, the Emancipation group, and the recently formed syndicats formally established the Fédération des Syndicats des Instituteurs et Institutrices at a special congress in Paris.

The years 1905–1906 were fortunate ones for the young syndicats. With the Right defeated, the Radical government took power with great hopes for reform. In the absence of government prohibition, the teacher syndicats continued to exist. But in October, 1905, the question of syndicalism for teachers became an important political issue. On the twelfth, the syndicat of the Seine deposited at the prefecture its statutes and the names of its officers, as required by the law of 1884. Immediately the press, in particular *Le Temps,* attacked the organization of teachers into syndicats. *L'Eclair* ran articles headed "L'Ecole Rouge" (the red school) and "L'Internationale au Village" (the International in the village).[65] On October 19, the prefect announced that he would not give permission for the syndicat to continue. On November 4, forty syndicalists were brought before the tribunal of the Seine, "indicted for having, as public fonctionnaires, illegally formed a syndicat."[66] The question came before the Chamber on November 8, and the government asserted that the 1884

63. *Revue Politique et Parliamentaire,* July 10, 1906, pp. 86–87, quoted in Musée Social, *Le Droit d'association,* 145.

64. Ferré, *Instituteurs,* 73.

65. *L'Eclair,* October 29, 1905.

66. Ferré, *Instituteurs,* 76.

law did not authorize syndicats of teachers. The deputies were assured, however, that the government did not mean to penalize the teachers but merely to establish clearly the limits of the law. The government's position was supported by a vote of 305 to 35, with 235 abstentions. Immediate amnesty was proposed, and the next day the syndicalist teachers of the Seine were released. The legal proceedings against the Seine teachers had rallied many teachers and left-wing political groups. The ideas of the syndicalists were espoused in newspapers and at meetings. Marius Nègre, one of the leaders of the syndicalist movement, wrote in an article on the persecution of the Seine teachers: "We are convinced that our interests are tightly linked to those of the working class and that the syndicalist organization offers us . . . superior guarantees. Beyond our immediate demands we want to affirm the sentiments of deep solidarity which tie us to the working class and to show our sympathy for the vast movement of organizations and of proletarian emancipation which inevitably must transform the world." Nègre concluded that it was for these reasons that the amicales were moving toward syndicalism.[67]

The teachers welcomed the release of the Seine teachers and anticipated a "reign of tolerance" that would enable their movement to grow. In November, 1905, a manifesto of syndicalist teachers appeared. It declared that teachers did not teach in the name of the state but in the name of truth; they proclaimed the right to form syndicats:

> If one accepts that it is in the nature of things and in the higher interest of the state that the ability to have a syndicat should be refused to civil servants who hold a portion of the public power, one could not claim that power to deny teachers the right to form syndicats. Our teaching is not the teaching of authority. It is not in the name of the government, even a republican one, nor in the name of the state, nor even in the name of the French people that the teacher provides his teaching; it is in the name of truth. Mathematical relations, rules of grammar as well as historical, moral, and scientific facts, of which our teaching consists, will not be subject to the fluctuations of a majority.[68]

The number of syndicats grew; their first congress was held in Paris in February, 1906, presided over by Anatole France.

67. *La Nouvelle du Morbihan,* November 28, 1905.
68. Ferré, *Instituteurs,* 78–80. The entire text is in the appendix of Ferré's book.

One thousand teachers gathered at the Sociétés Savantes and greeted Jean Jaurès with frequent and prolonged applause as he spoke of the special role of instituteurs in a democratic society and of the necessity of joining the teachers to the syndicalist movement.[69] The meeting ended with a call for the improvement of curriculum, the ending of authoritarian administration, and cheers of "Vive le Syndicat."[70] But the question of affiliation to the CGT was left for the next congress because, as the militant syndicalist Bouët explained, "through fear of not being followed by the mass of members," the CGT was still a "bogeyman" even in the eyes of instituteurs with advanced ideas.[71]

The entrance of Aristide Briand into the Ministry of Education, first under Sarrien and then in the Clemenceau government of 1906, was welcomed by the instituteurs. For the first time, the reactionary administration would have at its head a man who was not only a socialist but had been the leading advocate of the general strike when the CGT was developing its program in the previous decade. Surely he would be better than even Millerand, who had never been a very strong socialist. But a lot of water had passed under the bridge in that decade. Briand had become the defender of the bourgeois state and, in the Ministry of Education, the defender of the status quo. He declared almost immediately that though he would not disband the existing syndicats, he would not allow the formation of any new groups. And indeed, while Briand headed the ministry, not one syndicat was formed.[72] His attempt to prevent the Rhône syndicat from joining the Lyons Bourses du Travail, though unsuccessful, clearly indicated his opposition to the syndicalism of teachers. The Guéry affair put him firmly in the camp of maintaining the arbitrary and hierarchical structure in education.

By the end of 1906, when the blue-collar labor movement was entering a period of intense activity and fonctionnaires were organizing and demanding the droit syndical, the battle lines for the teachers were drawn. Any attempts to form new syndicats were met with threats of legal proceedings, and a number of teachers found themselves in the courtroom in the years after 1906. Syndicalist teachers were harassed

69. L'Humanité, February 12, 1906.
70. L'Action, February 23, 1906.
71. Ferré, Instituteurs, 81.
72. Laurin, "Le Syndicalisme."

constantly; the secretary of the federation, Nègre, was fired in 1907 for his syndicalist activity and for signing an open letter to Clemenceau espousing syndicalism.

Still organization continued. *Répétiteurs, professeurs des Collèges, professeurs speciaux* (music and art), and *instituteurs laïcs* all formed amicales and associations. Many of these organizations became part of their local Bourses du Travail, and at the Nantes congress of 1907, the Fédération des Instituteurs affiliated with the CGT, issuing a statement of working-class solidarity: "The CGT is the living and active expression of proletarian solidarity and it is the indispensable link between all the syndicalist organizations. . . . The wage-earning teachers of the state, like other wage earners, have demands to present to their employer, *l'Etat-Patron*, that they will not uphold the governmental thesis that places a barrier between the administrative proletariat and the wage earners of industry." But then an important reservation was added: "By joining the CGT, they achieve their duty of working-class solidarity and *remain free in their methods and tactics.*"[73] The teachers entering the CGT would not agree to strike.

In reviewing all this activity, two questions come to mind. Why was the government so hostile, so fearful of the organization of teachers into syndicats, harassing, firing, and penalizing instituteurs as it did no other fonctionnaires? And, indeed, were the teachers as radical as the government seemed to think?

The secular teachers of the Belle Epoque were deeply republican. Hired to imbue their young charges with a devotion to the republican form of government and to France, to follow the great humanitarian and positivist traditions, and to substitute philosophy for theology, they did just that and for very little monetary gain. "Teachers have become an important force: the Radicals, the democratic socialists who follow Jaurès, count on them to dechristianize the people, to give devoted and educated citizens, and good voters, to the body politic."[74] The amicales were successful in part because they organized a group of young, vigorous men and women who adhered to everything the radical Republic stood for.

73. Ferré, *Instituteurs*, 106; italics added.
74. M. T. Laurin, "Les Idées socialistes: Les Idées socialistes des instituteurs et les amicales," *Le Mouvement Socialiste*, No. 150 (March 1, 1905), 297.

But it was just this devotion to democracy, to anticlericalism, and to the socialist humanitarianism of Jaurès that frightened the government. The future of the nation—its young—was in the hands of the teachers. Their position was very delicate. It was fine to be anticlerical but not in a radical way. It was fine to believe in democracy but not the way Jaurès interpreted the term. If one reads the personal memoirs in the impressive and touching study by Jacques Ozouf, *Nous les maîtres d'école,* one finds, time and again, that the universal hero of the teachers was Jean Jaurès, the humanitarian socialist, a frequent thorn in the side of the bourgeois state. A significant number of teachers also joined those Frenchmen who abandoned the nationalism of the nineteenth century and declared themselves openly against war. The line of support for the Republic was a narrow one; to overstep the bounds was anathema. To try to form a syndicat, to talk of solidarity with the working class, was unacceptable.

It is true that the syndicalist movement contained an influential group of militants, hostile to the bourgeois state, anxious for social reform, and determined to join with the blue-collar working class. This group was to grow in size and influence as the decade advanced. But for the most part, the teachers were just what they were supposed to be—devout republicans. An article in *Le Mouvement Socialiste* by a frequent defender of teacher syndicalism, M. T. Laurin (an instituteur whose real name was Marius Tortillet), summed up the political role of teachers: "Fonctionnaire of the state, I have never conceded that I could be led to rebel against this state." Most chose to remain in the tame amicales, many keeping a dual membership even when they joined a syndicat. Some found the amicales a bit too tame: "In my opinion, this amicale was nothing more than 'rose water'—official journal, banquet at the end of the year, various congratulations . . . that's all." And so they joined a syndicat or tried to influence the amicale to become one. "I thought it necessary to transform the amicale into a syndicat, without hiding that for me, our syndicat must be apolitical." Some saw the affiliation with the syndicalist movement as an act of solidarity with the working class: "It is through the union of all the manual and intellectual workers that we could improve our personal situation and make the society more fraternal for all."[75]

75. Ozouf, *Nous les maîtres,* 253–59.

But when these teachers joined a syndicat, they were not endorsing the general strike. Jacques Ozouf's teachers frequently expressed their views on the role of teachers' organizations: "I was favorable to a transformation of the amicales into syndicats with the condition that the strike would be excluded; teachers in the countryside enjoyed the growing confidence of the population and I feared that a strike would discredit them with their students, their parents and the population at large."[76] The syndicat of the Var declared that it was opposed to the general strike because it was illegal, and if the workers did hold such a strike, the place of the teachers was in the classroom with the workers' children.[77]

Some teachers who called themselves socialists were intellectual socialists, not revolutionaries. M. T. Laurin described the typical teacher: "He is humanitarian, lower middle class, secular, anti-clerical and above all, devoted to the state—but he is hardly a worker."[78] Some members of the CGT were fearful of allowing teachers into their organization because of their reformist tendencies.[79] Certainly there was a group of revolutionary socialists among the teachers, and this group would grow in influence, but the bulk of teachers were solidly republican, devoted to the ideals of the democratic republic, perhaps too devoted to ideals the bourgeois state never met.

The PTT and the Ministry of Education employed the largest number of fonctionnaires, and their organizations were the most important in size and influence. But thousands of other fonctionnaires, scattered in ministries and offices and courtrooms all over France, were also part of the massive movement that resulted in the growth of the organizations of all fonctionnaires. In the Ministry of Finance, the largest group to organize were the fonctionnaires of the Contributions Indirectes (tax office), whose numbers were to increase substantially as the central government expanded the taxation of French citizens and businesses. In the interwar period, the members of the Syndicat des Agents des Contributions Indirectes were to play an important role in the fonctionnaire movement. In

76. *Ibid.*
77. *L'Eclair,* February 3, 1906.
78. Laurin, "Les Idées socialistes," 304.
79. Gabriel Beaubois, "Les Employés de l'état et le socialisme ouvrier," *Le Mouvement Socialiste,* No. 152 (April 1, 1905).

the early part of the century, their organization, the Union Générale des Contributions Indirectes, though relatively small compared to those of the teachers and postal employees, grew steadily. At the first general assembly held in April, 1903, three hundred employees of this section of the Ministry of Finance came together to initiate their organization. Within a few months, they had 1,136 members; by 1907, L'Humanité reported that 9,500 of the 10,000 cadres in Contributions Indirectes were members of the Union Générale. The government's attempt to create a "yellow" union, the Association des Employés Supérieurs, according to the paper, made up of fils de papa (children of the privileged few) willing to do the bidding of the administration, was a failure.[80]

The Union Générale was at first rather conservative. In 1903, the administrative council of the union talked about "deferential visits before the finance minister and the director-general." In 1904, the council was still trying anxiously to get politicians to be honorary members, making plans to ask Gaston Doumergue, who was then minister of the colonies, and delighted that the socialist Alexandre Zévaès had become a member. But gradually the members of the Contributions Indirectes began to move away from their deferential position. By November, 1905, when the state and ministerial budgets were discussed, the Union Générale decided that instead of issuing the usual appeal to the minister to consider its interests in the budget, it would organize a campaign against him. By the time plans were being made for the 1906 congress, it was decided that the issue of syndicalism would be discussed at that meeting and that there would not be a banquet at the congress so they would not have to invite the minister of finance.[81] At the April congress, when syndicalism was discussed, the issue of the droit syndical was clearly separated from the right to strike. In an order of the day presented by the secretary-general, the congress voted in favor of the law of 1884 and the council was instructed to take all legal steps to obtain the benefits of the law.[82] The demand for the droit syndical was to be made again and again at the prewar meetings and congresses.

Whereas most teachers and postal workers were primarily concerned

80. Procès-Verbaux du Conseil d'Administration, Union Générale des Contributions Indirectes, meeting of October 19, 1903; L'Humanité, May 13, 1907.

81. Procès-Verbaux, May 15, 1903, May 10, 1904, November 23, 1905, January 16, 1906.

82. Le Matin, April 8, 1906, and Procès-Verbaux, April 2, 1906.

about their low wages, the members of the Contributions Indirectes were more interested in improved advancement procedures. Apparently the Ministry of Finance was a more desirable placement than the post office or the village school and favoritism was a more serious matter. Those who worked in the Contributions Indirectes were most anxious for advancement; the earliest demands all revolve around advancement procedures.[83] The Ministry of Finance attempted to improve working conditions in 1905, but when the advancement procedures were published in 1906, the fonctionnaires of the Contributions Indirectes found them highly unsatisfactory and the issue of advancement continued to be a major demand.[84]

A second important group under the Ministry of Finance was the *douaniers*. They were organized into two categories: the *sédentaires*, who dealt with import taxes, and the *actifs*, whose duties involved surveillance of coasts and frontiers. The larger group of actifs lived up to their name by being much more active in organizing and presenting their demands. The *sédentaires*, meeting in congress in 1907, praised the work of the ministers and listened to speeches assuring the government of their devotion. The closing banquet was addressed by one of the leaders of the Union Générale des Douaniers Actifs, who declared that the douaniers were not revolutionary and would not join the Bourses du Travail or the CGT. When his talk became more passionate about the demands of the douaniers and how their patience might run out, a gesture of impatience from the chairman of the *sédentaires* did not escape the speaker, who ended with a toast for the democratic and social Republic.[85]

The actifs were much more clamorous in demanding increases in their very modest wages and government guarantees against arbitrary behavior and injustice and against "secret notes and anonymous letters" placed in their dossiers. But the main problem faced by the douaniers was the illegality of their organization even into associations. Because they were armed, douaniers actifs were faced with an *ancien régime* governmental attitude; not even the 1901 Law of Associations was open to them, let alone the 1884 law allowing syndicats. Jacques Salis, deputy of the Hérault, supported an amendment to the finance law allowing the

83. Procès-Verbaux, November 19, 1903.
84. *L'Humanité*, February 7, 1906.
85. *Ibid.*, April 29, 1907.

actifs as civil fonctionnaires to use the law of 1901,[86] but in 1906, when twenty thousand of the twenty-three thousand douaniers were members of the Union Générale, associations and syndicats were still technically illegal. At the first congress in 1906, after several days of discussing salary, clothing allowances, and pensions, the actifs firmly declared themselves eligible for the 1884 law: "Contrary to the opinion expressed by the government, the douaniers consider themselves as agents of administration. . . . The congress adopts the principle of the syndicat."[87] In the 1907 congress, they asked their leaders to prepare the way for the transformation of the Union Générale into a syndicat. But the question, "The douaniers, are they civilians or military?" continued to be debated by douaniers and government officials.[88] The organizations remained illegal.

A different problem was faced by the *préposés des manufactures de l'état* (section heads and cadres of state-owned manufacturing facilities), who were considered workers when they demanded the prerogatives of fonctionnaires but fonctionnaires when they wanted the rights of workers, particularly regarding the droit syndical. The secretary-general of the Association Générale des Préposés asked for a definition of their positions. "Sons of workers, workers ourselves, we are deeply attached to republicanism," he reassured the government.[89]

The employees of the Trésoreries Générales (treasury) and the Recettes des Finance (tax collector's office) simply formed a syndicat, affiliating with the blue-collar Union Fédérative des Travailleurs de l'Etat.[90] Other fonctionnaires of the Ministry of Finance who organized were those in the Contributions Directes and the Octrois.

At the Ministry of Justice, a host of organizations sprang up: Association Amicale des Cours et Tribunaux, Association Amicale de la Magistrature, and Syndicat des Mandataires au Tribunal de Commerce. At the 1907 congress of the *mandataires,* the secretary-general declared it their duty to fight privilege in the justice system. Several lawyers of the Court of Appeals voiced the same devotion for the struggle for equal

86. AN, F7 13712.
87. *L'Action,* June 27, 1906.
88. *La Bataille Syndicaliste,* December 6, 1913.
89. *L'Action,* June 1, 1907.
90. AN, F7 13728.

justice: "As young lawyers, we have also had the dream of gaining access to the Court of Commerce and thanks to you, we will see it come true because what we all desire is this dream: a free bar in a free state."[91] The Service Pénitentiaire, with seventeen hundred members in 1908, also organized for a ten-hour day, a weekly day off, sick leave, vacations, memberships on councils of discipline, twenty-four hours' rest after night duty, and, like so many fonctionnaires, an end to favoritism and arbitrary decisions.

Not even the police were to be bypassed by the tremendous rush of organization. But the police who tried to organize were denied not only the right to form syndicats but frequently the benefits of the 1901 Law of Associations as well. After several attempts at organizing—an amicale had been formed in Marseilles in 1904—the police enjoyed a spurt of activity and success in 1906. Dozens of associations of *gardiens de la paix* and *agents de police* sprang up in cities such as Toulon, Rennes, Toulouse, and Rouen. A congress was held at Lorient, and a national federation was formed.

From the beginning there was a conflict between the police, who saw themselves as citizens fighting for improved working conditions, and the government authorities, who saw the police as a military arm of the state. Prime Minister Aristide Briand, addressing the amicales in 1909, told the police that there was a difference between a totally free citizen and a fonctionnaire demanding his rights; that difference was loyalty. "You as police," he added, "have an even more delicate situation. You are fonctionnaires and you are soldiers."[92] The amicales, treading softly, assured the government that they were not revolutionaries or syndicalists, nor would they think of striking against the public. Their demands were simple: salary increases, improved pensions, and a more democratic disciplinary procedure.[93] But a week-long strike of Lyons police struck fear in the hearts of national and municipal authorities.

In the course of meeting about pension difficulties, a discussion was begun about the other needs of Lyons police employees. The result of the meeting was a declaration which stated that if anyone was fired, all

91. *Ibid.*, Comby, avocat à la cour d'Appel, speaking at the 1908 banquet.
92. *L'Action*, December 6, 1909.
93. *L'Echo*, July 9, 1906.

would stop work. The prefect promptly fired sixty *gardiens*, and the strike became general. Gendarmes and foot soldiers brought in to replace those who refused to work could not prevent the increase of crime. Pressure mounted; the elected officials accused the prefect of refusing to pay sufficient attention to the needs of the police. Finally, the police were promised that their demands would be seriously considered and they returned to work.[94]

In Paris, the *commissaires* (superintendents) sent a letter to Louis Lépine, the prefect of police, saying that they had organized because the prefecture had neglected their needs. They claimed the rights of other fonctionnaires: "Even at the Prefecture of Police, we are fonctionnaires with the same titles as the others and without wanting to stress the services which we render to the population of Paris, we are right to demand from you, M. Prefect, and from your immediate staff, the respect and consideration which are our due."[95] Some of the police even talked of forming a syndicat; a letter that was circulated among the Paris agents urging them to join such a group caused great alarm not only at the prefecture but at the Ministry of the Interior to which any information about the possibility of such an organization was immediately relayed.

The demands of the Paris police were similar to those of other fonctionnaires, centering around questions of discipline, the weekly day off, and salary schedules. Although starting salaries were not as low as those for teachers and postiers—fourth-class gardiens received 1,900 francs; third-class, 2,100; second-class, 2,200; and first-class, 2,300—the maximum was low and the differences between the levels was small. Even a *chef-brigadier* could expect a maximum of only 3,000 francs. One had to wait fourteen years to reach the maximum gardien salary.[96]

Lépine declared that he would never meet with the representatives of an association, and those who might plan to form a syndicat were told that they would face dismissal.[97] *L'Aurore* explained that the police were asking only for the 1901 law and not for the right to have a syndicat or to join the CGT, but most of the press raised the specter of the CGT and the police on strike. *L'Autorité* expressed its horror: "It is anarchy in the

94. Georges Cahen, *Les Fonctionnaires: Leur action corporative* (Paris, 1911), 137–39.
95. *La Petite République,* July 31, 1906.
96. *L'Echo de Paris,* July 25, 1906.
97. *Le Journal,* July 3, 1906; *La Patrie,* July 27, 1906.

police."[98] Clearly the organization of police, even in associations, was a severe blow to the government authorities.

The list of organized fonctionnaires grew. In the *travaux publics* (public works), the commis of the *ponts et chaussées* (bridges and roads) organized a society, as did the fonctionnaires of the *eaux et forêts* (waterways and forests). Among prefectural workers, the *secrétaires de mairies* (town hall secretaries) complained that they were hired and fired at will by the mayors and that there was no standardization of salaries; they asked the government to pass laws granting them stable working conditions.[99] Employees in central ministries, in departmental offices, communal workers from hospital to pawnshop, and employees of the Bibliothèque Nationale (the National Library) all formed amicales, societies, associations, and, occasionally, syndicats.

Many of the demands made by fonctionnaires in this early period of organization were similar to those of blue-collar workers; issues involving wages, holidays, vacations, and hours rallied workers in both the private and public sectors of the economy. But there were other demands that were unique to fonctionnaires and reflected the hierarchical structure of their environment. Few blue-collar workers could advance very far, but advancement was of great concern to all fonctionnaires, especially those in the Ministry of Finance. Teachers were concerned about the government's control over their teaching and their private lives; they demanded the freedom of conscience that was supposed to be the right of all French citizens. All fonctionnaires complained about nepotism, favoritism, and arbitrary decision making, the same problems that plagued the brave souls who tried to organize in 1848 but which seemed even more incongruous in the era of the democratic and social Republic. Fonctionnaires who enjoyed the job security that was denied to blue-collar workers, who sold their labor on the open market, demanded representation on the councils of discipline that fired or transferred or demoted "violators" of the organizational rules. They demanded the end of secret letters and free access to the dossiers upon which their professional advancement depended. Fonctionnaires were also concerned with the efficient running of the public services, exposing inefficient methods

98. *L'Autorité,* July 25, 1906.
99. *La Petite République,* March 10, 1908.

and understaffed bureaus. Talk of returning government monopolies such as the telephone service to private hands brought howls of protest from the government workers.

As the twentieth century opened, fonctionnaires, anxious to voice their demands and have them met, joined the only organizations open to them—the associations and the amicales. It is difficult to ascertain just how content fonctionnaires were with the associations. Clearly, many accepted the 1901 law, separating themselves from blue-collar concerns and actions. But other fonctionnaires, often remaining in associations because they were the only organizational form that was legal, were desirous of forming and joining syndicats. The syndicat was preferred by those who felt its effectiveness was a direct consequence of its attachment to the blue-collar movement. Some associations had only a few syndicalists; others, like the Association Générale des Agents des PTT, were associations in name only. Other fonctionnaires broke from their associations or transformed them into syndicats. As 1906 drew to a close, the blue-collar workers entered a period of intense activity, and the fonctionnaires faced the state with the new strength of organization, the legality of syndicats for fonctionnaires became a critical issue. Anatole France, addressing the teachers' congress of 1906, extolled the growing unity of "those who hold the pen and those who hold the pick." He concluded, "Teachers, it will be to your eternal honor to have taken the greatest role in this harmonious effort and to have organized the proletariat of the schools and to have held out your hand to the proletariat of the offices, of the toll house and of the roads." [100]

The battle for the droit syndical, pitting fonctionnaires against the employer-state, was on.

100. L'Action, February 23, 1906.

3

Le Droit Syndical, 1906–1909

The fonctionnaires, pressing ever harder for improved working conditions and preparing to do battle with the government for the droit syndical, found themselves thrust from behind their anonymous desks and *guichets* (windows and counters) into the central arena of Third Republic politics. With the Dreyfus affair a painful but quiescent memory and the separation of church and state a smoldering but much diminished controversy, the Radical government under Clemenceau stood face to face with the product of a half-century of economic growth and the syndicalism of the working class. Although they were latecomers to the syndicalist movement, the fonctionnaires, by virtue of the essentially white-collar nature of their work and their unique relationship to the government as employees of the state, not only raised the issue of the expansion of blue-collar syndicalism to white-collar and professional workers but opened for public discussion and question the very nature of the modern state.

The Third Republic, committed to serving the growing needs of an urbanizing and industrializing nation and heir to the highly centralized state of the Revolution and the two Napoleons, expanded government monopolies and public service and thus government employment at a breathtaking pace. Inheriting a bureaucracy of approximately 200,000 the Third Republic made the fiscal control of the state all-encompassing, added education to its services, and expanded state monopolies, thereby nearly quintupling that number by the period 1906–1909.[1] Employment statistics are difficult to ascertain because the bases of determination changed from year to year, but by a conservative estimate the central

1. André Macaigne, *Le Fonctionnarisme et les syndicats des fonctionnaires* (Paris, 1907), 18–19.

government now employed more than 600,000 fonctionnaires (excluding blue-collar workers). In addition, the need for clean streets, public transportation, and new and improved roads brought the number of departmental and communal workers to nearly 300,000. In 1909, the central fiscal agencies employed 116,000, 200,000 were involved in public education, 113,000 serviced the postal and other communications needs of the nation, and the Ministry of the Interior employed 236,000.[2] If blue-collar workers (*ouvriers d'état*) and state railroad workers are added, the number of government employees on all levels goes well over 1 million. Writing in 1911, an observer counted the one-half million in the military and arrived at a figure of 1.8 million or 4.5 percent of the population as employees of the state.[3] One of every forty living Frenchmen and Frenchwomen and, even more impressive, one of every ten voters received a salary paid out of public funds. Almost 300,000 were retired and receiving state pensions.[4]

In a little over a generation, the state had emerged as the most formidable of employers, and it was evident that this trend would continue. At the 1905 congress of the Radical party, a commitment had been made to continued expansion of public service and monopolies. Although no specific industries were mentioned, it seemed logical that the state would eventually complete its control of the railroads and move on to the sources of energy that were vital to the industrial and military well-being of the nation. Suddenly the public became conscious of the vastness of state involvement in their daily lives.

The public, often critical of the inefficiencies and high cost of public goods and services, began to organize, not only to counteract the take-it-or-leave-it attitude sometimes engendered by monopoly service but to have some control as well over the state's role in their lives. Since 1881, the Ligue de l'Intérêt Public (League of Public Interest), sporting such famous early sponsors as Victor Hugo, Louis Blanc, and Clemenceau himself, had long been defending citizens against "illegalities" that might arise from state monopolies, public administration, and authority, and the Dreyfus affair had brought into existence the influential Ligue pour la Défense des Droits de l'Homme et du Citoyen. Caught up in the general

2. Paul Louis, *Le Syndicalisme contre l'état* (Paris, 1910), 81.
3. Pierre Harmignie, *L'Etat et ses agents* (Louvain, 1911), 351–52.
4. Alexandre Lefas, *L'Etat et les fonctionnaires* (Paris, 1913), 41.

wave of organization at the beginning of the century (the League Against Pornography, for example), the users of public services formed dozens of groups. The administration of finance was watched over by the Ligue des Contribuables (League of Taxpayers), and the inefficiencies of the telephone service were challenged by the Association des Abonnés (Association of Subscribers). The malcontents of the Ouest-Est Railroad line formed a Ligue des Voyageurs (League of Travelers), and even the tramway riders of Lille had their very own pressure group. Most influential was the Ligue de l'Enseignement (the Education League), founded in 1866 under the Second Empire, which became, after the laicization of the schools, a federation of societies dedicated to the application of the principles of free tuition and secular education. By the period 1906–1909, it had grown in influence to be a "real organ of inspection," verifying curriculum and books. Its religious counterpart was the Ligue des Pères de Famille (League of Heads [fathers] of Families).[5] Most of these organizations went beyond their primary role as critics; they began to press for reform.

Critical of the inefficiencies of public service, the public was disturbed as well by the explosion in the number of fonctionnaires. Peasants in particular were incensed at the number of state employees paid by their hard-earned and grudgingly paid taxes. To some it seemed that France would be divided into two enemy classes, not the bourgeoisie and the proletariat but the payer and the payee.[6] The growth of bureaucracy beyond efficiency and control was derisively attacked as *fonctionnarisme*. Innocent people were often the victims of this frustration; individual fonctionnaires, powerless themselves, were attacked for the faults that were inherent in the system. It was much easier to shout at the tax collector than at the minister of finance. But as the fonctionnaires, in their quest for improved working conditions and the right to organize, raised these issues themselves, citing the low pay, the stifling hierarchy, and the favoritism as barriers to the performance of their duties, as well as to their professional and personal integrity, the public began to rally to their support and call for the reform of the state administration.

If the expansion of government service and bureaucracy was impress-

5. These organizations are discussed in Georges Cahen, *Les Fonctionnaires* (Paris, 1911), 268–78.

6. *Ibid.*, 24.

ing itself on the general consciousness, the politicians, journalists, academics, and political thinkers were becoming concerned about a more basic problem—the relationship of this vast administrative machine to the democratic process. As early as 1895, the deputy Paul Deschanel had asserted, "France is not a democracy, it is a bureaucracy."[7] By 1906, the problem was even more obvious. By attacking the authority and hierarchy of the state administration, the fonctionnaires had brought into the open incongruities that had purposely been forgotten, ignored, or papered over as the Third Republic was trying to establish and legitimatize itself. Now these incongruities were not only openly discussed, they were discussed with an eye for the future, with an awareness that the growth of state function was a permanent feature of the modern democratic state.

If the political culmination of the social and economic changes of the nineteenth century had been the democratic Republic, the administration, designed for a Bonapartist monarchy, had not changed. If the legislature had been established on democratic principles, the administration had remained hierarchical and authoritarian. Article ten of the Constitution of February 25, 1875, had transferred the powers of Napoleon III to the president of the Republic.[8] The Third Republic had become a compromise between the "democratic idea installed in the organs of government and the aristocratic idea surviving in the bureaus."[9] What, then, was the relationship between these two arms of government? What was the nature of the state? Was it a simple conglomeration of individuals, or did it evolve historically to become a separate entity, something higher than the sum of its parts, imbued with a necessary and sacred power? For left-wing socialists such as Paul Louis, the state was the tool of the bourgeoisie, direct democracy was nonexistent, and parliament was a fiction behind which the possessors sheltered their sovereignty. The possessors vilified the collectivism of the socialists, but it was the "liberals," theoretically committed to individualism, who had made the individual economically and politically impotent.

7. *La Centralisation,* quoted in Macaigne, *Le Fonctionnarisme,* 21.
8. Louis Salaün, *Pour Enrayer le favoritisme il faut organiser la réforme des fonctions publiques* (Paris, 1912), 11.
9. Felix Garas, *La Sélection des cadres administratifs* (Paris, 1936), 26.

What individual could hope to influence the legislation or administration of laws?[10]

But except for the syndicalists and socialists of the Left, most legal and political theorists accepted the view that the state transcended its parts and was the embodiment of civil society. For administrators such as Henri Chardon (maître des requêtes, a high position in the Council of State), the aim of the parliamentary regime was to organize public service in such a way that citizens could register their satisfactions and dissatisfactions and be able to achieve changes when necessary. Chardon agreed with politicians such as Léon Bourgeois that parliament was only a collection of individuals who changed from election to election. To guarantee the continuity necessary for the proper functioning of the state, a permanent administration was needed. Parliament was created to oversee the administration, not to administer the country. Since the minister was responsible to parliament and the fonctionnaires responsible to the minister, it followed that the minister, to shoulder his responsibilities before the representatives of the nation, must have absolute authority over his permanent fonctionnaires. This authority was inherent in the Bonapartist administrative structure inherited by the Third Republic. Chardon argued that the granting of such formidable power to a minister was not antidemocratic, for the minister was the delegate of the parliament and the parliament was the voice of the people. But this haut fonctionnaire of the democratic republic voiced an opinion about the weakness of parliament that was to crop up again during the life of the Third Republic. He did not suggest that parliament disappear, but he did not think this legislative body, political in nature and nonpermanent in composition, was vital for the life of the nation. But the nation would cease to exist if the administrative services stopped. For the proper administration of those vital services, the hierarchy and authority now under attack must be preserved. To abandon authority was to invite anarchy.[11]

Chardon's identification of the administration as the vital center of the state is still accepted by many analysts of government functions. An-

10. Louis, Le Syndicalisme, 42, 132–33.
11. Henri Chardon, Le Pouvoir administratif (Paris, 1912), 14–15.

other haut fonctionnaire, Robert Catherine, wrote in 1961 that though governments come and go, the state is continuous and that fonctionnaires, entering public service almost as one enters a convent, are part of the continuity.[12] Chardon's contemporaries echoed his support of administrative power and authority even more strongly. Fernand Faure, the editor of *Revue Politique et Parliamentaire,* wrote in that influential journal in 1906 that "the state in the service of democracy and within the framework of its prescribed powers could not be too strong."[13] Others, firm believers in the sacredness of the state and reacting to the concept of election of administrators which had been tried during the Revolution and continued to be put forth as an ideal, were terrified that the *syndiqués* might choose their own superiors.[14] Even Maxime Leroy, a prolific writer on the subject of fonctionnaires and state administration and a supporter of the droit syndical for the fonctionnaires, accepted the need for authority as long as the ministers were to be responsible to parliament. For Leroy, the die was already cast for the modern state. The hierarchy was all-encompassing; not even the lowest road repairman could escape the line of command that held the state administration together. Parliament, more interested in political than in legal and technical questions and unable to monitor every aspect of state activity, had already subjugated itself to the administrators. Parliament had relinquished its role as chief legislator and had become the "steward" of the government. Ministerial bureaus, preparing laws, were becoming the true legislators. "The administration proposes, parliament accepts or rejects."[15]

Another *maître des requêtes* of the Council of State, Georges Cahen, who had been one of the first administrators to sympathize with the plight of the fonctionnaires and had supported their right to organize in a series of articles in the *Revue Bleue* in 1905, defended the centralized state in his 1911 book *Les Fonctionnaires.* Cahen urged mitigating bureaucratic authoritarianism with "collaboration" but agreed that the modern state could not function without discipline and hierarchy. Yet, unlike his colleague Chardon, he had hopes that the antidemocratic tide would be stemmed by reform and that cooperation between state ad-

12. Robert Catherine, *Le Fonctionnaire français* (Paris, 1961), 14, 15, 22.
13. Quoted in Cahen, *Les Fonctionnaires,* 367.
14. Macaigne, *Le Fonctionnarisme,* 17; Garas, *La Sélection,* 23.
15. Maxime Leroy, *La Transformation de la puissance publique* (Paris, 1907), 167–73.

ministrators and state employees would reestablish the solidarity of fonctionnaires, the elected representatives of the nation, and the public.[16]

Above all this analysis of the modern state there hung the question of syndicalism. If the state was based on hierarchy and authority, if the state was the embodiment of the people, what would be the position of fonctionnaires? Could the fonctionnaires, citizens and employees of the state at the same time, be permitted to form syndicats, to challenge collectively the authority of the state?

Faced with the agitation of the fonctionnaires and the public's demand for reform, the Clemenceau government of 1906 was forced to come to grips with the problem of reorganizing the archaic administration of the civil service. Anxious to preserve social peace and prevent the move toward syndicalism, especially after the strike of the sous-agents, the government offered the fonctionnaires the promise of a statute that would regularize recruitment, advancement, discipline, and salary schedules. It was a step which most European states, notably Germany, had already taken. The Republic, slow with all social reform, had been hesitant to tamper with the Second Empire's position against such a statute. Minor ineffectual reforms had been attempted, but a real statute had been opposed by those republicans who felt that the state must have absolute power over its employees. If the state employees did not like their working conditions, they could always leave public service; no one forced them to stay. By 1906, mindful of the warning that "men who do not get their legal rights will use extralegal methods," parliament readied itself for the first of a host of statutes to be proposed by the government.[17]

There were two ways to approach the formulation of a statute. Questions of advancement, discipline, and the like pertained to the individual, *le statut individuel*. Questions of organization pertained to the group, *le statut collectif*. Since the fonctionnaires were asking for the right to join associations, syndicats, and the larger worker federations and demanding legal guarantees against the arbitrary decisions and favoritism of the administrators and politicians, and since the state found it impossible to

16. *La Revue Bleue,* June 3, 7, July 8, 22, August 5, 19, 26, 1905; Cahen, *Les Fonctionnaires,* 380–83.

17. Jacques Busquet, *Les Fonctionnaires et la lutte pour le droit: La question du statut* (Paris, 1910), 12.

disassociate fonctionnaires as individuals from the public service, the statute was to cover both aspects, the individual and the collective.

The problem was complicated. If the administration used the examination (*concours*) as the basis of recruitment and advancement, how could the Republic be sure it would be getting the most dedicated and loyal employees? If advancement were to be based on seniority, meritorious people might be lost, ambition stifled. Seniority, however, could identify experience; examinations did not. Discipline presented an even more difficult problem because the threat of dismissal or reprimand gave administrators their greatest power over individual fonctionnaires. Certainly the rules of behavior should be clear and the accused able to defend himself. But should fonctionnaires sit on the councils of discipline in judgment of their peers? If the Clemenceau government found the problems of the *statut individuel* complex, it found the *statut collectif* relatively simple. The statute, meant to render both the 1884 and 1901 laws obsolete, would allow the fonctionnaires no syndicats, no federations, no attachment to either the Bourses du Travail or the CGT, and, most emphatically, no right to strike.

The government, hopeful that it would end the problem of fonctionnaire discontent and stop the spread of syndicalism with a statute, offered for public and parliamentary approval in the 1906–1907 session the project Clemenceau-Guyot-Dessaigne. Indeed, the government had reason to be optimistic. For years the fonctionnaires had been calling for such a statute. This demand was to crystallize in early 1908 with the formation of the Comité d'Etudes des Associations Professionnelles des Fonctionnaires de l'Etat, des Départments et des Communes, founded to study ways to get a statute. Representing amicales and associations with approximately two hundred thousand members, the Comité d'Etudes was headed by Georges Demartial of the central administration. Its *membre consultatif* was none other than Henri Chardon of the Conseil d'Etat.[18]

For the syndicalists among the fonctionnaires, however, the government's attempt at promulgating a statute came too late; they wanted instead the droit syndical. In late November, 1905, galvanized into action

---

18. Other officers were Emile Courrèges of the Instituteurs and Charles Laurent of the Dépôts and Consignations.

by the struggles of the instituteurs to have their syndicat accepted by the government, these syndicalists came together to form the Comité Central pour la Défense du Droit Syndical des Salariés d'Etat, des Départements et les Services Publiques. Headed by Marius Nègre of the instituteurs, the Comité Central included among others the syndicats of the ouvriers des PTT, the sous-agents, and the teachers, as well as the Associations Générales of the agents and the jeunes facteurs. Nègre made their position clear at an early meeting: "It is time, comrades, to abandon an impossible position. We no longer want a regime of tolerance. We want to have the droit syndical formally recognized by law."[19]

Between the years 1906 and 1909, there thus came into existence two fonctionnaire organizations: the more moderate Comité d'Etudes, established to pressure the government for an acceptable statute, and the Comité Central, committed to organized and concerted action for the droit syndical. The Comité d'Etudes, with a large number of associations and amicales in its ranks, was at first numerically much stronger than the syndicalist Comité Central. But the Comité Central had taken immediate action. Thousands flocked to hear the syndicalist speakers at meetings held all over France, and the influence of the Comité Central spread rapidly. Cognizant that the government was planning to present legislation on the question of fonctionnaires' rights during the 1906–1907 session, the Comité Central called for the government to pronounce immediately for the extension of the 1884 law, stating "that the employer-state is subject to the same obligations with regard to its wage earners that the law imposes on other employers; that they must set the example of respect and of the application of the laws."[20]

In January, 1906, two months after its inception, the Comité Central gathered a huge crowd of six thousand Parisian fonctionnaires at the Manège Saint Paul. The speakers were received enthusiastically: Adrien Meslier of the SFIO told them that their dignity was being insulted by the police state; Lucien Caron of the instituteurs accused the government of preferring the associations because they were weaker than syndicats. He declared that teachers wanted not only their rights as citizens but the opportunity to contribute to the proletariat's struggle for emancipa-

19. *L'Humanité*, January 19, 1906.
20. AN, F7 13724.

tion.[21] But the biggest cheer of the evening was for Victor Griffuehles of the CGT, who said, "Instead of begging for the droit syndical, you have taken it."[22]

While the Parisians were listening to the speeches at the Manège Saint Paul, fonctionnaires all over France were attending simultaneous meetings in sixty different towns and cities. Two thousand met at Brest, six hundred at Bordeaux, three thousand at Lyons, fifteen hundred at Marseilles, five hundred at Rennes. The meetings continued into February, all asking for immediate legislation to extend the 1884 law to the fonctionnaires.[23]

At the beginning of 1907, the government offered instead the Clemenceau-Guyot-Dessaigne statute. It was a disaster. Not only did it forbid syndicats, federations, and strikes, but it gained the sarcastic label "the statute *against* the fonctionnaires" because it imposed specific fines and prison terms for those who joined illegal syndicats or failed in the performance of their duties. (The strike of the sous-agents had been duly noted by the government.)[24] Not even the part of the statute pertaining to individuals was acceptable. Although some provisions had been made for hearing grievances, the rules for recruitment, advancement, and discipline, the areas in which favoritism was the biggest problem, had so many loopholes that the statute could not be considered a serious effort at reforming the administration. The moderate fonctionnaires were disillusioned; the syndicalists were incensed.

The Comité Central decided to reject any idea of a statute and to work for the droit syndical. On March 30, 1907, the Comité Central issued a remarkable *lettre ouverte* (open letter) to Clemenceau. Published in newspapers and plastered on walls all over France, the letter, reminding Clemenceau, Briand, and Viviani of their previous syndicalist sympathies, declared that the 1884 law should be extended to fonctionnaires because state employees were not representatives of the public service but, like workers in private industry, were merely exchanging their labor for a salary paid by the state. The state was a boss like other bosses,

21. *Ibid.*
22. Cahen, *Les Fonctionnaires,* 129.
23. AN, F7 12538 and F7 13724.
24. M. T. Laurin, "Le Syndicalisme et les instituteurs," *Le Mouvement Socialiste,* No. 185 (April 1, 1907), 313–14.

and the fonctionnaires, like other workers, possessed only their labor. When the state employee sold his labor, he did not sell either his liberty or his independence. The letter went on to assert that the employer-state, possessing all the political and coercive power belonging to modern governments, was even more powerful than an ordinary employer; in addition to the privileges of the capitalist boss, it had the right to be arbitrary. The fonctionnaires, allying themselves with the true creators of wealth, the workers, were prevented from joining these workers in the Bourses du Travail by a state that defended only capital and its privileges. The letter ended with a description of the history of the state as murderous and bloody and promised intense struggle against "the tyrannical and bloody monster" and for the droit syndical.[25]

The letter, signed by the representatives of eleven organizations belonging to the Comité Central, provoked surprise and anger in a government already engaged in bloody struggle with the working class. The beginning of 1907 had brought a bitter and violent lockout of the shoe workers at Fougères, a dockers' strike at Nantes, and an electricians' strike in Paris which left the "city of light" in unexpected darkness. Within a few weeks of the open letter, the winegrowers of the south were in open revolt against the government. The troops brought in to suppress the huge demonstrations at Narbonne had refused to fire on their brothers and cousins.[26] In the midst of this panic came the letter from the fonctionnaires, public servants, who dared to identify themselves with the working class, which was now battling not only their bosses but the government as well. It seemed even more menacing that the letter appeared at the same time as the syndicats of the instituteurs were meeting at their second congress. Following the exhortations of the secretary of their federation, Nègre, the teachers had voted to affiliate with the CGT.

Clemenceau reacted quickly and sharply to both occurrences. A strong letter, addressed specifically to Nègre and another syndicat leader, Charles Désirat, but published first in the newspapers, warned

25. The complete text of the open letter appears in several sources, including M. T. Laurin, *Les Instituteurs et le syndicalisme* (Paris, 1908), 57–60.
26. Clemenceau had made an absurd decision to use the Seventeenth Line Regiment, most of whose members were from the Languedoc. See Leo A. Loubère, *Radicalism in Mediterranean France* (Albany, 1974), 192.

the teachers of the danger of their illegal move into the "antipatriotic" CGT: "In any case, France could not hand over its children to you so that you could practice on them the 'sabotage' of young minds."[27] The signers of the open letter were immediately called before their ministers to explain that indeed they had written and signed the letter, but as representatives of their organizations responding to the mandate of the membership, not as individuals.

In an effort to weaken the Comité Central, the government decided to pursue the most outspoken and militant of the signers: three members of the Association Générale des Agents des PTT who were prime movers in the syndicalist group, Amalric, Clavier, and Paul Quilici; Louis Simonnet of the jeunes facteurs; a leader of the 1906 strike, Henri Grangier of the Syndicat des Sous-Agents; Janvion of the Syndicat des Travailleurs Municipaux; and the secretary of the Comité Central, Nègre, who had been most responsible for the instituteurs' vote to join the CGT. Brought before the Council of Discipline of the PTT, the three agents were judged guilty of *délits d'opinion* (the offense of opinion) and dismissed from service. (Quilici had not even been in Paris when the letter was issued; his signature was added automatically because of his position in the Association Générale. In a gesture of solidarity, he did not remove his name.) Nègre was acquitted by the Council of Discipline of the Seine but was fired when the prefect, obviously under government orders, refused to accept the decision of the council. By the end of April, all seven men were no longer employees of the state.

The firings and Clemenceau's attack on the teachers caused an uproar among fonctionnaires and blue-collar syndicalists: "O Légalité! O Justice Dreyfusarde!"[28] The syndicalist teachers, intimidated by the government's warning, abandoned their decision to enter the CGT but immediately joined other members of the Comité Central as they rallied around the victims of Clemenceau's "justice." Letters of protest and delegations from the syndicats and associations all over France arrived at the ministerial bureaus to register displeasure with actions they considered "unrepublican" and illegal. A letter from the teachers' amicale of

27. Laurin, *Les Instituteurs*, 64.
28. Gabriel Beaubois, "L'Etat, les partis et le syndicalisme," *Le Mouvement Socialiste*, Nos. 189–90 (August 15–September 15, 1907), 122.

the Loire asked Clemenceau how Nègre's actions could possibly hurt the Republic to which they were all so loyal.[29] Clemenceau's response to one of the PTT delegations that he had acted strongly because he had been faced with a "real revolt" of fonctionnaires only intensified the feeling against him.[30] In a vote of confidence, the members of the Association Générale overwhelmingly elected the fired agents Amalric and Quilici as representatives to the Council of Discipline.[31] A defense committee was organized. It was not simply a question of protesting the government's actions; funds had to be collected. The low wages of the fonctionnaires, most of whom were family men, had not permitted them the luxury of financial reserves; they needed money for survival.[32] Quilici described the reaction to the open letter as a turning point in his thinking: "I believed that it was now or never for all state workers to stand shoulder to shoulder and bellow (excuse the expression) at Clemenceau."[33]

Blue-collar syndicats joined the protest, well aware that it was not only fonctionnaires who were being attacked but the blue-collar movement as well. Nègre's letter of dismissal had referred to his influence on the decision of the teachers to enter the CGT as well as his role in the publication of the open letter. The connections between the events of 1907 were not missed by the syndicalist orators. The Clemenceau government was the "government of assassins, of infamy, because of the shootings at Narbonne, the war in Morocco and the firings of citizens Simonnet, Nègre, etc." Thousands of blue-collar workers joined the fonctionnaires in protesting the judicial proceedings against the teachers and the signers of the open letter at a meeting at the Tivoli-Vaux Hall in Paris in response to a letter from Nègre which told them that "today it is the organizations of state wage earners who do not enjoy the legal droit syndical. . . . Tomorrow it will be those who enjoy this legal right now, then the working-class organizations themselves will have their turn."[34]

29. L'Humanité, April 20, 1907.
30. L'Action, May 2, 1907.
31. AP, BA 1427.
32. Not much money was collected. The organizations themselves tried to aid the men (Nègre was supported for a while), but most had to find other employment. See Quilici Papers, Centre de Recherches d'Histoire des Mouvements Sociaux et du Syndicalisme, Paris.
33. From a letter in the Quilici Papers.
34. AN, F7 12538, from a meeting held at Marseilles on March 16, 1908.

The first part of the statute, *le statut individuel*, was almost forgotten. The organization of the fonctionnaires became the critical issue. Should fonctionnaires be allowed to join syndicats, to join the CGT, to strike? The discussion of these questions and the campaign for the reintegration of the signers of the open letter quickly moved from the level of the syndicats into the national political arena. Immediate support came from many politicians on the Left. Francis de Pressensé of the Ligue des Droits de l'Homme issued a statement of "regret" that a republican government would punish subordinates for voicing opinions, a right all citizens had received at the dawn of the Revolution from the fathers of French democracy. A letter to Briand, the minister of education, defended Nègre, who, said Pressensé, was acting, not as an individual, but on a mandate from the collective.[35] At a congress held several weeks after the firings, the Ligue des Droits d'Homme, which was influential with liberal Radicals and socialists, voted to recommend that fonctionnaires be granted the droit syndical.[36] Most socialists also sprang to the defense of the fonctionnaires; the SFIO delegation in the Chamber was particularly strong in its support of the militants of the Comité Central as well as the droit syndical. When the question of the droit syndical was extended to the CGT and the right to strike, however, some socialists balked. While Guesde spoke at meetings all over the country and Zévaès and Jaurès defended the syndicalists in the Chamber—Jaurès declaring that the entrance of the fonctionnaires into the CGT was a revolutionary step that would help bring about a social revolution—others who called themselves socialists were not anxious to see the fonctionnaires join the revolutionary syndicalists in the CGT. Professor Paul Painlevé of the Institut de France and later a Republican-Socialist deputy, for example, supported the droit syndical as the only positive action that could be taken against favoritism but would not support the entrance of the fonctionnaires into the larger worker federations.[37] Nevertheless, the battle for the reintegration of Nègre and the others was carried to the Chamber floor and passionately defended by the SFIO.

The Right, of course, considered Clemenceau's actions against the

35. AN, F7 13724.
36. *L'Action*, May 21, 1907.
37. *L'Humanité*, April 23, 1907.

militant syndicalists appropriate. By demanding the extension of the 1884 law, fonctionnaires were attacking the nation itself and threatening the administration with anarchy. "If state fonctionnaires are allowed to unionize, the state will crumble into small pieces," wrote the spokesman of the ultraright, Charles Maurras, "no more hierarchy, nor discipline, nor order."[38]

The situation was much more complex for those who allied with the Radicals. Clemenceau, of course, considered the fonctionnaires public servants ineligible for the droit syndical. The former socialist Viviani, now head of the newly created (1906) Ministry of Labor, had written a year before, "As strong as an association is, it is not worth as much as a weak syndicat." But Viviani was now a "clemenciste," as was the former revolutionary syndicalist Briand. Briand had told the postiers in 1905: "Unionize! Your right of association is not enough; you must win the syndicat."[39] As minister of education, however, he had prevented the formation of new syndicats. Concurring with Viviani and Clemenceau, he had been instrumental in the attack on Nègre. Less clear was the position of the former socialist Barthou, who had earlier been a partisan of fonctionnaire organization. It was thought in 1906 that, instead of the Guyot-Dessaigne statute, the government would put forth a statute proposed by the minister of public works, Barthou, which would allow the droit syndical for certain government employees. Now his position was compromised. Barthou's proposal had been disavowed by the government and he was moving closer to the stricter government position.

Some Radicals in the Assembly supported an extension of the 1884 law, and Jeanneney was to offer his own statute, which would allow the droit syndical. Recognizing his long-term service to their cause, the fonctionnaires asked the old Radical Socialist Camille Pelletan to aid them in the Chamber. Immediately after the firings, the executive committee of the Radical and Radical Socialist party refused to take up Nègre's case, saying that it was not within its jurisdiction. But the Comité Central appealed to the party as the "embodiment of republicanism"[40] and at the next meeting of the executive committee on April

38. J. Paul-Boncour, Les Syndicats des fonctionnaires (Paris, 1906), 25.
39. Harmignie, L'Etat, 78, 208.
40. L'Humanité, April 20, 1907.

25, a passionate discussion ended with the formation of two clear camps. Adolphe Maujan, under secretary of state for the interior, Fernand Dubief, former minister of commerce and industry, and Louis Puech, later to be minister of public works and the PTT, and others, approved the conduct of the government, and when the more left-wing Radical Socialist group, in the confusion of the discussion, rammed through an order of the day which recommended that the charges against the fonctionnaires be dropped until the Chamber had time to discuss and vote on the issue of the droit syndical, the antisyndicalist Radicals, led by a furious Maujan, left the meeting.[41] One week later, the executive committee voted another, more acceptable order of the day voicing regret for the action taken against the signers of the open letter and asking that the revocation be reversed.[42] Maujan could not easily be reconciled; almost daily in the pages of Le Radical, he had demanded the heads of the guilty fonctionnaires, traitors to the Republic.[43]

If some Radicals were willing to accept the droit syndical for fonctionnaires, they were not willing for the fonctionnaires to enter either the Bourses du Travail or the CGT. The idea of a strike, of course, was anathema. One of the confusions that constantly arose in discussion was the linkage of the droit syndical with the grève générale. To many Radicals (and most conservatives), syndicalism was synonymous with revolutionary syndicalism. The pro-working-class tone of the open letter exacerbated this fear. Thus though most fonctionnaires who were pressing for the droit syndical considered the strike issue irrelevant—the teachers especially would not dream of striking—strike and syndicat were linked irrevocably in the hearts and minds of many stalwarts of the bourgeois Republic.

All this came to a head on May 7, when the Chamber of Deputies, in response to questions regarding the teachers, the firings, and the general handling of fonctionnaire syndicats, began a week-long debate that demonstrated not only how far the Radicals were from unity on this issue but how strongly, when the vote was taken, most Radicals, fearing a ministerial crisis, rallied to Clemenceau.

41. AN, F7 13724.
42. L'Action, May 2, 1907.
43. Beaubois, "L'Etat," 122.

The SFIO deputies opened the debate with an attack on Clemenceau and his policies. Alexandre Blanc castigated the government for its treatment of teachers and other fonctionnaires, quoting Briand and Clemenceau from earlier days and adding most pointedly, "You saved the Republic with these very workers." He chided the Radicals in particular, much to the amusement of the deputies, who erupted in laughter when he told them, "You have two choices: either you call the Bourses du Travail hotbeds of revolution and calumniate the workers whom you praise on election day or you approve of the Bourses du Travail and let the fonctionnaires in."

The Socialists continued the debate the next day as Edouard Vaillant told the deputies that there was parliamentary stagnation because, of all his reform promises, Clemenceau had kept only the one made in Lyons when he declared war on syndicalism and socialism. The violence and repression were called republicanism but were in reality a reactionary program of government by police. Vaillant welcomed the penetration of syndicalism into the ranks of the fonctionnaires because they were needed as allies by the working class. He stated what all knew: the question of the droit syndical was fast becoming the premier domestic issue of the era.

Deschanel defended the government, saying that it was wrong to think that the public services belonged to it; actually the post offices, the arsenal, and the schools belonged to the people, not the workers. Briand reminded the fonctionnaires and their defenders that the state was not the same as an employer in private industry, that an attack on Clemenceau's government was an attack against the nation. Moreover, it was not a question of syndicats but one of discipline. Even if the fonctionnaires were to be allowed to form legal syndicats, the state could not allow such things as the open letter to appear on the public walls of France. Then Barthou, moving rapidly to take his position at the side of Clemenceau, Briand, and Viviani, added further weight to the firings by reminding the deputies of the role played by Simonnet and Grangier in the 1906 strike.

After a week of such speechmaking, the debate narrowed down to the two men who best represented the two sides of this question and, indeed, most of the political questions of the prewar Third Republic,

Jaurès and Clemenceau. The two devout republicans argued back and forth on the nature of the government: Clemenceau for the authority of the state, Jaurès for a society based on social and economic justice. Clemenceau claimed that he had dismissed men who had been instigating violence, murder, and antipatriotism. Jaurès rose and said, "You were never enough of a revolutionary to be so reactionary now."

The voting began. A motion proposed by the socialist Vaillant affirming the droit syndical and blaming the government for its actions went down to overwhelming defeat, 460 to 75. A much weaker motion proposed by Alexandre Blanc, which left out the syndicalist issue and merely condemned the government for firing Nègre against the advice of the council of discipline, received only a few more votes, 410 to 109. A third socialist proposal, made by Albert Willm, gave the Chamber the opportunity to defend liberty of opinion by ordering the government to release all people in prison or on trial for délits d'opinion went down to overwhelming defeat, 381 to 121.

The left-wing Radicals, Théodore Steeg and Charles Dumont, then offered the Assembly a way out by asking the government to be generous to the poor fonctionnaires: "The Chamber, standing resolute against arbitrariness and favoritism and for the legitimate interests of state fonctionnaires, asks the government to be benevolent toward those whom it had penalized without having instructed them about the legal limits of their rights." Most Radicals did not even respond to this benign statement; it lost, 309 to 152. Finally, Maujan, Alfred Gèrault-Richard, Paul-Jules Gouzy, Arthur Dessoye, Chaumet, and Marc Reville proposed the motion of approval the government was waiting for; it passed 343 to 210.[44]

May Day, 1907, brought the arrest of Jean Bousquet, Albert Lévy, and André Delalé of the CGT. Even as the debate on the fonctionnaires was taking place in the Chamber, the crisis in the southern vineyards widened. On May 5, 50,000 winegrowers demonstrated at Narbonne; on the twelfth, 150,000 rallied at Béziers. By June 9, a demonstration at Montpelier brought out an incredible 700,000. There was a troop mutiny. From May to August, from Narbonne to Perpignan, the countryside was in revolt. In July, a strike of shoe workers at Raon-L'Etape brought out the troops and resulted in one dead and thirty-two workers

44. *Journal Officiel,* May 8–15, 1907.

injured. One year later came the horrible events of Draveil-Vigneux and Villeneuve–Saint Georges. More blood was shed, and three more died. The record of Clemenceau's war against the syndicats during his first two years in office was impressive: 104 years of prison sentences, 667 workers wounded, 20 killed, and 392 fired. "Gouvernement d'Assassins" cried the posters of the CGT. "And parliament whose stomach is tight with fear . . . has given a blank check to the sinister trio who symbolize power: CLEMENCEAU—BRIAND—VIVIANI."[45]

But these developments did not push the question of the droit syndical or the victims of the open letter repression from the political scene. If anything, it heightened the realization among fonctionnaires and workers alike that their causes were linked. The terrible trio and, in particular, Clemenceau, the "Chief Cop of France," the "Emperor of Finks," the "Strikebreaker," fired postal and shot construction workers with the same aplomb. The firings and the droit syndical were discussed over and over again at meetings and by the socialists in the Chamber. Pelletan and Buisson continued to press the Radical and Radical Socialist party. Nègre, Janvion, Grangier, and Simonnet traveled to meetings of blue-collar workers and fonctionnaires all over France—to the Bourses du Travail at Angers, Brest, Marseilles, and Montpelier, to St. Etienne and Rive de Gier to speak to the miners. At all these meetings, the fired men were defended, the droit syndical was upheld, and Clemenceau, Briand, and Viviani were vilified. The response among fonctionnaires was enthusiastic but far from unanimous. Many who remained in associations and amicales were sympathetic, but others, particularly in areas far from industrial and commercial centers, wanted nothing to do with syndicalism. Barthou, having abandoned his more moderate policies of the year before, was roundly applauded by the agents of Pau, for example, when he spoke in favor of retaining the legal associations.[46]

In early March, 1908, the Comité Central launched a campaign to move public opinion against yet another statute and for reinstatement of the fired men. Meetings were held in dozens of cities, and the sympa-

---

45. Edouard Dolléans, *Histoire du mouvement ouvrier* (3 vols.; Paris, 1968), II, 143–45. For a description of the events at Draveil-Vigneux and Villeneuve–Saint Georges as well as an interesting analysis of Clemenceau's policies, see Jacques Julliard, *Clemenceau briseur de grèves* (Paris, 1965).

46. *La Petite République*, August 22, 1907.

thetic press published their appeal. A few days later, the minister of war, General Georges Picquart, went before the Chamber to request the reintegration into the army of Joseph Reinach. The Chamber urged that other officers dismissed from service, as Reinach had been, for délits d'opinion should also receive pardons from the government. The socialist Paul Constans then strode to the lectern and offered a counterproposal to reinstate fonctionnaires who had been fired for the same reason. Clavier had already been reinstated by the PTT, so why not the others? Constans urged the Chamber to support the position that délits d'opinion did not exist for fonctionnaires. Everyone waited for Clemenceau's expected tirade, but the president of the council sensed the mood of the session and sent Julien Simyan, the under secretary of state for the PTT, to explain that the fonctionnaires had been dismissed not for their opinions but for indiscipline; they would be considered for reinstatement only by the authority of their respective ministries. He urged a vote of confidence for the government. Simyan's weak argument was countered by the moderate voice of the president of the Commission of the Army, Maurice Berteaux, who asked why the government deserved his confidence when it had not even come up with a statute. His accusation, "You don't keep your promises and you do nothing," was greeted with tremendous applause. The Chamber, clearly wanting to slap the hands of government, voted for the Constans motion, 352 to 147.[47]

Three days later, the brave gesture of the Chamber of Deputies was repudiated. Both Barthou and Clemenceau went before the Chamber to attack the decision on the fonctionnaires. Never one to mince words, Clemenceau told the deputies that the decision was clear—they could vote for rebellious fonctionnaires or for the government of the Republic. Faced with this dilemma, the deputies, unwilling to cause a ministerial crisis, reversed their decision by a vote of 352 to 130 and gave full confidence to Clemenceau.[48] It seems incredible that Clemenceau would risk the life of his cabinet by asking for a vote of confidence on so insignificant an issue as the rehiring of a few troublesome postmen and teachers. But to Clemenceau, already the "Tiger" who would accept no challenge to his authority, the droit syndical was indeed an important issue. When

47. L'Humanité, March 17, 1908.
48. L'Action, March 15, 1908.

the fonctionnaires had been content to remain in associations and ami-cales, their organizational activity was allowed. During periods of rela-tive political calm, even a few syndicats were tolerated. But now the situation had changed. The government was locked in violent struggle with the blue-collar working class, and the fonctionnaires were moving closer to syndicalism. The state could not allow this enormous group of employees, servants of the state, to have any connections, no matter how tenuous, with working-class syndicalism. Clemenceau had de-clared war against the blue-collar syndicats, but he would not even allow the fonctionnaires into the fray.

Of the three agents of the PTT, Clavier had been reinstated at the be-ginning of March, Quilici and Amalric in May.[49] The other révoqués active in the 1906 strike or the CGT were not reinstated. In December, 1908, Jaurès made another attempt to shame the deputies into rejecting the government's intransigent position. The government had just am-nestied the brigadier who had ordered the shootings that had killed two and wounded ten at the strikers' meeting hall at Draveil, but for Nègre, Janvion, Grangier, and the young facteur Simonnet, amnesty had to wait another two years.[50] If they had promised to restrict their activities, their jobs and their security would have been returned to them, but this they did not do. Marius Nègre, born of a poor miller's family in the wine country of the Hérault, whom Max Ferré calls "one of the most beautiful and highly esteemed figures of teacher syndicalism," still clung to his principles in a letter asking for reinstatement in 1909: "I cannot disavow my ideas nor erase my past, I will continue my propaganda; I have been and I remain favorable to the affiliation of the teachers to the CGT and if tomorrow I am reinstated I will continue to demand this affiliation."[51]

49. Quilici was to be fired again for his activity in the 1909 strike, reinstated in 1910, and fired once again a few months later after he ran against Millerand for a deputy's seat in Paris. His defense lawyer at the hearing was none other than the then defender of workers' rights Pierre Laval. Quilici was wounded and gassed in the war but never allowed back in the postal service. He maintained his political activity, running for office for the SFIO in 1919. Finally, in 1931, he received a letter from the president of the Council informing him that he had been automatically reinstated as an agent by the amnesty of 1919. See Quilici Papers.

50. F. Bernard, L. Bouët, M. Dommanget, and G. Serret, *Le Syndicalisme dans l'enseigne-ment* (Avignon, 1953), 89.

51. Max Ferré, *Histoire du mouvement syndicaliste révolutionnaire chez les instituteurs* (Paris, 1955), 109; Harmignie, *L'Etat*, 119.

The issue of the reintegration of those who signed the open letter and others who had been penalized for syndicalist activities was raised once again in February, 1909. During a discussion of a government-sponsored proposal to amnesty those workers who had suffered dismissal or jail after the events of Draveil-Vigneux and Villeneuve–Saint Georges, Sembat of the SFIO demanded to know why the amnesty was so limited. Perhaps, he suggested, the government was trying to amnesty itself for its actions at Draveil and Villeneuve–Saint Georges. Sembat and a host of cosponsors, including all the great names of parliamentary socialism—Jean Allemane, Maurice Allard, Jules Guesde, Jean Jaurès, and Paul Brousse—proposed an amendment that would have included in the amnesty all those who had been punished for syndicalist activities. Clemenceau, once again, decided to make the amendments to the amnesty bill the basis for a vote of confidence. Only a handful of Radicals joined the socialists, and the amendment was voted down, 247 to 93.[52]

The amnesty debate continued the next day. The right wing wanted amnesty for those who had suffered judicial action for defending the church. Other groups pressed for amnesty for those who were in tax difficulties. The Radical Socialists Louis Dumont, Justin Godart, Frédéric Buisson, and Henri Binet then offered an amendment specifically referring to fonctionnaires who had been punished for délits d'opinion or political actions. Dumont regretted that Clemenceau was making the issue the basis for a vote of confidence. After all, before being forced to reverse itself, the Chamber had the previous year voted amnesty for these fonctionnaires. Quoting from Nègre's frequent attacks on the government, Clemenceau rose to say that amnesty was not a question of personality but of government authority.[53] He was reported as having told the deputies that he would never amnesty diehards such as Nègre. If the Assembly voted such an amnesty, it could look for another government.[54] By a wide margin, 337 to 135, the Chamber voted to amnesty only those who had committed infractions relating to Draveil and Villeneuve–Saint Georges between May 2, 1908, and January 14, 1909. The fonctionnaires were clearly excluded.

52. *Journal Officiel*, February 12, 1909.
53. *Ibid.*, February 13, 1909.
54. AN, F7 13725, from the police report of February 13, 1909.

The repercussions of the vote were felt in the press. *La Patrie* wrote what all knew: there was no hope now for the fired fonctionnaires, who numbered about twelve. Under the headline "Under the Knout," *L'Humanité* wrote that the Radicals, by supporting Clemenceau, had not only failed the fonctionnaires but had declared war on them. Nègre and Simonnet told an interviewer, "They wanted war, they will have it."[55] The politics of appeal was losing ground.

While the battle of words raged in parliamentary circles, a change was taking place in fonctionnaires' attitudes which had started before 1906 and gathered momentum as the disillusionment with the government's handling of the statute, the affair of the open letter, and the general repression of the working class hammered away at the consciousness of state employees. More fonctionnaires were coming to the conclusion that the statute would grant them little or nothing and that they would still be dependent on the whims and interests of politicians. The fonctionnaires were moving closer to the conclusion that only the droit syndical would grant them the economic benefits and the political freedom they were seeking.

The fonctionnaires were split into three groups. Those in the largest group thought of themselves as separate from the working class and were content with the amicales and associations, which sent delegations to the government to ask for wage increases or changes in advancement procedures. The second group was made up of the highly vocal, highly active, highly militant, but small number who linked the administrative proletariat with the blue-collar proletariat in the private sector. They agreed with the socialist Paul Louis, who declared that public service was identical with concentrated private industry and that the postier and the instituteur were perhaps even "more disinherited" than the metallurgist or the printer.[56] Had not experience taught them that the chain that linked them to the employer-state, "for being more golden, is only heavier?"[57] They agreed with Nègre, Simonnet, and other signers of the open letter that capitalist society was divided into two classes and that

55. *La Patrie*, February 13, 1909; *L'Humanité*, February 13, 1909.
56. Louis, *Le Syndicalisme*, 204.
57. Hubert Lagardelle, "Le Droit syndical et les employés des PTT," *Le Mouvement Socialiste*, No. 176 (July, 1906), 206.

for fonctionnaires, workers themselves, to bring about the emancipation of the "intellectual and manual proletariat" they must ally themselves with the working class by joining the Bourses du Travail or the CGT.[58] For revolutionary syndicalists such as the PTT employee Charles Le Gléo, who used the name Oegel to avoid administrative retribution for his pamphlet *La Guerre sociale,* it was necessary for the fonctionnaires to join the CGT so that they could be radicalized by the blue-collar working class: "We do not wish to join the CGT in order to make the working class movement deviate from its revolutionary aims and to give our comrades in the private sector lessons in calmness and balance. On the contrary, we join so they can show us our path and to get from them the lessons in audacity and boldness which we need."[59] Even the ultimate workers' weapon, the strike, was accepted by many in this group. The sous-agents had already shown themselves willing to strike public service. Others agreed that though they might not choose to use it, the freedom to strike was coupled with the freedom to form and join syndicats; indeed, they could not be separated. Both rights belonged to every French citizen.

Although clearly a minority, these syndicalists had more adherents than the government would admit. Thousands came to their meetings. In Paris alone, fifteen hundred sous-agents attended a meeting in 1908 to affirm the affiliation of the Syndicat National des Sous-Agents to the CGT, and within the associations, there were other fonctionnaires who, fearful of the illegality of their position, did not openly state their preference for the working-class organizations.[60] It is always difficult to ascertain the strength of political ideology and activity. Among the large, voiceless majority who remained in associations and amicales, how many felt strongly about their organizational form and how many could be moved to other positions, to activity, by events? Those favoring affiliation with the CGT voiced a minority opinion, but they were an active minority, and as new political situations developed and working conditions changed, they were capable, as militant minorities often are, of moving large masses toward their position.

58. Remarks of Nègre quoted in Harmignie, *L'Etat,* 106.
59. AP, BA 1437. A rare copy of the pamphlet is in the Centre de Recherches d'Histoire des Mouvements Sociaux et du Syndicalisme, Paris.
60. *L'Humanité,* April 25, 1908.

The pressure of events and activity led to the growth of a third group who wanted the droit syndical without affiliation to the blue-collar organizations and without the right to strike. These fonctionnaires, still a minority but rapidly gathering adherents from the more conservative majority, recognized the strength of the 1884 law and, adamant about having the freedom all other French citizens possessed, abandoned the concept of a statute granted by a benevolent government and chose to press for the droit syndical. Though willing to support working-class efforts and to receive working-class support, they maintained that they were different from blue-collar workers and hence did not belong in working-class organizations. Warroquier of the Contributions Indirectes wrote, "Like two rivers flowing toward the same shore, they must follow their own particular course, they cannot use the same bed."[61] At their 1909 congress, the employees of the Contributions Indirectes, while protesting against the restrictions of fonctionnaire freedom, declared that they did not want to be in the CGT because they were fonctionnaires, not workers.[62]

This separation of fonctionnaires from the blue-collar working class was emphasized in a "referendum" sent in 1907 to teachers in the department of Pyrénées Orientales, signed by dozens of instituteurs and institutrices, who wanted a syndicat but no affiliation with working-class organizations. As salaried employees, they did not claim to be superior to blue-collar or agricultural workers. Each métier (trade) had its importance and its dignity, and they were not unaware of the difficulties facing the working class. They simply had to be realistic. The teachers of Pyrénées Orientales could not afford to be associated with the Bourses du Travail, which was affiliated with the CGT, because that meant association with "dangerous anarchists who currently run the CGT and where the guiding principles are direct action, sabotage and anti-patriotism."[63] Fearful of the revolutionary aspect of the CGT and even more fearful of being identified with these views by the government, these instituteurs wanted to use the syndicalist form only as a means to achieve their goals. They would not, or could not, accept the goals of revolutionary syndicalism. Of course, not all blue-collar workers fol-

61. *La Revue Syndicaliste,* December, 1907, quoted in Cahen, *Les Fonctionnaires,* 358.
62. AN, F7 12538, May 18, 1909.
63. AN, F7 12536, November 15, 1907.

lowed the official program of the CGT either. Still, the fonctionnaires were demanding the droit syndical, and it was just this which was significant. The demand for the droit syndical was becoming less the province of a militant revolutionary fringe; ordinary fonctionnaires were moving toward this position.

It seems appropriate at this point to ask why in the year 1907 or 1908, one fonctionnaire would want to ally himself with blue-collar workers in the Bourses du Travail or the CGT, yet another fonctionnaire would be hesitant about affiliating with the working class but still be willing to use the syndicat form, and still another would consider himself a professional with little or no connection to working-class ideology and institutions. Obviously one cannot speak for thousands of individual fonctionnaires, but armed with information about their origins, their work, their actions, and the society in which they lived, one may attempt some analysis about the development of fonctionnaire consciousness.

Unfortunately, no enterprising cliometrician or sociologist has yet seen fit to pore through hundreds of thousands of personnel dossiers to feed into the computer data on the social origins of fonctionnaires who were employed under the Third Republic. But even without a thorough statistical analysis, social origins can be generally determined. From random samplings of personnel files, collections of memoirs such as Ozouf's study of instituteurs, the états-civils of those arrested in demonstrations and strikes, individual biographies and memoirs, and personal interviews, it can be determined that most petits fonctionnaires came from agricultural or artisanal and, of course, from fonctionnaire families. For the young postier, instituteur, or douanier of the Belle Epoque, to become a fonctionnaire was one step, albeit a small step, up the ladder from poverty, tightening rural opportunities, and job insecurity. Most of the fonctionnaires of the period came from small villages and communes; just as an army of young people left the farms and villages to go into factories and mills of the industrial areas, so another, smaller army of sons and daughters of winegrowers, millers, carpenters, and other village inhabitants flocked to the larger towns and administrative centers to deliver mail, to clerk for the prefect, to teach in the schools, and to scrutinize the tax forms. Some, particularly those in education or postal service, remained in rural areas but not usually in their home commune.

Young, aspiring fonctionnaires came not only from small villages but usually from villages in the poorer, most isolated areas, where there was little opportunity to find work in a factory or mine. One still often hears the distinguishing southern accent of those who entered public service from the poor areas of the Landes or the Pyrénées. When I was interviewing retired or near-retired fonctionnaires, I was convinced that all business could easily have been conducted in Gascon rather than French (had I but known Gascon). Certainly, the Pyrénées department of L'Ariège has supplied more than its fair share of militants in the syndicats of fonctionnaires. This pattern continues today: the latest area to send its children into the public service is Corsica. Just as Irish immigrants filled the ranks of the police forces of Boston, New York, and Philadelphia, so the Corsican has become the mainstay of the police departments of Marseilles and other cities. And one can already begin to hear the lilting accents of the Martiniquens and Senegalese who are beginning to appear in the uniforms of public service.

In interviews with fonctionnaires who had entered public service after World War I, I found that almost all remembered most vividly the poverty of their youth. One, born in L'Ariège, reminisced about a constant diet of potatoes; the only work available was poorly paid road construction. With little formal schooling, he took correspondence courses and was able to pass the examination to enter the Contributions Indirectes. The mother of another fonctionnaire, widowed in the war and left with small children, eked out a living as a sharecropper in an area of the Landes where this ancient mode of exploitation still held sway even after the relative prosperity of World War I had improved the conditions of many peasants in other areas. The free state school system opened opportunities previously unknown to untutored and poorly educated peasants. A postier reminisced about how easy it was to enter service in 1906 as an aide in the PTT: "In 1906, what could a young man do who did not have his baccalaureate and who, like me, left high school after the third form (first is senior) without money, without having a trade, but having been imbued with a general culture; what could be better than for him to prepare for the exam to enter a state department which did not require a baccalaureate."[64] It was the dream of many peasants, one

64. From the unpublished memoir "Histoire de ma vie" by Robert Jourcin, kindly lent to me by Professor Alfred Grosser.

woman told me, to have a son become a postier and a daughter an institutrice. The pay was not high, but it was a living wage, it was secure, and the position commanded more respect than most peasants could ever hope to receive. Some peasants, of course, identified fonctionnaires with the *messieurs* who exploited and ridiculed them; they would not think of allowing their children to join the "enemy." But for the many village youths whom the farms could no longer support, in 1906 or even 1926, the choice was between the worker's blue blouse or the black coat and white collar of the fonctionnaire. For those who lived far from the mills and factories of the north and northeast, the black coat and white collar, though somewhat tattered, represented a welcome opportunity.

Not all fonctionnaires came from poverty-stricken families. Some came from families who had long been in public service. Teachers begat teachers, postmen begat finance workers. These families rarely knew the extreme poverty of the day laborer. Other recruits were the children of masons or other such small town artisans. Few came from the industrial working class at this time because the industrial proletariat itself was young and growing, recruiting from the same farms and ateliers. Practically no petits fonctionnaires in the early part of the century came from the wealthier entrepreneurial class or the liberal professions. A few less affluent shopkeeping families, that is, the petite bourgeoisie, might provide candidates for the Ministry of Finance or the corps of teachers, but it was usually the poorer families. The business or professional families supplied the hauts fonctionnaires, the professors of lycées or the middling cadre, not the clerks or telephone operators.

Before World War I, women fonctionnaires, as a group, apparently came from a somewhat higher background and had more education than the men who entered public service. With job opportunities limited for educated women and alternative work in factories and shops frequently paying less than subsistence wages, public service was attractive not only to poorer working-class women but to those who were considered petites bourgeoises. A survey done in 1896 noted that many young female teachers came from a milieu *plus aisé,* that is, from the families of fonctionnaires or small tradespeople.[65] More women teachers than men

65. Maurice Tallmeyer, "Les Femmes qui enseignent," *La Revue du Deux Mondes,* June, 1897, quoted in Danielle Delhome, Nicole Gault, and Josiane Gonthier, *Les Premières institutrices laïques* (Paris, 1980), 34.

passed through the more prestigious and academically superior lycées rather than normal schools and almost all had the *brevet supérieur* (a higher diploma than necessary for primary school). Persis Hunt, in her study of women teachers, maintains that of 115,000 teachers employed by the state on the eve of World War I, 60,000 had their brevet supérieur and 35,000 of these were women. Of those who went to normal school and had no brevets, 9,310 were men and only 4,308 were women. On the other hand, 12,238 had not attended normal schools and had brevets mostly from lycées, but only 1,681 men had received this superior education.[66] Wages, of course, were lower for women. Although the postal services required less education and women with any bourgeois background would be more inclined to enter teaching, Susan Bachrach indicates that PTT women, though still largely from poor or modest origins, were more likely than men to come from urban areas and to have parents who were artisans or small traders.[67]

The social origins of fonctionnaires have changed over the years. The villages have fewer children to yield, small businesses have been swallowed up, and the industrial proletariat has grown, as have the ranks of the fonctionnaires themselves. But if the occupations have changed, the economic levels have not. Most petits fonctionnaires still come from families with modest or low incomes. In 1950, Max Ferré conducted a survey of teachers who had been militants or leaders of the syndicats. This was a unique group consisting of very active, politically aware people. Still, the results are useful. Only four said they came from families who had been *aisés* (comfortable), only one was rich, twenty-two said they had come from modest circumstances, and twenty-eight listed themselves as poor or scholarship students. Twenty were children of either artisans or workers, fifteen of petits fonctionnaires, six were born of business families, and only four were of peasant background.[68] The états-civil of hundreds of fonctionnaires other than teachers who were arrested in the huge demonstrations of 1926 and 1934 show an even

66. Persis Charles Hunt, "Revolutionary Syndicalism and Feminism among Teachers in France, 1900–1921" (Ph.D. dissertation, Tufts University, 1975), 134–35.

67. Susan Dimlich Bachrach, "The Feminization of the French Postal Service, 1750–1914" (Ph.D. dissertation, University of Wisconsin, 1981), 176; see fuller discussion in Bachrach, "Dames Employées: The Feminization of Postal Workers in Nineteenth Century France," *Women and History,* No. 8 (Winter, 1983), 50–54.

68. Ferré, *Instituteurs,* 308–17.

more pronounced rural bias. A few were born in Paris or Bordeaux or Ajaccio, but the vast majority came from such places as Mallement (Bouches-du-Rhône), Lonzac (Corrèze), Brassac (Ariège), Péliceto (Corse), Carges-sur-Bray (Loire et Cher), Jouagnes (Aisnes), Magnac-Laval (Haute Vienne), Boboc (Ariège), or Bedarique (Vaucluse).[69]

Results of a census of the PTT done by the Institut National Statistique et des Etudes Economiques (INSEE) published in 1974 indicate that the PTT, perhaps more than the Ministry of Education, was still drawing its recruits from the peasantry, at least in the years before 1974.[70] Twenty-one percent of male agents and 16.8 percent of female agents came from agricultural backgrounds with *employés* (salaried office or sales workers) accounting for about 16 percent. Twelve percent of men and 17.8 percent of women came from artisanal or small commercial families. The largest group, nearly 30 percent, were children of blue-collar workers, a significant change from the prewar period. Only 3 percent came from the liberal professions or the upper cadre. Even more interesting was the breakdown according to categories. Of the sons of those in the liberal professions or upper cadre who were in the PTT, more than one-third were in the highest-paid category. Conversely, more than 80 percent of agricultural sons were in the lowest category, along with 73.2 percent of workers' sons. For women the picture is different. Only 4 percent of daughters of the upper cadre or professionals were in the highest category; most went to the next level or to the lowest-paying jobs. Daughters of peasants or workers, however, were more likely than their brothers to go into a higher category, though not the highest. It seems, then, that women whose origins were more humble did relatively better than women of higher standing. Few women of any class were in the highest-paid category, which is not surprising. In 1907, however, children of peasants and artisans, trying to take their leave of village poverty, took advantage of the republican school system and flocked into public service.

Depending on the administration he or she served, the young fonctionnaire worked in widely differing conditions, which helped shape his or her consciousness. For those in the Ministry of Finance, the place of work was often an office in a large administrative center, most likely

69. AP, BA provisoire 305.
70. "Généologie PTT," *Postes et Télécommunications,* May, 1974.

Paris, or in the case of the douanier, isolated border areas. Separated from workers in other occupations and the community at large, employees of the Finance Ministry were less likely to feel the attachment to blue-collar workers or even to other fonctionnaires than would an employee of the PTT, for example. It has already been shown that employees of the PTT as a whole were much more militant in their syndicalist activity than other fonctionnaires. In close contact with the workers and peasants they served as postmen and clerks, these fonctionnaires, still close to the poverty of their youth, identified more quickly with each other and with blue-collar workers than did either the finance employees or the teachers. Furthermore, although finance workers often had been the beneficiaries of a more rigorous education and worked in a white-collar atmosphere, the postal employees worked at positions not too far from what might be considered blue-collar work. For the hundreds of women herded into the central telephone offices of Paris, there was only the slightest difference in the alienation and monotony of work, which involved endless manipulation of a switchboard, and the work done by their working-class sisters who tended the textile looms of the north. Naturally, the milieu of work is but one determining factor in the development of consciousness, yet it is difficult to disagree with an haut fonctionnaire who wrote in 1934 that as one went down the hierarchy of public service, one more and more lost the idea of serving the state; on the lower levels, the petit fonctionnaire was involved in a work contract similar to those of private industry.[71]

The teachers, particularly the instituteurs, the primary school teachers, intellectuals as well as fonctionnaires, deserve a more detailed analysis. Perhaps the lowest paid of all fonctionnaires with comparable education and experience, these teachers, the champions of secular school education, the defenders of the democratic Republic, and the anticlerical transmitters of French culture, present perhaps the widest spectrum of attitudes toward syndicalism, from the most cautious defenders of professionalism to the most ardent fighters for the unity of manual and intellectual workers.[72] Despite authoritarian administrators and low salaries, which often made it difficult for teachers to maintain their pro-

---

71. Pierre Dietsch, *De la légalité des syndicats des fonctionnaires* (Paris, 1934), 38.

72. For a comparison of salaries of teachers and other fonctionnaires in France in 1907, see Ferré, *Instituteurs,* 197.

fessional dignity, almost all teachers remained in the more professional amicales. Fearful of CGT anarchism, fearful of direct action by workers, fearful of government repression, and, most significant, cognizant of their duty as public servants of the Republic, teachers took only the most cautious steps toward syndicalism and resolutely rejected the use of the strike. A leader of the Fédération des Amicales voiced the sentiments of these teachers and of many government leaders, as well:

> I do not favor the fonctionnaire strike; here's why. The public services are the essential organs of the state. Suppose the tax collectors cease to collect taxes, that teachers no longer instruct their classes, that the police abandon their work, that a part or the whole of the public services no longer function. What happens? The nation is struck at its very core. Who will suffer the most in this situation? The humble people, the little people. Fonctionnaires who have guarantees that blue-collar workers do not have must renounce these tactics.[73]

Among these children of poverty, poverty-stricken still, teaching children of peasants and workers among whom they lived, anticlerical, politically active in the creation of a more progressive republic, readers of Jaurès and Tolstoy, the potential for syndicalist activity was great. Indeed, a dedicated but tiny minority did emerge in this crucial period to plead the case for the syndicalism of the working class. It was made up of the teachers who had been instrumental in the establishment of the Comité Central. Recognizing the tremendous role played by the schools in the development of young minds, these teachers wanted not only to join the syndicats of the working class but to influence the curriculum so that the children of workers and peasants could be educated in schools that would reflect their class needs. "We are proletarian. . . . We understand how to approach other proletarians . . . to instruct them, to develop their intelligence." It was to be instruction for a better world. It was to be "a red, pacifist, socialist, syndicalist school." Proposals for model working-class schools were made but never realized. At their 1908 congress in Lyons, the syndicalist teachers, anxious to make contact with the working class both as fellow workers and as parents, pro-

---

73. P. Courrèges, quoted in *La Petite République,* December 21, 1910, and in Musée Social, *Le Droit d'association des fonctionnaires* (Paris, 1912), 171.

posed to invite the Bourses du Travail to a mixed congress of teachers, other fonctionnaires, and blue-collar workers. The aim was to "work together toward the adaptation of academic programs responsive to the needs of the working class." The minister of education, Doumergue, forbade such a unified congress, but finally in 1910, electricians and masons, teachers and postmen, met together at Angers. Following addresses by the instituteurs Nègre and Louis Léger and by Jouhaux of the CGT, the congress passed resolutions in favor of more humane, rationalistic, and coeducational (a very advanced proposal) schools. They demanded that class size be diminished and that the age at which a child could leave school be raised from thirteen to fifteen. One motion stated clearly the aim of the congress: teachers must work to create a milieu favorable to the development of worker solidarity. The congress closed with a call for the unity of teachers and workers, for fonctionnaire syndicalism.[74]

The government, of course, shuddered at the idea of syndicalist teachers creating schools for fostering independence of thought and working-class solidarity. The schools were supposed to teach loyalty to the Republic, not to the working class: "The school must teach scientific method, progress made by peace and brotherhood, judicious collective work learned from the evolutionary model given us by nature, love of one's neighbors and *respect of the law,* in a word, the republican spirit."[75]

The government's design for education was well known to the working class. Despite the efforts of syndicalist teachers, many revolutionary syndicalists in the blue-collar movement distrusted the schools and the teachers who taught in them. Aware that the control of education was crucial to social change, the revolutionary syndicalists attacked the bourgeois schools. The republican schools were there to exalt the state, to teach conformity, to combat subversive ideas, to prepare fonctionnaires for service to the state, and to prepare workers for the rigors of industrialism. Above all, the bourgeois school was there to convince the children of the working class that the existing social structure must remain

74. E. Julien, quoted in Bernard *et al., Le Syndicalisme,* 43; Ferré, *Instituteurs,* 49; Musée Social, *Le Droit d'association,* 156–57.

75. Alphonse Aulard, an instituteur, in *La Dépêche de Toulouse,* quoted in Beaubois, "L'Etat," 124; italics added.

the same. Anarchists, of course, made no distinction between the teaching of state dogma and the teaching of religious dogma. They saw no difference between priests and lay teachers, "the intellectual cops of the capitalist class." Janvion, a signer of the open letter, called the republican school "the academic antechamber of the barracks and the vestry." Teachers who taught radicalism and republicanism instead of socialism were no friends of the working class.[76]

The majority of instituteurs, understandably cautious considering how severely the government treated any teacher who deviated from political norms, were as dedicated to the working-class and peasant children they taught as they were to the Republic. This dedication was deeply affected by the events of 1907–1908. The open letter, the shooting of blue-collar workers, the unexpected conservatism of the Clemenceau government, and the continued attack by the conservatives on the free, anticlerical schools all helped move the teachers closer to the syndicalist position. Most teachers remained in the amicales, but the lines between amicales and syndicats were growing fuzzier. More and more talk of the droit syndical was heard at amicale meetings. More teachers belonged to both organizations, hoping to move the amicales further along the road to syndicalism. Courrèges, the second secretary of the Fédération des Amicales joined the Syndicat of the Seine. In 1909, the amicales held a congress at Nancy at which a sizable minority presented the syndicalist position. The congress maintained its moderate tone and emphasized allegiance to the Republic. Yet the sympathy for the syndicalist position was obvious; the government was chastised for its failure to enact legislation that would end favoritism and arbitrary authoritarianism. Of the eleven members of the permanent commission of the federation at Nancy, five were syndicalists, partisans of teacher adherence to the Bourses du Travail.[77] By 1909, the teachers were responding to fast-moving political events and beginning to take the moderate syndicalist position of support for the droit syndical.

Despite the activity of left-wing militants and despite the advance of large numbers of state employees toward a moderate syndicalist posi-

---

76. Louis, Le Syndicalisme, 107–12; Lorulot, quoted in Ferré, Instituteurs, 153; ibid., 154.
77. Musée Social, Le Droit d'association, 165.

tion, most fonctionnaires were still unwilling to identify more closely with the blue-collar working class. If their origins and their work and political experiences were similar, there were enough differences between blue-collar workers and state employees to maintain the barriers that separated the consciousness and activity of these two segments of the working class.

As hard-pressed as they might have been financially and as frustrated as they were with the restrictions on their independence, the fonctionnaires enjoyed many privileges denied to blue-collar workers. Fonctionnaires in 1906 or 1909 were assured of pensions, sick pay, and automatic pay increases and advancement, whereas blue-collar workers had to fight bitterly for every small pay raise. Not that all these benefits came automatically for the fonctionnaires; they had to press hard for increases in the salary scale, for the weekly day off, and, starting at this time, for some paid vacation. But these demands were answered with parliamentary refusals, not soldiers' bullets. Most important, the fonctionnaires had security. An occasional fonctionnaire might be fired or transferred for political or personal reasons, but the bulk of them never suffered the uncertainty of seasonal or cyclical unemployment. Blue-collar workers were at the mercy of all the uncertainties of the capitalist economic system as well as dead-end employment with little hope for professional improvement. Senior fonctionnaires received the highest pay; older blue-collar workers were most often discarded by the industrial process.

The life-style of the fonctionnaire was also different. Even fonctionnaires at the lowest level of employment were likely to have had more education than blue-collar workers and to aspire more to bourgeois standards of dress and habitation. They even had fewer children. A radical revolutionary syndicalist fonctionnaire complained that the French had fewer children than other Europeans, but the fonctionnaires had fewer still, and the least prolific of all were those fonctionnaires who did not work with the pen, the employees of the PTT. The same syndicalist was not anxious for the fonctionnaires to enter the CGT because they were too bourgeois. Fonctionnaires could never be part of the working class, he wrote, because they came from the world of the petit bourgeoisie: the small peasant proprietors, the artisans, the small shopkeepers. These privileged employees, certain of all things in life except the day of death, would never know the black poverty or the deep uncertainty of working-class life. They could never understand the struggles of those who had died at Fourmies and other places of atrocity. These petits bourgeois strove for more education for their children, and their wives drove them to work harder so they could buy fancy furniture at the new department stores. They fought for advancement and would never understand class struggle, never battle the state, never be real syndicalists. It was better to keep them out of the CGT.[78]

The fonctionnaire also did not experience the same type of exploitation the blue-collar worker did. The loom operator knew his or her wages, the amount of work produced, and the price the product would command. The blue-collar worker was keenly aware of the profit made by bosses who dined in fancy restaurants, lived in grand houses, and sent their wives to take the cure at elegant spas. For the fonctionnaire, the exploitation was less clear. The fonctionnaire produced no goods; he supplied a service. It was impossible to determine the profit, the surplus value, of delivering letters or teaching children. Moreover, for the fonctionnaire there was no fat boss visible for all to see; the boss was the state. Fonctionnaires did feel exploited; they knew they worked hard for little pay. But only a few syndicalists and socialists connected service to the state with service to the bourgeoisie.

The differences between blue-collar workers and fonctionnaires kept the fonctionnaires isolated from the blue-collar movement. Yet almost from the beginning of organization, there was a strong nucleus of fonctionnaire syndicalists, and over the years, more and more fonctionnaires moved closer to the working class and its movement. How, then, does one determine fonctionnaire consciousness and activity? In his survey of militant teacher activists, Max Ferré asked what had influenced them to join syndicats and to become militants. Most answered that they had been influenced primarily by their origins, by pacifism (most of the respondents had been active in the World War I period), and by the social and political climate. Few cared about political parties, struggles within the administration, or injustice in the state system. They indicated that their primary concern, once in the syndicats, had not been wage in-

---

78. Gabriel Beaubois, "Les Employés de l'état et le socialisme ouvrier," *Le Mouvement Socialiste,* No. 152 (April 1, 1905).

creases or other specific material benefits but the desire for a better society for all workers.[79]

In my own interviews with a later generation of syndicalist militants (active in the interwar period and just after World War II), a similar predilection for social change was evident when these fonctionnaires answered questions about the origin of their syndicalism and their attachment to the working-class movement. The economic injustice of their childhoods had helped to determine their identification with the victims of injustice, the poor. When faced with injustice in their work and in the society at large, they allied themselves with those who struggled against these injustices; they joined a syndicat. Being part of the syndicalist movement was a way for them to change society. One or two spoke of being influenced by teachers or by reading *L'Humanité*. One man came from a "red" family. But even these men placed these influences on a lower level of importance in determining their syndicalist action. It was the events of the 1920s and 1930s that had affected their already strong predilection for social action. Most critical, a movement existed for them to join.[80]

In 1906, most fonctionnaires were isolated from the working-class movement. But as events unfolded, as the state increased its economic role, as the Radical party failed to live up to their aspirations, as working conditions changed, and as fonctionnaire syndicalism itself grew and changed, more fonctionnaires began to move closer to working-class syndicalism.

The government, distressed at the possibility of even the moderate syndicalism espoused by those who wanted only the extension of the 1884 law, continued to propose statutes. Between the Guyot-Dessaigne project and 1914, more than a dozen proposed statutes were presented to parliament.[81] Some Radicals, sincere in their desire to reform the admin-

79. Ferré, *Instituteurs,* 314.

80. Most of these interviews are on tape in my possession, but some information comes from unrecorded conversations.

81. It is difficult to give an exact number because some statutes were debated and amended and acted upon and some never got beyond the proposal stage. I read through most of these proposed laws. I must confess that I did not read them all. For those hearty souls who might want to undertake this task, the more important proposals for a statute are in the Archives Nationales F7 13725 and in the appropriate *Journaux Officiels.*

istration of fonctionnaires and most anxious to support moderate fonctionnaires against the militant fringe, proposed a number of statutes that included the extension of the 1884 law or the right to form federations. Such proposals, no matter how weak or ineffectual, never had a chance of passage. The government, fearful of any connections between fonctionnaires and the working–class movement and reluctant to admit that state employees were anything but servants of the state, would allow neither the droit syndical nor the formation of federations.

Some academics, notably law professors such as Henri Barthélemy, tried to make a distinction between *fonctionnaires de gestion,* those who, like blue-collar workers, lower clerical workers, and most employees of the PTT, made no decisions, merely performing services, and *fonctionnaires d'autorité,* those who might make individual decisions or be responsible for public opinion such as policemen or teachers. The fonctionnaires de gestion would be covered by the 1884 law, the fonctionnaires d'autorité would not. A debate among political theorists raged over the pros and cons of such a distinction and the difficulties of making any distinction at all among different categories of state employees, but the debate was really academic. Neither the government nor the fonctionnaires cared about such fine points of definition; whatever decisions were to be made would affect all fonctionnaires.

After the failure of the Guyot-Dessaigne statute of early 1907, the Radical deputy Jeanneney proposed a statute that would allow fonctionnaires to choose either the 1901 or the 1884 law.[82] Then came a second government-sponsored statute which had more individual guarantees but changed nothing in the *statut collectif.* The finance workers union expressed its anger: "You call this a statute. They're just trying to pull the wool over your eyes."[83] In 1908, Demartial, the haut fonctionnaire who headed the Comité d'Etudes, was instrumental in formulating a statute proposed by the Radical deputies Buisson, Dubief, Reinach, Dejéante, and Maurice Violette. Because the government considered it too extreme, another Radical deputy, Gabriel Chaigne, attempted to tone this proposal down by introducing another statute that did not allow federa-

82. Jeanneney's erudite and informative introduction to the proposed law was published as a book: *Associations et syndicats de fonctionnaires* (Paris, 1908).

83. AN, F7 13724, statement of the Union des Associations de Personnelle des Administrations Centrales.

tions. Despite the constant promises of the government for a statute, none of these moderate projects ever became law. Chaigne complained that the government had no real intention of reform. The moderate newspaper *Le Temps* editorialized in 1909, "The delays involved in the discussion and in the vote on the fonctionnaires' statute has had its natural results: the flabbiness of the Public Powers of course begat the boldness of the fonctionnaires." Even the government-sponsored Briand project, considered urgent because of the PTT strike of 1909, fell by the wayside. Poincaré worried about the agitation of fonctionnaires and the inactivity of parliament: "While our eyes are fastened on our constituencies and we believe ourselves secure, we are sliding gently into anarchy."[84] The last important attempt at a statute before World War I, the Maginot project of 1912, had as much chance of passage as did his plan for halting the advance of the German military machine in 1939.

The fonctionnaires, already hesitant about the statute, lost patience with the government. It was clear that the government would not allow a meaningful statute to pass into law. Their only recourse was the droit syndical. The Comité Central gathered more adherents. The Comité d'Etudes was fast becoming isolated from the mainstream of fonctionnaire attitudes. In early April, 1909, the Comité d'Etudes held a large open meeting in Paris on the question of the statute, which was attended by fonctionnaires belonging to both the Comité d'Etudes and the Comité Central. The PTT agents had just ended their March strike, and the mood was turbulent. When Demartial of the Comité d'Etudes spoke of the statute, Nègre interrupted to demand the committee's support for the droit syndical and for permission to enter the CGT. The Radical deputies Dubief, Buisson, Reinach, and Joseph Paul-Boncour were hooted down by postiers shouting "Vive la grève." Emile Pataud, the eccentric leader of the electricians, shouted to Paul-Boncour to bring his boss Viviani, "the worker's friend," before the group.[85] Then they would see what he thought of the "common law" for fonctionnaires. The syndicalists took over the meeting; the statute was condemned as

84. AN, F7 13724; *ibid.*, November 26, 1909.
85. Paul-Boncour listed himself as Republican-Socialist, but he voted with the left-wing Radicals. Pataud was famous for his fiery oratory and rash behavior. He threatened in December, 1909, to turn out the lights of Paris for the eating and drinking festivities of New Year's Eve, a threat that French gastronomes and celebrants did not take lightly.

one further attempt by the government to separate fonctionnaires from the working class. The poor Radical deputies, clearly out of touch with the swiftly evolving fonctionnaire movement, appeared at a loss to explain this distressing behavior.[86] The report of the meeting sent to the Ministry of the Interior by its "observer," ended with the comment: "If the government does not insist on having the question of the fonctionnaires' statute discussed, there is an excellent reason. The interested parties do not want it."[87] Amicales and associations began to pass resolutions against this statute.[88]

At the end of the year, at a critical meeting of the Comité d'Etudes, despite the intense opposition of the committee leaders Demartial and Chardon, the bulk of the amicales and associations belonging to the Comité voted to transform it into the Fédération des Associations de Fonctionnaires. This moderate and reformist group was to place itself between the conservative Comité, now headed by Chardon, in the wake of the resignation of the furious Demartial and the more radical syndicalists. Under the leadership of the instituteur Courrèges, the new organization declared that "loyal servants of the republican regime determined to remain out of party struggles, anxious not to create any disturbance in the public order, the federated fonctionnaires unanimously state that the strike will not be considered as a method of professional defense."[89] But the federation also voted to support the extension of the 1884 law, the droit syndical. Despite its extremely moderate position, the new federation was never received by any minister and never recognized by the government, which continued to uphold its intransigent position against any form of syndicalism. By the end of 1909, however, it was clear that despite government opposition to any extension of the 1884 law, the fonctionnaires had moved beyond the government's position. While the government continued to talk of reform through a statute, the majority of fonctionnaires now rejected the statute. The majority of fonctionnaires, radical or reformist, demanded the droit syndical.

86. *Le Journal, Le Petit Parisien, L'Action, Le Temps,* April 4, 1909.
87. AN, F7 13725.
88. See, for example, *Bulletin de l'AG,* August, 1909.
89. Musée Social, *Le Droit d'association,* 203.

4

The Struggle Intensifies:
The Postal Strikes of 1909

On Tuesday morning, March 16, 1909, thousands of Parisians awoke to find that their morning mail had not been delivered. By afternoon, the women of the central exchanges had stopped telephone service, and by the next evening, no letters, no telegrams, no communication service of any kind was available to banks and businesses, government offices, or private citizens. In an age of advanced technology, a massive strike of PTT employees had left Paris isolated from the rest of the world. The strike had begun officially on the evening of March 15 at a mass meeting, when six thousand agents had declared themselves on strike, but in reality, the movement had begun several days earlier with demonstrations, work stoppages, and arrests at the central telegraph office. To the ordinary Parisian and to many politicians, it seemed at first that the strike was hardly more than a personality conflict; the under secretary of state for the PTT, Simyan, had antagonized the members of the Association Générale des Agents with foolhardy rudeness and arrogance. But as with most strikes, the final events that caused the ultimate strike action were only the proverbial sparks that lit the fire. The grievances had been building for months.

The heart of the PTT employees' discontent was their increased work load. For years, the volume of correspondence had been growing at a rapid pace. Billions of letters, millions of telegrams, and millions of postal checks, packages, and pieces of registered mail passed through the hands of PTT agents and sous-agents.[1] This flood of communication pressed heavily on a staff whose numbers did not increase as rapidly as the work. The telegraph and telephone services with large numbers of

---

1. In 1909 the PTT handled 3.5 billion letters (Rapport PTT Charles Dumont Budget 1910, cited in Georges Frischmann, *Histoire de la fédération CGT des PTT* [Paris, 1967], 145).

female employees were particularly affected. By 1909, 254 million telephone messages were handled manually at the central telephone exchanges in Paris. Linesmen could not keep up with the growing demand for new phones; lower-paid auxiliaries, mostly day workers, were hired. Inadequately trained, unskilled telephone operators were pressed into service. These *téléphonistes*, mostly female, were herded into obsolete, dirty, and crowded "centrals." When one of these centrals, Gutemberg, had a fire, it was discovered that there were no fire boxes or fire escapes. Throughout 1908, there was talk of "une crise téléphonique."[2]

All this came to a head under the administration of Julien Simyan.[3] Whatever administrative and political qualities Simyan possessed which led Clemenceau to make him part of his 1906 cabinet did not endear him to the employees of the PTT and especially to the Association Générale des Agents. Arrogant, authoritarian, capricious, and seemingly disdainful of the growing organization and militancy of the PTT employees, Simyan carried out Clemenceau's policies in the most heavy-handed way. None of Clemenceau's political acumen had rubbed off on his appointee. A host of grievances began to accumulate. The director of the Caisse Nationale d'Epargne, the one haut fonctionnaire on the Council of Discipline who had had the courage to vote for the acquittal of the three agents who had signed the open letter, soon found himself retired from office. Favoritism continued to be a major problem. The PTT employees were particularly incensed by the appointment of a certain M. Bure. A young man with no PTT experience, but who had been Clemenceau's secretary at *L'Aurore*, Bure now became Simyan's leading adviser on PTT policies; skilled technicians were ignored. Complaints about inefficiencies of service led not to reorganization or better hiring and training policies but to a tightening of work rules. Circulars were sent out, rescinded, and new ones drafted, encompassing a host of petty but very annoying regulations. The operators of the Gutemberg central, who had fled their switchboards during the fire, were outraged when the administration, indignant at the abandonment of service during the alarm, posted a notice which declared that in case of fire, operators were

2. *Bulletin de l'AG,* October, 1908.
3. The PTT was part of the Ministry of Travaux Publics, Postes et Télégraphes, headed at the time of Simyan's term of office, from October, 1906, to July, 1909, by Louis Barthou. Simyan was under secretary of state for the PTT.

forbidden to leave their posts without permission.[4] Sick days were entered in employees' dossiers under the heading *cote d'assiduité* (note of regular attendance) to be considered in questions of advancement. Overtime pay was rescinded for postmen at railroad stations who had to work late when trains were held up. Iron discipline was maintained at the telephone centrals. It was forbidden to move, to push one's chair back, to lean on furniture, or to talk. The téléphonistes told a reporter, "We are treated like little girls . . . reprimanded if we sit sideways, given a bad note if we are thirsty and ask to peel an orange."[5] To discourage operators from seeking transfers from overloaded lines to more desirable positions, special bonuses on the preferred jobs were lowered. The activities of the Association Générale des Agents were particularly restricted. It was forbidden to collect association dues at the Gutemberg office and to post notices or minutes of meetings in the rest room at the central telegraph office. Activists could no longer switch hours with sympathetic comrades at work so they could attend meetings. Association militants were harassed and switched from post to post.[6]

Finally, after months of this petty harassment, Simyan moved his campaign against the PTT employees and their organizations into high gear. He attacked the advancement procedure of the PTT administration. Because salary increases had to be voted by difficult and lengthy legislative action, PTT employees recognized that most wage increases would have to come through advancement. Indeed, one of the advantages fonctionnaires enjoyed was a regular system of advancement, neatly laid out in steps, according to length and satisfactory completion of service. Simyan's plan would make advancement more difficult. The fonctionnaires of the PTT correctly interpreted this not only as an attack on their professional dignity but as a serious attack on their livelihoods. A curtailment of advancement meant a curtailment of wage increases.

Simyan's plan was to have advancement determined by *tiercement* (thirds). One-third would be advanced *à choix* (by choice), one-third *à demichoix* (half-choice), and one-third *à l'ancienneté* (seniority). The

4. Gabriel Beaubois, *La Crise postale et les monopoles d'état* (Paris, 1909), 54.

5. Susan Dimlich Bachrach, "The Feminization of the French Postal Service, 1750–1914" (Ph.D. dissertation, University of Wisconsin, 1981), 344.

6. A. Monbrunaud, "La Grève des postes," *Le Mouvement Socialiste*, No. 209 (April, 1909); Frischmann, *Histoire PTT*, 147.

existing advancement system was determined by choice without limitation, and because it allowed more men and women of the PTT to advance more rapidly, the postal employees wished to retain it. The method worked simply. At the end of a given time period, usually three years, a given number of employees were eligible for advancement if their work was deemed satisfactory. A supervisor would determine if the work was indeed satisfactory, indicate this on the employee's record, and recommend advancement. Until Simyan's plan, about three-fourths of eligible employees were promoted this way. Simyan's proposal was to restrict such advancements à choix to only one-third of those eligible. The rest would have to wait a longer period: one-third for three months more, one-third to be advanced by seniority three months after that. A supervisor would thus automatically have to restrict advancement to one-third even if he had, as was usual, many more satisfactory employees. Thus only one-third would get the pay increase that had earlier gone to more than two-thirds of the workers involved.

Simyan had unveiled the plan in July, 1907, causing great consternation among postal employees. The Radical deputy Steeg and others brought the employees' reaction to the attention of the Chamber. Eventually the plan was withdrawn. In the fall of 1908, however, le tiercement was once more introduced. The Association Générale rallied to the defense of the existing advancement procedure. In October, a special open letter was sent to Barthou, the minister of public works, on the subject of this regressive move. It stated: "Not only are our hopes disappointed, not only are our most unquestionable rights being ignored, but our more urgent material and moral interests are seriously threatened." A special appeal was sent to the rank and file on the danger "of delaying your promotion, of lowering your salary." Throughout October and November, meetings were called to alert the membership and PTT employees in general; on November 7, two thousand came to a protest meeting in Paris. At the end of November, parliament began its discussion of the PTT budget. Simyan explained le tiercement, proudly displaying letters of approval from dozens of postiers. Simyan's advancement plan and his general handling of the PTT were attacked by Charles Dumont and other left-wing Radicals and Socialists. But once again, the parliamentary "liberals," worried about a ministerial crisis, approved Clemenceau's policies with regard to fonctionnaires, though some of the more perceptive politicians might well have sensed disaster in the air. The Ligue des Droits de l'Homme had already criticized Simyan for overstepping his boundaries by declaring war on the Association Générale.[7]

With the new year, agitation intensified. Despite the repressive measures taken by the government through Simyan, the Association Générale was growing by leaps and bounds. Meetings grew larger; discontent increased. Under Simyan, the association members declared, salaries were decreasing and postal employees were treated like pariahs. On January 18, when a delegation from the Association Générale went to see Simyan, a violent argument ensued between the minister and the volatile Subra of the association.[8] The pressure continued to mount. On February 8 and 9, the central telegraph office erupted. For months the telegraph workers had been agitated about Simyan's infamous changes in work regulations and rules. Then in early 1909, he made yet another announcement: the workday, which normally ended at nine o'clock in the evening, was to be extended to ten for some employees.[9] Although the extension of hours affected only a few, the telegraph operators, knowing how often changes in working conditions and salaries were slipped in through the back door in just this manner, feared that this was merely the first step in extending the workday for all. They were even more distressed by the appearance, at the same time as the ten o'clock announcement, of a new regulation concerning the determination of individual productivity. All telegraph operators were to note on their *fiches* (index cards) the number of telegrams handled per day. Since the number did not take into account the intensity of labor, that is, the length of the telegram, the condition of the line or apparatus, accidents, and so on, the telegraphers insisted that it could not be considered a valid indication of productivity. On February 8, work stopped at the central telegraph office; a meeting was held. When Simyan arrived, he was greeted with hoots, whistles, and the traditional *chahut* used by students. The next morning, the telegraph operators, moving their demonstration into the street, were met by the police. Two arrests were made,

---

7. *Bulletin de l'AG,* November, December, 1908, February, 1909.

8. Frischmann explains that the volatile Subra was from L'Ariège (*Histoire PTT,* 147).

9. This would not mean an increase in the number of hours worked because these men could report to work one hour later in the morning.

and the telegraphers became more vociferous. Even after the release of the two men, the demonstrations continued. Simyan and his notorious *fiches* were jeered, and the courtyard rang with cries of "Démission! Démission" (Resignation!). The "International" was sung. Finally, a conciliatory Simyan agreed to withdraw the regulations concerning the ten o'clock closing and the *fiches*. Immediately, the demonstration stopped. An important lesson had been learned; direct action had worked.

Throughout February, the agents held meetings. The telegraph workers were extolled for their determination in the face of police action and for their victory. Simyan's actions were decried. On the evening of the eighteenth, three thousand Parisian agents came to a meeting of the Fédération des Groupes Parisiens de l'Association Générale des Agents. Subra was elected president and Mme Pech, representing the five hundred women who were present in the room, was named honorary president. The presence of such a large number of women at the meeting was an important development in the association. And indeed, the women workers were to play an important role in the strike, a fact duly noted by the press and by the association itself. The mood was militant. Simyan and the *tiercement* were attacked. Telegrams of support came from the provinces. The Ligue des Droits de l'Homme pledged its support. The government agent who reported on the meeting to the Ministry of the Interior noted that the meeting was turbulent. It was his opinion that it did not matter that the agents were organized as an association rather than a syndicat; the threat of a strike was very real.[10]

One month after the incidents at the central telegraph office, the *ambulants* (postal workers who worked on railroad trains and in train stations) called a meeting to protest the threatened curtailment of their service as well as the implementation of the *tiercement*. On March 12, one thousand, about one-half of the Parisian ambulants—the other half were on duty and thus traveling—met at the Salle Vianey on the Quai de la Rapée. In the course of the meeting, the ambulants, hearing that a delegation from their association was at that moment meeting with Barthou, decided to go en masse to the offices of the minister of public works to hear the results of the interview. As the crowd streamed across the Seine and onto the Boulevard St. Germain, they met the returning

10. AN, F7 12792.

delegation. The ambulants were told that once again Barthou had put them off. He had gone off to the Chamber to participate in the debate on recent events in Algeria. The cortege of ambulants moved on, intent on reaching Barthou's office on the rue de Grenelle. Passing the back of the Chamber, the marchers were met by the police, who, under orders from the prefect of police, Lépine, tried to disperse the crowd. The regrouping ambulants finally reached their destination, where a battle broke out with charging policemen in the street. Seven agents were arrested. Police barricaded the streets, and the marchers retreated to the courtyard and up into the corridors of the central telegraph office. The shift was changing, and the ambulants were joined by a large number of telegraph operators, veterans of the February incidents at this very place. The police, directed by Simyan himself, began to arrest all those who came to hand. "Take all who are in street clothes," shouted the minister.[11] Thirty-seven agents were apprehended, seven in the street and thirty at the central office. The latter group was kept in custody, threatened with a violation calling for a penalty that could bring them a sentence of up to two years in prison. Attempts by friendly legislators to secure their release were unsuccessful. The agents were treated as ordinary criminals, handcuffed, and taken at two in the morning in a police van to the Conciergerie.

The next morning, a Saturday, police filled the courtyard of the central telegraph office. The operators, waiting for news of their arrested comrades, refused to send telegrams (*une grève des bras croisés*). Simyan blustered that it was all the work of anarchists.[12] By afternoon, the judicial hearing had been held. The majority of the arrested agents had been released, but eight were kept, ordered to face judgment, not allowed even their provisional liberty. The news spread quickly—thirty-two suspended, eight in prison. The telegraph operators left their machines and some ambulants refused to go on their tours of duty. Meetings were organized. On Saturday evening and all day Sunday, telegraph and telephone operators, ambulants, agents of all kinds, facteurs, and line workers flocked to meetings all over Paris to pledge solidarity with the imprisoned agents and to demand the resignation of Simyan. A strike

11. *Bulletin l'AG,* March–April, 1909.
12. AN, F7 12792.

seemed inevitable; only the official declaration and the organization of the action remained. Messages of support came from the provinces; work stoppages were reported in Lyons and Marseilles. Subra and Quilici addressed the crowds. It was time to fight back. Pataud pledged the support of the electricians. He agreed with the PTT speakers that it was time to "get involved." The CGT declared that the fonctionnaires, by stopping the government from operating, would be the principal force of the revolution.[13]

A call was issued for a mass meeting at the Tivoli Vaux-Hall for Monday evening, March 15. Throughout the day, the agitation increased. Work had again ceased at the central telegraph office. Simyan was greeted with jeers and cries of "Our Pals, Our Pals," "Down with Simyan." Word spread rapidly that the furious secretary had insulted the female employees, calling them *saloperies* (sluts), *fripouilles* (scum), and *putains* (whores). Lépine, the *goujat* (cad) had also insulted the ladies.[14] The police, wielding truncheons, had to be called in to restore order. The judicial tribunal met: the seven agents (one was at the funeral of his child), charged with *délits d'opinion* for shouting for Simyan's resignation, were sentenced to six days in prison.[15] The strike movement gathered strength. The ambulants had voted to strike, and the ouvriers had agreed to join the ambulants. The *dames téléphonistes* had taken no official vote, but hundreds had signed a petition for either a strike or a slowdown, and it was clear that they too were ready. The big question was what the sous-agents would do. Would the facteurs join the agents or would they repay the agents for their lack of solidarity in the 1906 strike?

The hall was filled to capacity with six thousand agents and other PTT workers. Eugène Guerard of the railroad workers cheered the agents on. Nègre spoke for the teachers. Some agents thought that perhaps the action should be delayed until the Chamber met, but when the strike declaration was read, all doubts fell by the wayside. "All those who are in favor of voting for an immediate general strike, raise your

13. AP, BA 1391.
14. *Révolution,* March 15, 1909.
15. It was noted among the agents and the CGT that just a few days before the sentence, several members of the Action Française had received a small fine of 50 francs for shouting "A Bas la République."

hand." All hands shot up. Hats flew in the air. Vive le Grève! Pauron spoke for the line workers; they would meet the next day. Grangier spoke for the sous-agents; the syndicat was ready to join the movement. The strike of the PTT was to be general.

The next morning, the sixteenth, the strike began to take effect. In the next forty-eight hours, the telegraph office was completely idled—women had stuck hatpins in the machines to short-circuit them—the ambulants refused to work, the téléphonistes closed their offices, and post offices in most arrondissements ceased to function. The Prefecture of Police estimated that 60 percent of agents were not at work. A notice was issued by the strikers explaining the causes of the strike to the public: it was with heavy hearts that this action was taken by fonctionnaires dedicated to public service, but Simyan's policies and insults had driven them to this extreme. More meetings were held. The employees of the PTT central administration voted to join the strike. The line workers met. The strike issues did not directly concern the blue-collar workers, but in a significant gesture of solidarity they voted to make the strike complete. On the evening of the seventeenth, a crowd of nearly ten thousand PTT employees filled the Manège Saint Paul to overflowing.

Messages of solidarity were read. The Association des Abonnés des Téléphones (telephone consumers organization), though disapproving of the strike action, nevertheless sent its sympathy to the strikers. The association had long called for reform of the telephone service; it hoped that the strike would be settled quickly and reform instituted.[16] Finally, word came from the sous-agents; the facteurs had joined the strike. Barbut of the Syndicat des Sous-Agents had told the strikers: "There is no longer any division between us all: agents, sous-agents, telephone operators, and workers, we are united by the same bond of solidarity. The duty of each is to continue the struggle. It is now a question of dignity where everyone must do his utmost to achieve justice for our demands."[17] In actuality, as had been the case in 1906, the strike was to be strongest among *facteurs d'imprimés;* the *facteurs des lettres* were less anxious to join the movement. The meeting ended with tumultuous cheers; the strike had indeed become general in Paris. A federated strike com-

16. *Bulletin de l'AG,* March–April, 1909.
17. AN, F7 12792.

mittee, a precursor of the Fédération Postale, which was later to emerge from the strike, was formed. It included the three major PTT organizations: the Association Générale des Agents, the Syndicat National des Sous-Agents, and the Syndicat National des Ouvriers des PTT. This unity was to be one of the most important results of the strike.

In the corridors of the Chamber of Deputies, everyone talked of the strike. It was impossible to find any supporters for Simyan; his outrageous behavior was blamed for all the difficulties.[18] On Wednesday, the seventeenth, a small delegation of the Left had gone to see Barthou and Clemenceau to urge them to support proposed legislation that would establish a council to look into reform of the PTT. Immediate action was necessary; everyone feared that commerce and industry would be paralyzed. Clemenceau acknowledged the seriousness of the situation; the government was sending telegrams to Berlin through Brussels. But, Clemenceau continued, the agents had gone on strike for no reason and the government would not consent to any discussions of a parliamentary project at this time. He was already taking steps to replace the striking workers. And by the next day, Barthou had signed a decree which permitted the head of the PTT to fire strikers without going before the Council of Discipline as was ordinarily the case. The striking workers received an ultimatum: return to work within forty-eight hours or be fired.

By Thursday, the eighteenth, telegrams and letters were piling up at the central offices. Businesses were making arrangements to send couriers out of the country with important messages. The amazingly effective strike was equally amazingly peaceful. After the difficulties of the first day, there were only a few incidents of shouted insults and some pushing of nonstrikers. An offer of help from the Action Française was turned down by the police.[19] The government made a special request. There was a crisis in the Balkans. The Ministry of Foreign Affairs asked for eight workers to keep the vital telegraph lines open to Vienna. Amid applause and laughter, the strikers agreed to send eight of the originally fired telegraphers. At yet another gigantic meeting, the strikers received more messages of solidarity from the teachers, from other fonction-

18. AP, BA 1391. One deputy was overheard telling a colleague what was the general consensus, "Simyan is an ass."
19. *Ibid.*

naires, and from the police. The Paris police, "partners in misery," had sent eight hundred francs.[20] Two big questions remained: what would the PTT employees in the provinces do and would the blue-collar workers in either the public or private sectors support the striking fonctionnaires? The CGT had just undergone an internal crisis. In February, Griffuehles had been forced to resign and the leadership of the federation was now in the hands of the more moderate and less capable Louis Niel.[21]

On the eighteenth, the CGT leadership met. Most agreed that some solidarity must be shown, but some of the CGT militants were uncertain that the Association Générale wanted the CGT to enter the movement; the press might use its support of the strike as an excuse to brand the strike revolutionary. Finally it was agreed to issue a simple solidarity statement. The statement, posted in the traditional manner on walls all over Paris, began with an explanation that the CGT did not want to interfere in the PTT strike; it wanted to alert CGT supporters to the situation. The blue-collar workers were told that once again the government was using all its forces, the judiciary, the army, and the police, against workers. This time the striking postiers were the victims. It was the duty of all workers, of all men of good heart, to show the utmost sympathy for these strikers and to encourage them to persevere until victory was attained.[22] No action was mentioned. The PTT strikers now waited to hear from the railroad workers and the electricians. The leaders of both groups had pledged solidarity on the first evening of the strike; results of membership meetings were not yet known.

Friday, the nineteenth, was to be a critical day. The strike committee, flushed with success, issued another statement thanking the public, and especially the *abonnés,* for their support. The strike was a success, and they would press on to victory. They would not return to work until

20. This information was found in the archives of the Ministry of the Interior, AN, F7 12792. In the Archives of the Prefecture of Police of Paris, there is also mention of the action with an apologetic note that indeed the police had contributed some money to the strikers but only 140 francs (AP, BA 1391).

21. Edouard Dolléans says that the CGT leaders, Latapie and Lévy, were used by Briand, either willingly or unwillingly, to force the more aggressive Griffuehles out of the leadership. His resignation marked a turning point in CGT history (*Histoire du mouvement ouvrier* [3 vols.; Paris, 1968], II, 52–55).

22. *Bulletin de l'AG,* March–April, 1909.

they were assured that their demands would be heard by a chief of the PTT other than Simyan. The strike committee pledged that when the strike was over, all PTT employees would work toward restoring service as quickly as possible, using their vacation time if necessary.[23] Friday was also the day the imprisoned agents were to be released. A huge meeting was called for the afternoon, and by three o'clock, nearly twelve thousand fonctionnaires filling two halls were waiting to welcome their released comrades and to hear the results of the discussion taking place in the Chamber of Deputies. The parliamentary debate went on late into the evening. Although Simyan was severely criticized by the deputies, once again the parliamentarians defended Clemenceau's position. A three-part order of the day, introduced by the Radical Reinach, was finally voted on. It said: "The Chamber, resolute in not tolerating fonctionnaires' strikes" (458 to 99 in favor) "and confident in the government's ability to restore order in the PTT" (346 to 147 in favor) "approves its declaration" (raised hands).[24] The entire statement was passed 368 to 211.

Instead of convincing the strikers of the futility of their actions, the Chamber vote had the opposite effect. Their hopes for parliamentary intervention gone, the PTT strikers, riding the crest of a successful movement, had no choice but to continue to strike until they forced the government to give in. Late on the nineteenth, an appeal was sent to the provinces telling of the failure at the Chamber and saying it was time to extend the strike.[25] The next morning, at yet another mass meeting, strikers voiced their disdain for the parliamentary decision, referring to "the servile Chamber which has not yet shown the depth of its cowardice."[26] Word of provincial action began to come in. A general strike of the PTT was in effect at Lyons, Chartres, and Marseilles, and a large number of employees had stopped work at Lille, Nice, Rouen, Nancy, Brest, Le Havre, St. Etienne, Limoges, and Quimper. Troops had been ordered sent to Marseilles. Dozens of sympathy meetings were held in cities and towns all over France. Workers in some of the provincial cities such as Bordeaux did not wish to become involved with the Parisian

23. *Ibid.*
24. The government's declaration of opposition to the illegal strike, *ibid.*
25. *Bulletin de l'AG,* March–April, 1909.
26. AN, F7 12792.

actions. In others, smaller towns such as Angoulême, Besançon, and Evreux, sympathy was high for the Parisian cause, but workers hesitated to take any action until they were sure that all the larger cities had joined the strike. One could probably correlate the militancy of PTT employees with the strength of the blue-collar movement in their area. Thus Marseilles was on strike, Montpelier was not.[27] But clearly the provinces were affected. With Paris, Lyons, and Marseilles on strike, postal service was severely curtailed and telegraph service was practically nonexistent. The king of England, vacationing in Biarritz, appealed for special service, and special facilities were set up for English tourists in that resort town. Norwegian and British fonctionnaires sent solidarity messages. Belgian postiers held a sympathy strike. There was agitation in Algiers. Most important, there were rumblings that other state and municipal employees might extend the strike.

The government began to have second thoughts. Despite the intransigence of Clemenceau and Barthou, despite the Chamber vote, despite the charges of sabotage launched in the press to anger the taxpayers, the strike was effective. It is difficult to ascertain just how many PTT employees were actually on strike. The government issued figures of just over five thousand, but the Paris police estimated on March 19 that at the central post office and the central telegraph office alone, four thousand were out. The government listed fifteen hundred facteurs on strike—mostly *facteurs d'imprimés*—and if the line workers, the telephone operators, and the ambulants are included, the number goes well over six or seven thousand. The strike committee kept no official count. It knew only that the meetings were drawing enormous crowds; at two meetings, the attendance was estimated at about ten thousand. It is likely that between eight and ten thousand, or about 60 percent of PTT employees, participated in the strike action in Paris.[28] At least eight hundred were on strike in Marseilles. Whatever the number, the strike was clearly effective. But the federal strike committee also knew that the strike could not be prolonged indefinitely without losing support. Soli-

27. AN, reports of provincial meetings are in a separate folder of prefectural reports under F7 12792. It is clear that many blue-collar workers attended these meetings to show solidarity with the fonctionnaires.

28. AP, BA 1391. In May, 1908, there were twelve thousand agents and sous-agents and five thousand ouvriers in Paris.

darity statements were still coming in from other state employees and from the blue-collar workers, but their militant rhetoric did not necessarily mean they would join the strike.[29] The electricians had voted to strike, but now their capricious leader, Pataud, was dragging his feet. The railroad workers were still hoping the government would give in and eliminate the need to extend the strike.

By Saturday, the twentieth, however, the Chamber was beginning to reflect on the meaning of the carte blanche it had given Clemenceau the night before. The SFIO was apparently amazed at the militancy of the postal workers. Sembat (former reporter for the PTT budget and a strong supporter of the Association Générale) had reportedly told a colleague that he would never have believed the postiers capable of such a movement. A central council meeting of the party was told that since the strike most section meetings of the SFIO had been deserted. Louis Debreuilh worried openly that the strike would favor the extension of syndicalism at the expense of political action. He was also concerned with how the postiers would take the silence of Jaurès, who had been absent from the Chamber during the critical vote on the nineteenth. The Radicals and their supporters were just as agitated. The Radical and Radical Socialist party counted on the fonctionnaires for electoral support. Mougeot, the former secretary of state for the PTT, worried about the repercussions of the government's position. He told the deputies that perhaps Clemenceau and Barthou did not fully comprehend the situation. The government was threatening to fire eight to ten thousand PTT fonctionnaires (another admission of a high number of strikers). Did Clemenceau realize that with fathers, brothers, and other relatives, each worker had to be multiplied by five or six and they represented fifty thousand votes? And the general election was to be held in a few months. More than that, was it possible, because of the new apparatus, to train thousands of new telegraph and telephone operators quickly? The PTT was already charged with squandering money; this would be an unacceptable waste of funds. Besides, even if the government replaced the entire personnel of the PTT, what guarantee was there that

29. AN, F7 12792. Strong messages of support came from dozens of syndicats and associations, including teachers, hospital workers, employés, miners, mint workers, arsenal workers, Contributions Indirectes, penitentiary employees, and, of course, the Paris police. The Gardes Municipaux officially declared their unwillingness to replace strikers.

the conditions that prompted this strike would not cause the new employees to organize and strike also? Because of the important position he had held in the PTT in the previous government, Mougeot's comments were taken seriously. A group of left-wing Radicals, led by Steeg and Maurice Berteaux, came to a similar conclusion—it was madness to push the postiers to the wall just before the election. The government would have difficulty standing under such conditions. Moreover, such intransigence was likely to encourage the supporters of the Camelots du Roi "and those gentlemen of the Action Française" in their antirepublican efforts.[30]

Barthou and Clemenceau, having made the necessary public demonstration of refusing to recognize "fonctionnaires in revolt," began to let it be bruited about that they would look for a solution of the strike. On Sunday afternoon, March 21, Barthou agreed to receive a delegation from the Syndicat des Ouvriers, who were given a mandate from the strike committee to negotiate a basis for settlement. The committee had chosen the delegation of blue-collar workers because that group had no direct interest in the outcome of the settlement; they had joined the strike in a gesture of solidarity.[31] The workers' delegation used this opportunity to deny vigorously the charges that equipment had been sabotaged and then went on to present the conditions under which the PTT workers would return to work. There were three conditions: that Simyan resign, that no strikers be fired or punished in any way, and that the delegation be assured that representatives of the strikers would be received directly by the minister of public works, Barthou, so that demands could be submitted by the PTT personnel.

Barthou replied that it was impossible for him to agree to the first condition because only parliament could demand a minister's resignation. He agreed to the other two demands. Since no one had yet been

30. *Ibid.* Grangier, a member of the SFIO as well as a syndicalist, had appealed for the SFIO's support on the sixteenth. At that time Debreuilh did not see how the SFIO could be of any help.

31. I have seen speculations in police reports and in the press that Pauron of the line workers' syndicat was accused of pushing his syndicat into a position of control of the strike, to the detriment of the Association Générale. It is true that Pauron was criticized at several meetings for being in too great a hurry to end the strike, but it is probably correct, as the *Bulletin de l'AG* reports, that the workers' committee was chosen by the strike committee specifically for the reasons given—to act as neutral negotiators.

fired, if the PTT employees went back to work by Tuesday morning, no punitive action would be taken. The minister assured the delegation of the goodwill of the government; after their return to work, he would agree to meet with representatives of the PTT employees to discuss their problems. He closed the interview with an appeal to the republican sentiments of the PTT personnel to end the strike, which was so painful to the public. The delegates were also invited to see Clemenceau later that day.[32]

As the delegation was calling on Clemenceau, two huge meetings were in progress. The crowd was so large that two manèges, Saint Paul and Pantheon, had to be used.[33] Victory was in the air. Nevertheless, the railroad workers assured the strikers that in case the government did not agree—but, of course, it would—plans were being made for a strike on railroad lines belonging to the state. The delegation arrived to give its report to the strike committee. After hearing that Clemenceau had concurred with Barthou's statement, the strike committee urged the meeting to vote an end to the strike. Pauron of the line workers was particularly anxious to see work resume. But the bulk of the strikers felt that Clemenceau's statements were not precise enough, and they did not want to wait for parliament to fire Simyan. The strike was to continue. Another meeting was called for the following morning.

At the Monday morning meeting, it was agreed to send three members of each participating organization (nine in all) as a second delegation to Clemenceau. They would tell the minister that the PTT employees were willing to return to work if he would make more formal his assurances on amnesty and Simyan. This expanded delegation returned to an afternoon meeting with the news that Clemenceau had confirmed the statement he had made to the previous delegation. No one would be fired if there was an immediate return to work, but he refused to consider the reintegration of Simonnet and Grangier, who remained fired

32. The account of this interview is taken from the *Bulletin de l'AG* (April, 1909), which took its account directly from the statement Barthou gave the press.

33. One of the characteristics of a bygone era was the use of huge indoor riding halls (a manège or the Hippodrome) for large meetings. In a horseless era, political rallies or large union meetings are more often held in exhibition halls like the one at the Porte de Versailles, or in the case of the Left, in the pride of the "red" suburbs, the huge athletic stadium.

because of the open letter.[34] He also refused to fire Simyan, but the delegates were convinced that a constitutional technicality prevented him from accepting this demand. Clemenceau assured the strikers of his sincerity; the government would see to the reorganization of the PTT.[35] Both Barthou and Clemenceau had indicated that discussions between PTT employees and the government would involve direct contact with Barthou; Simyan was to be bypassed.

By the afternoon, the Havas news agency received the government statement and the newspapers began to herald the end of the strike. *Le Temps* wrote, "The complete victory of the strikers must not be questioned."[36] A final meeting was called for the twenty-third. The spirited Vallet spoke for the agents. Since the government had agreed to the conditions at two separate interviews, it was foolhardy not to return to work immediately. Barbut of the sous-agents agreed that they could return to work with their heads held high. Pauron of the line workers assured the strikers that if Clemenceau dared to renege on the agreement, a new, more devastating strike would ensue. Dozens of speakers lauded the solidarity of the strike. It was decided to pass an order of the day pledging renewed dedication to the reintegration of Simonnet, Grangier, and Nègre. It was proposed that the strike committee be transformed into a vigilance committee. Finally, in the utmost calm, the vote was taken. The strike would end at two o'clock in the afternoon. The statement ending the strike began, "Considering the precise authorized guarantees conceded to them by Monsieur Clemenceau."[37] The unity of the postal proletariat was cheered, and a permanent federation containing the three organizations that had participated in the strike was established. Finally, the public and the organized working class were thanked for their support. At two o'clock, a huge cortege was formed, and long

34. AN, F7 12792. The police report adds that Clemenceau also warned that if the strike was continued, there would be an endless number of firings.

35. *L'Humanité*, May 5, 1909. The report of the interview goes as follows: "Don't ask me to say what I cannot; have confidence in the government's word. You are men, you have a brain, do you understand; I am asking you for few days' leeway; you have satisfaction on all your points." He repeated the last sentence when asked about the reform of the PTT, adding, "even that which involves the reorganization of the postal administration."

36. Quoted in Frischmann, *Histoire PTT*, 154.

37. *Bulletin de l'AG*, March–April, 1909.

lines of victorious strikers marched back to the telegraph offices, the telephone switchboards, and the post offices. At the central post office, the red carpet was unrolled on the main staircase. The next morning, *L'Humanité* described "the victorious return of joy, of dignity, of fervor."[38]

The PTT employees returned to work deservedly proud of their successful movement. Not until the 1930s would fonctionnaires be able to organize such an impressive show of strength. But even as the victory cortege was winding its way through the streets of Paris, the victory was already in doubt. Could Clemenceau, the notorious strikebreaker, be trusted to fulfill the promises he had been forced to make to fonctionnaires he considered in rebellion? Almost immediately, the postal employees had a hint of what might be expected from the old tiger. As soon as the strike was ended, the federated strike committee issued a public statement entitled "Thank you to our Citizens." The statement, posted on the walls of Paris, not only included a message of gratitude to the Parisians who had been so supportive during the strike and a pledge to work toward improved public service, it contained an attack on Simyan and his administration. The opening paragraph explained that the workers had been "pushed to the wall by the excessive malevolence, the vulgarity and the authoritarianism of M. Simyan." It went on to declare that PTT employees would no longer deal with Simyan as *chef:* "We have been promised that we will see his pernicious work disappear . . . it is the legitimate revenge of 'right' against arbitrariness."[39] Clemenceau, outraged at what he considered an impermissible attack on his government, wanted the heads of the members of the strike committee who had signed the offensive document. Only the threat of a renewed strike stopped him from acting. The matter was dropped.[40]

But there was another aspect to the strike which was perhaps even more threatening to Clemenceau. As a result of the strike action and the solidarity shown by the blue-collar workers, the PTT and other fonctionnaires had moved closer to the blue-collar movement. Had not an association joined with two syndicats affiliated with the CGT to run a strike which they heralded as a grève générale? Had not money and mili-

38. *L'Humanité,* March 24, 1909.
39. *Bulletin de L'AG,* March–April, 1909.
40. Monbrunaud, "La Grève des postes."

tant solidarity messages come from state workers and blue-collar workers alike? Now there were plans for uniting the organizations of agents, sous-agents, and blue-collar workers into the Fédération Postale. Moreover, there was a strong possibility that the Association Générale, having gained hundreds of new members as a result of the strike, might turn itself into a syndicat.[41] At the March 29 meeting of the administrative council of the association, six leaders who had not participated in the strike were forced to resign their posts. The Association Générale was now in the hands of the militants who had successfully organized and led a strike. At a mid-April meeting, the members voted to push for the transformation of the Association Générale into a syndicat at the next congress. A number of the more militant syndicalists expressed their disappointment with the council for not doing this during the strike. Even CGT affiliation was not out of the question. The CGT, which had traditionally maintained an ambivalent attitude toward the fonctionnaires—some revolutionary syndicalists were most wary of the moderate petit-bourgeois state employees, while others considered the petits fonctionnaires necessary allies—now, impressed with the organization and success of the strike, planned more activity among state workers. For their part, fonctionnaires who had been hesitant to join with the revolutionaries, found that their strike experience and the solidarity shown by the leadership of the CGT had made them less hesitant about allying themselves with the organization of the blue-collar working class.

In the wake of the strike there was also increased activity on the question of the droit syndical. Throughout late March and April, fonctionnaire meetings declared their opposition to the statute for the extension of the 1884 law. On April 2, there occurred the meeting of the Comité d'Etudes at which Nègre and other militants forced an organizational split which reflected the move toward the syndicalist position among most fonctionnaires.[42] Two days later, on April 4, a solidarity meeting of ten thousand fonctionnaires and blue-collar workers took place at the Hippodrome. The call for the meeting, "To all workers (Manual and Intellectual)," was launched by the masons, puisatiers-mineurs (well and

41. *Bulletin de l'AG,* May–June, 1909. The Association Générale gained more than eight hundred new members from April 1 to April 15.
42. This meeting was discussed in Chapter 3.

sump diggers), the electricians, and the *terrassiers* (street pavers and repairers).[43] Thousands of fonctionnaires responded. An observer described the crowded hall: black-coated teachers were rubbing elbows with masons in corduroy trousers, facteurs in uniform sitting next to *terrassiers,* distinctively girdled with bands of red flannel.[44] All the speakers stressed the solidarity of the working class, the rejection of the statute, and the demand for the droit syndical—the right to strike. Pataud spoke for the electricians, Le Du for the *terrassiers,* Georges Yvetot in the name of the Bourses du Travail, Alphonse Merrheim for the CGT, Grangier, Simonnet, and Nègre for the fonctionnaires. The meeting concluded with a pact of solidarity; fonctionnaires and blue-collar workers were to be united: "They pledge to support the fonctionnaires vigorously in the struggle they are waging against the employer-state and in case repressive measures might be taken against them, they declare themselves to use all the means in their power, including a general strike, to defend those who might be legally charged."[45]

As the Hippodrome meeting concluded, a similar meeting began at Lyons. The postal strike had been successful in that industrial center, and now workers in both the private and public sectors came together to listen to their victorious Parisian comrades as well as their own leaders. Telegrams of solidarity were exchanged with Paris.[46] The meetings of April 2 and 4 were covered by most of the newspapers in Paris and the provinces. Detailed reports were sent to the government. The import of the meetings, especially the ones joining blue-collar workers and fonctionnaires under the smiling leadership of Merrheim of the CGT, was not lost on the government. The government was particularly sensitive to foreign reaction, especially in Germany. The Paris paper *Le Journal* reported that the Germans viewed events in France as an indication that the Republic was in danger. The newspaper *Lokal-Anzeiger* referred to the period April 2 to 4 as a new 1793. Even the more moderate *Berliner Tageblatt* considered the situation grave.[47]

Clemenceau bided his time. Simyan remained in office. A delegation

43. AN, F7 12538.
44. Georges Cahen, *Les Fonctionnaires* (Paris, 1911), 171.
45. *La Petite République,* 1909.
46. AN, F7 13725.
47. *Le Journal,* April 6, 1909.

of PTT employees, granted an interview with Barthou to talk about reform, was told to wait until the middle of May. A special request was sent to all prefects asking for information on all fonctionnaires active in fonctionnaire organizations in the provinces; the most militant were to be put under surveillance.[48] The strike leaders in Paris, LeGléo, Raoul Montbrand, Jean-Louis Chastenet, Barbut, Grangier, Simonnet, Fouquet, Pauron, and others, were also under surveillance. Finally, the tiger sprang.

Toward the end of April, reprisals against the strikers began. The leaders of the Association Générale and a group of militants from the provinces were brought before administrative committees and questioned about their strike activities. The first days of May brought suspensions for strikers who had spoken too radically at strike meetings or had urged their comrades to stop work. Charged with délits d'opinion, dozens of postiers were fired. On May 1, eight telegraphers were fired; on May 2, thirty-nine line workers; CGT members who had left work as they had done without incident in previous years to celebrate May Day were also dismissed from service. On May 3 and 4, six more agents and on the sixth, another group, including Pauron, the secretary-general of the Syndicat des Ouvriers, were all fired. On May 8, the most militant of the Association Générale leaders, those who had signed the statement "Thanks to our Citizens," Chastenet, LeGléo, Montbrand, and four others were dismissed from service by the Council of Discipline (Simonnet and Grangier of the sous-agents, were, of course, still under revocation from the affair of the open letter). The employee representatives on the council resigned in protest. L'Humanité headed the story "Clemenceau and Barthou traitors to their word."[49]

Each day brought news of more firings and more attacks on the fonctionnaire organizations. Simyan, interviewed on the subject of fonctionnaire syndicalism by L'Eclair, declared: "No! We will not yield. We will not accept the syndicat."[50] The postal workers and their allies were up in arms. Why had Clemenceau broken his promises? What had happened to their victory? A new strike seemed inevitable. Meetings were held all

48. AN, F7 12792.
49. L'Humanité, May 9, 1909.
50. L'Eclair, May 7, 1909.

over France; fonctionnaires in Lyons, Le Havre, Lille, and other cities pledged to strike. In Paris, mass meetings of agents and line workers calling for a strike were held on May 5, 6, and 7. The railroad and lighting workers pledged support.[51] The press talked of the coming strike; the only question was when.

Clemenceau continued his attack. The politicians of the Left criticized him in the Chamber and in the press. The SFIO issued a statement defending the rights of the postiers and other fonctionnaires as citizens. It pledged to do all it could in meetings and in the Chamber to see that justice was done to the PTT workers.[52] The Ligue des Droits de l'Homme held a solidarity meeting. Even the Radicals were shocked at the government's behavior. Charles Dumont had urged the Chamber to give the fonctionnaires what they asked for. Let them join even the CGT, he declared, they would probably be a moderating influence.[53] Now the executive committee of the Radical and Radical Socialist party, worried about the gravity of the situation, issued a statement disaffiliating itself from the actions of Clemenceau, "who had frustrated the hopes of the republican democracy and intensifies the misunderstandings between the different factions." The party declined "any solidarity with a cabinet whose governmental methods go against the tradition of the party."[54]

Everyone, including the press and the politicians, worried that the inevitable outcome of Clemenceau's policies would be another strike. But his actions indicated that another strike was just what Clemenceau wanted. In March, the government had been surprised by the militancy and organizational success of the postiers. Clemenceau and Barthou had been forced to concede to the strikers. Now Clemenceau would be in control. Plans were made to keep the postal services functioning, troops were readied, and replacements were waiting. Even pigeons were to be pressed into service.[55]

More meetings were held. On May 9, at the Manège Saint Paul, once again the government "without guts" was blamed for not keeping the

51. Frischmann, Histoire PTT, 159.
52. Bulletin de l'AG, May–June, 1909.
53. AN, F7 13725, April 25.
54. Bulletin de l'AG, May–June, 1909.
55. See "Les pigeons mobilisés," Le Matin, May 7, 1909.

promises made at the end of the previous strike. A pledge was made to cease all work until the fired men were reintegrated into the postal service.[56] Still the federated committee hesitated, realizing that they were being drawn into a strike on Clemenceau's terms and that this time, hundreds, perhaps thousands, might be fired.[57] But there was no choice. Without any moral compunction, Clemenceau had reneged completely on the strike agreement. Not only was Simyan still in office, he was gloating to the press that fonctionnaire syndicalism would be crushed. No moves toward reform had been made, and, most important, the PTT organizations were under severe attack. Each day more people were fired; the postal fonctionnaires were losing all their activists.

Finally, the decision was made. On May 11 the newly created Fédération Postale declared a strike. Crowds cheered. This time one of the strike demands was the droit syndical. The next day, the debate in the Chamber was bitter. Sembat defended the postiers; they had trusted Clemenceau. Paul Deschanel reproached the government for not voting a statute. Louis Louis-Dreyfus told Clemenceau and Barthou that they had been dishonest in their dealings with the postiers. Willm warned the Chamber that such arbitrary behavior was dangerous; it could be used on anyone, even themselves.[58] On the same day, an article by Paul-Boncour appeared in *La Lanterne*. The Radical deputy urged the government to acquiesce and give the fonctionnaire movement the droit syndical. The government would have to give in eventually, and it was "better to give it to them early than to yield too late."[59] But on the thirteenth, when the critical vote was taken, the resolutions in defense of fonctionnaire freedoms were forgotten. Most Radicals deserted the fonctionnaires. In an overwhelming vote (454 to 69), "The Chamber, determined to refuse the right to strike to all fonctionnaires, is firmly resolved to require of them the absolute respect of the law, of discipline and of their obligations to the Nation." A vote of confidence in the government passed 365 to 159.[60]

The strike began. Thousands stopped work, but thousands more

56. AP, BA 1437.
57. AP, BA 1392.
58. *Ibid.*
59. AN, F7 13725.
60. *Bulletin de l'AG*, May–June, 1909.

hesitated. The momentum had been lost. In March, the majority of PTT employees had joined the movement; all postal services were stopped or curtailed. This time the majority did not strike.[61] The army and the police kept many services open. The speeches were just as fiery—the strike would continue until victory—but this time the crowds numbered no more than three or four thousand, not ten thousand. Parliament offered the postiers no hope, and Clemenceau had them just where he wanted them. Immediately, the government began to fire the strikers. The first group numbered 228, many of them female telephone and telegraph operators. Within a few days, 303 more were dismissed from service. The government once again launched sabotage stories, and the newspapers picked up the cry: "Telephone Lines Cut." *Le Temps* gave more coverage to a fire in a letter box than it did to important foreign news for the day.[62] The meetings continued; the strike was supposedly growing bigger, and hesitants were joining.[63] But the atmosphere was becoming more acrimonious. Perhaps only two hundred sous-agents were out. Nonstrikers were cursed and kicked.

The only hope for the postiers lay in the blue-collar workers. But once again, the *cheminots* (railroad workers), the *gaziers* (gas workers), and the electricians had failed to fulfill their promises of solidarity. Yvetot told the postiers he could not order the Bourses du Travail into action; each corporation had to make its own decision. The Union des Syndicats de Paris issued a solidarity statement. They were ready to join a general strike when their leadership chose the day and moment.[64] Finally, the isolated postiers turned to the CGT.

On the seventeenth, the CGT called a meeting of its member federations to decide what to do about the postal strike. The situation was desperate. The time for solidarity statements was past; only a general strike would suffice. Opinion was divided; only the building and electrical federations were ready to strike immediately. The miners said they might be able to get a strike organized, the metallurgists were not ready, and

61. Once again, it is difficult to ascertain the strike figures. Frischmann says eight thousand were on strike in Paris. The Paris police estimated about three thousand. Probably the figure is somewhere in between.
62. *Le Temps,* May 14, 1909.
63. AP, BA 1392.
64. *Le Petit Parisien,* May 16, 17, 1909.

the railroad workers were not in attendance. Later, at a larger evening meeting, the cheminots voiced their hesitation; they did not think their members were ready for a general strike. But something had to be done. Niel was attacked for not being militant enough. Griffuelhes, aware of the weakness of the CGT organization and knowing that the call for a general strike was at best risky, nevertheless told the council: "It is nobler to risk a defeat than to remain inert." A vote for a strike in the Parisian area was approved, 86 to 18, with 6 abstentions.[65]

An executive strike committee was formed: it included Niel, the secretary-general of the CGT; G. Thil, the adjunct secretary; Raymond Pericat of the building federation; Pataud of the electricians; Pauron of the PTT ouvriers; Yvetot, secretary of the Bourses at the CGT; and Thuillier, secretary of the Union des Syndicats de Paris. Le Journal remarked that the majority were revolutionaries. The call went out, and posters were rushed all over Paris. They carried the rallying cry: "The victory of the postiers will be that of all the proletariat, just as their defeat will be. . . . The proletariat will not fail in its duty of solidarity."[66]

The striking postal workers felt renewed hope. The building workers ceased to work on the nineteenth. The naval recruits had also voted to strike, and the electricians were expected to follow—but when was not clear. Jaurès took the occasion of the strike declaration to write a sober front-page editorial in L'Humanité. The calling of the general strike in the name of worker unity was a solemn occasion, he said. No one knew if it would succeed. He hoped, in the name of the SFIO, that the working class would remain united. Jaurès's comments did not sound optimistic. On the twentieth, building workers and PTT strikers filled the Manège Saint Paul. It was like March again—ten thousand were in attendance.

More strikers were fired. The PTT launched another appeal to the blue-collar workers. Despite the efforts of the PTT militants and the CGT committee and despite the support of the building workers, the strike did not become general. The miners did not respond. Pataud,

---

65. AN, F7 13570. The CGT meetings were secret, yet a full report of the proceedings appears in the Archives of the Ministry of the Interior. This box contains a host of information on prewar CGT activity and some marvelous photographs, including Nègre, Subra, a mangy-looking "chien de Bourses du Travail," and Pataud and his pet rats.

66. Le Journal, La Petite République, and others, May 19, 1909.

a member of the central strike committee, did not bring in the electricians. Most important, the railroad and gas workers decided to remain out of the struggle. The general strike was aborted, and the PTT strike was at an end.

On the twenty-first, the PTT voted to return to work and the CGT concurred. The first attempt at fonctionnaire–blue-collar unity had been a failure. The supporters of the general strike were bitter toward Pataud, Guerard of the railroad workers, and other syndicat leaders who did not put into action what they said so gloriously in words, a fault not uncommon in the prewar CGT. But the seeds of cooperation had been planted—both CGT and PTT militants expressed the hope that such unity would be more successful in the future.[67] In July, Niel was replaced as secretary-general by Léon Jouhaux, under whose leadership the CGT was eventually to move away from its revolutionary syndicalist position.

For the PTT employees, the defeat was dreadful; more than eight hundred strikers had been fired. "We are vanquished. The government has its revenge. We have our 16th of May," declared the Bulletin de l'AG.[68] The organizations were in disarray. The Syndicat des Sous-Agents, declared illegal once again, its leaders fired, was in particular distress.[69] But gradually the pieces were picked up. A campaign was mounted to aid those who had been fired and to press for their reintegration. Plans for changing the Association Générale des Agents into a syndicat were necessarily shelved, but the unified Fédération Postale became a reality.[70]

Then in July, the government fell. The final blow to the Clemenceau cabinet came on the question of naval resources, but discontent in the Chamber had been growing for months. Postiers had no doubt that the events of March and May had contributed to Clemenceau's defeat. Briand came in as head of the new government, and Millerand was now given the Ministry of Public Works and PTT. The position of under secretary for the PTT was abolished, and Simyan was finally displaced

67. Descriptions and strike statements appeared in all the newspapers, May 22, 1909.

68. Bulletin de l'AG, May–June, 1909.

69. At the congress of the rival Association Générale des Sous-agents in November, 1909, the president told the delegates to be proud of having avoided the pitfalls of a strike and illegal syndicalism (Musée Social, Le Droit d'association, 132).

70. Immediately after the strike, a group of syndicalist agents, unwilling to wait for the congress of the association to make such a change, formed a syndicat. It was declared illegal.

from office, never again to serve in a cabinet position—a belated but sweet victory for the postiers. A policy of appeasement that historians associate with Briand began. The *tiercement* was abolished, and gradually the strikers were rehired, albeit very slowly. At the end of 1909, some 163 PTT employees still had not yet returned to their jobs: 70 agents, 62 sous-agents, and 31 ouvriers; 6 were women. The more militant of the strikers had to wait for months, some for years, to regain their positions. Raoul Montbrand, one of the last to be rehired because of his leadership position in the strike, was to die at Verdun. His obituary proudly read, "révoqué de 1909."[71]

To many contemporary observers familiar with strikes that occurred for specific economic reasons such as wages and hours, the postal strikes of 1909 were difficult to understand. To some, the strikes appeared to be mere personality disputes, first with Simyan, then with Clemenceau. Even Jean Jaurès, who was to defend the postiers vigorously in the Chamber and in *L'Humanité,* temporarily succumbed to this superficial interpretation.[72] By stressing the personality of Simyan and making his resignation the prime aim of the first strike, the postiers contributed to this misinterpretation. Fire the obnoxious Simyan first and then we will tell you what reform we want was essentially the message in most of the public statements made by the strike committee. Although reforms were indeed discussed at meetings, many rank-and-file postiers stressed the insults of Simyan, the arrest of their fellow workers, and the attack on their professional dignity as reasons for striking. The personalities of the two ministers certainly exacerbated the discontent in the PTT administration, but the true significance of the strike goes beyond the arrogance of Simyan or the vindictiveness of Clemenceau.

As the employer-state expanded its economic and public service role, adding hundreds of thousands of employees to its domain, the organization and administration of government enterprise became more and more similar to that of private industry. Indeed, given the monolithic nature of state enterprise, one might say that the state had organized its

---

71. *Bulletin de l'AG,* September, 1916.

72. AN, F7 13792. The police report for March 25 read: "The representatives, notably M. Jaurès, persist in denying the importance of the postal strike which was, he told Dubreuilh, only a movement of ill humor against personality and not a direct action against the public powers."

workers in large, concentrated, monopolistic enterprises long before most French private industry had reached that stage of development. The state's aim, of course, was not direct profit; it was to provide the services that would enable private industry to function. And its workers had the security private industrial workers lacked. Nevertheless, thousands of fonctionnaires felt that the organization and administration of their work was no different from that in private industry. This was particularly true in the PTT. The fonctionnaires responded to this development by organizing, by moving closer to the blue-collar organizational form, the syndicat. Now the postiers had used the main tactic of the working class, the strike. The postal strikes of 1909 were declarations to the government as employer-state that the state was a boss no different from other bosses and that the state workers were like other workers. In striking, the postiers were attacking the omnipotence of the employer-state.

The syndicalist fonctionnaires, Le Gléo, Quilici, Simonnet, and others, stressed this more fundamental aspect of the strike. In their speeches to mass meetings and their interviews with the press, they emphasized the conflict with the employer-state and the solidarity of the working class. Left-wing socialists also analyzed the strike in these terms. Charles Rappoport and Henri Ghesquière, writing in the Guesdist paper Le Socialisme, saw the strike as an indication of the bankruptcy of the notion of state socialism and the beginning of working-class unity: "We have greeted with joy the entrance of the petits fonctionnaires of the PTT in the workers' struggle, as a decisive step toward proletarian unity."[73] Ironically, it appears that Clemenceau understood what many left-wing Radicals and liberals did not. Reacting immediately to this attack on the government and to the growing unity of fonctionnaires with the blue-collar working class, he refused to yield any ground to the postiers and vigorously pursued the strikers, particularly the syndicalists. The employer-state could tolerate striking workers no more than private industry could, perhaps even less so, because public service was vital to all industry. Moreover, having declared war on the syndicats and on socialism, how could he allow the fonctionnaires, a growing segment of the work force, to unite with the blue-collar workers? Having

73. Le Socialisme, Charles Rappoport, April 10, 1909; H. Ghesquière, April 3, 1909.

refused the droit syndical for this reason, Clemenceau knew that the strike, though far from complete (even the first strike involved less than half the PTT employees in France), had been a big step toward working-class unity. In earlier years, the blue-collar workers had thought of fonctionnaires as separate from their lives and their movement. Many in the CGT had wanted to keep the moderate fonctionnaires out of their organization. As the fonctionnaires moved closer to syndicalism, the blue-collar workers moved closer to the fonctionnaires. The fonctionnaires' strike further convinced the blue-collar workers of their common destiny. Indeed, the syndicalists understood as never before how necessary it was to have the fonctionnaires as allies in the struggle for the social revolution. When state workers could stop the government from functioning, the general strike would be at hand. The CGT failed to mount a successful general strike not so much because of the division of blue-collar and state workers, an all too real division fostered by the nature of their employment and by the government itself, but because of the general weakness of the CGT. The call for a strike in 1909 was made on behalf of postiers, but there is little indication that a general strike would have been any more effective if it had been called on behalf of miners or textile workers. Indeed, the much vaunted general strike did not occur during the huge railroad strike of 1910, when Briand called out the army, nor did it occur in 1914 to stop the war, nor in 1920, the year of so many general strikes, when once again railroad workers called for that ultimate act of solidarity. But the very decision to try for a general strike in 1909 was important. Despite its failure, the concept of unity of action had taken root.

Another, less obvious aspect of the strike is reflected in further changes in political alignments. The moderate fonctionnaires had been important supporters of the république sociale and the Radical party. Disillusioned over the failure of the Radicals first to grant a statute, then the droit syndical, these fonctionnaires now had the further example of the Radicals' failure to come to the aid of the postiers during the strike. The second strike was particularly significant because the Radicals, perfectly aware of Clemenceau's perfidy, nevertheless supported his policies. Moderate fonctionnaires, eschewing strike action, were to turn in these last years before the Great War to electoral politics. Fonctionnaires ran and actively campaigned for their own candidates. But increasingly, the candidates they supported were not Radical but SFIO. The fall of the Clemenceau government in 1909 was certainly not the end of the Radical party, but it does represent a turning point in Radical history. The Radical party as the voice of the progressive and social republic had passed its peak. Having failed and thus lost the votes of the working class, the Radicals were now losing the support of the fonctionnaires. Without this mass base, the Radicals were to become, by the 1920s, the party of small town shopkeepers, farmers, and professionals.

It would be incorrect to overemphasize the significance of the postal strikes of 1909. They did not change the nature of the employer-state or bring about a social revolution. They did not forge permanent unity with the working class or even succeed in uniting all the postiers—the sous-agents had not supported the strike. But in the evolution of the fonctionnaires' consciousness and organization, the strikes mark a large step made by fonctionnaires toward unity of organization and action with the blue-collar working class.[74]

74. The 1909 strikes were studied in detail by Danielle Tartakowsky in her 1969 master's thesis at the University of Paris, "La Grève des postiers de 1909." I read her very fine thesis after completing my own research; our sources were similar.

5

The End of an Era, 1909–1914

Many historians of the French labor movement refer to the years 1909–1914 as a period of crisis for the CGT.[1] The intense organizational and strike activity of 1906, 1907, and 1908 rallied hundreds of thousands of workers to syndicalism and to the CGT. From a mere 100,000 members in 1902, the CGT grew, during the peak year 1907, to an impressive 600,000.[2] But this organizational strength was built on a very fragile foundation. For most of the period 1906–1910, the CGT could count on only about 350,000 paid members. By the eighteenth congress held at Le Havre in 1912, the membership had grown again to the 1907 figure of 600,000 and the number of syndicats had doubled, but it is evident that from 1907 to 1912, the CGT had managed only to maintain the support it had gathered in the 1906–1907 strike years.[3] By January, 1914, the growing CGT membership had advanced to over 800,000 but was only a small fraction of the nearly 8 million industrial workers in France.[4] Compared to the 4 million trade union members in Great Britain and the 4.3 million who belonged to the highly organized German unions, the CGT membership appears even less impressive.

It would be incorrect, however, to overemphasize membership figures as the only determinant of CGT strength. The influence of syn-

1. Edouard Dolléans says that the crisis ended in 1913 (*Histoire du mouvement ouvrier* [3 vols.; Paris, 1968], II). See also Henri Dubief, *Le Syndicalisme révolutionnaire* (Paris, 1969), and Peter Stearns, *Revolutionary Syndicalism and French Labor* (New Brunswick, 1971). Jean Bron prefers a milder analysis of the period as one of "tension" (*Histoire du mouvement ouvrier français* [2 vols.; Paris, 1968–70], I).

2. Dolléans, *Mouvement ouvrier*, II, 189. Bron gives 700,000 (*Histoire du mouvement*, I, 56).

3. Here again, Dolléans gives 600,000 and Bron gives the figure issued by the congress, 700,000.

4. Roger Picard, *Le Mouvement syndical durant la guerre* (Paris, 1927), 19.

dicalism and the CGT had always been more extensive than the dues-paying membership would indicate. Even during this crisis period, the organization of the workers of the new petroleum industry into a federation was completed, as was the important Fédération des Métaux under the leadership of Alphonse Merrheim. Both groups adhered to the CGT, which already had within its loose federation the critical industries of printing, electricity, textiles, railroads, and mining.[5] By 1912, the last of the independent Bourses du Travail had dissolved and the unity of the syndicalist movement under the aegis of the CGT was nearly complete.[6] The crisis period also continued to be one of great activity—the campaigns for the eight-hour day, for the *semaine anglaise* (the English week—half-day Saturday and Sunday off), and against the government retirement plan, derisively called *les retraites des morts* (pensions for the dead) were waged with the CGT's usual intensity.[7] And by 1910, syndicalists, aware of the threat of war with Germany, began to organize opposition to the coming capitalist conflict. In early 1911, Merrheim wrote several articles on the crisis of overproduction and the threat of war in *La Vie Ouvrière*. Antiwar meetings and speeches soon became a part of CGT activity. The three-year law was opposed, the *sou de soldat,* the sending of a stipend to workers in the army, was organized, and, in the summer of 1911, at the time of Agadir, workers in both Berlin and Paris held huge peace meetings. The vitality of the CGT was also evident in the publication of *La Vie Ouvrière,* begun as a periodical in 1909, and *La Bataille Syndicaliste,* the widely read newspaper that began publication in 1911. Strike activity, though somewhat diminished in intensity, continued to rally a large number of workers. The railroad strike of 1910, the Parisian taxi drivers' strike of 1911, and the dockers' strike of 1912 were no less militant than the strikes of 1906–1908.

This activity, however, could not cover up the basic weaknesses of the syndicalist movement and the CGT. The years dominated by the con-

5. The miners joined the CGT in 1908.
6. There were several independent syndicats and a federation of "jaunes" (company unions), but the vast majority of organized workers were in the CGT.
7. In 1910, after a delay of many years, the government finally put forth a retirement plan for all workers (the railroad workers had been granted pensions the year before), which called for a pension of eighteen sous a day at age sixty-five. Since only 15 percent of the population reached that advanced age and certainly very few of those were miners, railroad workers, or metal workers, the *retraite pours les morts* seems an accurate description.

cept of class struggle had brought some economic gains and a significant growth in working-class consciousness but had brought neither the grève générale nor the social revolution the general strike was supposed to initiate. Years of government oppression, arrests, shootings, firings, and conscription had caused many militants to become discouraged. The use of *agents provocateurs* further disillusioned the faithful.[8] Briand, the former revolutionary syndicalist, was particularly skillful at luring the more reformist syndicalist leaders into agreements with industry and government; some even entered government service, following the path of so many socialists. Merrheim wrote in 1910 that the CGT was not having *une crise domestique* (a domestic crisis) but *une crise de domestication* (a crisis of domestication).[9] The crisis of domestication indicated that there was an internal crisis; ideological and tactical differences within the CGT could no longer be papered over. The CGT had begun as a loose amalgam of federations which included anarchists, reformists, revolutionary syndicalists, and a handful of Marxists. Except for the powerful and radical building federation, most larger federations tended to be more moderate than the smaller ones. Since the federal organization emphasized equality in voting, the revolutionary syndicalists, whose strength often lay with these smaller groups, had more power than their actual numbers would indicate. The principles agreed to at Amiens in 1906 managed to hold together these disparate tendencies throughout most of the eventful strike years before 1914. But the capitalist system was evolving; industrial enterprise was becoming more concentrated and complex; production processes used more advanced technology. Strong employers' federations were being organized, and resistance to the organization of workers and strike activity was becoming more sophisticated and effective. Increased use of lockouts and firings, the establishment of paternalistic company unions (*syndicats jaunes*), and effective use of collective bargaining, previously avoided by factory owners zealous in defense of their individual authority, all contributed to the grow-

8. It was revealed, for example, that Métivier, the syndicalist who had been the prime enthusiast for the ill-fated Villeneuve–St. Georges demonstrations, was in the pay of Clemenceau.

9. Merrheim's articles on the crisis appeared in *La Vie Ouvrière* and *Le Mouvement Socialiste* in November and December 1909, and are discussed in Dolléans, *Mouvement ouvrier*, II, 166.

ing failure of syndicalist organization and tactics.[10] The spontaneous, individualistic tactics of direct action championed by the revolutionary syndicalists were more suited to the isolated smaller shops of the nineteenth century than to the new industrial enterprises. Tighter organization, more planning, and more unity of action were needed. The CGT had yet to come to grips with these new developments. In these years just preceding the Great War, differences in ideology and tactics once again surfaced. This time the revolutionary syndicalists found themselves losing ground to the reformists, who preferred "everyday practicality" to the spontaneity of the general strike. These reformists also rejected the extreme antimilitarism of the revolutionary syndicalists, whose intense feelings about the French military had been influenced by the role the army had often played in the suppression of strikes. By 1913, revolutionary syndicalists such as Merrheim of the metallurgists and Péricat of the building federation were having trouble maintaining the leadership of their syndicats, and anarchists such as Jouhaux were becoming more moderate.[11] The isolation from the SFIO was also beginning to be bridged. Despite its antiparty rhetoric, the CGT had always accepted the intervention of socialists such as Jaurès, Vaillant, and Sembat on behalf of the CGT in the Chamber of Deputies. At the Le Havre congress of 1912, the 1906 debate on party connections was once again opened. The proposal for contacts with the SFIO was not passed, but it was clear that the political "purity" of the CGT was no longer as strong as it had been. Although the war accelerated the developments that eliminated revolutionary syndicalism from the working-class movement and brought into leadership the reformist element of the CGT whose antagonism toward the new left-wing Marxist faction would culminate in the split of 1921, it was in this period of crisis, 1909–1914, that the "myth of the general strike" had already begun to die.

10. The growth of employers' resistance is discussed by Peter Stearns, "Against the Strike Threat: Employer Policy Toward Labor Agitation in France, 1900–1914," *Journal of Modern History*, XL (December, 1968), 474–500, and in *Revolutionary Syndicalism and French Labor*. Although I do not concur with Stearns's general thesis, his analysis of this aspect of the failure of revolutionary syndicalism is most useful.

11. Revolutionaries also began moving to the extreme Right. In 1913, Janvion (open letter) and Pataud (electricians) were expelled from the CGT. Their well-developed anti-Semitism led them to close relationships with the Action Française.

For the organized fonctionnaires, the period 1909–1914 was a time of consolidation and growth. The postal workers, of course, had to expend an enormous effort on the campaign for support and reintegration of their fired comrades, but after the brief hiatus following the strike, all fonctionnaires, including the postal workers, were ready to push harder for their demands. The strike had in no way diminished the strength of fonctionnaire organizations; even the Association Générale des Agents was able to maintain its membership. Indeed, the strike had been a stimulus for membership growth in many associations. In April, 1909, the Union Générale des Contributions Indirectes could announce that out of about ten thousand eligible fonctionnaires in this branch of the Ministry of Finance, ninety-five hundred were members of the organization.[12]

As the established associations grew and consolidated, more and more fonctionnaires from every ministry and from all levels of the administration—museum guards, workers at the national printing offices, nurses, municipal pawnship workers, sous-officiers at the prefectural offices—joined the flood of state employees forming organizations and issuing demands. Fonctionnaires who worked at the seats of government authority were not exempt from the movement; even the employees in the administration of the Conseil d'Etat formed an amicale in 1912.[13] At the second congress of the Association Professionnelle du Personnel Civil des Administrations Centrales in 1913, favoritism at the ministerial offices was still considered a major problem. For these fonctionnaires, advancement à choix, so dear to the hearts of the postal workers, meant nepotism, favoritism, and the politicization of the central administration.

The police had begun to organize earlier; by 1909, their membership was growing rapidly. The reactionary newspaper La Libre Parole worried that there might even be a syndicat of police in the city of Paris.[14] Indeed, by the end of 1909, stimulated perhaps by the postal strikes of that year, Paris police, desiring more than a benevolent society, were again organizing and were to bring a new militancy not only to the Pari-

12. AN, F7 13727.
13. AN, F7 13720.
14. La Libre Parole, December 13, 1909.

sian amicale but to the national organization as well. Forced to meet in secret, the Paris police, under the leadership of Paul Rigail, created an underground network that discussed demands and created an organization. In December, with a membership of 450, a delegation was ready to bring these demands to Prefect of Police Lépine, whom they respectfully addressed as the "father of us all."[15] Lépine agreed to go to the Municipal Council to ask for more money for salaries and for a more reasonable shift system.[16] But, he added, he would never permit a professional association.[17] The newspapers had a field day. Were the police involved in secret meetings and secret groups?[18] The influential Le Temps warned in an editorial entitled "Anarchy in the Police" that if police, who already had a respectable amicale, organized into an association or, worse yet, a syndicat, they would become contaminated with the air of syndicalism. Sooner or later, they would "tie themselves, first by friendly relations, then by feelings of solidarity, to groups who were more or less revolutionary."[19] Clearly, the great fear was that the police, despite their assurances to the contrary, would join hands with blue-collar workers organized in the revolutionary syndicalist CGT. But despite this disapproval, the Paris police continued to agitate and by 1912 had created the Association Professionnel de la Préfecture de Police.

In the meantime, the national federation grew. A newspaper, Le Gardien de la Paix, was begun. The congress of 1910, held in Paris but without Parisian delegates, had representatives from seventy-five cities. While calling for wage equity and the nationalization of all police, the leadership continued to assure the government of its loyalty: "We will never betray you: we are republicans, we will remain republican."[20] The Paris police joined in 1911; Rigail, the head of the new Paris association, was elected a vice-president, and one year later the national congress voted to affiliate with the major organization of civil service workers, the Fédération des Fonctionnaires. By 1914, with a membership of over

15. Le Syndicalisme Policier, pamphlet of the Syndicat Général de Police (December, 1977), 2.
16. Six hours of duty, followed by twelve hours of rest, then six hours of duty; it was called the three sixes.
17. L'Action, December 6, 1909.
18. Le Journal, December 7, 1909.
19. Le Temps, December 29, 1909.
20. AN, F7 13043.

thirteen thousand, the police federation had become, save in name only, a union.

The 1912 congress of the Fédération des Fonctionnaires was opened by Delhomme of the Fédération des Amicales de la Police, who declared his support for the extension of the 1884 law.[21] In 1911, Georges Cahen was able to ask how, with the police involved, anyone could continue to view the fonctionnaire movement as superficial or a passing phenomenon.[22] Even the judges organized a syndicat. The old chairman of the Comité d'Etudes, Demartial, not without some tongue-in-cheek, expressed his amazement: "So now, there will be a syndicat of judges. We already have syndicats of professors from the college of letters and law, a syndicat of diplomats and of state council members. I truly hope that by the second decade of the twentieth century we will have a syndicat of military officers. We will have quite a crowd."[23]

The consolidation of many of the fonctionnaire associations and syndicats into large federations was another important development of this period. Permission to form federations was one of the demands inherent in the droit syndical. In early 1910, the Fédération Nationale des PTT was officially constituted, and the Fédération des Fonctionnaires, founded in 1909 after the stormy meeting of the Comité d'Etudes on April 2, was able to hold its first congress in early 1910. Taking a position of support for the 1884 law without the right to strike, a position that had, a decade before, been considered radical but was now moderate, the federation drew together, through its member associations, about two hundred thousand fonctionnaires, including the teacher amicales, the Association Générale des Sous-Agents, the Contributions Indirectes, Douanes, and a host of smaller groups. Charles Laurent of the Caisse des Dépôts et Consignations was to dominate the leadership until the end of the Third Republic. In 1913, the Fédération des Fonctionnaires began publication of *La Tribune des Fonctionnaires,* the longest continuous fonctionnaire newspaper. In these last years before the war, the federation, though eschewing connections with syndicalist campaigns, began to take a more vigorous stand for fonctionnaires' rights and salary increases. It was to grow in influence among the enormous

21. AN, F7 13727.
22. Georges Cahen, *Les Fonctionnaires: Leur action corporative* (Paris, 1911), 194.
23. *Le Matin,* October 27, 1909.

number of moderate state employees, emerging from the war as a formidable organization, the most powerful voice of the fonctionnaires.

By 1914, the majority of blue-collar workers remained unorganized, but in contrast almost all fonctionnaires were members of associations, amicales, or syndicats. This amazing organizational strength of state workers as compared to blue-collar workers was not because of lack of blue-collar militancy—syndicat membership had never been the sole determinant of militancy—nor was it a result of the nature of the social relationships of fonctionnaires, who came in daily contact with the public; the fonctionnaires were more easily organized into professional groups because of the nature of state service and the relationships of employer to employees inherent in state employment. In these years before the war, although French industry was becoming more concentrated, the bulk of blue-collar workers, largely unorganized, still worked in small shops more akin to artisanal ateliers than to giant industrial plants. These smaller establishments, isolated one from the other, where employees often had personal relationships with the employer, were much more difficult to organize than larger establishments where hundreds of workers were in daily contact with each other and the strength of numbers enabled workers to weather harassment or threats of firing for syndicalist activity. Even in the larger plants, the predominant mode of private industrial relations, in nonfamily firms as well as family establishments, was paternalistic. These relationships would have to be destroyed before syndicat organization could fully penetrate the industrial working class. Fonctionnaires, on the other hand, no matter how separated they might have been geographically, had as an employer the centralized state, the employer-state. Teachers, postmen, and tax assessors all were employees of the state, which determined the conditions of employment—salaries, advancement, work load. In addition, most state employees entered service as youths, and no matter where they might be transferred, they remained in the same service, serving the same state. This continuity and unity of employment helped fonctionnaires develop an identity, a consciousness of themselves as fonctionnaires. Moreover, France had a tradition of professional organization, with shopkeepers, lawyers, and producers coming together in organizations, frequently called syndicats. The fonctionnaires, though influenced by blue-collar activity, found a legitimacy in professional organizations which did not touch the blue-collar workers. Blue-collar organization in France was considered illegitimate. Even after syndicats were made legal, employers and the state made organization and activity difficult. Because of the nature of industrial development and because of the repression they often faced, French blue-collar workers, except perhaps for the printers in the Fédération du Livre, did not develop the organizational tradition which English workers, for example, had inherited from their artisans.[24] French blue-collar workers in the prewar period were more likely to express their dissatisfaction by work stoppages, demonstrations, and other forms of direct action than by joining a syndicat. Fonctionnaires, eschewing direct action, formed organizations to express their dissatisfactions and their demands for improved working conditions. In the period 1909-1914, with large numbers of fonctionnaires facing rapidly changing political and economic conditions, these organizations were increasingly active in making these demands known to the public and to the government.

Of critical importance to organized fonctionnaires in this period was the continuing campaign against the statute and for the droit syndical. The agitation against a statute, which had gained momentum during the postal strikes, continued unabated throughout the summer and fall of 1909 as fonctionnaires of all categories held meetings, heard speeches, and wrote articles voicing their demand for the 1884 law. The more militant fonctionnaires in the Association Générale des Agents or in the syndicats viewed the statute as an attempt by the government to create a chasm between blue-collar workers and fonctionnaires, "to create, for the benefit of the ruling class, two categories of wage earners," but even those syndicalists who desired affiliation with the CGT stressed other arguments in favor of the 1884 law which were also put forth by the moderates in the Fédération des Fonctionnaires.[25] The fonctionnaires had legitimate demands for improved working conditions and against favoritism and authoritarian bureaucracy. Only the 1884 law gave fonctionnaires the ability to negotiate with the state for their professional interests. If the fonctionnaires received the droit syndical, if their demands

24. See, for example, E. P. Thompson, *The Making of the English Working Class* (London, 1967).
25. *Bulletin de l'AG,* August, 1909.

were granted, all state services would be run more efficiently; service to the nation would be improved.[26]

As might be expected, throughout the years before the war, the more radical fonctionnaires in the syndicats, the Fédération Postale, and the Comité Central intensified their activity on behalf of the droit syndical. But of particular significance was the increasing agitation against the statute on the part of the more moderate fonctionnaires in the Fédération des Fonctionnaires. As more and more fonctionnaires abandoned support of the statute and as the Fédération des Fonctionnaires grew in strength, so did the intensity of the demand for the droit syndical. The first congress of the federation had been concerned with establishing an organization, but by the second congress, held at the end of 1911, there was already an indication of the development of a more militant position on the part of federation members. The congress voted unanimously to instruct the federal committee, under the leadership of the secretary-general, Charles Laurent, "to allow an energetic policy of combat and resistance" against a statute and for the extension of the 1884 law.[27] In early spring 1912, news of yet another proposal for a statute brought an even stronger response. The federation stated that since the individual statute did not offer the guarantees claimed by the 1911 congress and since the collective statute did not allow fonctionnaires to federate, the Fédération des Fonctionnaires "rejects the text put forth by the Commission and asks the 300,000 fonctionnaires of the federation to launch a strong and lively protest with their deputies in all the departments of France."[28] Then, once again, government action against the teachers pushed the fonctionnaires even further along the path to more militant support of the droit syndical.

Syndicalism had continued to penetrate the ranks of the instituteurs. Even as they adhered to the CGT—"teachers are men who work for a living like all those who have nothing"—the Syndicat National encouraged its sympathizers to remain in the amicales where they could best influence the majority of teachers toward syndicalist activity and ideology.[29] Although the majority of teachers remained in the amicales, the

26. AN, F7 13525 and F7 13802, see reports of meetings of 1909–1910.
27. *La Bataille Syndicaliste,* November 6, 1911.
28. *L'Humanité* and *La Bataille Syndicaliste,* March 3, 1912.
29. Fédération Nationale des Syndicats des Instituteurs et Institutrices, *Instituteurs, Syndiquez-vous* (1910).

syndicats continued to grow. In August, 1912, the syndicalist teachers, with representatives from forty-four groups containing six thousand members, held the largest congress of their history in the town of Chambéry. Many important votes on pedagogic matters were taken, including one for coeducation, but the government was much more interested in the pro-CGT statements issued by the delegates: "The teachers are watching with particular attention the daily struggle waged by the working class to better its living conditions and to defend its dignity. Sharing its agonies and its hopes, they are proud to be active in their ranks and to declare themselves once again solidarized with all unified wage earners under the flag of the CGT."[30] If the government cast a wary eye on the teachers singing the "International" in the streets of Chambéry, the newspapers paid most attention to a vote on the *sou du soldat*. Following the policy established by the CGT of sending financial aid to workers doing their military service, the teachers voted, "in order to maintain relations between the soldiers who are syndicat members and their organization, each syndicat shall institute a syndicalist benefit called *sou du soldat* aimed at bringing moral and monetary aid to these men." Immediately the syndicalist teachers were denounced as antipatriotic and antimilitarist. The Balkan crisis was threatening to erupt into open conflict, and the teachers' support of the *sou du soldat* was put to use in a general press campaign against the CGT; this "organ of revolution" would render the army useless in the coming war. *Le Temps* was particularly vigorous in its demands for the dissolution of the illegal syndicats and the dismissal of their leaders, but other newspapers such as *Le Journal des Débats* echoed the same demands. The Catholic newspaper *La Croix* used this opportunity to attack the secular school system under the control of "anarchists and antipatriots." Even the amicales were not exempt from criticism.[31] At the end of August, the government responded to the "scandale de Chambéry."

The minister of public education, Gabriel Guist'hau, issued a circular to all prefects: "The government cannot accept that teachers who are entrusted with national education publicly profess views which will alienate from the school all those who care about the morality of childhood,

30. AN F7, 13724.
31. Max Ferré, *Histoire du mouvement syndicaliste révolutionnaire chez les instituteurs* (Paris, 1955), 162, 168.

human dignity and national security." The syndicats had been tolerated while the vote on the statute was awaited; now, because of the incidents at Chambéry, these illegal syndicats were to be dissolved within two weeks. The teachers responded with a "manifesto" attesting to their "patriotism": "If to be a patriot means to desire a France even more prosperous, but also more humane and more just, well then, we are determined patriots!" But the syndicalists also defended their pacifism, protesting "against the chauvinistic provocations and the maneuvers of politicians and financiers who risk provoking a general conflagration at any time."[32] Many of the eight hundred teachers who signed the manifesto were to carry these ideas into war; the antiwar movement of the 1914–1918 period had considerable teacher participation.

The syndicats refused to disband. André Maginot, the prime creator of the new statute, chastised the syndicalist teachers for rejecting the authority of the state: "Too many fonctionnaires are totally committed to pure syndicalist theories; their organization seems less a way of defending their legitimate professional interests than a breeding ground for battle against the state which employs them." Four departmental syndicats were brought before the tribunal and officially declared illegal; their leaders were threatened with legal proceedings for disobeying the government's instructions.[33] In December, when the case was debated in the Chamber, most deputies recognized that it was incorrect and injudicious to label all teachers antipatriotic. They cautioned the militant minority, however, not to ally itself with the CGT; such connections would be construed as acceptance of CGT antipatriotism.[34] Eventually, on the accession in 1913 of Raymond Poincaré to the presidency of the Republic, an amnesty ended this particular affair, but the government's attack on the teachers' syndicats had already had its effect on fonctionnaires. Fonctionnaires, radical and moderate alike, were greatly shaken by the fragility of their ability to maintain their oganizations. Without the droit syndical, the government could, as it did with the teachers, dis-

32. This was the first Poincaré cabinet, which remained in office from January, 1912, to January, 1913. The teachers' statements are quoted in Ferré, *Instituteurs,* 169–70.

33. *Le Journal,* August 28, 1912. The Maginot statute also failed to extend the 1884 law to fonctionnaires. The syndicats were those in the departments of Seine, Bouches-du-Rhône, Rhône, and Maine-et-Loire. The lawyer for the teachers was Pierre Laval.

34. Debates of December 8–13, 1913, cited in Ferré, *Instituteurs,* 171.

solve any syndicat, or indeed any federation, because they were also technically illegal.

Although public attention was focused largely on the *sou du soldat,* Chambéry was important for yet another reason; it marked the further development of the feminist movement among women teachers. The original Groupes Féministes evolved into the Fédération Féministe Universitaire (FFU), and at Chambéry they held a separate meeting. Although most male teachers were less hostile than blue-collar workers to the feminist movement, there were still sharp ideological and emotional differences between the sexes. For many men and some women in the syndicalist movement who were committed to class struggle and the social revolution to bring about the end of capitalism, the existence of a separate feminist group with connections to the bourgeois suffrage movement was anathema. They feared bourgeois feminism as antimale, anti-working-class, and antirevolution.[35] If women wanted to be active, they should join the syndicat. It fell to Marie Guillot, Cécile Panis, Marie Guérin, and others in the FFU to raise the special concerns of women and women teachers and to stress the connections between civil and political rights for women and the syndicalist movement.

In October, 1910, the teachers' syndicat had issued the first of its weekly periodicals, *L'Ecole Emancipée* (the emancipated school). Though filled with lesson plans and teaching information, its mission went far beyond pedagogy. *L'Ecole Emancipée,* with a revolutionary syndicalist orientation, brought to its readers issues of concern to the union and to the working class in general, as well as discussions of wider political significance. From its inception, the editors encouraged women to air their views. A weekly column, "La Tribune Féministe," written by Marie Guillot, but often printing the views of other feminists, discussed votes for women, the problems of housework, economic independence for women (not until 1907 could married women legally keep their wages), reproductive freedom, and, of course, issues of concern to women teachers—coeducation, equal pay, and open employment in all schools. Often debates on women's issues spilled over from the column into the general political pages. With the founding of *La Bataille Syndicaliste,*

35. The attitude of male workers toward female workers is described in Marie-Hélène Sylberberg-Hocquard, *Féminisme et syndicalisme en France* (Paris, 1978) esp. chap. 3.

these issues were raised in the columns of the CGT paper as well. Marie Guillot used her column in *L'Ecole Emancipée* and in *La Bataille Syndicaliste* to answer the criticism of bourgeois feminism by emphasizing that it was through political activity that women came to syndicalism and that millions of women had to be brought into the political mainstream before they could be active in a changing society. "You are paying now," she charged, "for the political ignorance of women."[36]

Underlying this discussion was the question of whether activist working women should put their energies in the syndicalist movement or in the feminist movement. For most of these feminist teachers, there was no choice. As Cécile Panis explained, the struggle for workers' rights and women's rights were inseparable. Marie Guillot further explained why women's rights had to be a special part of the working-class struggle: "We have as women a double battle to wage, the common struggle of all the proletariat against economic servitude and the special struggle for the conquest of our rights as human beings. As long as women are treated differently in society, they must have separate organizations," she wrote. "We must be feminists *and* revolutionaries."[37]

While these debates were taking place, fonctionnaires, galvanized by the attack on the teachers, continued their quest for their rights. Throughout the autumn of 1912, fonctionnaire meetings issued resolutions of solidarity for the teachers, opposition to the Maginot statute, and support for the droit syndical. The members of the militant postal organizations were most active in the campaign, but meetings of finance workers (Contributions Indirectes, Douanes) and amicalist teachers were also issuing strong statements of similar content.[38] At the end of October, the Association Générale des Agents called a meeting of organizations representing five hundred thousand fonctionnaires.[39] CGT speakers or members attended most of these meetings. The CGT had already issued a statement of support for the teachers at the Le Havre congress; now it continued to press the issue of worker-fonctionnaire solidarity. A report to the Ministry of the Interior by one of its agents warned that the campaign against the teachers was allowing the CGT to

36. *L'Ecole Emancipée*, September 2, 9, 1911.
37. *Ibid.*, various issues 1910–1913, esp. July 12, 1912.
38. See newspapers from August to December, 1912.
39. *La Petite République*, October 31, 1912.

make headway among the fonctionnaires.[40] In late September, the SFIO issued an official protest against the persecution of the "secular teachers": "In order to defend the freedom of organization and the droit syndical of fonctionnaires, we must call on all the energy of socialist democracy and of the proletariat." *Le Journal* reported that all fonctionnaires, including one hundred thousand teachers, had vowed to fight against the statute.[41] Since most of the teachers were in amicales belonging to the Fédération des Fonctionnaires, where they constituted the largest bloc, their strong rejection of the statute is most significant.

At the end of December, the Fédération des Fonctionnaires, now grown to thirty-one associations representing over three hundred thousand members, held its annual congress.[42] The opening speaker, Emile Glay of the instituteurs, immediately set the tone of the meeting by observing that the question of the rights of fonctionnaires took on even greater importance in the wake of the government's suppression of teacher syndicats. To defend their rights, state employees must be unified as never before. Charles Laurent also stressed unity of action. One of the major difficulties with the Maginot statute now under consideration was that it did not allow federations. The debate on the statute was vigorous. Almost all agreed that the collective statute would only continue the authoritarian regime the fonctionnaires were trying to reform. But most delegates did not support the *syndicalisme intégral* proposed by the representative of the *professeurs adjoint* (adjunct professors) and sustained by Laurent. A compromise, introduced by Glay, was reached providing that an individual statute might be acceptable if fonctionnaires were allowed to collaborate fully in its determination. There was actually little hope for such collaboration, but apparently the teachers, the douaniers, and the delegates of the Contributions Indirectes were hesitant to abandon the possibility. But the main vote was for a total rejection of any collective statute and for a vigorous campaign for the droit syndical.[43]

40. AN, F7 13725.

41. *L'Humanité*, September 29, 1912; *Le Journal*, October 23, 1912.

42. The most important addition of the year had been the Fédération des Amicales de la Police, but the Association Générale des Sous-Agents, losing influence to the more radical syndicat, had dropped its affiliation.

43. Most newspapers reported on the congress. See, for example, *La Bataille Syndicaliste*, December 23, 1912.

The growing strength of the Fédération des Fonctionnaires and its increasing support of the droit syndical were welcomed by blue-collar militants. Jouhaux, carefully indicating his hesitation to interfere in the affairs of the federation, nevertheless wrote in an article for the widely read CGT paper La Bataille Syndicaliste that the evolution of fonctionnaire organization and activity was an integral part of what was happening within the working class. He foresaw the realization not only of immediate goals but of a regime in which "the arbitrary behavior of the state will be prevented by the common will of workers and fonctionnaires, united and joined together within the CGT."[44] This recognition of the fonctionnaires' strength and militancy was echoed by the old leader of the Bourses du Travail, Emile Pouget. Slowly but surely, he wrote, syndicalism was infiltrating everywhere, even among the professions that would have been thought immune to new ideas. After the syndicalism of blue-collar state workers, there was now developing the syndicalism of fonctionnaires, of those intellectuals whom shortsighted ouvrièrists had formerly treated as anathema.[45] Moreover, not only was there the syndicalism of the demi-intellectuals such as teachers, there were now syndicats of professors and of fonctionnaires of the central administration.[46]

Indeed, the extremely moderate Union des Personnels Civils des Administrations Centrales had, at its 1912 congress, expressed its strong dissatisfaction with the Maginot statute. In no way did these middling and upper cadres of the twelve ministries envisage themselves as the "proletariat of administration"; they had certainly not affiliated with the Fédération des Fonctionnaires, the organization of lower-level fonctionnaires. Viewing themselves as part of the government, primarily interested in curbing favoritism and achieving better advancement procedures and more "democratic" participation in decision making, they did not press for the 1884 law and they totally rejected the right to strike.

44. La Bataille Syndicaliste, December 29, 1912.
45. Ouvrièrists were followers of an earlier ideology, workers who believed that only the worker, the ouvrier, was capable of making the social revolution. No alliance with middle-class intellectuals would thus be possible. Jean Allemane had been one of the original leaders of the Ouvrierist party, but he had sat for years as a deputy of the SFIO, and by 1912 the ouvrièrist position had few adherents.
46. La Guerre Sociale, December 23, 1913.

Many thought that even lower-level fonctionnaires should be denied that right. The statute under consideration, however, did not correct the abuses that prevented the state administration from being a true instrument of the democratic Republic. The rejection of the statute by these upper-level, conservative fonctionnaires was discussed widely in the press.[47]

Even as the Fédération des Fonctionnaires moved closer to the syndicalist position, there was not complete unity among fonctionnaires. A steadily shrinking minority still hoped for a statute. A far larger minority was more radical than the federation and had formed syndicats adhering to the CGT. The Association Générale des Agents, though still not a syndicat—it was to vote this transformation at the 1914 congress—had close ties to the blue-collar movement and refused to bring its twenty-two thousand members into the federation. In 1912, a *comité de liaison* between the Fédération Postale and the Fédération des Fonctionnaires was established, and several unity meetings were held in 1913 with representatives of numerous administrations. But the Fédération Postale and the more militant members of the Contributions Indirectes were planning independent actions to push for salary increases and the droit syndical; the rift between the more radical fonctionnaires and the federation remained. In 1914, another appeal was made to the postiers to join the Fédération des Fonctionnaires. The secretary-general of the agents refused; the Association Générale would not adhere to a federation that opposed the major organizational arm of the working class, the CGT. Laurent replied that the federation was not antagonistic to the CGT; any association belonging to the Fédération des Fonctionnaires could, if it desired, belong to the CGT as well. The main aim was unity of action—all fonctionnaires in one federation. The unity of organization that Laurent desired was to come to pass after the war in a brief interlude before the CGT itself bitterly split apart.

By 1914, even though the unity of the fonctionnaires was not complete, the movement toward syndicalism, begun hardly more than a decade before, had made enormous advances. In the spring of that last year of a dying era, the newly founded *Tribune des Fonctionnaires* would write:

47. Reports of the congress are in AN, F7 13727, as well as many newspapers of March 5 and 6, 1912.

Little by little, we have become used to the word *syndicat,* which at the beginning alarmed so many devoted activists, and the question of the droit syndical has ceased to be the apple of discord which only recently caused divisions in the fonctionnaire associations. Thus, time has done its job and progress has been made. How far we have traveled since that period, still so near, when the old Comité d'Etudes carefully avoided raising the question of syndicalism.[48]

The failure of the government to grant the droit syndical was viewed by the fonctionnaires as a curtailment not only of their organizational activity but of their rights as citizens as well. Miners, farmers, doctors— all had the right to organize freely; only fonctionnaires were denied that right, placed in the position of second-class citizens, *citoyens diminués:*

> Why should those who work for the state voluntarily accept a decrease in their rights as citizens? Why would they agree to be placed outside the bounds of common law? Why would they allow themselves to be thus separated and imprisoned? I know of no concept more monstrous than the one which separates the fonctionnaires from the rest of the nation, which makes them a separate caste, which places them outside the law—which governs all other citizens.[49]

The fonctionnaires wanted their rights as citizens, *le droit commun,* their right to organize, the droit syndical, and they wanted as well the right to speak out publicly on all political and professional matters; they wanted the *droit d'opinion,* freedom of speech.

As the fonctionnaires became more active in organizing and articulating their demands, the question of the droit d'opinion took on added importance. For years, fonctionnaires in all areas, but especially teachers, were expected to conform to the political and moral standards established by the communal or state government leaders. Deviation from this norm brought reprimand, transfer, or even dismissal from service. Examples of *la guillotine sèche* (the "dry" guillotine), some bordering on the absurd, abound. A teacher who visited the curé in an anticlerical town, a douanier who helped put up a poster against the three-year law, and a teacher whose private love letters were illegally confiscated by the police—all were fired. Postiers who had applauded a speaker at a meet-

---

48. *La Tribune des Fonctionnaires,* April, 1914.
49. Maurice Allard in *L'Humanité,* February 1, 1912.

ing were called before their superior the next morning to describe the opinions they had applauded.[50] But to the fonctionnaires, the fear of dismissal or transfer for délits d'opinion was not absurd; it was a threat to their organizational and professional activity. The charge délits d'opinion had been used frequently against the militants of the associations and the syndicats; the ambulants whose arrests had triggered the postal strike of March, 1909 and the signers of the open letter of 1907 had been charged with délits d'opinion. In 1911 and 1912, two more causes célèbres involving syndicat members made fonctionnaires of all persuasions press even harder for the freedom of speech that was their right as citizens of the Third Republic.

The first case involved a Corsican teacher named Paoli, who had sent a letter to his inspector that was considered insolent. Charged with délits d'opinion and insubordination, the luckless instituteur was threatened with transfer. Immediately, Louis Léger, the secretary of the "illegal" Fédération des Syndicats des Instituteurs et Institutrices (this was before the Chambéry congress), sent a letter of protest to the vice-rector of Corsica. The letter was published and Léger was censured by the Council of Primary Education in his home department of the Rhône. Censure and transfer was hardly a severe punishment; but to the fonctionnaires, it was an attack on their rights as citizens to protest against an illegality. More significantly, it was an attack on the right of a professional organization to defend its members. Even though the federation of teacher syndicats belonged to the CGT, not to the Fédération des Fonctionnaires, the latter leaped to the defense of the syndicat secretary, whose protest on behalf of the illegally threatened teacher was not only his *droit naturel* but his duty as an elected official of his professional organization. The CGT, of course, issued a protest, and the federation pledged its members "to defend the right of organizations to protest and to intervene against the breaking of the law, especially when such violations are the work of a leader charged with the application of the law."[51] After several months of agitation, the censure of Léger was rescinded, the "injured" inspector was sent in disgrace to Algeria, and Paoli was returned to his post in Corsica.

50. AN, F7 13727, examples from a speech by Professor Pinault at the 1913 congress of the Fédération des Fonctionnaires.
51. AN, F7 13727, statement of January 4, 1912.

The Paoli-Léger case had involved the small but active teachers' syn-dicats; the second droit d'opinion case involved the equally militant syn-dicat of sous-agents. This active organization was rapidly drawing sup-port away from its more conservative rival, the Association Générale des Sous-Agents. In the spring of 1911, postal employees participated in an election for representatives to an extraparliamentary committee to dis-cuss wages and working conditions. The Association Générale des Agents and the Syndicat National des Ouvriers, presenting unified slates, won the seats for the agents and the blue-collar workers. Al-though the results of the election for the representatives of the sous-agents gave the victory to the Association Générale slate, the vote had been extremely close; of the 48,961 votes cast, 21,654 had gone to the syndicat, 22,368 to the association. The Association Générale des Sous-Agents and the government had long maintained that, except for the area around Paris, the influence of the syndicat among sous-agents was negligible; the membership of the Syndicat National des Sous-Agents was estimated at under 10,000. The results of the 1911 election strongly indicated that the syndicat's strength had been greatly underestimated.[52] The Syndicat National des Sous-Agents, affiliated to the Fédération Postale and the CGT, was clearly a powerful force.

Throughout 1911, the Fédération Postale had sponsored meetings to discuss ways to achieve salary increases, the droit d'opinion, and closer ties of all postal workers, including the Association Générale des Agents, with the blue-collar working class and the CGT. On the night of December 2, 1911, a crowd of eight thousand postal employees at-tended the largest meeting of the year. Julien Bordérès, the secretary of the Syndicat National des Sous-Agents, was one of the main speakers. Bordérès stated that the postiers would never accept certain government regulations, which had been made by "the so-called republicans of today nastier (plus vaches) than those they had fought in the past."[53]

Within a few weeks of the speech, Bordérès, an active member of the Fédération Postale and a leader in the drive for the syndicalization of all postal employees, was fired. Immediately, the postiers in the syndicat of sous-agents and the Fédération Postale organized to defend Bordérès as

52. Georges Frischmann, *Histoire de la fédération CGT des PTT* (Paris, 1967), 179.
53. AN, F7 13802.

well as the droit d'opinion of all fonctionnaires. Posters were put up and meetings organized. Bordérès himself sent circulars to all the Bourses du Travail stating: "You must not be oblivious of the struggle which our syndicat leads for proletarian emancipation. Those in power continually hammer away at us but we won't let them intimidate us."[54] The *Bataille Syndicaliste* connected the Bordérès affair with the Paoli-Léger case. It was no accident that Bordérès and Léger were leaders of syndicats. Just as the government had attempted to destroy the workers' movement, so it now attacked the syndicats of fonctionnaires.[55] On January 26, Bordérès went before the Council of Discipline. The government worried that the sous-agents might strike.[56]

Bordérès defended his work record to the council; he was an excellent employee. What he did after work was his own business. He had attacked the government because he was furious at the political pressure it put on the working masses.[57] After the hearing, more meetings were held in Paris and in the provinces. Although the mood of the meetings was militant, no strike was declared. Although the sous-agents were growing in strength and influenced by their membership in the CGT, they were not anxious for a strike at this time. Nor was it clear that the agents would join a strike of sous-agents, who had not fully supported the agents in 1909. The agents did, however, join the campaign for Bordérès and the droit d'opinion.

It appears that although the Fédération des Fonctionnaires defended Léger and the syndicalist teachers threatened after Chambéry, they did not involve themselves in the defense of the more militant Bordérès. Nevertheless, the Bordérès case, as yet another example of the fonctionnaire's position as *citoyen diminué,* had made its mark. The droit d'opinion was becoming an issue of prime importance.[58]

Freedom of speech, the droit d'opinion, was vital to the fonctionnaire associations and syndicats; the ever-present threat of an arbitrary charge

54. AP, BA 1438, January 15, 1912.
55. *La Bataille Syndicaliste,* January 13, 1912.
56. AN, F7 13802.
57. *Ibid.*
58. Apparently, in the summer of 1913, the minister of commerce, industry and PTT, Massé, was favorable to the reintegration of Bordérès, but the head of the government, Barthou, was opposed (AP, BA 1438). Bordérès reported at a meeting in April, 1914, that he had received notification of his reintegration.

of délits d'opinion was a severe deterrent to the voicing of demands or to vigorous fonctionnaire action of any kind. In the period 1909–1914, the campaign for the ability to speak and act openly on professional and political issues took on added importance as the fonctionnaires' organizations grew larger and more militant. It was in this period that yet another development made the droit d'opinion even more significant. The fonctionnaires entered the realm of electoral politics, participating openly and actively as a unified group in electoral campaigns. For years, state employees had gone hat in hand to their parliamentary and communal representatives to voice their demands for improved working conditions and for the droit syndical. Most Socialists and many Radicals had been responsive, but the majority of deputies and other elected officials had consistently failed the fonctionnaires. Pay raises and social legislation, passed only after enormous pressure, were usually too little and too late. In the critical years 1906–1909, the fonctionnaires, increasingly disillusioned with parliament and the Radical party in particular, had watched parliamentary votes go against the extension of the 1884 law, amnesty for fired fonctionnaires, and finally a proper settlement of the postal strike. By 1909, the fonctionnaires decided to challenge those politicians who did not support their demands.

The first political activity began on the Left with the syndicalists, yet another indication of the disparity between the syndicalism of the fonctionnaires and the theoretical revolutionary syndicalism of the blue-collar workers, which was still officially separated from party politics. In June, 1909, intensely bitter about the amnesty vote and parliamentary support of Clemenceau during the postal strikes, Nègre's Comité Central began to organize for the 1910 election campaign. On June 10, several newspapers printed and commented on an open letter from the committee calling on all fonctionnaires to make their electoral power felt: "Above all, it is necessary that our class enemies, all the discredited members of parliament who took positions against us by associating themselves with arbitrary and violent governmental acts against the working class, bite the dust next year." Within a few days, the Comité Central had decided on a course of action: it would publish a brochure on the candidates so fonctionnaires would know their enemies, inaugurate an inquiry into the electoral situation in each constituency, and make new efforts to convince the Radical and Radical Socialist party to intervene in favor of the fired postiers and fonctionnaires. "The silence of the committee of Radical deputies will be considered as a hostile act." Nègre declared that henceforth the fonctionnaires must carry on their actions on the *terrain electoral*. Each fonctionnaire organization would have to extract from its representatives a written pledge to defend fonctionnaire interests in the Chamber; without guarantees, the promises of politicians were too often violated.[59]

By the end of 1909, the Association Générale des Agents had reached a similar position. Vowing to maintain absolute neutrality in political matters, the Association Générale at its December congress, nevertheless, recognizing the self-interest of PTT employees in defending themselves against the hostile actions of certain politicians, asked all agents to take a position, either individually or collectively, in the next election "to oppose without distinction all the renegade members of parliament who have systematically disregarded their rights and their interests."[60]

The postiers not only took an official collective stand on regular candidates; some individual postiers ran for office. In the 1912 municipal elections in Paris, the fonctionnaires officially supported sympathetic candidates such as the SFIO representative of the eighteenth arrondissement, Marcel Cachin (later a founder and leader of the French Communist party). Two men who had signed the open letter, Quilici of the agents and Grangier, the former secretary of the Syndicat National des Sous-Agents, ran a strong campaign to represent the fourteenth arrondissement, and Grangier was elected.[61] Earlier, in the national elections of 1910, Quilici, as president of the Comité Electoral de Défense des Travailleurs des Services Publics (representing PTT and railroad employees), had been the leader of a vigorous campaign to defeat the deputy representing the twelfth arrondissement, the minister of public works, and the PTT, the former Socialist Alexandre Millerand. Millerand was campaigning as the friend of the postal workers, claiming responsibility for the institution of the eight-hour day and the nine-franc per diem minimum wage. The agents plastered the district with posters declaring this boast to be a lie: only line workers had benefited from those improvements. Indeed, Pauron of the ouvriers' syndicat had

59. AN, F7 13725.
60. *Bulletin de l'AG*, March, 1910.
61. AP, BA 1438 and the Quilici Papers.

signed Millerand's posters, an indication of the fragility of the fonctionnaires' unity. In addition, election posters and speakers at electoral meetings emphasized Millerand's ties to the repressive administration of the new *premier flic* (chief cop), Minister of Justice Barthou; a vote against Millerand was a vote against Barthou. Voters were informed that Millerand had voted against amnesty for the fired fonctionnaires. The battle cries were "Get rid of Millerand." "When voting, don't forget that Millerand is the friend of the big shots, the enemies of the little people. DON'T VOTE FOR MILLERAND." A color poster done for the SFIO by the renowned artist Paul Poncet read: "Organized, the producers will crush the octopus."[62] Millerand won handily, but he was not to forget Quilici's role in the campaign. In May, hardly a month after the election, Quilici was assigned to a lower-paid position in Laon, far from the center of his activity in Paris.[63] Claiming hardship—he had a new baby, an aging mother, and outstanding debts from the time of his unemployment in Paris—Quilici took a leave from Laon and asked to be reassigned to Paris. In July, Quilici was fired, another victim of the *guillotine sèche*.

The concern with electoral politics that had begun with the left-wing syndicalists soon spread to the larger organization of fonctionnaires. As the Fédération des Fonctionnaires grew larger and more dedicated to the active defense of fonctionnaires' rights, electoral strategy became an important part of its activity. The first important test of this involvement was to be the national elections of spring 1914. Even before the congress of December, 1913, plans were made to send out questionnaires to candidates of all political persuasions; to be favored, candidates would have to agree to grant the fonctionnaires the droit syndical and freedom of opinion.[64] At the congress, the campaign for these two demands was made official. Fonctionnaires were asked to form electoral committees and to take an active role in this critical election. The same election posters were sent to fonctionnaire associations all over the country, leaving a blank space for insertion of the names of candidates who would vote for the extension of the 1884 law and guarantee the fonctionnaires'

62. All these posters and election cards are in the Quilici Papers.

63. The newspaper *L'Authorité* chastised Millerand; only Quilici had been sent to a "hole" like Laon (Quilici Papers).

64. AN, F7 13727, December 3, 1913.

droit d'opinion. Articles in the *Tribune des Fonctionnaires* emphasized the importance of this election, not only for the liberty and dignity of fonctionnaires but for better working conditions and a greater role in administrative decision making.[65] The left bloc won the election; the fonctionnaires were quick to acclaim their part in the victory: "The victory of the parties of the left is also the victory of syndicalist fonctionnaires. Now, we can acknowledge our hope, our conviction: the newly elected house will not make us second-class citizens."[66]

The outbreak of hostilities was to dash these hopes, but the involvement in electoral politics, begun before August, 1914, was to be of critical importance to the parties of the Left and to the fonctionnaires in the years following the war.

The fonctionnaires' campaign for the droit syndical and the droit d'opinion was determined not merely by the desire not to be second-class citizens but by the need for these rights in their quest for improved working conditions. With strong, active organizations, fonctionnaires could pressure the government more effectively to end favoritism, to lighten work loads, and to raise salaries. In the early years of fonctionnaire organization, agitation for improved advancement, against arbitrary discipline, and against favoritism had often obscured the basic demands for higher salaries and a shorter workweek. Slowly but steadily, advances had been made. First, the *repos hebdomadaire,* the weekly day off, had been granted, vacations were instituted, and some services were on the eight-hour day. Salaries, always low, had usually kept pace with the slight changes in the cost of living. With security of employment and retirement benefits to look forward to, most fonctionnaires, particularly those with more than one wage earner in the family, though clearly not far from the poverty line, could maintain somewhat more than a subsistence standard of living.

By 1911, this economic stability had begun to erode. The fixed income of fonctionnaires, renewed at intervals by the legislature, was satisfactory only as long as prices remained stable. In these last years before the war, the cost of living began to rise, continuing to increase during

65. *La Tribune des Fonctionnaires,* March, 1914, article by Rattazzi.
66. *Le Rappel,* May 10, 1914, article by Pinault of the Professeurs Adjoints des Lycées.

the war and spiraling uncontrollably into the great inflation of the early 1920s until the reforms of 1926 finally restored financial stability. This long inflationary period lowered the standard of living of many workers, but the fonctionnaires, whose salaries were determined by budget-minded legislators, were particularly hard hit. The prewar rise in prices, though insignificant compared to what was to follow, was serious enough for the fonctionnaires to feel their standard of living, already weak, severely threatened. The government did not issue a cost-of-living index; indeed, the first official salary index for fonctionnaires, planned for five-year intervals, was initiated by the Ministry of Labor only in 1911.[67] Nevertheless, every fonctionnaire could see and feel the increase in rents, in food prices, and in clothing.

In the century since the Napoleonic bureaucracy had been established, a concept of remuneration for fonctionnaires had undergone a vast change. The nineteenth-century concept of a traitement for the fonctionnaire who was a "semiprofessional" had been eroded by the expansion of government employment. Now, the fonctionnaires, few of whom had outside resources, needed enough money to live on—they needed a living wage. In the forty years that the Third Republic had been the government of France, teachers' salaries had doubled and facteurs' salaries had increased by a third, but in comparison with the rising cost of living and the salaries of civil servants in other industrialized nations, the French fonctionnaires were recipients of a very low wage indeed.[68] Shortly after the war, the haut fonctionnaire Henri Chardon wrote, "The Third Republic has maintained, to an extent beyond all justification, starvation wages for almost all the civil servants of the nation.

67. The first *Rapport au Ministre du Travail relatif aux échelles des traitements des fonctionnaires* was issued in September and October, 1911. Because of the war, the report due in 1916 was left undone. The next report appeared in a supplement to the *Journal Officiel* of December 2, 1921, but the series was again interrupted when the 1926 report was abandoned because of the financial crisis. It was not until 1931 that another report appeared. Thus in the crucial period 1911–1931, we have salary statistics for every ten years, and these figures are far from complete. François Perroux calls French interwar statistics "unworthy of a great state" (*Les Traitements des fonctionnaires* [Paris, 1933], vii).

68. Salary figures for 1913 were as follows: instituteurs—minimum 1,250, maximum 1,666; préposé des douanes—minimum 900, maximum 1,250; facteurs—minimum 750, maximum 1,000 francs. In 1911, police agents got 1,400 and gardiens de la paix, 1,900 francs (Perroux, *Traitements*, 58). Civil servants' salaries are analyzed more fully by Perroux, *ibid.*, 18–28.

I would blush to write down the wages we still paid at the beginning of 1914, to the most indispensable instruments of communal life."[69] The fonctionnaires were fully aware of the erosion of their real wages; the question of la cherté de la vie (high cost of living) began to dominate their meetings.

If the fonctionnaires in general were paid low wages, certain categories of "forgotten" fonctionnaires were even more grossly underpaid. The newspapers chronicled the pay difficulties of postiers, douaniers, and other petits fonctionnaires, but the public was largely unaware of the personnel secondaire, the huissiers, museum guards, gardeners, and garçons of the Bibliothèque Nationale. The median wage for these subalterns was only fourteen hundred francs, and they did not get the living indemnity awarded to other urban fonctionnaires. The secondary employees also complained that salaries differed from ministry to ministry. A huissier at the Ministry of Foreign Affairs received a maximum salary that was three hundred francs below the maximum at the Ministry of Justice, and at the Academy of Medicine, a huissier received five hundred francs below the salary at Foreign Affairs.[70] As the cost of living rose, these and other forgotten fonctionnaires began to make more determined demands for pay raises. The agents (or garçons) of the lycées, for example, formed a syndicat in 1906 and had always made modest demands; as late as 1907, they were still seeking the repos hebdomadaire. By 1911, the agents were desperate enough to send an open letter to the minister of education stating that their pay was the lowest of all fonctionnaires, and if they did not get a wage increase, they would have to go on public assistance.[71] The lycée agents continued to press for a wage increase until June, 1914, when Viviani, then minister of education, promised that the budget would include money for this hard-pressed group.[72] L'Humanité wryly commented that so far the agents had gotten only promises.[73] The fonctionnaires of Eaux et Forêts also began to clamor for higher wages. The armée forestière consisted of hundreds of

69. Henri Chardon, L'Organisation de la République pour la paix, 44, quoted ibid., 18.

70. AN, F7 13726, booklet issued in 1912 by the Fédération des Associations Professionnelles des Ministères de l'Etat.

71. AN, F7 13743, letter of June 11, 1911.

72. Le Matin, June 1, 1914.

73. L'Humanité, June 12, 1914.

guards in state domains who made only from nine hundred to fourteen hundred francs a year; communal *forestiers* had a starting wage of only seven hundred francs in 1914.[74] In the postal services, the youngest workers received wages well below those paid to young men in private industry. Jeunes facteurs (apprentice postmen), starting at age thirteen, received a monthly salary of forty-one francs. In 1914, these young men, whose apprenticeship lasted four years and whose salaries were often vital to their families, had asked for a minimum wage of eight hundred francs; the government promised six hundred after one year of service. A similar situation existed for the young telegraph workers, *tubistes* and *boulistes,* those bicycle-riding carriers of *pneumatiques* and telegrams.[75]

Employment of women, mostly at lower levels, continued to increase. At the 1913 congress of the Union des Administrations Centrales, the opening speaker commented on the presence of women *dactylographes* (stenographers) at a congress for the first time. Women, he asserted, would play an increasingly important role in the central administration in the years to come; the "gracious ambassadors" were most welcome.[76] The Association Générale des Agents was already pressing for women to be allowed to take examinations for higher positions in the postal service, but the question of equality of wages was of prime importance.[77] Women in all the services, but particularly in the PTT, were demanding salary increases to bring their earnings to the same level as those of the men in the same service doing similar work. A téléphoniste told the congress of the Association Générale about the position of women in the PTT: "Equal pay for equal work, that's true feminism." She asked that the question of wage parity for women be seriously studied so that it could be discussed at the 1915 congress.[78]

Although the salary crisis was most obvious among lower-paid fonctionnaires, the higher-level state employees were also affected by the loss of real wages; even the judges, plagued by "political tyranny" as well, complained that they were underpaid.[79] A new problem began to be dis-

74. *L'Humanité,* May 2, 1914, article by A. Luquet.
75. AN, F7 13802.
76. AN, F7 13727, speech by Salaün.
77. *Bulletin de l'AG,* April, 1912, report on the congress of the Association Générale.
78. *La Bataille Syndicaliste,* June 7, 1914, speech of Mlle Chaudel.
79. *Le Journal,* April 18, 1914, congress of Association Amicale de la Magistrature.

cussed—the crisis in recruitment. Bright young men and women were no longer willing to enter state service for starvation wages. The prison guards worried about the *grève de candidats* (strike of candidates); the 1912 budget had called for 130 new employees, but only 20 suitable candidates could be found.[80] The July, 1913, issue of *La Tribune des Fonctionnaires* devoted a large article to the problem of recruitment. Commercial and industrial employment was now superior to public employment: "The fonctionnaire, shackled within the ranks of a control ever tighter and more complex, has no other hope for the future than a precarious and monotonous existence."[81]

The crisis of recruitment, though serious at all levels, was particularly distressing to the middling and upper cadres. An army of peasant boys and girls was still available for the lesser posts; the employees of the central administration were most worried about losing qualified candidates to private industry. In 1899, for four places in the Ministry of Education, there had been forty candidates; in 1913, for eight vacancies, there were only twenty-eight candidates.[82] In Public Works, forty candidates had been advanced for eight positions in 1903; in 1912, thirty-five candidates vied for fifteen places. In the Finance Ministry, the number of candidates had nearly doubled from 1899 to 1912 (from forty-six to eighty-two), but there were seven times the number of vacancies. In the War Ministry, there were twenty places but only nineteen candidates.[83] At the 1914 congress of the Fédération des Employés des Administrations Centrales, the secretary-general, Roquès, accused the minister of finance, Joseph Caillaux, who had refused to put wage increases for these state employees in the budget, of being hostile to the employees of the central administrations. There was a terrible malaise among the fonctionnaires, even though they continued to be "aware of their dignity and their professional duty."[84]

The government, already cognizant of the deteriorating salary situation, had established in 1911 an extraparliamentary commission to study

80. *Le Journal,* January 3, 1912.

81. *La Tribune des Fonctionnaires,* July, 1913.

82. Nominations were made from a larger list of applicants, but not all were deemed qualified.

83. *Le Matin,* May 5, 1913, meeting of the Union des Personnels Civils des Administrations Centrales.

84. AN, F7 13727.

the question of fonctionnaire traitements. The result of the inquiry was a recommendation that wage increases be granted to the PTT employees in steps over a five-year period from 1912 to 1917. When the implementation of the recommendations was delayed, the PTT employees held a series of mass meetings to pressure the legislature to enact the first increment. The Syndicat des Sous-Agents went as far as planning a demonstration in the Jardin du Luxembourg; the postiers and their families were to assemble peacefully in small groups shouting, "Cent sous! Cent sous!" (Five francs! Five francs!).[85] A government promise to speed up the granting of salary increases put an end to plans for that particular demonstration, but in the months to come, as the cost of living continued to rise and the increases were not forthcoming, the fonctionnaires became more vociferous.

By 1913, a new crisis had arisen. The first step in the new salary schedule had finally been proposed to go into effect on January 1, 1913. In the budget discussion, the Chamber had voted increases for the PTT, the Contributions Indirectes, and the Douanes, only to have the Senate postpone the increase until June. A ministerial promise of a raise for teachers was also delayed by the Senate; the equalization of male and female salaries had already been eliminated from the budget by the government. Pinault of the Professeurs Adjoints des Lycées charged that the teachers were being punished for their antimilitarism.[86]

If the PTT employees had always demonstrated their willingness to act firmly in presenting their demands, the employees of the Ministry of Finance, the douaniers, and the employees of the Contributions Indirectes had traditionally been more cautious. By 1909, both services had voiced support for the extension of the 1884 law (without the right to strike) and had actively maintained this position in the Fédération des Fonctionnaires, but during the postal strikes, both groups hesitated to act. The congress of the Union Générale des Contributions Indirectes, held in the middle of the second strike, had sent a sympathy message to the beleaguered postal agents but made it clear that this was not their struggle.[87] A motion to send five hundred francs to the fired strikers was defeated. At the same congress, any connection with syndicalists who

85. AP, BA 1427, 1911.
86. *La Tribune des Fonctionnaires*, May, 1913.
87. AN, F7 13729.

belonged to the CGT was also rejected; revolutionary syndicalism and the general strike would never be acceptable to these employees of the Ministry of Finance.[88] Both douaniers and Contributions Indirectes employees continued to send delegations to ministers and deputies to plead the case against favoritism and hierarchical rigidity, which were particularly serious in this ministry. By 1911, however, it was more than favoritism that troubled the finance workers; the salary issue now became important. "Indemnity of residence," subsidies for living expenses for finance workers assigned to posts far from home, was of particular significance as the cost of living rose.

The declining standard of living, coupled with the dissatisfaction with hiring and advancement policies, pushed the usually moderate finance workers closer to the activist position of the PTT. At the 1911 congress of the Contributions Indirectes at Montpelier, a militant faction rejected the moderate pleas to be "prudent." Referring to the *grèves des bras croisés* (sit-down strike) of the PTT and the *grève perlée* (slow down) of the cheminots, these activists called for a *grève des yeux fermés* (strike of closed eyes) on the part of the finance workers.[89] A compromise with moderates was reached at this congress, but a year later, at the 1912 congress, the situation had deteriorated enough that such a "strike" was possible. The effects of such an action would be incalculable—think what would happen to the alcohol revenue, for example, if the Contributions Indirectes closed its eyes to irregularities.[90] The douaniers also became more vocal; the government was accused of *gabegie,* squandering tax money through administrative inefficiency while employees of the ministry struggled to survive on subsistence wages. Moreover, the *douaniers actifs* were faced once again with the possibility of being declared a military service, losing their ability to organize even under the law of 1901.

By the time the Senate rejected the January 1 increase, the finance workers, disillusioned with the inactivity of the Fédération des Fonctionnaires on the wage issue, were ready to join the Fédération Postale in mass meetings. Throughout France, in all the major cities, the three services sponsored open meetings; fonctionnaires in all areas pressured the

88. *L'Action,* May 21, 1909.
89. *Le Journal,* May 24, 1911.
90. Report of congress in *Le Matin* and *La Bataille Syndicaliste,* May 20, 23, 1912.

Senate for their wage increases.[91] In Paris, the Manège Saint Paul was once again host to nearly ten thousand fonctionnaires.[92] Telegrams of solidarity sped from one meeting to another. Finally, the Senate yielded and the increases, retroactive to January 1, were granted. But once again, it was too little and too late. The increases of one hundred francs a year for agents and a mere forty francs for sous-agents were hardly enough to compensate for rising prices.

Then, at the end of 1913, the government, anxious to improve conditions in the military services as war with Germany became more probable, granted a substantial increase to military personnel. Astounded, the fonctionnaires immediately demanded that the 1914 budget include provisions for granting the rest of their increases at once—all four steps in one. Meetings were held in Lille (December 26), Brest and Valenciennes (January 18), Verdun (January 25), Montpelier (February 1), Arras (February 2), St. Mihiel, Toulon, Reims, and Toul (February 8), La Rochelle, Bayonne, and Boulogne (February 15), Toulouse (February 19), Marseilles (February 21 and 26), Lyons and Bordeaux (February 28). Another eight thousand met at the Manège Saint Paul—every day brought more meetings.[93] PTT employees, employees of the Contributions Indirectes, douaniers, instituteurs—fonctionnaires were as valuable as the military. Particular reference was made to the increases granted to *officiers* and *sous-officiers*: "Today fonctionnaires see that they have been suckers." The fonctionnaires would look for the "means of action which would affect the Public Powers."[94]

In February, even the Fédération des Fonctionnaires joined the movement for an immediate increase in fonctionnaires' wages. In February and March, the *Tribune des Fonctionnaires* carried lead articles on the cost of living and the military raises. On March 2, the federation called a mass meeting at which speakers decried the raises for military personnel, who, in times of peace, ran less risk than many fonctionnaires, who did service that was just as honorable. The government and the Chamber were reminded of the recruitment crisis. The warning was issued: if salaries were not increased, the results would be visible in the next elec-

91. AN, F7 13730 has reports on these provincial meetings.
92. *Le Rappel* and *L'Humanité*, April 6, 1913.
93. AN, F7 13804. The list of meetings goes on for three pages of the report.
94. AN, F7 13802, meeting of February 21, 1914.

tion.[95] Several weeks later, Laurent, the secretary-general of the federation, wrote an article for Le Petit Parisien assuring the public that fonctionnaires were interested in more than ameliorating their working conditions. The rising cost of living had forced the salary issue to the forefront, but fonctionnaires were still primarily interested in better administration and better service to the public.[96] The federation was clearly not ready to do more than hold meetings and make electoral threats; direct action was to be avoided.

If the Fédération des Fonctionnaires eschewed direct action, the more radical syndicalists did not. Throughout the spring of 1914, meetings and demonstrations grew more heated. The syndicalist ranks swelled with new adherents. The ineffective and inactive Association Générale des Sous-Agents, once the dominant force among facteurs, was rapidly losing whatever strength it had maintained in the provinces as new syndicats were organized in dozens of cities.[97]

Finally, the Association Générale could hold out no longer; the syndicalists within the association were now a majority. At the annual congress in March, the membership voted not only to support the extension of the 1884 law but to proceed, without regard to the question of legality, with the transformation of the Association Générale into a syndicat. The question of joining the already existing Syndicat National des Sous-Agents was avoided because it belonged to the CGT and not all sous-agents were ready for this advanced position.

The sous-agents of the more radical Syndicat National saw the action of the "yellow" Association Générale as an attempt to split the sous-agents into two syndicats.[98] Speaking from a position of continued growth—eight hundred new members in January and February—the secretary-general of the Syndicat National, Bordérès, urged the syndicalists in the Association Générale to join them in a single syndicat in the Fédération Postale and in the CGT.[99] The Syndicat National continued to reaffirm its connections with the blue-collar working class. In October, 1913, its members had met for the first time at the Paris Bourse

95. L'Humanité, March 3, 1914.
96. Le Petit Parisien, March 22, 1914.
97. AN, F7 13802, reports of February 17, 1914.
98. Ibid.; see report of April congress.
99. La Bataille Syndicaliste, March 24, 1914.

du Travail. The CGT newspaper *La Bataille Syndicaliste* made much of the presence of the fonctionnaires in the *grand salle* of the Parisian working class.[100] Now, in March, in a significant gesture of attachment to the working class, twelve hundred sous-agents met once again at the Bourse. At yet another meeting, Titignac of the agents asked the sous-agents, "Do you want to become an intermediary class and fight against the workers who are at your side?" The assembly roared back "NON."[101]

A scant ten days after the Association Générale congress, the Syndicat National held its annual congress at Lyons. Once again, the Association Générale was attacked: "Considering that the Association Générale of the Sous-Agents no longer represents the aspirations of the large majority of the sous-agents, that by its acts of servitude, the bad faith of its leaders, it has alienated the sympathy and the confidence of all the proletariat, both public and private," and once again, sous-agents were asked to unify under the aegis of the Syndicat National, "the only organization capable of realizing the union."[102] At this congress, the Syndicat National also reaffirmed its affiliation to the CGT and, significantly, its continued pacifism.[103] By the summer of 1914, then, whether in theory or in deed, almost all the nearly fifty thousand sous-agents were syndicalists.

By midsummer, the entire postal service had rallied to the syndicalist cause. The Association Générale des Agents, which had remained an association even though it had initiated such "syndicalist" activity as the strike of 1909 and had joined the two CGT affiliates in the Fédération Postale, took official action. At the annual congress, in June, 1914, held as agitation over the salary increases intensified, the twenty-two-thousand-member association voted to transform itself into a syndicat. Titignac proclaimed: "Our origins, our methods of action, our corporative past, the nature of our work, one of exploitation rather than strictly speaking, administrative, and above all, our syndicalist views, make it a pressing duty as well as a necessity to turn with determination toward the great workers' organizations."[104] A week earlier, at the con-

100. *Ibid.,* October 20, 1913.
101. AP, BA 1438.
102. AN, F7 13802.
103. AP, BA 1438.
104. AN, F7 13802, June 6, 1914.

gress of the Union Générale des Contributions Indirectes, the finance workers, though avoiding the term *syndicat,* had withdrawn from the Fédération des Fonctionnaires and cast its lot with the more militant PTT employees for communal action for "common interests." [105]

The rapidly growing syndicalism of the PTT employees and the movement of the Fédération des Fonctionnaires toward support of the syndicalist position were welcomed by the CGT leadership. Fearful of antagonizing the more moderate fonctionnaires, who still thought of the CGT as revolutionary, Jouhaux, the secretary-general, had been hesitant during and just after the postal strike to press the issue of fonctionnaires' adhesion to the CGT too strongly. And, of course, within the CGT, there still remained those revolutionary syndicalist *ouvrièrists* who mistrusted any allegiance with non-blue-collar workers. But in these last years before the war, as the CGT itself was evolving toward a new position, its leaders began to speak more openly and enthusiastically for the unity of the two arms of the working class under the aegis of the CGT. The CGT was particularly interested in the fonctionnaires' gaining the right to strike. CGT speakers appeared regularly at antistatute fonctionnaire meetings, calling for the right to strike, a right no statute would ever guarantee: "The right to strike is not something you ask for; it's something you take." [106] Alexandre Bracke and Marcel Cachin, writing in *L'Humanité,* echoed these sentiments—the fonctionnaires must syndicate, they must have the right to strike, they must join other workers: "There are not two proletariats, that of the factories and that of the administrative offices, but only one working class which wants to emancipate itself from all subordination and which wants to win its well-being and its freedom from those who oppress it." [107]

Syndicalists in the CGT who still opposed fonctionnaire membership in the CGT were rapidly becoming a weak minority. At the 1913 congress of the metalworkers federation, Gaspard Ingweiller, the Parisian secretary, proposed a motion to prohibit fonctionnaire membership in the working-class organization. He complained that since the *Bataille Syndicaliste* had refused to print an antifonctionnaire article, the news-

105. AN, F7 13729, May 30, 1914.
106. *La Bataille Syndicaliste,* July 7, 1912, Jouhaux at a July 6 meeting of the PTT.
107. See, for example, the issues of *L'Humanité,* June 1 and June 14, 1912.

paper, far from being the impartial organ for the working class, was, in reality, the organ of syndicalist fonctionnaires. Ingweiller's motion was strongly attacked by Merrheim and was overwhelmingly defeated. As if to emphasize the CGT's position, Jouhaux told the congress delegates that "to behave as 'antifonctionnaires' is to arrive at the desperate idea that all activist workers should be put on the same level as those who have betrayed the working class."[108]

The differences between fonctionnaires and blue-collar workers could not be ignored; in February, 1914, the treasurer of the CGT, Charles Marck, told attendees of a meeting in Paris that the fonctionnaires should not be guaranteed the "sinecures" that made it "appear" to the public that they were not hardworking.[109] But clearly, the two great groups of French workers were moving closer together. Although numerous events such as changing social origins, an eroding standard of living, routinization and expansion of work, and blue-collar strikes and militancy contributed to the change in fonctionnaires' consciousness and to the alliance of fonctionnaires and blue-collar workers, most critical was the role played by the state. The centralization of state employment and the state's authoritarian response to fonctionnaires' demands were crucial factors in making fonctionnaires identify themselves as part of the working class. And as the government's failure to grant the fonctionnaires their political and professional rights and their much needed salary increases helped to push the fonctionnaires closer to syndicalism, the CGT, as it passed through its "crisis," was abandoning much of the revolutionary rhetoric and ideology that had helped keep the two groups of workers apart. The war merely accelerated the process that had been developing in the tumultuous decade before 1914.

As the summer approached, activity reached a fever pitch. Action on the droit syndical, the droit d'opinion, and salary increases, could no longer be delayed. The forty thousand blue-collar state workers who belonged to the Union Fédérative des Travailleurs de l'Etat and to the CGT added another dimension to the demands; they pressed for the reduction in the workweek known as *la semaine anglaise*—Saturday afternoon off to make a long weekend. There was to be no reduction in the

108. AN, F7 13770.
109. *Ibid.*

forty-nine-hour week: Monday to Friday would be nine-hour work-days, Saturday morning would add four more hours. Various ministers of war and finance had promised the shorter workweek only to have the Senate hold up the necessary legislation. Fearful of the effect such a move would have on workers in private industry, the elected officials who sat in the Luxembourg chamber rejected every attempt to include the semaine anglaise in budgetary legislation. The government did not press too hard. Delegation after delegation of workers went before the ministers to urge that more pressure be put on the Senate. By June, 1914, patience was at an end; a strike in the critical war industries loomed as a grave possibility.[110]

To the fonctionnaires, the most critical issue was still the salary increase they had been demanding for months. By June, their patience was also at an end. Even before the congress of PTT agents which made the decision to transform the Association Générale into a syndicat had ended on June 9, the newspapers were speculating about a general strike.[111] But the PTT employees, though verbally committed to strong action, did not envisage such a grave gesture. On the evening of June 9, the Fédération des Fonctionnaires, which had earlier asked the Fédération Postale to join it in pressing for salary increases, only to be rebuffed for being too moderate, held a mass meeting at which five thousand Parisian fonctionnaires expressed their doléances.[112] Within a few days of the PTT congress, while the Senate was still debating the budget, there was talk not of a general strike but of a slowdown strike. The Fédération Postale denied that it had any such intentions; the public would not be made to pay for the difficulties created by the Senate. But as the days passed, the possibility of a grève des bras croisés or a grève perlée increased, particularly among the sous-agents. The Senate, in discussing the budget, had agreed to grant wage increases but had left inequities. In particular, it had failed to grant the sous-agents the same living allowance, the frais de séjour, that it awarded to the agents; the facteurs were to get only three hundred francs instead of the four hundred francs they considered their due as equals of the agents.

110. "Sera-çe la grève des Travailleurs de l'état?" L'Humanité, June 27, 1914.

111. See, for example, La Dépêche de Toulouse, June 8, 1914.

112. AN, F7 13802, Report M / 9234, May 21, 1914; La Tribune des Fonctionnaires and Le Radical, June 10, 1914.

On June 22, there were half a dozen meetings of sous-agents and plans for a *chahut* (noisy demonstration) were made, and finally, the next day, the sous-agents of the central post office abandoned work and poured into the street, cursing the Senate and calling for their four hundred francs. To the tune of the student song "L'Air des Lampions," they sang "Nous voulons nos quatre cents francs, ton taine, nous voulons nos quatre cents francs, ton ton" (We want our four hundred francs). The strains of the "Carmagnole" alternated with those of the "International."[113] By evening, responding to a ministerial promise that the Senate would include the additional money for facteurs, the "demonstration-strike" ended. Two days later, thousands of postiers met once again at the Bourse du Travail to make sure the promises were kept. Pierre Laval, the Socialist deputy, brought greetings of support from the SFIO: "You are defending your kids' bread, what is more just and natural." Grangier, now a municipal councillor, recalled the struggle of 1906, when he had been a leader of the first strike. A speaker from the agents supported the claim of the sous-agents to equality of *frais de séjour,* and Marck of the CGT offered the hand of solidarity of the blue-collar working class. The meeting ended with cries of "Frais de Séjours" and "Vive le Syndicat."[114]

Finally, on July 11, the Senate voted the wage increases for the fonctionnaires, agreeing to the principle of equalization of wages between the Contributions Indirectes, the Douanes, and the PTT, the full living indemnity for the sous-agents, and the semaine anglaise for the blue-collar state workers. Part of the increase was to be granted retroactive to January, 1914; the rest was to be granted the following December.

Even as the Senate was voting, the threat of war mounted. The organized working class, antagonistic to a war that would pit worker against worker, had bitterly opposed the three-year conscription law and had held a large number of antiwar meetings at which votes were taken pledging the CGT to a general strike if the expected capitalist conflict erupted. Many fonctionnaires concurred with this antiwar position. Syndicalist teachers had displayed their hostility to war at the Chambéry congress and had continued to speak out against the three-year law.

113. *Le Matin* and *Le Petit Parisien,* June 24, 1914.
114. *La Bataille Syndicaliste,* June 26, 1914.

The teacher syndicat of Haute Savoie, for example, issued a statement against the three-year law, declaring that it was more beneficial to the enemies of the Republic and the "big businessmen" than to the defense of the nation.[115] Bordérès of the sous-agents had supported the votes on the general strike. Fonctionnaire meetings in 1913 and 1914 often ended with resolutions against the conscription law and for peace. The PTT listened to speakers who encouraged them to tell their departing soldiers that conscription would guarantee the tranquillity only of the bourgeoisie: "You mustn't falter when there is an armed conflict or a strike; your duty is the opposite of what they tell you."[116] But as July drew to a close and France's greatest humanist voice against the war—that of Jean Jaurès—was brutally stilled by an assassin's bullet, the SFIO and the fonctionnaires capitulated. All plunged into a war that was to drain the lifeblood of France. The world would never be the same again.

115. *Ibid.*, June 12, 1913.
116. AP, BA 1436, Dutailly to a meeting on March 14, 1914.

6

Champs d'Honneur, Champs de Carnage, 1914–1918

Inheritors of the nationalism of the Revolution and the Commune—the Commune, after all, had originated in an effort to continue the war with Germany—and the internationalism of the socialist and anarchist movements, the French working class had always been ambivalent toward "La Patrie." Devoted to republican principles, devoted to *la France révolutionnaire,* the organized working class had rallied frequently and ardently to the defense of the young Republic in its struggles with right-wing monarchists and stalwarts of the church. But even as they defended the Republic, many workers, particularly those who adhered to a revolutionary syndicalist or anarchist position, recognized the bourgeois state as their enemy. For workers who believed in class struggle, the state remained the most formidable tool of the class enemy, the bourgeoisie, for the regimentation and repression of the working class. Antimilitary feeling also ran high among CGT and other workers whose syndicalist activity had often been thwarted by the government's use of the French army. As the threat of war with Germany increased, so did this antimilitarism. The French working class had no quarrel with German workers. War would benefit only the bourgeoisie of both countries, and the workers would be bloody victims of the bourgeois conflict. The campaign against the three-year law, the creation of the *sou de soldat,* and the frequent antiwar meetings and demonstrations have already been discussed. The CGT had pledged to respond to any European war with a general strike.

But though the CGT had often taken antimilitary and even antipatriotic positions, declaring at the Marseilles congress of 1908, "Workers have no country," it was never clear that the French working class was as antipatriotic as its official statements indicated.[1] To be antimili-

---

1. Roger Picard, *Le Mouvement syndical durant la guerre* (Paris, 1927), 46.

tary and antiwar might be acceptable, but to be antipatriotic was a step many workers could not take. The state was not the nation. France, after all, was also the France of Valmy, of 1848, and of the Commune. This France belonged to the working class. Still, as the war drew closer, both the government and the workers wondered whether the working class would support the threatened conflict. Its support seemed less likely as it became obvious, as it did in the summer of 1914, that Europe was sliding toward a war that was truly without value for the working class, a war that could only result in the meaningless slaughter of young workers and peasants. Just a few days before the outbreak of hostilities, in an obvious reference to French workers, the Radical war minister, Adolphe Messimy, told the Council of Ministers, "Let me have the guillotine and I will guarantee victory."[2] The government readied the Carnet B, the infamous list of political activists and militant syndicalists to be detained in time of crisis.[3] Would there be a general strike against the war?

On July 26, 1914, Jouhaux warned in *La Bataille Syndicaliste* that the people knew that the massacres, the famine, and the butchery of war would mean an end to their hopes and dreams, perhaps an end to a civilization.[4] Under the headline "We Don't Want War," *La Bataille Syndicaliste* stated CGT policy: "The workers must respond with an immediate general strike to any declaration of war." On the twenty-seventh, an appeal was launched for a mass demonstration on the Grands Boulevards: "It's our last hope to avert the catastrophe: let us be our own saviors."[5] But even as thousands poured into the streets shouting their opposition to the impending disaster, other crowds jammed the very same boulevards crying, "A Berlin! Vive la guerre!" A call for a mass meeting, to be held at the Salle Wagram on the evening of the twenty-ninth, was issued by the Federation of the Seine. The launching of a Parisian general strike would surely emerge from this meeting. The Wagram meeting, forbidden by the government, drew an enormous crowd. No strike declaration emerged, but plans were made for further meetings with socialists, who were also trying to stem the tide of war. At a meeting in Brussels, Jaurès, speaking for the French socialists, and Hugo

---

2. *La Bataille Syndicaliste,* July 30, 1914.

3. See Jean-Jacques Becker, *Le Carnet B* (Paris, 1973).

4. Jean Maitron and Colette Chambelland, *Syndicalisme révolutionnaire et le mouvement ouvrier français* (Paris, 1967), 16.

5. *La Bataille Syndicaliste,* July 27, 1914.

Haase, speaking for the Germans, their arms entwined, pledged to continue the struggle to avert the impending conflict. Fonctionnaires joined the peace efforts. At meetings of postiers and teachers, resolutions against the war were adopted.[6]

Then on July 31, an assassin's bullet struck the apostle of peace, Jean Jaurès. It was announced that the CGT and the socialists would join in a huge antiwar meeting on August 9, but the movement toward war was accelerating. Mobilization was initiated in Germany. Even as *La Bataille Syndicaliste* proclaimed the CGT's opposition to the war, Jouhaux was already acquiescing. At the bier of Jaurès, the CGT leader declared that the French workers, who never had wanted war, were ready to punish the "bloody despots who had unleashed it." The French workers were to be soldiers of liberty.[7] As Jouhaux was preparing the way for cooperation with the state, Louis Malvy, the minister of the interior, had, probably with the government's approval, refused to carry out the orders of the minister of war, Messimy, to use the Carnet B. By not arresting the three thousand syndicalists on the list, the government apparently hoped to indicate its confidence in the working class, a confidence that was surely not ill-advised.[8]

By August 3 Germany had declared war on France. *La Bataille Syndicaliste* wrote: "The irreparable is now done . . . it's atrocious. It's unbelievable. But there it is."[9] And on August 4, as the National Assembly heard the call for the Union Sacrée of all classes, all parties, the syndicalist newspaper stated, "In the face of the rule of the mailed fist, we must save the democratic and revolutionary tradition of France."[10] Within a few days, workers and fonctionnaires alike were mobilized for battle. Class warfare was to be forgotten. All headed for the front: "Without a word, without a gesture, without a regret, they left for the border where the winds of death awaited them."[11]

6. AP, BA 1438, July 30, 1914.

7. Picard, *Le Mouvement syndical durant la guerre*, 48.

8. Malvy's instructions to the prefects read: "Don't apply the strict instructions of Carnet B completely even in case of mobilization. The current attitude of syndicalists allows us to be confident in those who have been drafted. Use only a careful but discreet surveillance of them" (Edouard Dolléans, *Histoire du mouvement ouvrier* [3 vols.; Paris, 1968], II, 216). Actually a number of syndicalists were arrested in the north, and during the war there were other arrests.

9. Annie Kriegel and Jean-Jacques Becker, *La Guerre et le mouvement ouvrier français* (Paris, 1964), 133.

10. Maitron and Chambelland, *Syndicalisme révolutionnaire*, 17.

11. *L'Humanité*, August 10, 1914, quoted in Kriegel and Becker, *La Guerre*, 150.

The CGT's adherence to the Union Sacrée has been defended by Jouhaux and others: the German unions would not cooperate, there was fear of government repression, there was no choice, mobilization came too soon. Merrheim gives perhaps the most cogent explanation. The leader of the metalworkers, disapproving of Jouhaux's wartime devotion to the Union Sacrée, nevertheless agreed that a general strike had not been possible in August, 1914: "At that moment, the working class, aroused by an incredible burst of nationalism, would not have left it to the representatives of the public powers to shoot us, they would have shot us themselves." The young soldiers—workers, peasants, fonctionnaires, bourgeoisie—rushed to the front lines, bursting with *élan vital.* The CGT militant Péricat poignantly described the frustration of the antimilitarists as they moved toward the front: "How is it possible that I, an antipatriot, an antimilitarist, I who acknowledge only the International, that I would go as far as firing on my comrades in poverty and perhaps to die fighting against my own cause, my own self-interests, for the benefit of my enemies?"[12]

But even as the Union Sacrée was sealed and the soldiers enthusiastically streamed to the front, a small core of militants continued to oppose this most abominable war. Isolated at first, this tiny group of *minoritaires* was to grow in strength as the war stretched endlessly and the casualty lists lengthened. Eventually, those who had flocked to the Union Sacrée would have to defend themselves before the working class. But much suffering would occur before the war could be discredited.

In the chaos of mobilization and siege—the war had moved quickly into French territory—syndicalist activity among blue-collar workers and fonctionnaires alike was suspended. During the last months of 1914, syndicat membership plummeted and meetings were practically nonexistent. In July, 1914, 109 strikes had been recorded. Between August and December, there were only 17 strikes, involving fewer than one thousand workers, mostly in the textile industry, which suffered from severely depressed wages.[13] Marie Guillot, an institutrice from Saône-et-Loire and a militant in the teachers' syndicat, wrote to Pierre Monatte on October 15: "The thing that terrifies me more than all the carnage is

12. Dolléans, *Mouvement ouvrier,* II, 222.
13. Picard, *Le Mouvement syndical durant la guerre,* 104.

the tide of hate which is rising higher and higher and which deflects the workers' efforts from their goal."[14] She had hopes, however, that the syndicat militants would soon come to their senses; syndicat membership had remained strong in their local.

By early 1915, it became obvious to both blue-collar workers and fonctionnaires that organizational activity would have to be resumed. Working conditions had deteriorated rapidly for those in both private industry and government service. Gone was the eight-hour day; everyone was expected to work harder and harder. In many government services, vacations and weekly days off were eliminated, health and sanitation forgotten. In critical areas such as railroads, metalwork and munitions, a quasi-military regime was instituted. Some railroad lines and many factories were put under direct military command.[15] Food prices rose rapidly, but there were no wage increases. Women who replaced men sent to the front received only a fraction of the wages the men had received, and many, especially those in munitions factories, worked under extremely unhealthy and dangerous conditions.[16] The victims of war had to be cared for. Pensions for the wounded, the widowed, and the orphaned and aid for those whose homes had been destroyed had to be organized. The CGT distributed aid to widows and orphans. In July, 1915, a delegation of metalworkers was told by the minister of war, Millerand, "There are no longer any workers' rights, no longer any social laws; there is only the war."[17]

May 1, 1915, is generally regarded as the date of the rebirth of syndicalist activity and propaganda. On this day of commemoration of working-class solidarity, a few organizations managed to uphold the tradition of celebration with work stoppages; the Parisian *terrassiers,* for example, ceased working despite the threats of the military. But the majority of syndicats used this opportunity to publish appeals to workers

14. Maitron and Chambelland, *Syndicalisme révolutionnaire,* 26–27.

15. Picard, *Le Mouvement syndical durant la guerre,* 79.

16. The employment of women rose from 199,000 in August, 1914 (a low figure for the prewar period), to 400,000 in July, 1915, and to 626,881 in July, 1917 (Picard, *Le Mouvement syndical durant la guerre,* 99). Of particular significance was the increase in female employment in metallurgy. By November, 1917, of the 1.7 million metallurgy workers, 430,000 were women (Mathilde Dubesset, François Thebaud, and Catherine Vincent, "Les Munitionnettes de la Seine," in Patrick Fridenson [ed.], *1914–1918: L'Autre front* [Paris, 1977], 195).

17. Dolléans, *Mouvement ouvrier,* II, 229.

and to state syndicalist positions on working conditions and the war. On this May 1, Merrheim's federation began once again the publication of the newspaper *L'Union des Métaux*. In this first issue since the outbreak of hostilities, the metallurgists not only criticized the CGT's total support of the Union Sacrée, they also chastised the government's repression of syndicalist activity and reproached the employers for using the opportunity of war to lower the wages of metalworkers.[18]

Even before May 1, fonctionnaires had begun to rekindle their organizational activity. In January, 1915, the *Bulletin Officiel de l'Association Générale des Agents des PTT* once again appeared. Explaining that circumstances forced them to publish only irregularly, the association leaders pledged to issue the *Bulletin* when they could, to defend the rights of agents, and to work for the maintenance of the postal service despite the massive mobilization of postal workers. The first issue was concerned largely with maintenance of service and equipment under difficult conditions. By the next issue (March), there was talk about regrouping around the Association Générale and rebuilding its strength. Maintenance of advancement for mobilized fonctionnaires was also discussed, an issue that was to be raised frequently during the war. Three other issues of the *Bulletin* appeared in 1915; their main concern was with aid for mobilized soldiers, suffering families, and war wounded, who were returning to the postal service. Each issue carried its list of dead.[19] By March, 1916, the *Bulletin* was able to announce that the creation of a central bureau was almost complete; the Association Générale was back in action.

Among the sous-agents, a provisional council had been organized by March, 1915, and in May, the syndicat's newspaper *Le Cri Postal* had resumed publication.[20] The first issue of the *Cri* gave its reason for appearing: "[*Le Cri*] must circulate everywhere to disconcert our adversaries who have not disarmed and who are still trying to smash the syndicalist organization."[21] The syndicalist postiers immediately dealt with the issue of who was being sent to the front; some sous-agents felt that they were being mobilized more rapidly and in larger numbers than

18. *Ibid.*, 230; Picard, *Le Mouvement syndical durant la guerre*, 81–82.
19. *Bulletin de l'AG*, January, June, September, December, 1915.
20. AP, BA 1438.
21. *La Bataille Syndicaliste*, April 5, 1915.

the agents. At a July meeting, several speakers accused the War Department of sacrificing only workers, peasants, and lay teachers and asked whether the ministry was tied to Action Française. The August issue of Le Cri was censored by the government. In October, Jouhaux, addressing a meeting of six hundred sous-agents, many of them in military uniforms, told the fonctionnaires that their syndicat must not be forgotten, even in time of war.[22] By the end of 1915, the syndicat council reported growth in membership. Bordérès told the council that the syndicat of sous-agents would be in the first rank in the fight against any reactionary or imperialist movements.[23]

Despite its commitment to the CGT in the name of the Union Sacrée, the government still refused to recognize the fonctionnaire syndicats. In 1915, it would not even permit representatives of syndicats to participate in personnel policy decisions, including those involving the now common placement of war wounded, decisions that were supposed to be made by cooperative committees representing both the state and the employees. In December, 1915, Le Cri Postal published a letter of complaint written by a group of postal workers at the front. The issue of the Cri with the letter was suppressed by the censor, but the sous-agents quickly put out a second edition of the newspaper, defiantly including the offending letter under the headline "Our Doughboys Protest." What was the meaning of the Union Sacrée, the letter asked, if the true representatives of the sous-agents could be replaced by those who did not serve their interests? (The government had appointed nonsyndicat worker representatives to the committee.) At the front, there was no distinction between syndiqué and non-syndiqué; all were Frenchmen saving their country from a barbarous invasion. They demanded to be represented at home by their chosen leaders, representatives of the syndicats.[24]

For the blue-collar workers of the PTT, the main issue in 1915 was the loss of their hard-won eight-hour day. In early February, a meeting of 150 workers, angry about an administrative circular that preserved the wartime ten-hour day, was addressed by the secretary-general of their

22. AP, BA 1438, October 18, 1915.
23. AN, F7 13803, November 15, 1915.
24. Le Cri Postal, December 4, 1915.

syndicat, André Dutailly. Scarcely a year before, the same speaker, a CGT militant, had called for a general strike against the war.[25] Now Dutailly told the blue-collar fonctionnaires that German social democracy had failed in its duty to the working class by not joining the struggle against the war; it was thus the duty of the French working class to fight against German militarism. It was not for the preservation of the present bourgeois Republic that they were fighting but for the république sociale, which would surely come to pass after the war. The workers made it clear that they were willing to do their duty, even if it meant working long hours, but they insisted on the principle of the eight-hour day.[26]

By the summer, feeling had intensified among the blue-collar workers of the PTT that the government was taking advantage of linesmen and other workers, who, despite the mobilization, were doing extraordinary service for the government by keeping telephone lines repaired and running. There were reports that several linesmen who had complained about working conditions had been fired. It was clear that the syndicat was needed to maintain decent working conditions. The long-awaited announcement of government amnesty for those who still remained discharged from service for their activity in the 1909 strike eased the tension somewhat, but even that government decision was seen as a victory for the syndicat and yet another reason to support that organization.[27]

With most of the men mobilized—by 1915, twenty-five thousand male teachers had been drafted and replaced by women—the teachers' organizations floundered.[28] It was to be the women, the institutrices, who would emerge as the wartime leaders of the teachers' syndicat. For the first year of the war, Fernand Loriot and the syndicalist women—Marie Guillot, Marie Mayoux, Hélène Brion, Julia Bertrand, and Gabrielle Bouët—managed to hold the syndicat together and keep publishing L'Ecole Emancipée, now heavily censored by the government and forced to change its format and its name to the less provocative L'Ecole

25. AP, BA 1436, report of March 15, 1914.
26. AN, F7 13803, February 1, 1915.
27. Ibid., August 29, September 10, 1915. Eventually, in December 1915, even the 1906 strikers were granted amnesty.
28. Persis Charles Hunt, "Revolutionary Syndicalism and Feminism among Teachers in France, 1900–1921" (Ph.D. dissertation, Tufts University, 1975), 196.

de la Fédération. It was forbidden to print anything connected with peace; issue after issue appeared with huge gaps; whole pages except for the ever-present casualty lists were often blank. Almost from the beginning, these syndicalist teachers attached themselves to the peace movement; Marie Guillot, Marie Mayoux, and Julia Bertrand were in frequent contact with the minority leaders of the CGT and the SFIO—Pierre Monatte, Alfred Rosmer, Merrheim, and the Fédération des Métaux.[29] Through the initiative of Marie Mayoux, teachers who wanted to take a stand against the continuation of the war met at Tours on June 15, 1915. Although Hélène Brion, representing the governing committee of the teachers' union, was in favor of continuing the war until the victory of the Allies was complete, the "pacifist" position was upheld. The question was, considering the repression of syndicat and pacifist activity, how they could be most effective in making their position known. Within two weeks there appeared a manifesto, edited by Marie Mayoux and signed by the syndicats of Charente and Bouches-du-Rhône and a few individuals. The manifesto called for an immediate end to the war:

> Organized teachers and syndicalists, members of the great family of French and worldwide workers, we believe we must publish our opinion of the present situation.
> Enough spilled blood. Our deep-seated and profound conviction is that at present a peace proposal could be humanely offered by any of the adversaries, but that this gesture would bring great honor particularly to the Allies.
> Because this war has no meaning, if it isn't a conscious revolt by free men against barbarous militarism.
> France must conclude its defense action with a frank and open peace offer to end the butchery. Such an act would be to France's eternal honor.
> We consider that the foundations of peace must be the following:
> 1. Freedom of the people of the world to decide their destiny for themselves.
> 2. General disarmament by obligatory arbitration.[30]

At first, the federal bureau of the syndicat, considering the manifesto too strong, refused its support, but at a small congress held at Paris on

29. See letters of Monatte and Rosmer in Maitron and Chambelland, *Syndicalisme révolutionnaire.*

30. Max Ferré, *Histoire du mouvement syndicaliste révolutionnaire chez les instituteurs* (Paris, 1955), 176.

August 14, Brion and Loriot came over to the pacifist side, and the teachers' syndicat officially took a stand in favor of the resumption of international relations and for peace.[31] Thus Loriot was able to go to the conference of bourses, unions, and federations which had been called by the CGT for the next day and support the resolution presented by Merrheim and Albert Bourderon, which began with the words they had uttered a year before, "This war is not our war." The peace resolution, supported only by the federations of teachers, barrelmakers, hatmakers, ceramics makers, brushmakers and, of course, the metalworkers, whose leader, Merrheim, was rapidly becoming the main syndicalist voice for the antiwar forces, was defeated. Within a few weeks, Merrheim and Bourderon were on their way to Switzerland to take part in the international conference at Zimmerwald. Marie Mayoux, who had already met with the international socialist women at Berne in early March, was refused a passport to leave France and was thus unable to take part in the Zimmerwald meeting.

The efforts of the *minoritaires* (minority) were brave, but this small group did not represent more than a handful of syndicat members in France. As 1915 drew to a close, though the minoritaires were beginning to gather strength, most workers and fonctionnaires, though anxious to keep their syndicats alive, still supported the war and the Union Sacrée.

If for the first two years of the war, the fonctionnaires were proud to be doing their part in defending civilization against the *boches,* by 1916, the situation had changed. A few days before the beginning of the new year, Joseph Gallieni, the recently appointed war minister, had told the Senate: "Eighteen months ago France wanted peace for herself and others. Today she wants war. . . . This great struggle will be ended only when France, in accord with its allies, says, 'I have obtained full satisfaction. I will cease fighting and resume the work of peace.'" Above the applause of the senators could be heard the voice of Clemenceau shouting, "jusqu'au bout!" (to the bitter end). But 1916 would only bring more hardship and more casualties. For most of the year, the battle of Verdun raged, the "victory" that literally drained the blood of a genera-

---

31. Rosmer wrote to Monatte that he was pleased with the teachers' declaration, even if it was a bit "lukewarm"; it would attract attention (Maitron and Chambelland, *Syndicalisme révolutionnaire,* 180).

tion of Frenchmen. While the battle dragged on, yet another meeting of the Socialist International was held in Switzerland. The one at Zimmerwald had been attended only by Merrheim and Bourderon of the CGT; this time, in April, 1916, several French socialist deputies, including Pierre Laval, joined an even larger number of German socialists at Kienthal. A resolution calling for an immediate peace without annexations and without indemnities issued from this historic meeting: "Neither victors, nor vanquished, or more likely all vanquished, all exhausted; such will be the result of this insane war."[32]

But it was not just the casualties that disturbed the workers and fonctionnaires who were keeping the factories and the state apparatus functioning. While their brothers were living "the hell of Verdun," while war profiteers were amassing fortunes, the standard of living was falling rapidly for most French workers. Prices were rising rapidly—the cost of food and housing hit workers the hardest—and salaries did not keep pace. Indeed, in 1915, salaries were lowered in some industries. For most of 1915, miners, whose workday had been lengthened considerably, were still earning the same five francs a day they had received in 1914—the wage index for miners in 1915 was 89 based on an index of 100 for 1914—and in the textile industry, the workers, mostly female, were receiving in 1916 a bit more than half their 1914 wages.[33]

Slowly the workers turned to their syndicats; the CGT began to regain its prewar strength. There are no official statistics for CGT membership during the war. With so many men mobilized, it was difficult to keep membership figures. But finance reports issued by the CGT give some idea of its growth. In 1914, the federations took 2.5 million *timbres* (membership stamps) from the central office. In 1915, that number had fallen to only five hundred thousand. By 1916, the figure went over 1 million, and by 1917 it had surpassed the 1914 figure to reach 3 million. By 1918, the number of *timbres* was up to an amazing 6 million.[34] Of particular import was the growth in CGT membership in building, railroads, and metallurgy, critical industries from which many workers had not been sent to the front.

32. Jacques Chastenet, *Histoire de la troisième république, 1906–1918* (Paris, 1957), 247–48, 255.

33. The wage statistics are from Picard, *Le Mouvement syndical durant la guerre*, 113.

34. *Ibid.*, 88. These figures do not represent actual membership, but the growth pattern is obvious.

More significantly, the number of strikes also began to rise in 1916. In 1915, there had been only 98 strikes involving nine thousand workers. In 1916, more than forty thousand workers were involved in 314 strikes, and this figure would pale when compared to those of 1917.[35] The government was most concerned about strikes in the critical war industries in which the number of women workers had increased dramatically. Agitation over wages had been building. For example, at a meeting of the syndicat of the *cartoucherie* of Valence at the end of 1915 an audience of 60 men and 150 women nodded agreement when a speaker told them that the military commander who had proposed a wage reduction had no concern about workers starving to death at this moment when the cost of living was rising at an alarming rate.[36] The government managed to keep the situation under control until the end of 1916, when suddenly a series of strikes erupted.

On November 6, fourteen hundred munitions workers at Wilcoq-Regnault struck when there was a proposal to lower wages from eight francs a day to six francs fifty for women and from ten francs a day to eight francs fifty for men. The minister of armaments intervened, promised to maintain the wages, and the strike ended. At the end of December, two thousand workers, of whom eleven hundred were women, struck Panhard-Lavassor. This strike received much publicity as the left-wing press used the opportunity to attack the enormous profits being amassed by armaments producers and, in this case, automobile manufacturers, who had transformed their production lines to manufacture shells, while the right-wing press spoke of "strikes against the Fatherland." Once again the minister had to intervene; there was a minimal wage increase, but production was maintained at the same rapid pace the workers had complained about.[37] In 1917 such a deluge of strikes occurred that the minister of armaments had to issue regulations on salaries and arbitration in case of salary disputes. The regulations did not prevent the enormous outbreak of strikes that summer.

Fonctionnaires suffered particularly from the rise in the cost of living. Workers in private industry could, by threatening a strike or some other

35. *Ibid.*, 105.
36. AN, F7 13739, report of Commissaire Spécial de Valence to the Prefect of the Drôme, September 6, 1915.
37. Picard, *Le Mouvement syndical durant la guerre*, 109-10.

action, force some improvement in their wages. Fonctionnaires' salaries, determined by the legislature upon recommendation of the government, were to remain nearly stagnant throughout the 1914–1918 period as the government, asserting that the war had top priority, showed little concern for the wages of state workers. By the summer of 1916, the fonctionnaires could no longer be told about their patriotic duty; they wanted more money. Moreover, there was talk once again of the droit syndical. There were numerous rumblings in the Association Générale des Agents about the high cost of living, but it was the syndicat of the sous-agents—the association was just about finished—who began seriously to pressure the government for more money. Twelve hundred postiers attended a meeting in April and complained about the use of military replacements (*vaguemestres*) for postmen sent to the front, as well as the cost of living. It was noted at that meeting that because of these and other difficulties, their devotion to the CGT was more important than ever.[38] The leader of the syndicat of sous-agents, Bordérès, who stood with Jouhaux and the *majoritaires* (majority), nevertheless was disturbed enough by the rise in the cost of living to tell a Paris meeting in July that the fault for this dismal situation lay with the government and the elected representatives of the Socialist party, who were failing in their duty; they should be taxing profiteers and requisitioning the necessities of life for the working population. To the contrary, he charged, the government was favoring the "hoarders," who were growing richer and richer. The German government was actually doing a better job. Later in July, a special report on the cost of living was sent by the syndicat on behalf of its twelve thousand members to the government.[39]

In August, at a council meeting, the notion of a strike was rejected; it was decided to try to reach the public with their demands. On August 20, a huge meeting attended by more than two thousand postiers was held in Paris. Bordérès, addressing the meeting, stated that the fonctionnaires appeared to have more duties than rights. Two important resolutions were voted: one for an immediate indemnity of two hundred

38. AP, BA 1438 and *L'Humanité*, April 3, 1916. It is difficult to get the sense of this meeting because much of the article reporting the event had gaps where the censor had done his careful duty. The police agent covered the meeting as well, and I was able to piece together the information from the two sources.

39. AN, F7 13803.

francs to offset the rise in the cost of living, the other for the droit syndical. In this time of crisis, when thousands of postal workers were sacrificing themselves at home and at the front and the CGT was working in collaboration with the government as part of the Union Sacrée, it was unacceptable that only the sous-agents, because of their position as fonctionnaires, were excluded from the rights granted to other members of the CGT.[40]

Throughout the fall, fonctionnaires of numerous ministries, including education, continued to meet to discuss these two issues. By October, there was evidence of the continuing formation of a minoritaire position within the CGT; the CGT was not doing enough to promote international meetings and peace. At a large meeting in December, leaders of the sous-agents attacked the CGT and the SFIO for abandoning the workers and for not pressing hard enough for salary increases and other improvements in working conditions. The alliance with the government was defended by Bordérès and the Socialist deputy Pierre Laval, who urged the postiers to unite so they would be able to press their demands after the war. Laval recognized the financial problems faced by the sous-agents; he supported the fonctionnaires of Paris who had refused to pay their rapidly increasing rents.[41] A few days later, the syndicat of the sous-agents voted confidence in the CGT, but five members of the eighteen-man council voted negatively and two abstained.[42]

Even the fonctionnaires of the Administrations Centrales began to move. In December, 1916, more than five hundred came to a meeting organized by the fonctionnaires of the Ministry of Finance to demand an indemnity similar to the one granted the railroad workers.[43] A leader of the Caisse des Dépôts told the meeting: "Whereas in commerce and industry, the bosses have agreed to healthy raises, up to now, only the employees of the state have not seen any improvement in their condition. Today they turn toward their 'employer' to ask him for a small sacrifice."[44] At the end of 1916, some municipal workers in Paris and in the suburb of St. Ouen went out on strike.[45]

40. *La Bataille Syndicaliste* and *Le Journal,* August 21, 1916.
41. AN, F7 13803, December 11, 1916.
42. AP, BA 1438.
43. AP, BA 305 provisoire.
44. AN, F7 13726.
45. AN, F7 13933.

The winter of 1916–1917 was a hard one, and the meager worldwide wheat harvest in 1917 intensified the difficulties. Bread was scarce, and prices escalated. In August, 1917, not enough wheat remained to bridge the gap until the autumn harvest; soldiers and civilians alike went hungry. The year 1917 opened with a wave of strikes, which was to intensify during the critical summer and fall. In the month of May alone, nearly one hundred thousand were on strike.[46] By the end of the year, there would be a total of 696 strikes involving three hundred thousand workers.[47]

The war had particularly exacerbated the economic exploitation of women workers. With prices rising and working conditions deteriorating, women workers in textiles, food, and other feminized industries were told by employers making huge profits that demands for higher wages and shorter hours would have to wait until the end of the war. Women working in munitions plants were told that they would be unpatriotic, that they would be hurting their sons and husbands, if they dared demand any improvement in their long hours and dangerous working conditions. Feminists and socialists such as Louise Saumoneau and Mathilde Duchêne and the feminist-syndicalist teachers Marthe Bigot and Marcelle Capy had continuously publicized these wretched conditions in their publications and through organizations like the CGT-sponsored Comité Intersyndical d'Action Contre l'Exploitation de la Femme. Finally, in the late spring and early summer of 1917, a wave of strikes erupted. The working-class movement and the entire country were stunned by the enormity and intensity of these totally female actions. Textile workers, dressmakers, trolley conductors, laundry workers, sugar refinery workers, and munitions workers demanded and won more pay and a shorter workweek: Saturday afternoon off (the semaine anglaise), fifty-four hours' work for sixty hours' pay.[48] On the backs of the signs demanding the shorter workweek, there appeared the words, "We want our doughboys" and "Down with war."

46. Georges Frischmann, Histoire de la fédération CGT des PTT (Paris, 1967), 195.

47. Picard, Le Mouvement syndical pendant la guerre. The precise figure given by Picard is 293,810.

48. The strikes are recorded in Fonds Brion 14AS 183 (4), in Institut Français de l'Histoire Social, and in James McMillan, Housewife or Harlot: The Place of Women in French Society, 1870–1940 (New York, 1981), 145–57. A very thorough analysis of the strikes appears in Jean-Louis Robert, "Ouvriers et mouvement ouvrier parisiens pendant la grand guerre et l'immédiate après-guerre" (Thèse du Doctorat d'Etat, Paris I, 1989).

The fonctionnaires continued their agitation for relief from the soaring prices. Letters of protest about the cost of living began to appear in association and syndicat publications.[49] In March, the Association Générale des Agents sent a letter to its minister saying that agents were proud of their wartime efforts but could not live on their salaries, and that same month the first meeting of a new PTT organization formed by auxiliaries of the PTT heard Marcel Cachin support its demands for an indemnity.[50] As the summer approached, more and more mass meetings were held to pressure the government into action. On June 10, twelve hundred line workers attended a meeting at the Bourse du Travail. Later that afternoon, douaniers and employees of the Contributions Indirectes joined postal workers at a meeting called by the syndicat of sous-agents. A crowd of fifteen hundred filled the Bourse to hear calls for wage increases and for an immediate indemnity to help relieve the economic difficulties suffered by all fonctionnaires. The fonctionnaires were particularly incensed at the government's failure to grant a proper indemnity because private companies, notably in transportation, had been obliged by the same government to grant indemnities. All state employees would soon unite to force these increases, Métayer of the douaniers predicted.[51] At another meeting, one thousand agents, half of them women, heard one of their leaders proclaim: "This same government demands that the low-level fonctionnaires pay their rent [there had been a movement among Parisian fonctionnaires not to pay their rent], even though it is materially impossible to live. The people are tired of being exploited and since the government, in agreement with the big financiers, does nothing for the little people, these people have decided finally to make their voices heard."[52]

In April, the legislature had allowed a temporary daily indemnity—the government called it a supplement—of one franc to one franc fifty per day with a family allowance of one hundred to two hundred francs a year for children under sixteen. But the fonctionnaires had asked for three francs a day, and as the summer wore on, it was clear that the government's indemnity was not nearly enough. In fact, during the entire war period, real wages for all workers remained consistently below the

49. *Bulletin de l'AG,* 1917.
50. AN, F7 13804, meeting of March 16, 1917.
51. AN, F7 13803.
52. AN, F7 13804, July 2, 1917.

1914 level. It was not until 1921, when there was a brief respite of lower prices before unemployment depressed wages, that the 1914 levels were once again attained.[53]

In May and June of 1917, even the fonctionnaires joined the strike movement. In late May, two thousand female employees, mostly temporary auxiliaries of the Ministry of Finance, staged a victorious twenty-four-hour strike, and a few days later a group of young telegraph workers in Paris, mostly boys, refused to report to work. Promised a cost-of-living indemnity and the opportunity for advancement, they returned to work after two days, but not before they had declared themselves ready to join a syndicat.[54] Brief walkouts occurred among PTT employees at Tours and Bordeaux as well as the Central Militaire in Paris.[55]

It was not just the rising cost of living that distressed fonctionnaires and blue-collar workers. The war was dragging on, with more and more men being sent to the front to live and die amid unbearable filth and destruction. In the spring of 1917, the much heralded Nivelle offensive failed; morale in the armed forces and at home tumbled. The summer brought a wave of antiwar protests in the army. Soldiers returning from leave cried out against the war from the windows of the trains carrying them back to the front. When the military police surged onto the platforms and trains in town after town, they found bits of tissue paper, some printed, some handwritten in the careful penmanship common to women of the period: "Women want peace and their rights." "Soldiers on leave. Your wives and your children cry out to you. Don't go back to the front where a stupid death awaits you."[56] There were mutinies, brutally suppressed, at the front.[57]

The pacifist position began to gather strength. The government, wary of all syndicalist activity and quick to react to any talk of social revolution or peace, which the government called defeatism, had kept a

53. Picard, *Le Mouvement syndical durant la guerre*, 114.
54. AN, F7 13933; Frischmann, *Histoire PTT*, 196.
55. AN, F7 13933, Bordeaux, June 17, and Tours, July 20. No date is given for the Paris strike, but it appears to have been in May or June. There were probably other work stoppages; police reports mention trouble in Lyons in June and in Marseilles in October, but data from the provinces are too scarce to report any solid information (AN, F7 13803).
56. AN, F7 13370.
57. See Guy Pedroncini, *Les Mutineries de 1917* (Paris, 1967).

careful watch on all militants, meetings, and publications. The former minister of the interior, Malvy, stated that there was also a "red book" made up of special reports sent directly to the chief of the police intelligence, the Sureté, by the prefects of each department.[58] Newspapers were frequently censored or banned, meetings prohibited, and militants imprisoned or restricted in their movement.[59]

As in the prewar period, the government paid particular attention to the teachers. From the moment of the outbreak of hostilities, the syndicalist teachers had been in the center of propeace activity. In 1917, this activity intensified. In May, the Charente section of the teachers' syndicat published a sixteen-page tract, signed by Marie and François Mayoux. Called *Les Instituteurs syndicalistes et la guerre,* it echoed in stronger terms the manifesto of 1915. Throughout 1917, pacifist tracts and letters were circulated to teachers on all levels. From école maternelle to lycée, teachers passed around statements like the one found at the Lycée Edgar Quinet, which began, "Enough dead: Peace!"[60]

Amid accusations that even the children were spying on their teachers—certainly the government was—hosts of teachers had been fired or otherwise punished for their pacifist views. Now the government decided to take even stronger action against the newest defeatist propaganda. The Mayoux were condemned to prison for a term of two years. Hélène Brion, the feminist-pacifist member of the central bureau of the syndicat, was arrested. Campaigns were initiated to raise money for the Mayoux and to have Brion released. A letter signed by syndicalist teachers, including Marthe Bigot, secretary of the Fédération Féministe Universitaire, attacked the government and the newspapers, which, without justification, accused Hélène Brion of being defeatist. Brion, they stated, was not a defeatist; there were no defeatist teachers. Teachers, whose colleagues were dying on the field of battle, had only the future of their country at heart.[61]

By this time, many of the syndicalist institutrices were attached not

58. Louis Malvy, *Mon Crime,* 85, quoted in Picard, *Le Mouvement syndical durant la guerre,* 147.

59. In the midst of a war and manpower shortage, the Ministry of the Interior could manage to spare enough men to cover every syndicat meeting, no matter how small.

60. AN, F7 13743.

61. AN, F7 13743, letter of February, 1918.

only to the antiwar movement among syndicalists but to feminist peace groups as well. Brion and Marthe Bigot joined the feminist lycée professors Jeanne Halbwachs and Madeleine Rolland as well as Mathilde Duchêne, creator of the 1915 pacifist tract *Un Devoir pour les femmes,* in the Section Française du Comité International pour la Paix Permanente, the organization started by, among others, Jane Addams of the United States, which became, after the war, the Women's International League for Peace and Freedom. Brion's trial, begun in March, 1918, brought dozens of feminists and syndicalists to testify on her behalf. She was convicted but given a suspended sentence.[62]

Syndicats of blue-collar workers and fonctionnaire organizations from all over France expressed their outrage at the treatment of the teachers. From Marseilles, from the Cantal, from Orléans, from Le Havre, from Rochefort, came statements of support for Brion and the others. In February, 1918, the Fédération des Syndicats des Instituteurs et Institutrices sent a direct appeal to the CGT. Once again the syndicalist teachers were victims of government repression, the appeal began. But it was not just their little federation that the government wanted to break, "it's the secular school, the entire working class, it's the republican idea itself" that was under attack. Having adhered to the CGT with all their hearts to safeguard working-class solidarity, the teachers now called on the CGT to join in the resistance against the government's attacks on their syndicats and their activists.[63]

Jouhaux responded positively to the teachers' appeal. Copies of their letter, sent to each member federation and the Bourse, were accompanied by a letter from Jouhaux himself, asking for support for the

---

62. A note on the chanciness of finding historical evidence: When researching Hélène Brion for a paper on French feminist-pacifists I gave at the Berkshire Women's History Conference in 1984, I went to Paris to see the Brion files at the Bibliothèque Marguerite Durand. The archive included a rare printed résumé of the trial (*Le Defaitisme et les defaitistes: Le procès Hélène Brion et Mouflard*). I spent several hours taking careful notes and photocopying important sections. One week later, at the lesser flea market near the CGT headquarters at Montreuil, I spied a battered copy of the same pamphlet lying on a ratty blanket. The seller was amazed that anyone would want such a thing, and I was able, in true French fashion, to bargain him down from five francs to three. Brion's feminism is discussed briefly in Huguette Bouchardeau, *Hélène Brion, la voie féministe* (Paris, 1978). For a more detailed analysis of the pacifist-feminist movement, see Judith Wishnia, "Feminism and Pacifism: The French Connection," in Ruth Roach Pierson (ed.), *Women and Peace: Theoretical, Historical and Practical Perspectives* (New York, 1987).

63. AN, F7 13743.

teachers in the name of working-class solidarity. In spite of existing political differences, it was necessary to defend the liberties of the syndicats. In March, when the government arrested Loriot, a leader of the teachers' syndicat, because it was suspicious of his political activity, the central committee, protesting the government's treatment of the teachers, issued a formal statement of solidarity.[64]

The persecution of militant syndicalist teachers was to continue even as the war was drawing to a close. The teachers had planned to hold their annual congress on August 3, 1918. The government had arbitrarily forbidden the 1916 and 1917 congresses, but in 1918 there was no indication that the congress would be banned. All other fonctionnaires, including the syndicat of sous-agents, had held congresses during the summer, and the teachers had received no official notice from the government. Then on the morning of the congress, as the delegates, among them Jouhaux, entered the Impasse Chaudron, which led to the Maison des Syndicats, they were met by a cordon of police who refused to let them enter the building.[65] The government, in a surprise move, had decided to ban the congress. The teachers, joined by the recently released Hélène Brion, held their congress in a local restaurant. The CGT issued a formal protest—Jouhaux wrote an article for La Bataille (the wartime replacement for La Bataille Syndicaliste)—as did the Ligue Pour la Défense des Droits de l'Homme et du Citoyen. On November 4, 1918, there was a call for a general amnesty for all teachers who had been arrested or fired for their syndicalist activities which stressed that the German socialist leader Karl Liebknecht had been released by the German government. Was France less democratic?[66]

Blue-collar and CGT support for the teachers during the winter of 1917–1918 reflected changing attitudes among the syndicalists in the CGT. Of primary importance was the gradual shifting of policy toward the war. In the beginning, Merrheim, Bourderon, and a handful of

---

64. Ibid.

65. The home of the CGT, the Maison des Syndicats, was situated officially on rue de la Granges-aux-Belles, but the entrance is set back in a passageway. It is a small building, especially when compared with the newly built center in Montreuil.

66. AN, F7 13743. Marie Mayoux was not released until April, 1919, and François Mayoux had to wait until November, 1919, one year after the end of the war. For a description of their activities and trial, see Marie Mayoux and François Mayoux, Notre Affaire (Epône, 1918). The campaign for their release is outlined in various issues of l'Ecole Emancipée of 1918–1919.

other minoritaires had stood dangerously alone; Jouhaux and the majoritaires considered the war effort more important than the corporative interests of the working class. The confederation leadership, as a matter of principle, had attended no international peace conferences. By the summer of 1917, however, when the Swiss syndicalists invited the CGT to send delegates to an international workers' conference for peace to be held in Berne, the CGT council decided to attend. The government, worried about the renewal of international relations with an "official" delegation from France in attendance, refused to grant passports. The CGT protested: "With this refusal, the government indicates that it suspects the intentions and actions of delegates properly designated by the syndicalist organizations, that by doing this, they are attacking the dignity of the workers without considering the enormous sacrifices made by them since August 1914." [67] The government also refused to allow the CGT to attend a joint syndicalist-socialist conference to be held in Stockholm, which never did take place. During the entire war, no official CGT delegation attended any of the international working-class peace conferences attended by delegates from non-Allied nations.

In the fall of 1917, two events further influenced the shifting positions in the CGT. One was the assumption of executive power by the old enemy of the syndicalists, Clemenceau; the other was the Russian Revolution. The shadows of both Lenin and le tigre lay over the CGT congress of December, 1917, held at Clermont-Ferrand. The minoritaires saw in the Russian Revolution a real hope for peace, yet they worried that the new Russian government might make a separate peace agreement that would jeopardize the stated objectives of no reparations and no annexations. The majoritaires were more anxious than ever to press for international accord on ending the war, yet they did not wish to antagonize Clemenceau or endanger the Union Sacrée. The minoritaires read a resolution urging the CGT to reaffirm its independence and to break from the Union Sacrée to continue the class struggle. Profound support for the Russian revolutionaries was reaffirmed. But to preserve the unity of the CGT against Clemenceau, the minoritaires joined the majoritaires in unanimously accepting a peace resolution which declared that the formulas of Wilson and Lenin—no annexation, the right to self-

67. Picard, *Le Mouvement syndical durant la guerre,* 144.

determination, no economic reprisals, obligatory arbitration of international disputes, and the creation of a society of nations—had always been the principles of the working class.[68] Another motion, calling for an end to secret diplomacy, was also passed.[69] The CGT had finally adopted, as Merrheim correctly reminded the delegates, the original 1915 resolutions of Zimmerwald—"no annexations, no punishments."

The changing attitude toward the war was not the only indication of shifting positions within the working class and the CGT. The prolongation of the slaughter, the deterioration of the standard of living, the continued repression of syndicalist activity, and the realization that while workers were starving and dying, rapacious *accapareurs* (hoarders) and "ordinary" capitalists were, often with government support, reaping huge profits from the war, weakened support for the Union Sacrée. Once more, the workers turned to their syndicats; the Fédération des Métaux alone went from a membership of 18,000 in 1916 to 204,280 by the end of 1918.[70] Increasingly, the strikes, which in 1916 and early 1917 had revolved around economic demands, began to take on the character of dissatisfaction with the war, with the government, and with the social structure. In the spring of 1918, yet another gigantic wave of strikes began, the largest of which was the wildcat strike of 180,000 metalworkers. These strikes were further indication of the dissatisfaction with salaries, working conditions, and the government's handling of the working class and the war. When the metalworkers' strike ended, many of the leaders were punished by being fired or sent to the front.

For many workers, the class struggle, temporarily shelved by the policies of Jouhaux in 1914, had never disappeared; Jouhaux's majoritaire position of collaboration with the state was no longer tenable. But revolutionary syndicalism, having lost much of its strength before 1914, had been further weakened by the war and the Russian Revolution. Increasingly, the working-class movement was shifting toward new alignments—the class collaboration of Jouhaux and the majority socialists or the revolutionary class warfare of Lenin. These shifting alignments would be the basis for intensifying divisions within the CGT after the war and would lead eventually to the great schism of 1921.

68. Dolléans, *Mouvement ouvrier*, II, 270.
69. AN, F7 13743.
70. Picard, *Le Mouvement syndical durant la guerre*, 88.

The fonctionnaires were also deeply affected by the continuation of the war and the deteriorating standard of living. The failure of fonctionnaires' salaries to keep pace with the cost of living further proletarianized the state workers; little remained in the salary structure to distinguish white collar from blue. As the blue-collar workers turned to their syndicats in an effort to maintain their standard of living and fight for improved working conditions, so the fonctionnaires turned to their organizations. But for the fonctionnaires, there were still no legal syndicats; the *droit commun* was still denied to state workers. A 1917 article in *La Bataille* pointed out that the rights permitted all workers in private industry were denied to fonctionnaires. The government had been fearful of the CGT, but that had been before the war. Now with the Union Sacrée, with the sacrifice of so many workers and fonctionnaires, how could the government continue to deny the fonctionnaires their *droit commun?* [71] By the summer of 1917, more and more fonctionnaires began once again to demand the droit syndical. There was no longer thought of returning to the ineffective amicales and associations of the prewar period. Among the PTT employees, the Syndicat des Sous-Agents continued to increase its membership, and by the fall of 1917, the Association Générale des Agents had begun a campaign to turn the association into a syndicat and to demand that the syndicat be made legal. [72] Efforts were made to mend the old Fédération Postale and to unite once again the ouvriers, sous-agents, and agents of the PTT.

Throughout the winter and early spring of 1918, fonctionnaires of all kinds—douaniers, postiers, teachers—held huge meetings to demand a cost-of-living indemnity and the droit syndical. More and more there was talk of joining the working class in the CGT. A speaker at a Marseilles meeting in February told the fonctionnaires that to struggle it was necessary to unite with the working class. Only Clemenceau could benefit from the bourgeois snobbery that separated blue-collar workers from fonctionnaires. The association was for "worker demands"; the syndicat was for "struggle." [73] Quilici wrote in his memoirs, "If now we have in mind joining the CGT, we cannot imagine that it might be forbidden: our sympathies are with the organized working class." [74]

71. *La Bataille,* June 30, 1917.
72. *Bulletin de l'AG,* October, 1917.
73. AN, F7 13803, Canavelli, commis de poste and municipal councillor, February 2, 1918.
74. Quilici memoirs.

In April, meetings were held at Le Havre, St. Etienne, Lyons, and Paris. Jouhaux told the Paris meeting that the fonctionnaires belonged in the CGT. The St. Etienne meeting declared itself "strongly united with all the organized proletariat" and closed its meeting with cries of "Vive le syndicat."[75] The Fédération des Fonctionnaires also began to move.

In the summer, congresses were held. In May, the Association Générale des Agents met at Versailles and passed a motion stating that if by January 1, 1919, a law was not passed giving the fonctionnaires the droit syndical, the Association Générale would automatically become a syndicat.[76] On December 31, 1918, the Association Générale did indeed become a syndicat. In June, while Zeppelins rained their bombs on Paris, the Syndicat National des Sous-Agents held its congress. The backbone of the new Fédération Postale must be the syndicat. An order of the day was passed stating that the sous-agents "send their cordial greeting to the organized working class . . . regret that after four years of war endured under the aegis of the Union Sacrée, government after government have not believed it their duty to end the administrative ostracism which has weighed upon their syndicat since its inception and to grant the droit syndical to all fonctionnaires."[77]

In July, it was the turn of the douaniers. Buteux of the Fédération des Fonctionnaires assured the douaniers that all the important organizations belonging to the federation "will move forward in their march toward the CGT."[78] Prefectural and communal workers also expressed their dissatisfactions and a new militancy. The March issue of the *Bulletin Officiel* of the Union Nationale des Secrétaires et Employés de Mairie, using warlike imagery, published a call to its members: "The hour has come, to pursue to the bitter end, to the final victory, our very legitimate demands. . . . Rise Up activists . . . and others, to defend our bread."[79]

The women fonctionnaires had begun to move toward syndicalist activity as well. The war had upset old patterns. Women were originally hired to replace men at the front, but their numbers were now swelled by war widows, who had suddenly become the heads of their families.

75. AN, F7 13804.
76. Frischmann, *Histoire PTT,* 201.
77. AN, F7 13803.
78. *L'Humanité,* July 4, 1918.
79. AN, F7 13728.

But the government had kept them as auxiliaries, at the lowest pay level, without job security or pension benefits. They had been told by the syndicalist leaders that they must show more interest in the syndicat, but the male-run associations and syndicats had not pushed hard enough for their special needs.[80] The Fédération Féministe Universitaire and the syndicat (not the larger amicale) had pressured the administration to regularize the position of substitute teachers. This was done in 1917. The women jammed the meeting halls, separate feminine sections of syndicats and associations were formed, and the auxiliaries formed their own organizations. A newspaper, La Lutte Féministe, "the rigorously independent and unique voice of feminism," made its appearance. Hélène Brion and other feminist teachers were associated with its publication. In Dijon, fifteen hundred female employees met to demand an indemnity, the semaine anglaise, and sick-pay benefits.[81] In September, the auxiliary agents threatened a strike. Persuaded by the Association Générale to stay at work, not to risk a debacle like that of 1909, and not to let down the men at the front, the women vowed, nevertheless, to do all they could to sabotage the next advancement examinations. In October, the women at the central telegraph office struck briefly and noisily for the indemnity.[82] The women had clearly become a force in the fonctionnaire movement. In the postwar period, women syndicalists would use this strength to press even harder for syndicalist support of their demands for wage parity, improved advancement, and general economic and social equality.

Europe was exhausted; the war was nearing its end. In August, twenty-five hundred postal workers—sous-agents, agents, and ouvriers—united once again, met in Paris; there was talk about the unity of the PTT and the cheminots.[83] Yvetot wrote that syndicalism was the future, and the fonctionnaires know this well.[84] The suffering of the war had yielded its fruits: the organizational unity of the fonctionnaires and the working-class was imminent.

80. AN, F7 13804; see meeting of January 27, 1918, at the Bourse du Travail.
81. AN, F7 13738, August 25, 1918.
82. AN, F7 13804, October 26, 1918.
83. Ibid., August 5, 1918.
84. L'Heure, August 9, 1918.

7

Vive le Syndicat, 1918–1920

After four years of death and deprivation, the French working class
stood ready to press its demands for an improved living standard, for
participation in political and economic decisions, and for the république
social, which had been denied to them in the prewar period. But if the
CGT was now stronger than ever, so was the bourgeoisie. Grown rich
with war profits, more tightly organized into cartels and *comités,* with a
state apparatus more centralized and more capable of aiding financial
and industrial enterprise than ever before, the bourgeoisie was firmly
committed to stopping the CGT from wielding its potential power. The
CGT also faced internal problems. Though the Russian Revolution,
viewed as the first proletarian victory, had been welcomed almost unanimously by the syndicalists, the more "reformist" elements of the CGT
were considerably less enthusiastic about Lenin's soviets than the more
"revolutionary" members of the labor confederation. The creation of
the Third International further dampened the ardor of the reformists
and gave the revolutionaries a focus for their ideological and tactical
struggles. As the "red" revolutions flashed across Europe, the divisions
between those who supported the revolutions and those who wanted to
continue the wartime collaboration with industry and the state continued to deepen. But despite these ideological divisions, the CGT, reformists and revolutionaries alike, was committed to making certain
that the working class would receive the economic and social rewards
that were its due and desperately tried to maintain its tenuous unity.
Throughout the turbulent years 1919 and 1920, the unity held; the CGT
continued to grow at a phenomenal rate.

Even before the war had ended, the CGT had begun to experience
one of the cyclical spurts of growth characteristic of French syndicalist
history. A similar period of growth had occurred in 1906–1910; it was

to be repeated in the era of the Popular Front (1934–1938) and again in the aftermath of World War II (1944–1947). As Annie Kriegel has postulated in her analysis of the CGT's growth, in the period 1918–1920, the CGT increased not only in the number of individual adherents—the membership was officially estimated at over 1 million in 1920, compared to a 1911 estimate of almost seven hundred thousand—but also in the number of syndicats and federations, as well as penetration of syndicat organization out of the commercial and industrial centers into almost every department in France.[1] A more recent study by Jean-Louis Robert makes the growth seem even more impressive because he lowers the prewar estimate to under three hundred thousand in 1914 and raises the 1920 figure to 1.6 million.[2] Although much of this growth was based on the enormous increase in syndicalist membership in such critical industries as metallurgy, railroads, mining, paper, clothing, and textiles, the addition of fonctionnaires, particularly the nearly two hundred thousand PTT employees and teachers, further bolstered the CGT's strength. Riding the crest of increased membership, the CGT further strengthened its position by reorganizing the confederation into federations of industries and departments. Gone was the loose hodgepodge of bourses, local organizations, and small syndicats of *métiers* (trades). These groups continued to exist, but now they had to join a larger industrial or geographic federation in order to belong to the CGT. The reorganized CGT was to be more unified, more centralized, and more representative of the larger syndicats; it would also be more effective.

While the CGT was reorganizing, the rank-and-file workers were pressing for action. The main reason for the workers' dissatisfaction was economic—the cost of living continued to outstrip wages—but there were political reasons for proletarian unrest as well. The government under Clemenceau's authoritarian rule continued its repression of syndicalist and revolutionary activity. The judgment against the former

---

1. The geographic penetration was particularly impressive among metalworkers, printers, building workers, railroad workers, postal workers, and teachers. For a full statistical analysis of this growth and penetration, see Annie Kriegel, *La Croissance de la CGT, 1918–1920* (Paris, 1966). The above paragraph is a brief summary of some of her findings.

2. Jean-Louis Robert and Michel Chavance, "L'Evolution de la syndicalisation en France de 1914 à 1921," *Annales: Economies Sociétés Civilisations*, XXIX (September–October, 1974), 1092–1108. For the fuller statistical analysis, see Jean-Louis Robert, *La Scission syndical de 1921* (Paris, 1980).

minister of the interior, Malvy, for not having been repressive enough against striking or pacifist workers, had severely shaken the Union Sacrée. The majoritaire CGT leaders joined with the minoritaire syndicats of the Seine in protest: "It is with stupefaction and indignation that we have heard the judgment of the high court; a judgment which is an attack on the working class. Four years of sacrifices, of self-sacrifice, gives us the right to claim a clearer understanding of our needs and our aspirations."[3] In March, 1919, the acquittal of Raoul Villain, the assassin of Jaurès, was the occasion for mass demonstrations in Paris. The shock waves of the Russian Revolution only intensified the desire for social change. In the spring of 1919, the collaboration of the CGT with the state was abruptly broken by a series of bitter strikes that tapered off only after the failure of the railroad strike in the summer of 1920.

Once again, May 1 was a critical date. At the end of April, 1919, the eight-hour day, the focus of CGT agitation since 1890, was finally voted. For thirty years, each May Day celebration had begun with the call for this most continuous demand of the working class. Now, in 1919, the CGT decided that the emphasis of the first postwar May Day would be the demand for the rapid implementation of the new law. Under pressure from the minoritaires to go beyond the issue of the eight-hour day, the May 1 statement of the CGT included demands for general demobilization, amnesty for condemned workers and soldiers, the end of armed intervention in Russia, and the adoption of the newly formulated "minimum program" of the CGT. Fearful of the revolutionary spirit sweeping across Germany, Hungary, and even Italy, the government forbade the demonstrations. The workers of France responded to the interdict of the Clemenceau government by stopping work and pouring into the streets of cities and towns all over the country. In Lyons, the line of march went on for hours, in Albi, Toulouse, St. Etienne, Dijon, Roanne, Toulon, and dozens of other cities, the factories, the stores, and the workshops remained closed; it was an impressive show of working-class strength. In the provinces, the demonstrations were peaceful, but in Paris, at the seat of the central government and the CGT, there was a return to the violence of the prewar period. At the rue Royale, soldiers sent to stop the demonstrators opened their ranks, but

3. Roger Picard, *Le Mouvement syndical durant la guerre* (Paris, 1927), 105.

at the Place de la Concorde, near the railroad stations, and around the Bourse du Travail, there were skirmishes. At the Place de l'Opéra, shots were fired and a young worker was killed, and on Boulevard Magenta, Jouhaux himself was struck and the Socialist deputy Poncet was wounded. More than six hundred demonstrators were arrested. The CGT was in shock, the Union Sacrée in shambles. A CGT statement reminded the people of Paris that the head of the government, Clemenceau, had used these bloody methods before—in 1908, at Villeneuve–St. Georges. The government was accused: "You are responsible because you have given the barbarous orders to the police; because you have transformed our soldier brothers into cops . . . you are guilty. We will remember."[4]

Within a few weeks of the May Day events, hundreds of thousands of workers, disillusioned with the repressive policies of the government and anxious for salary increases and the implementation of the eight-hour day, were on strike. In the northern textile centers, in the mines of Pas-de-Calais, in Bordeaux, in Lyons, in St. Etienne, Grenoble, Rennes, Belfort, in small towns and large cities, construction workers, truck drivers, metalworkers, glassworkers, shoemakers, department store employees, and bank employees abandoned their work. In Paris, strikes of metalworkers, chemical workers, and metro employees idled hundreds of thousands more. Throughout June and July, the strikes spread, but despite the large number of workers on strike and the efforts of the minoritaire supporters of the Third International to make the strike more political, France did not follow the path of proletarian revolution. The strength of the government, the underlying disunity of the CGT, and the hesitancy of the workers, many of whom were new to syndicalism, to go beyond corporative demands—all contributed to the failure of any movement for social revolution. On July 21, 1919, these difficulties led to the failure of a planned general strike.

Fonctionnaires, who had also experienced the severe trials of the war, reached a new level of organizational militancy. Gone were the amicales and the associations, victims of the terrible carnage and the plummeting standard of living. For the fonctionnaires, only one form of organization would do—the syndicat. As soon as the war had ended, the PTT employees, the teachers, the douaniers, and the agents of the Contributions

4. *Ibid.*, 206–207.

Indirectes all began clamoring for the immediate extension of the 1884 law. But even without waiting for the promised government action on the droit syndical, fonctionnaires in every category, in every department, in every town, organized new syndicats or transformed their old organizations into syndicats. Throughout 1919, at meetings all over France, fonctionnaires declared themselves beneficiaries of the droit syndical. More significant, many declared their solidarity with the working class and voted to join the CGT. "There cannot be any difference between the worker at the forge and the worker with the pen. They must all be united," a group of Toulouse fonctionnaires was told. "The goal that we have wished for, for twenty-five years, may finally be realized."[5]

In the PTT, the agents had joined the sous-agents and the ouvriers by becoming a syndicat at the end of 1918. Throughout the spring of 1919, the transformation of the Association Générale into the Syndicat National des Agents was ratified at huge, enthusiastic meetings. By June, when the first congress of the new syndicat was held at Valence, the alliance with the working class was sealed. Fraternal greetings were sent to the entire organized working class, and the political demands of the CGT were discussed and ratified. Among the sous-agents, most of the old Association Générale had also gone over to the syndicat, and in August the Fédération Postale was reestablished. The new Fédération Postale, with a membership of seventy-five thousand agents, sous-agents, and ouvriers, adhered to the CGT, becoming one of its largest federations.

The old Union Générale des Agents des Contributions Indirectes had also reorganized as a syndicat; each week brought new evidence of support from the departmental sections.[6] At the 1919 congress held in June, the secretary-general, Léon Coudert, told delegates, "Our syndicat will march resolutely toward the CGT, within which the fonctionnaires have a role to play, a role filled with nobility and grandeur, because in the new world which is painfully asserting itself, we have a role of action and of leadership to fill which we cannot shirk."[7] At the congress at which the douaniers also organized themselves officially into a syndicat,

5. AN, F7 13805, Bedel at Toulouse meeting of February 17, 1919.
6. See *Bulletin Officiel* of Syndicat National des Agents des Contributions Indirectes, August–September, 1919.
7. AN, F7 13729.

the delegate from Marseilles voiced the feelings of most fonctionnaires: "The Ministry has threatened us with breaking relations if we go to the extreme on the question of syndicalism. We don't care. What have we gotten with our visits and our respectful requests? We can't trust the ministers and the bourgeois deputies. They don't want to grant us the droit syndical. Let's take it."[8] The douaniers stood ready to bring their eighteen thousand members into the CGT.

The new militancy also permeated the ranks of the teachers. Even those who remained in the amicales were now ready to join a syndicat. But if the government had turned its back while the other fonctionnaires assumed the droit syndical on their own, the same tolerance would not be allowed the teachers. In February, Emile Glay, the leader of the Fédération des Amicales, had invited teachers who were in the army taking a special physical education course to come to a meeting to discuss the benefits of syndicalism. As with so many other teacher meetings, the meeting was banned, this time by the military governor of Paris. With six thousand dead on the field of battle, the amicales were indignant at the denial of their right to meet and organize.[9] But nothing the government was to do would stem the tide of syndicalization. The old prewar syndicat had never ceased activity, and now, one by one, the amicales transformed themselves into syndicats, many voting for CGT affiliation. "The teachers are joining the proletariat," declared the CGT newspaper La Bataille.[10] Even the teachers in higher education joined the movement. Professors at the lycées began to organize syndicats, and many voted to accept the principle of a strike, but they would not join the CGT.[11] At a special September meeting, the Fédération des Amicales officially transformed its amicales into syndicats and voted its affiliation with the CGT. The entrance of the instituteurs into the CGT made them the largest fonctionnaire federation in that organization.

The new fonctionnaire syndicats continued to press for the extension of the 1884 law, but for most of 1919 the campaign for the droit syndical

8. L'Humanité, May 14, 1919.
9. AN, F7 13743. Casualties among teachers had been high. In the department of the Seine, of 3,275 teachers, 1,750 had been mobilized. Of those, 397 had been killed, 723 wounded, 42 had received the Légion d'honneur, 49 the Médaille Militaire, and 735 received citations.
10. La Bataille, July 24, 1919.
11. In AN, F7 13743; see meetings at Clermont-Ferrand, April 9, and Digne, April 11, 1919.

was of secondary importance. Passage of a law granting fonctionnaires the right to join and organize syndicats was expected momentarily; the law had already been voted by the Chamber of Deputies. In the meantime, the actual law mattered little; the fonctionnaires had seized the droit syndical by themselves. Much more critical to the fonctionnaires was the continuing deterioration of their standard of living. The fonctionnaires had received small salary increases in the summer of 1919, and the 720-franc cost-of-living indemnity, awarded at the end of the war, had been temporarily renewed.[12] Despite these measures, the cost of living rose faster than the income of most fonctionnaires. By 1920, the inflationary spiral had pushed the index of retail prices to more than four times the 1914 figure.[13] The demand for salary increases and for more realistic indemnities was to be a major focus of syndicat activity throughout the postwar inflationary period.

The newly formed syndicats were also concerned with the improvement of working conditions. Most services had adhered to the eight-hour day or the forty-eight-hour week recently awarded the blue-collar working class, and the postal workers wanted their forty-eight-hour week to be arranged to ensure that Sunday would be a day of rest for all employees of the PTT. The weekly day off had been guaranteed before the war, but in many cities outside of Paris, including the large centers of Marseilles, Lyons, and Bordeaux, the law was never fully implemented. In the summer of 1919, the campaign for the *repos dominical* was intensified. Huge meetings of postal workers took place in numerous cities. By September, the newly formed Fédération Postale decided that it was time to go beyond meetings and delegations and take action. If the government would not close the post offices on Sunday, the postal workers would. On Sunday, September 14, post offices in dozens of cities remained closed for the day. Posters appeared on the walls asking the public not to do business on Sunday. The campaign was victorious. By the end of September, reduced Sunday service allowed the agents to have the day off, and sous-agents could voluntarily arrange their day off among themselves or use the service of auxiliaries.

Working conditions and salary increases were of major concern to

12. As of July 1, 1919, the minimum salary for fonctionnaires was 3,800 francs, compared with 1,200–1,500 in 1914 (François Perroux, *Les Traitements des fonctionnaires* [Paris, 1933], 49).
13. Alfred Sauvy, *Histoire économique de la France entre les deux guerres* (4 vols.; Paris, 1965–75), I, 501.

most fonctionnaires, but for many, the purpose of organizing syndicats was not just to improve the standard of living but to change the social structure. In the prewar period, only a handful of fonctionnaires were interested in more than their narrow corporative issues. Now, just as the war, inflation, and the example of the Russian Revolution had changed attitudes and tactics in the blue-collar working class, so the ideological and tactical changes that had begun to develop before 1914 among fonctionnaires were accelerated. The most important of these was the syndicalization of the fonctionnaires, but the attitude of most fonctionnaires toward politics also changed. Before the war, politics had meant supporting the campaigns of those who would promise to vote for the droit syndical or for salary increases for fonctionnaires. In the postwar period, politics involved support of the political parties' general ideology and broader societal goals. For most fonctionnaires, politics also meant the politics of the working class and of the CGT. The fonctionnaire federations rallied to the CGT's call for rapid demobilization, for amnesty, and for the end of armed intervention in Russia and Hungary. For still other fonctionnaires, politics meant the struggle for more basic social change, for the destruction of capitalism, and for social revolution. For these fonctionnaires, the Russian Revolution was of critical importance. On the first anniversary of the Armistice, the leader of the PTT ouvriers, Dutailly, told a huge meeting of Parisian postal workers that the question of salaries was insignificant compared to the "great social problem which faces us and which will continue to assert itself." The Russian Revolution was the key to this problem: "Either the proletariat will save the Russian Revolution and free itself from capitalism, or it will allow the Russian Revolution to be crushed and it will fall once again under the domination of capitalism for centuries to come." The postiers were asked to propagandize for syndicalism and for the revolution, which Dutailly believed was inevitable. When French sailors in the Black Sea refused to obey their commander's order to fire on the Bolshevik-controlled territory, many fonctionnaires joined the campaign to save "the Black Sea sailors."[14]

For the small group of teachers who had been members of the prewar syndicats and for those who had been active in the campaign to end the

14. AN, F7 13805.

war, politics meant ensuring international peace by reorganizing education to teach brotherly love instead of blind patriotism. At a special congress held in June, 1919, these instituteurs, noting that the teaching of hatred could only create the atmosphere for more killing, pledged to oppose the chauvinist propaganda of the *soi-disant* patriotic organizations: "The secular school must have as its goal to do all within its power for the realization of permanent peace and universal brotherhood." Calling ceremonies honoring the dead necrophilial, the teachers of Bouches-du-Rhône appealed to the working class not to let their children participate in this wrongful glorification of patriotism and death.[15] Most of these teachers were also dedicated to the concept of *l'école unique,* schooling for all children regardless of class or sex, for the improvement of school buildings, for smaller classes, and for raising the age at which children could leave school. Many of these veterans of syndicalism adhered to the Third International.[16]

Of all the political developments that affected the fonctionnaires, the most significant for the majority of them was their alliance with the blue-collar working class—their mass entrance into the CGT. A core of fonctionnaires had always advanced the cause of syndicalism and the alliance of blue-collar workers and fonctionnaires in the CGT, but the mass of fonctionnaires, though gradually coming to support the concept of syndicalism, had avoided the formal joining of blue collar and white. Now in 1919 and 1920, the voices of the few hesitants were ignored, and fonctionnaire syndicalists, one after the other, adhered to the CGT. The fonctionnaires had come a long way. In one generation, they had gone from being professionals organized in associations to being workers organized in syndicats and to membership in the CGT. The attachment to the working class and its main organizations was to be severely tested in the years 1920–1921 and in other crisis years, but in the end, despite enormous difficulties, the alliance would not be broken.

The year 1920 opened with another series of intense and bitter strikes

15. AN, F7 13743, conference of July 8, 9, 1919; *ibid.,* October 28, 1919.

16. See Program for Pupils, Syndicat du Finistère, May 15, 1919. The February, 1919, issue of *L'Emancipation,* the monthly bulletin of the syndicat of Maine-et-Loire and sections from Calvados, Charente and Sarthe, mourned the death of Karl Liebknecht and Rosa Luxembourg with a picture of the two martyrs and an analysis of their politics and death written by Gabrielle Bouët.

over wages and the still elusive eight-hour day. From Lyons, where in February an automobile strike had spread first to the dyers and then to the chemical, electrical, and metallurgical industries, the movement spread northward, where the strike of miners in the Nord and Pas-de-Calais was joined by dockers and building workers. In March, textile workers in the north declared a twenty-four-hour general strike of solidarity. But the strike with the most far-reaching consequences was to be the strike of railroad workers, some of whom, working for government-owned lines, were technically fonctionnaires. Like the postal strike of 1909, the railroad strike of 1920 was actually two strikes; one in February was, according to one's political affiliation, either partially or completely successful, and one in May, was, like the postal strike of May, 1909, a debacle.

The strike began when a syndicat militant of the PLM line, whose request for released time to attend to syndicat business was denied, was suspended from his job when he took time off without permission. The cheminots, particularly the more revolutionary ones, viewed this action as an attack on their droit syndical. As with most strikes, the event that sparked the action was merely the last straw. The railroad workers used this opportunity to strike for higher wages, for assurances of respect for the droit syndical, and, most significant, for the nationalization of all the rail lines. It was hoped by the more revolutionary members, who were a strong but minority faction in the Fédération des Cheminots, that the political demand for nationalization would help spark political strikes in other industries and lead ultimately to a general strike. As the strike spread from the PLM to other lines—only the cheminots of the Nord refused to participate—the federation leadership, faced with a fait accompli, quickly attempted to take over the leadership of the strike from the more revolutionary elements. The CGT, extremely distressed by this spontaneous action but anxious to support the concept of nationalization, which was part of its minimum program, eventually lent its support also. Messages of solidarity from other industries poured in to cheer on the railroad workers. The fonctionnaires were sympathetic to the cheminots' defense of their droit syndical but did not join the strike action. The Syndicat National des Agents des PTT expressed its "warm sympathies to the railroad workers who have not hesitated to launch a solidarity strike so that the use of the droit syndical would be respected. It appreciates this action as proof of considered and enormous strength.

This action was provoked by the necessity to resist the attacks which are openly being made on the liberties and rights of workers," but the only official word from the Fédération Postale was to order postiers to refuse to do "scab" work and to perform only postal duties.[17]

The government of the Bloc National, newly constituted under the leadership of none other than Millerand and reflecting the swing to the right of the elections of November, 1919, was determined to end the strike quickly.[18] The Millerand government launched a two-pronged campaign: military reserves were readied to run the idled lines and an attempt was made to galvanize public opinion against the cheminots. Paris restaurants were told to limit food consumption, and the populace was led to believe that Paris would soon be without food. But Millerand was also aware that the majoritaire federation leaders and the CGT were not happy with the strike, and when he offered to mediate, everyone accepted. The strike settlement included guarantees for the droit syndical, a new salary scale, and the promise of a government commission to study the reorganization of the railroad lines. There was also a promise that all syndicat militants who had been arrested or fired would be reinstated in their jobs. The Fédération des Cheminots celebrated its "victory," but the minoritaires felt betrayed by the nonpolitical settlement. When the railroad companies ignored the amnesty part of the settlement, the minoritaires used the opportunity to oust the reformist leadership of the Fédération des Cheminots at their April congress. On the night of April 30–May 1, a new strike began.

Starting with enormous demonstrations on May Day, a wave of solidarity strikes occurred. A nationwide general strike seemed imminent. But the cheminots themselves were not united. Even though almost 250,000 were on strike, two of the lines, the Nord and the Est, did not join the work stoppage. The Parisian cheminots, so strong in February and March, were now a weak point in the strike. Moreover, the *minoritaires* were tactically and ideologically divided between prewar revolutionary syndicalists and supporters of what would become the *unitaires* or Leninist position. The government remained strong, calling the strike a "foreign plot" against public order and arresting federation militants. Volunteers—military personnel and students from the Grandes

17. AN, F7 13804.
18. The new Assembly was referred to as "la Chambre bleu horizon" because so many war veterans were elected.

Ecoles—ran the trains. Paris was fed. The CGT ordered more strikes; electricians, dockers, miners, and maritime workers joined the action. Once again, the fonctionnaires, many of whom supported the demand for nationalization of all public services, sent messages of solidarity to all the strikers and protested the arrests of militants and socialists.[19] Individual local organizations tried to help as they could, the teachers of the Var voting to send money to the Toulon strikers and those in Marseilles pledging to finance soup kitchens, but there were no solidarity strikes.[20]

It was clear, however, that without more support from the rest of the working class and with many of the railroad lines still running, the strike would be lost. The CGT desperately tried to fix a limit to the strike and, eventually, the railroad workers were left alone. When some workers in other industries returned to work, they faced lockouts. On May 28, all was over. The defeat was complete. But Gaston Monmousseau (using the nom de plume Jean Brécot), one of the leaders of the strike, told the railroad workers to be proud of what they had attempted. The Grande Grève of 1920 had been a great milestone in the development of class consciousness; cheminots were no longer docile fonctionnaires.[21] With over twenty thousand cheminots fired, their leaders in jail, and their membership diminished, the cheminots suffered a terrible blow. The failure of the railroad strike was also a serious blow for the CGT. May, 1920, was to mark a turning point for the confederation. The railroad strike had heightened the antagonisms between reformists and revolutionaries, and on May 11, in the midst of the strike, the government had decided to start legal proceedings to dissolve the CGT. The CGT was accused of supporting the May Day demonstrations, of leading the campaign to end the intervention in Russia, of aiding and abetting the railroad strike, and of illegally allowing fonctionnaires to enter the CGT. The CGT fought back. A declaration appealing to the people of Paris was issued, stating, "The CGT will withstand this attack."[22]

19. AN, F7 13744; see, for example, the teachers' meeting at Tours, May 19, 1920.
20. AN, F7 13744; AN, F7 13804. The cheminots were bitter about the lack of fonctionnaire support long after the strike had ended. At the end-of-year meeting in Tours, when Bordérès of the sous-agents criticized the cheminots for not being more numerous at the meeting, a cheminot in the audience asked, "Where were you last May?"
21. Jean Brécot, La Grande grève de mai 1920 (N.p., n.d.), 4–5. The book was written while Monmousseau was in prison for his role in the strike. He later became head of the CGTU.
22. Most analyses of the strike say that approximately twenty thousand were fired. Picard gives a figure of thirty-five thousand and says that in 1925, when he was writing his book,

But the beleaguered CGT, whose membership had reached new heights on May Day, 1920, began to lose support. In January, 1921, the court declared the CGT "an instrument of social warfare" and officially dissolved the organization and fined its leaders.[23] Although the judgment had no practical significance, it was another blow to the faltering organization. By the time of the great schism of 1921, the CGT had lost most of its postwar membership gains.

The fonctionnaires were not to be spared by the government. In the midst of the railroad strikes and the attempts to dissolve the CGT, the government launched an attack on the fonctionnaire syndicats. In February, 1919, the Chamber of Deputies had voted to extend the 1884 law "to the liberal professions as well as to fonctionnaires and workers of the state, departments, communes and the public service."[24] Only the military, the police, judicial and administrative magistrates, prefects, and subprefects were to be denied the benefits of the 1884 law. The archconservative Senate, however, rejected the proposed law, and the question of the droit syndical remained in abeyance. Then on March 14, 1920, other legislation on the extension of the 1884 law, the *loi Chéron,* was made official. Syndicat powers were widened and the liberal professions were granted the right to organize as syndicats, but none of these benefits were extended to the fonctionnaires. The fonctionnaires' hopes for the droit syndical were dashed.

The political atmosphere in which these events unfolded is significant. In the spring of 1919, Clemenceau had told a CGT delegation that their aspirations were indeed legitimate: "In 1789, the worthless nobility was bankrupt. Today the bourgeoisie, incompetent, has shown itself inadequate to meet the needs of the nation. The hour of the worker has sounded. The time has come for you to succeed us."[25] Louis Bouët, the instituteur militant, wrote that during the war, even though militant syndicalists were harassed as defeatists by the government, it appeared that under the government of Clemenceau the syndicats of fonction-

seven thousand cheminots remained discharged from service. See Picard, *Le Mouvement syndical durant la guerre,* 226, 228.

23. Georges Frischmann, *Histoire de la fédération CGT des PTT* (Paris, 1967), 221.

24. From the session of February 4, 1919, quoted in Pierre Dietsch, *De la Légalité des syndicats des fonctionnaires* (Paris, 1934), 57.

25. *Le Matin,* July 3, 1919. Laurent related the story of the interview and Clemenceau's remarks of May, 1919, to the congress of the Fédération des Fonctionnaires in July.

naires would not be threatened. But after the elections of November, 1919, the government of the Bloc National changed its tune.

In the fall of 1919 and the spring of 1920, the government was terrified that there would be a social revolution in France. The Russian Revolution, the increasing strength of the CGT, and the widespread strikes seemed to confirm fears of the bolshevik menace. At the March 29, 1920, session of the Senate, Henri Chéron told the upper chamber of his fears of social revolution. He mentioned the fonctionnaires' support of the railroad strike and the activities of supporters of the Third International. Their aim, he asserted, was "revolutionary action in the public service, the interruption of these services and ultimately, the incitement of military disorder." There was no civilized country in the world where the coalition of fonctionnaires was not considered a criminal act. That was why the Senate had repeatedly declared itself clearly and resolutely opposed to the syndicats of fonctionnaires. Above all, there must be no interruption of public service; Chéron called for repressive measures. Millerand agreed. The job of the government was to save the Republic from revolution. The state must act as policeman to preserve public order. The fonctionnaires could form only associations; they had no right to the 1884 law, and they certainly had no right to strike: "In no case whatsoever can the negotiation rights conceded to the fonctionnaires result in a work stoppage. They must be warned by the law itself that collective work stoppages would abolish all guarantees and that they would find themselves open to immediate dismissal."[26]

Despite the passage of the Chéron law, the fonctionnaires continued to create syndicats and to join the CGT. The Fédération des Fonctionnaires, having declared itself a syndicat in early 1919, had voted its intention to adhere to the CGT: "We are not revolutionaries, we simply want to live."[27] But the bylaws of the CGT would not allow formal membership to any federation containing associations that had not yet become syndicats adhering to departmental unions. Throughout the year 1919, the Fédération des Fonctionnaires had mounted a campaign to ensure that all local associations became syndicats. The passage of the Chéron law made the campaign more critical. In March, April, and May of 1920, Laurent, the secretary-general of the federation, Michel Piquemal

26. The entire debate is in the *Journal Officiel,* Sénat séance of March 29, 1920.
27. M. Oualid in *Le Petit Journal,* March 12, 1919.

of the Contributions Indirectes, and other board members barnstormed the provinces, going from meeting to meeting pleading the cause of fonctionnaire-worker solidarity. To Nîmes, to Nantes, to Lille, wherever the federation leaders went, the talk was not of the revolution so feared by the government and the bourgeoisie but of "economic and social transformation under the leadership of the CGT."[28] Piquemal told a Mont-de-Marsan audience that the fonctionnaires must join the CGT, "which, without violence, wants to build a new society," and at a Perigueux meeting, Adrien Budon of the registry office explained, "The working class is powerful and we need its help in order to achieve our moral demands which are more difficult to obtain than material demands."[29]

Although almost all the provincial associations had become syndicats, not all adhered to the CGT. Not all fonctionnaires were willing to identify with the blue-collar workers and the tactics and ideology of the CGT. At a Paris meeting of the employees of the Ministry of Finance, for example, Betmale, the secretary of the Union des Employés des Administrations Centrales, declared his dedication to the Fédération des Fonctionnaires but countered the pro-CGT arguments of Laurent and Coudert (Contributions Indirectes) with an assertion that the politics of the CGT were contrary to the interests of the fonctionnaires.[30] At an April meeting at Auxerre, a group of fonctionnaires listened to a former deputy and fonctionnaire, Ulysse Pastre, speak passionately for the Fédération des Fonctionnaires and for the droit syndical but voted not to join the CGT.[31] There were similar hesitations among the teachers. The amicale of the Basses Pyrénées had become a syndicat; one group adhered to the CGT but another voted to stay out. In the department of the Isère, the former amicales were similarly divided. In the Hautes Pyrénées, a circular calling for the formation of an independent syndicat was sent to all the teachers in the department. Entitled "Why we don't belong in the CGT," the circular declared "that all the members of the CGT, from the anarchists to the moderates, want the same end by the same means: the seizure of power by direct action." The CGT was in

28. AN, F7 13721, Tours meeting, March 27, 1920.
29. AN, F7 13726, April 22, 1920; AN, F7 13731, April 29, 1920.
30. AP, BA provisoire 305, February 19, 1920.
31. AN, F7 13726.

favor of class struggle, of the general strike, of the destruction of individualism; it wanted the fonctionnaires to join to enhance its chances of making a violent revolution.[32] A group of dissidents opposed to the Fédération des Fonctionnaires' decision to enter the CGT organized, under the leadership of a Parisian instituteur named Sennelier, the Union Professionnelle des Fonctionnaires. In May, 1920, the first issue of the union's newspaper *L'Union des Fonctionnaires* appeared. The dissidents wanted the droit syndical but did not want this right to become "a weapon of attack against society."[33] The Fédération des Syndicats des Instituteurs et Institutrices attacked these dissident groups as *jaunes* (scabs or yellow unionists).[34]

There was opposition from the Left as well. Some of the more revolutionary teachers were hesitant about the affiliation of the moderate Fédération des Fonctionnaires to the CGT; Bouët and others claimed that the principle of trades might be lost. If the Fédération des Fonctionnaires was admitted to the CGT as a bloc, what would become of the more militant Fédération Postale and the teacher federation that had been allied to the CGT since 1907?[35] These teachers feared that the reformist amicales in the Fédération des Fonctionnaires, latecomers to the syndicalist movement, might have more influence than the smaller group of revolutionaries.

But the large majority of provincial fonctionnaires responded enthusiastically to the pro–CGT arguments. A Toulouse meeting voted: "In the face of the present disorder, only the organized working class is presenting to the Conseil Economique de Travail a program of economic reconstruction and social renewal, and thus we resolve to ally ourselves with all the workers under the banner of the CGT," and the Bouches-du-Rhône fonctionnaires voted to place themselves "on the same ground with the worker organizations, with whom, moreover, they intend to forge stronger and stronger ties."[36]

On May 25 and 26, just as the railroad strike was ending and the CGT

32. AN, F7 13744.
33. AN, F7 13727.
34. *Le Rappel,* April 5, 1920.
35. AN, F7 13744, St. Etienne meeting, February 8, 1920. See also *L'Eclair,* March 19, 1920.
36. AN, F7 13713, April 18, 1920; AN, F7 13702, April 24, 1920.

was facing legal dissolution, the Fédération des Fonctionnaires held its annual congress. Many corporative decisions were to be made at this congress, but from the opening session there was one overriding theme that was to dominate all the speeches and discussion—the adherence of the Fédération des Fonctionnaires to the CGT. Reporting on the congress for Le Rappel, René Parol wrote that despite government repression, the fonctionnaires wanted to adhere to the CGT because they knew "in union there is strength."[37] The tone of the congress was moderate; there was no talk of class struggle or revolution. The alliance of the working class and the fonctionnaires was to encourage economic and social change through cooperation. In his opening address, a federation leader, Pierre Neumeyer, told the delegates, "Thus we are going into the CGT without any regrets, with the one wish to work in perfect accord with our fellow workers, to find the means to get our country out of the current terrible economic and financial crises."[38] During the discussion, some delegates expressed their doubts about the CGT, but the federation leadership told the congress that working-class-fonctionnaire solidarity was necessary to resist repression. Adhesion to the CGT was "the normal result of the current which pushes the fonctionnaires and workers to organize together."[39]

When the vote was finally taken, the fifty votes of the instituteurs, the thirty votes of the douaniers, and the twenty votes of the Contributions Indirectes all were for "adherence without reservations to the CGT." The final vote was ninety-three in favor, thirty-eight against, with seventy-eight abstentions, mostly of smaller organizations.[40] Representing sixty-eight organizations with nearly four hundred thousand members, the Fédération des Fonctionnaires brought to the CGT both numerical and moral strength. In the interwar period, with blue-collar membership fluctuating, the fonctionnaires would represent an important source of strength in the CGT.

Within a few days of the congress' decision to join the confederation, the government, having already started legal proceedings to dissolve the

---

37. Le Rappel, May 25, 1920.
38. La Tribune des Fonctionnaires, June 20, 1920.
39. La Bataille, May 26, 1920, speeches of Glay and Métayer.
40. Le Matin, May 26, 1920. The Fédération Postale was not a member of the Fédération des Fonctionnaires.

CGT, turned its attention toward the fonctionnaires. On June 1 a statute was introduced which forbade the union of fonctionnaire federations from different administrations as well as federations of fonctionnaires and workers from the private sector. On the same day, a cabinet decision was made to disallow the existing "illegal" syndicats. Orders went out from the Ministry of the Interior to the departments. The fonctionnaires were to transform themselves back into associations in compliance with the law of 1901. If the order of transformation was disobeyed, the offending syndicats would be dissolved.[41] The fonctionnaires fought back. On June 2, Laurent and Piquemal went to the CGT to ask for formal acceptance of the Fédération des Fonctionnaires into the confederation of French workers. A Cartel des Services Publics, encompassing the Fédération des Fonctionnaires, the Fédération Postale, the railroad workers, and state blue-collar workers, was immediately formed. Within a few months, the cartel would represent over 1 million workers in the public sector.

On the evening of June 3, more than six thousand Parisian members of the Cartel des Services Publics gathered at the Cirque de Paris to inaugurate the counterattack "to protest the blow struck by the government against the fonctionnaires' liberties."[42] Speaker after speaker denounced government repression, "the consequence of the vote of adherence to the CGT." Jouhaux, calling the dissolution of the CGT "a new revocation of the Edict of Nantes," told the fonctionnaires that the CGT would emerge from this struggle stronger than ever.[43] Henri Lartigue of the Fédération Postale linked the attacks on the fonctionnaires and the CGT: "The government, after twenty years of reflection, wants to give the fonctionnaires a statute which is at the same time a monument of perfidy and of folly. With this statute, they want to make docile servants out of the fonctionnaires and to distance them from the CGT. This must not happen, and it is the duty of all fonctionnaires to work together with manual workers."[44]

Throughout the summer of 1920, fonctionnaires rallied once again, this time to defy the government's order to dissolve the syndicats, to protest the statute, and to reaffirm their attachments to the CGT. At

41. For the official cabinet letter to the departments, see AN, F7 13726.
42. AN, F7 13726, speech of Roussel.
43. L'Intransigeant, June 4, 1920.
44. The entire meeting is reported in AN, F7 13726.

Saint Etienne, Grenoble, Nancy, Lyons, and Bourges thousands filled the meeting halls. At a meeting in Toulouse, postal employees were told that the government wanted to turn them into serfs,[45] and a speaker from the Fédération Postale told a Châlons-sur-Marne meeting that "they are placing a *cordon sanitaire* between the working class and the intellectual working class." At Mézières in the Ardennes, fonctionnaires were told that they must remain with the CGT, "which already has arms and in which the fonctionnaires will be the brain." On June 13, three thousand workers and fonctionnaires in Marseilles answered the call of the cartel to protest the government's actions, and on July 14, another meeting was called "to affirm their strong will to resist to the utmost the orders for the dissolution of their syndicats . . . to show the Public Powers that the administrative proletariat forms an indissoluble bloc in the great workers' army against which Daudet's Bloc National will soon be smashed."[46]

Some fonctionnaire organizations adopted the interpretation of the law made by Paul Jourdain, the minister of labor, when he addressed the National Assembly on March 11. Until the statute was voted on, there was no law against the syndicats of fonctionnaires.[47] Placards appealing to "nos citoyens" appeared on the walls of Dijon, Montbéliard, and dozens of other towns. Entitled "Why fonctionnaires want to save the droit syndical," the appeal ended with the words, "if a fragment of the republican idea remains in this country, you will be with us."[48] On September 9, twelve hundred met in Lyons; on October 11, another five thousand met in Paris.[49]

The fonctionnaires defied the government. They would not dissolve their syndicats; they would not retreat from the CGT. In July, the congress of douaniers reaffirmed its adherence to the CGT.[50] The Fédération Postale refused to accept the "abusive use of government power."[51] In August, the congress of the Contributions Indirectes voted its support

45. AN, F7 13726, June 13, 1920.
46. All these meetings are described in AN, F7 13730.
47. AN, F7 13726. This argument was discussed at meetings and in *L'Ere Nouvelle,* June 17, 1920, in an article entitled "Invités à se dissoudre, les syndicats vont répondre en invoquant la loi et promesses de M. Jourdain."
48. AN, F7 13730.
49. AN, F7 13732; AN, F7 13804.
50. AN, F7 13713.
51. AN, F7 13804.

of the 1884 law and its attachment to the CGT. In October, Coudert told the council of the Contributions Indirectes, "The government has entered into open struggle against the syndicalism of the fonctionnaires." Two courses were open: they could push the struggle to the end, no matter what the consequences, or they could form a committee of defense. Much to the distress of Piquemal and other, more radical members of the council, Coudert opted for the second, more moderate course of resistance. But resistance there was to be.[52] The teachers also indicated their defiance. In August the Syndicat de l'Enseignement Laïc (the old syndicalists) held its congress, and in September the Syndicat National des Instituteurs (the old amicalists) had its; both pledged to fight the government.

While all these meetings were taking place, the government began its judicial action against the fonctionnaire syndicats. Sanctions had been imposed on militants in the PTT, the Contributions Indirectes (including Coudert), and the instituteurs (the Bouëts); now court proceedings were begun against the PTT and militant instituteurs. The CGT issued a special message to the fonctionnaires condemning "the reactionary and antidemocratic policies which have become a government trademark in France." The CGT assured the fonctionnaires:

> Comrades of Education and the PTT, grouped together under the banner of the CGT, you have thus rejoined the two million workers of Industry, of Commerce, of Agriculture, of the sea, and of the railroads. By that act, you have indicated that you share their poverty and their troubles, their ideals and their deepest hopes that human society will soon undergo a profound and salutary renewal. That is your "crime." Keep your head high. This "crime" does you honor![53]

But as the fall wore on, the judicial actions continued. Particularly hard hit, as always, were the teacher syndicats. In October there were reports of the forced dissolution of departmental syndicats in Sarthe, Vaucluse, and Gard. In November the tribunal at Bourges fined the leaders of the syndicat of Cher, and in Tours the leaders of the syndicat of Indre-et-Loire were fined and their organizations dissolved.[54]

Despite the prosecutions of their militants and the dissolution of the

52. *Bulletin Officiel des Contributions Indirectes,* No. 146.
53. AN, F7 13734.
54. In the carton AN, F7 13726, there is a report from the minister of public education to the minister of the interior listing the transformations. Written in pencil and full of erasures,

teacher syndicats, the fonctionnaires continued to meet and voice their defiance. A few days after their leaders were fined, the teachers of Tours met to protest the action. Meetings in dozens of cities in November and December closed with the vow "that nothing will separate them from the working class and that in spite of all the methods of intimidation and all the maneuvers, they will remain in the CGT in order to pursue the work of public reform and social reconstruction."[55]

The meetings and public outcries of protest continued, but the legal proceedings against the syndicats and their activists could only weaken the fonctionnaire organizations and their resolve to stay in the CGT.[56] At the fall meetings of the council of the Contributions Indirectes, provincial representatives voiced their regret at having voted affiliation with the CGT—perhaps they should just keep an "unofficial" alliance or at least try to operate independently within the confederation. The pro-CGT people countered the arguments of the wavering syndicalists by indicating that the government's attack, which had already affected the postiers and the instituteurs, was against the entire proletariat, "those with dirty hands, those with shirt cuffs or with jackets." There was no difference between manual workers and fonctionnaires. Piquemal assuaged the hesitants by pointing out that the fonctionnaires had linked themselves to the working class not to participate in the disorganization of society but to realize the social and economic program of the CGT. The council then issued a statement affirming its affiliation to the CGT. Nothing could separate the fonctionnaires and the workers, "who share origins and ideals."[57] As the turbulent year 1920 drew to a close, the unity of fonctionnaire and worker, so long in developing, was maintained.

The adherence of the fonctionnaires to the CGT was the culmination

---

it hardly seems an accurate document, but clearly the provincial syndicats were under severe attack.

55. AN, F7 13731, meetings at Nantes, December 12, 1920, and AN, F7 13730, Charleville, December 19, 1920.

56. AN, F7 13703. The Ministry of the Interior was most anxious to hear of voluntary dissolutions of syndicats, and the local police tried to please. I was amused to see a July 27 report from Bourges in which the local surété man assured the ministry that the fonctionnaires of Bourges would accept the statute and quit the CGT. That same evening, there was a city-wide meeting and the police agent in attendance reported that the fonctionnaires had voted for solidarity with the organized working class and gave their leaders a mandate to fight the government statute with all the means at their disposal.

57. *Bulletin Officiel des Contributions Indirectes,* November–December, 1920.

of twenty years of organizational activity and growth, of the gradual meshing of the economic and social goals of workers and fonctionnaires. The expansion and routinization of public service, the tribulations of the war, and inflation had moved the fonctionnaires closer to the working-class organizations. The CGT, having abandoned much of its revolutionary ideology and now under reformist leadership, had in turn moved closer to the fonctionnaires.

8

Unity and Disunity, Victory and Defeats, 1921–1926

The formal alliance of the fonctionnaires and the blue-collar working class within the CGT represented more than mere organizational unity. The adherence of the fonctionnaire syndicats to the CGT was also an indication of the maturation of the fonctionnaires' understanding and consciousness of their role as workers in a modern industrial society. Blue-collar workers and fonctionnaires now shared common values, common desires for social and economic change, and, indeed, common destinies. This merger of fonctionnaire and working-class values also meant that the fonctionnaires had reached a new level of political consciousness. Their concerns now went beyond the narrow issues of wages and hours to the larger political and social issues that affected the society at large. International relations, the defense of state monopolies, school curriculum, legislative elections, and equality for women all were of interest to the fonctionnaires. The activity of fonctionnaires in the 1920s reflected this heightened political and social consciousness; the postwar period was characterized by the blossoming of fonctionnaires' participation in political activity.

But if the shared goals of fonctionnaires and the working class were reflected in shared political interests and activities, they also involved the fonctionnaires in the ideological struggles of the blue-collar working class. Unity with the working class meant that the ideological differences that divided the working class would divide the fonctionnaires as well. This ideological and organizational schism was to dominate many of the discussions and actions of the interwar period, but it did not prevent the fonctionnaires from participating in numerous activities that reflected their heightened consciousness.

The organizational alliance of the fonctionnaires and the working class, which had managed to withstand the government's attacks of

1920, could not survive the internecine struggles that racked the Socialist party and the CGT. At the congress of Tours, held in December, 1920, the Socialist party underwent a schism, the supporters of the Third International calling themselves the Section Française de l'Internationale Communiste (later to become the Parti Communiste Français), the remaining group keeping the old name, SFIO. It was only a matter of time before the socialist split would affect the syndicats. Indeed, despite the efforts of many syndicalists to maintain working-class independence and unity, the year 1921 was to end with the CGT split apart and the fonctionnaires forced to choose sides or withdraw from the devastated remnants of the confederation.

The roots of the schism went back to the period before 1914 and the ideological and tactical differences between reformists and revolutionaries. The divisions intensified during the war because of disagreements over the prowar class-collaboration policies of the Union Sacrée and deepened with the success of the Russian Revolution and the establishment of the Third International. The leadership of the CGT, under Jouhaux, remained hostile to the Third International and to the Comités des Syndicalistes Révolutionnaires (CSR), which had been established within the CGT syndicats by supporters of the new International "to prepare revolutionary cadres in all the federations and to foster revolutionary ideas."[1]

The ideological orientation of the syndicalist movement and the existence of the Comités Révolutionnaires was to be the dominant topic at the CGT congress held at Lille in July, 1921. After much discussion, the congress approved, by a vote of 1,572 to 1,325, Georges Dumoulin's motion to reject the revolutionary position and to exclude the Comités Révolutionnaires from CGT membership. By voting the motion of exclusion, the majoritaires had, as the cheminot Monmousseau had warned, voted for schism. On September 20, the national committee of the confederation was asked to rescind the vote of exclusion, but when the minoritaires refused to adhere to syndicalist discipline by abandoning the Comités Révolutionnaires, the revolutionary position was once again condemned. The minoritaires met separately to form the Con-

---

1. AN, F7 13744, declaration of the Comité des Syndicalistes Révolutionnaires de l'Enseignement, voted at Bordeaux, August, 1920.

fédération Générale du Travail Unitaire (CGTU). Because of the complications of determining membership figures, it is difficult to state with certainty which federation had more members at the time of the split. Edouard Dolléans says that in 1922 membership in the CGTU had gone up to 500,000 and that of the CGT had fallen to just over 373,000. These figures were generated by Georges Lefranc. Antoine Prost submits approximately the opposite figures.[2] Whatever the case, the divisions and the resulting schism had weakened both organizations. Within a year, more than 1 million workers had abandoned the syndicalist movement. It would take over a decade, until the period of the Popular Front, for the working-class organizations to regain this lost strength. Thus at a time of government repression and intense economic hardship, the most important organization of the working class was weak and divided. The schism, which lasted until 1935, remains one of the tragedies of French working-class history.

The ideological struggle that divided the CGT affected the fonctionnaires as well. Newcomers to CGT political strife, most fonctionnaires tried to avoid the schism, but in the end, having allied themselves with the syndicalist movement, they were to share the internal divisions as well as the ideals and tactics of these working-class organizations.

The teachers had never known ideological or organizational unity. The prewar syndicalists who had been in the CGT since 1907 and had campaigned actively at great cost against the war and the Union Sacrée now belonged to the Fédération des Syndicats de l'Enseignement Laïc. Under the leadership of their secretary, Louis Bouët, these instituteurs were active in the formation of the Comités Révolutionnaires and adhered to the Third International. One of their leaders, Hélène Brion, had been a delegate to the congress of the Internationale Syndicale Rouge in Moscow, and another, François Mayoux, was to play a leading role in support of the revolutionary position at Lille. The old amicales, on the other hand, containing a majority of the teachers, had become the Fédération des Syndicats des Instituteurs et Institutrices. Led by Glay and Louis Roussel, the former *amicalistes* supported Jouhaux and the reformist position against the Third International and the revolutionary

2. Edouard Dolléans, *Histoire du mouvement ouvrier* (3 vols.; Paris, 1968), II, 351; Georges Lefranc, *Le Mouvement syndical sous la troisième république* (Paris, 1967), 280; Antoine Prost, *La CGT à l'époque du front populaire, 1934–36* (Paris, 1964), 35.

committees. In the summer of 1920, Glay's group, hoping to emulate the unity of the Fédération Postale, changed its name to Syndicat Unique. But whatever hope there might have been that the two groups could unify would never be realized. First, Jouhaux and the reformist wing of the CGT were extremely hostile to the Bouët group, and when, at a September congress of the Syndicat de l'Enseignement Laïc, the minoritaires affirmed their adhesion to the Third International—*Le Figaro* wrote: "The extremists of primary education—they are 13,000! Yes, you have read it correctly, thirteen thousand!"—any idea of unity collapsed. Long before the CGT underwent its schism, the teachers had already chosen sides.[3]

In the PTT, which had proportionally more revolutionaries than any other public service, the disparate forces had managed to forge a unity of organization within the individual syndicats and the Fédération Postale. Fully aware of the need for organizational strength in the struggle for the economic well-being of their members, both factions attempted to maintain that unity long as they could. A month before the CGT was to meet at Lille, the congress of Employés des PTT (formerly called sous-agents) debated its political orientation. Even as he defended the reformist position—the working class was not revolutionary—Louis Digat pleaded for unity: "In the face of unleashed imperialism, in the face of the forces of reaction who are winning, we are a divided proletariat, growing weaker from day to day. . . . It is an odious thing to think of the schism which is being prepared for Lille."[4] A few days later, at the congress of the Fédération Postale, the postiers moved closer to a schism as the position of the revolutionaries was rejected by a vote of 159 to 129.[5] The syndicat newspaper *Le Cri Postal* still attempted to avoid factionalism. In its July 2 issue, remembering other difficult times they had endured, the editors voiced their hopes of maintaining the impartiality of the paper: "Majoritaires and minoritaires, reformists and revolutionaries, will here have the right to enlarge upon and share each others' opinions. The open platform which we have had for such a long time is open to all."

3. AN, F7 13744, see police report of the Orléans congress, September 30, 1920; *Le Figaro,* September 30, 1920.

4. *Le Cri Postal,* June 18, 1921. Digat was clearly blaming the revolutionaries for the schism.

5. Georges Frischmann, *Histoire de la fédération CGT des PTT* (Paris, 1967), 232.

After the events at Lille and the formation of the CGTU, the postal workers abandoned all hopes of unity. In April, 1922, the three member federations of the Fédération Postale held their congresses. The ouvriers, who had been in the CGT the longest, stated their belief that "the working class, organized to fight for its freedom, need no longer limit itself to a battle waged in constant collaboration with the exploiting class. Instead it must depend on itself alone to obtain its complete emancipation" and voted, by a 60 percent majority, to break relations with the CGT and rally to the newly constituted CGTU.[6] At their congress, the sous-agents (employés) voted almost unanimously to join the CGTU as well. But at the congress of agents, the vast majority voted to remain in the CGT. Even though two of the three syndicats belonging to the Fédération Postale had voted to join the CGTU, there were enough CGT supporters among the ouvriers and the sous-agents to join the more numerous *confédéré* (member of the CGT) agents and constitute a majority of all PTT workers. For the Fédération Postale, the numbers did not matter; it existed as a voluntary union of the three syndicats. With the membership of these syndicats divided in their orientation, the congress of the Fédération Postale, meeting just a few hours after the agents had made their decision to remain with the CGT, could only be, as *L'Humanité* wrote, "a meeting of liquidation and it was thus that it happened, very unceremoniously, almost with serenity."[7] A resolution was passed to begin the process that would bring about the creation of the Fédération Postale Unitaire.

Although the teachers and the postal workers were ideologically and organizationally divided—the majority adhering to the CGT, the minority to the CGTU—other fonctionnaire syndicats tried to avoid the schism. In meeting after meeting, the disunity of the working class was lamented and the pitfalls of partisan politics decried. But after months of discussion, the only way for these fonctionnaires to avoid the doctrinal struggles that had split the CGT was to sever their official ties with the working-class syndicats, to eschew both the CGT and the CGTU, and to become autonomous.

Through most of 1920 and 1921, the syndicat of the Contributions Indirectes faced dissolution by the government. The arguments were

---

6. Frischmann, *Histoire PTT,* 234.
7. *L'Humanité,* April 23, 1922.

not between revolutionaries and reformists within the CGT but whether to remain a syndicat and to belong to the CGT and the Fédération des Fonctionnaires. The revolutionary Piquemal had always strongly supported membership in both the CGT and the federation, and at the March, 1921, congress, his position was upheld. By a vote of 162 to 142, the Contributions Indirectes committed itself to remaining in the CGT and to fighting the government's attempts to dissolve the fonctionnaire syndicats. A July election referendum further strengthened Piquemal's position as the membership voted overwhelmingly for the prosyndicat, pro-CGT slate. Even after the Lille congress, the Contributions Indirectes tried to avoid taking sides. Discussing the elections to be held at the congress of the Fédération des Fonctionnaires, the central council declared that unity was more important than support for either faction. But after the official founding of the CGTU, the schism could no longer be avoided. A January council meeting issued a statement that the Contributions Indirectes maintained its devoted attachment to the working class but deplored the "weakening stemming from the working-class divisions which were growing wider even as the employer organizations were tightening their alliances, imposing salary reductions and seeking to reduce all workers' rights." The council pledged to continue to work for unity but said that until unity was reestablished, it would "defer the taking of confederation membership cards and stamps."[8]

Throughout the spring of 1922, the syndicat of the Contributions Indirectes was primarily concerned with its struggle to survive—the syndicats of the teachers, the PTT, and the Contributions Indirectes had been declared illegal on March 10—but at the 1922 congress in June, debate over the choice of the CGT or CGTU finally took place. Several speakers declared their desire to be with the working class—but where was the working class? Finally, a resolution was passed. The Contributions Indirectes declared itself allied to the working class but against any split. The final decision, 253 to 16, was to stay out of both the CGT and the CGTU, to be an independent syndicat. With its sympathies largely reformist but its major spokesman, Piquemal, a revolutionary, the autonomous Fédération des Contributions Indirectes managed for a few years to maintain an independent existence and to avoid a schism.

8. *Bulletin Officiel des Contributions Indirectes,* April, August, November, 1921, February, 1922.

The Fédération des Fonctionnaires, having waged an energetic campaign to convince the fonctionnaire syndicats to join the CGT, also tried to avoid the partisan struggles of the confederation. Laurent told the 1921 congress, held just two months after Lille:

> As all our comrades know, the CGT is undergoing a great moral crisis. At this moment, two tendencies divide the world of the workers. We are striving to avoid being part of these internal battles, which we happily have not experienced in our ranks. And we ardently hope that there will be more harmony in the working-class organizations. Indeed, workers of all categories must seek the closest kind of union, the means to defend fervently the interests which are now threatened.[9]

But in January, 1922, though its sympathies were largely with the reformist CGT, the Fédération des Fonctionnaires formally withdrew from the confederation. Faced with government threats of dissolution and anxious to avoid a schism in its ranks, the Fédération des Fonctionnaires, despite some criticism that it had abandoned the CGT in a time of crisis, turned its attention to corporative issues of wages and administrative reform.[10]

The often bitter partisan arguments that had taken up so much time at the fonctionnaires' meetings in the winter of 1921 and the spring of 1922 continued to rage throughout the 1920s. To the confédérés the unitaires were bolsheviks and had caused the schism. To the unitaires the confédérés were collaborationists, content to sit at meetings instead of acting to protect the workers' interests.[11] Still the hopes for unity remained. In 1925 and 1926, as inflation spiraled out of control and the fonctionnaires fought for salary increases, the question of unity took on added importance. From time to time, there were joint meetings of fonctionnaires of all persuasions; Laurent and Glay joined the unitaires Pierre Semard, Lartigue, and Niles at a meeting in February, 1924, for example, and throughout the provinces, unitaire and confédéré fonctionnaires, men and women who had worked together all their lives, often attended each others' meetings or met in joint sessions to hear a particu-

9. *La Tribune des Fonctionnaires,* October 1–15, 1921.

10. The CGT newspaper *Le Peuple* (January 17, 1922), bitter about the federation's decision to return to its "isolation," petulantly commented that the fonctionnaires had hardly been in the CGT anyway.

11. AN, F7 13804; see, for example, one meeting of the Fédération Postale Unitaire, September 18, 1924; see also the syndicat newspapers of the period.

lar speaker or to support a particular demand.[12] Unitaires attending the congress of the Fédération Postale Unitaire in 1924 heard the representative of the Fédération Postale Confédérée, Digat, declare that unity was possible because "the syndicat is not an ideological grouping but a grouping of interests." What separated the unitaires (CGTU) and the confédérés (CGT), Digat asked—their methods were essentially the same. He had no fear of different tendencies—it would be awful not to have differing opinions. He had no fear of communists; "men are judged by their deeds."[13] But unification was not to be. Despite Digat's assertions that there would be no conditions placed on the unitaires, the confédérés did not offer an "equal" unification; rather, they demanded that the unitaires disband their organizations and, like the prodigal son, return to the fold of the CGT. This the unitaires would not do.

It is difficult to estimate the exact strength of either faction among the fonctionnaires. Most estimates concur that about three-fourths of fonctionnaires were sympathetic to the confédérés. Clearly, then, the majority of fonctionnaires preferred the confédéré position, and when, in the late 1920s, the autonomous syndicats returned to the working-class confederations, most went to the CGT. But once again, membership figures do not tell the whole story. Autonomous syndicats often contained both factions, and in the provinces, where it was sometimes difficult to maintain two organizations and where the confédérés were stronger, many unitaires could be found in confédéré syndicats. Despite the bitter antagonism, the hopes for unity among the fonctionnaires never died. In the early 1930s, when economic crisis and the threat of fascism made unity imperative, the fonctionnaires would be among the prime movers for the reunification of the CGT.

Although the ideological and tactical differences that caused the schism continued to plague the fonctionnaire syndicats, they faced numerous other problems in the years following the split. From the summer of 1920, when their syndicats had been declared illegal, to the spring of 1924, when the election of the Cartel des Gauches ended the rule of the Bloc National, the fonctionnaires had to struggle for their

12. AN, 13730. In the winter of 1923–1924, meetings for the eighteen-hundred-franc indemnity were attended by all three groups. See, for example, Troyes, January 13, 1924, where eight hundred attended the meeting.

13. L'Humanité, April 28, 1924.

very existence. In March, 1922, almost all the fonctionnaire syndicats, as a bloc, were declared guilty of "infraction of the 1884 law" by the court; their leaders were fined and their organizations ordered disbanded.[14] Most of the syndicat leaders did not even appear at the hearing, declaring once again that their syndicats were not illegal because the Chamber of Deputies had approved the extension of the law of 1884 to fonctionnaires. Following the interpretation of the minister of labor, Jourdain, until a statute was enacted, the status quo, that is, the existing syndicats, was to be respected.[15] The syndicats defiantly continued to exist, but there is no doubt that the government attacks, combined with internal difficulties, began to take a toll among the fonctionnaire militants; the less committed fonctionnaires abandoned their beleaguered syndicats. Most teachers remained in their syndicats but were unenthusiastic about CGT membership. In August, 1923, Glay complained that of the eighty thousand instituteurs belonging to the syndicat, only twelve thousand paid their membership dues to the CGT.[16] There are indications that the Bouët group also lost members.[17]

The Bloc National had essentially declared war on the fonctionnaires. Any fonctionnaire involvement in politics was used as an occasion to harass syndicat militants, especially the leaders of the unitaire syndicats. In the summer of 1922, metalworkers, dockers, and maritime workers in the industrial and shipping center of Le Havre were involved in a bitter 110-day strike that began when a 10 percent wage reduction was imposed on metalworkers, who had already endured previous cuts. The largely working-class population of the city was sympathetic to the strikers. The employer organization, the Comité des Forges, and the government were determined to break the strike, and when the mayor refused to arrest strikers who had committed no violent crimes, his police powers were taken away from him. Meetings were broken up, aid centers closed, strikers arrested. In August, when three workers were

14. *L'Humanité*, March 11, 1922. Eleven syndicats were involved: both teacher organizations, the syndicats of agents and employés of the PTT, the Douanes Sédentaires and Actives, the Contributions Indirectes, the syndicats of the Caisse des Dépôts, Eaux et Forêts, Ponts et Chaussées et des Mines, and the Géomètres du cadastre.

15. *L'Humanité*, May 11, 1922.

16. *Le Peuple*, August 4, 1923.

17. *Le Petit Journal*, April 30, 1921, reported that the Syndicat de l'Enseignement Laïc had gone from a membership of thirteen thousand to eight thousand in the spring of 1921.

killed after "the gendarmes used their weapons, a bit too precipitously, it seemed," some PTT employees took part in a twenty-four-hour solidarity strike called by the CGTU.[18] Two leaders of the Fédération Postale Unitaire, who had gone as representatives to Le Havre, were arrested. Henri Raymond, charged with calling the strike, was fired. Dozens of other postal workers were fired or suspended.[19]

In January, 1923, the secretary of the Fédération Postale Unitaire, Henri Gourdeaux, and two other postal leaders, Lartigue and Leopold Cazals, were arrested along with the secretary-general of the CGTU, Monmousseau, Marcel Cachin of *L'Humanité,* and others, accused of a plot against the government for organizing a campaign against the French occupation of the Ruhr, a policy that was opposed by all the left-wing parties and syndicats, reformist and revolutionary alike. The Senate, sitting as a high court, eventually condemned Poincaré's precipitous arrest of his left-wing opponents, but not before Gourdeaux had spent five months in prison.[20] Ideological differences were forgotten as the confédérés of the PTT joined the protest against the arrest of the unitaire leaders.[21]

The government's campaign of harassment was particularly pernicious against the teachers. The least infraction, the least involvement in politics, the merest expression of opinion, was the occasion for dismissal or suspension. One by one, the teachers were condemned: for participating in May Day activities, for writing pacifist articles, for publishing in socialist newspapers, for publishing in *L'Humanité,* for expressing ideas publicly, for having "watched the sale" of a brochure.[22] Following in the footsteps of previous secretaries of the teachers' syndicat who had been fired for syndicalist activity—Nègre in 1907 and Hélène Brion in 1918—Louis Bouët, the head of the Syndicat de l'Enseignement Laïc and a member of the national committee of the CGT, was fired in 1920 for having left work to attend a special syndicalist meeting.[23] Other syn-

18. Edouard Bonnefous, *Histoire politique de la troisième république* (7 vols.; Paris, 1959), III, 316.

19. Frischmann, *Histoire PTT,* 238–39.

20. The arrests had actually taken place the night before the French troops entered the Ruhr.

21. Frischmann, *Histoire PTT,* 240–42.

22. *L'Humanité,* October 30, 1924.

23. Max Ferré, *Histoire du mouvement syndicaliste révolutionnaire chez les instituteurs* (Paris, 1955), 240.

dicalist leaders were attacked as well; Marie Guillot, for example, was fired for signing a statement of the revolutionary committees.[24] Marthe Bigot, cleared by a council of discipline for having signed a protest against the mobilization of the class of 1919, was fired by the prefect of the Seine. In January, 1922, three hundred departmental council members, citing many other grievances, resigned in protest against her dismissal. These same councillors were overwhelmingly reelected two months later.[25] Another institutrice, Berthe Fougère, not only was fired by the prefect of the Nièvre for having written an article in support of Marthe Bigot but was fined five hundred francs for "anticonceptional propaganda."[26] The historian Maurice Dommanget, the secretary of the Syndicat de l'Enseignement Laïc of the Oise, was censured for sending an appeal for the fired teachers to the local papers. Dommanget responded that the *state* and the *government* must not be confused: "It must not be forgotten that, in effect, when entering the teaching ranks, the teachers have not made a contract with such and such government which has been put in power for a time by the vagaries of political life, but with the state, in its role as administrator of the schools. To charge them for criticizing the government and the current minister is to pervert the contract."[27]

The attack on the teachers continued. A teacher at a provincial normal school was fired because he wrote articles against Poincaré and attended political debates.[28] A Clermont-Ferrand teacher was fired because he spoke against the occupation of the Ruhr.[29] Another case was the occasion for an amusing headline in La Lanterne: "Monsieur Bérard [the minister of education] wants to fire a teacher guilty of not admiring Monsieur Poincaré."[30] Hundreds of teachers were put under surveillance, and reports on their activities were sent from the prefects of the departments to the Ministry of the Interior.[31] Even Emile Glay, the secretary of the confédéré syndicat, was not to escape. In May, 1923, for

24. Le Matin, April 30, 1921.
25. AN, F7 13745.
26. AN, F7 13746.
27. L'Humanité, May 14, 1922.
28. Le Journal, April 4, 1923.
29. AN, F7 13746.
30. AN, F7 13745.
31. AN, F7 13744. I have copies of some of these reports, which include amazing detail on the personal as well as the political habits of the observed fonctionnaires; one teacher had, in the

what one newspaper called "an offense of lèse-majesté," Glay faced an "administrative inquiry."[32]

The "witch-hunt against the teachers" and the denial of the fonctionnaires' right to participate openly in the political process became more critical with the approach of the legislative elections of 1924. The CGT and the fonctionnaires were determined to oust from power the conservative coalition that was attempting to destroy their organizations. Soon after the CGT congress at Lille, with the elections still more than two years away, the Fédération des Fonctionnaires pledged that in addition to organizing communal action against proposed wage cuts, it would mount an electoral campaign against the Bloc National.[33] Glay, the head of the confédéré teachers, called for a special subscription "where each fonctionnaire who contributes will only be paying a minimum insurance premium for the safeguard of his freedoms and his right to a decent living."[34] In June, 1922, the CGT newspaper Le Peuple announced that the Cartel Confédéré des Services Publics had called for a massive electoral campaign for 1924.[35] At the closing banquet of the November, 1922, congress of the Fédération des Fonctionnaires, the delegates were addressed by politicians active in the attempt to create a coalition of the Left. The fonctionnaires cheered as Painlevé raised his glass "à la loi de 1884." They cheered even more as Paul-Boncour called Painlevé "this past and future president of the council." The very mention of the Bloc National unleashed a chorus of hisses and boos. Paul-Boncour told them: "The Bloc National is placed in a tragic situation; if they leave you alone, you will oppose them. If they persecute you, you are still against them."[36]

By the spring of 1923, the government began to worry about the electoral activity of the fonctionnaires. Speaking at public meetings in April and May, Poincaré voiced his disapproval of the involvement of state servants in political matters; it was the fonctionnaire's duty to be loyal, to be obedient to the government. At a speech at Bar-le-Duc, the head of

---

course of his numerous activities, been instrumental in the creation of a temperance society. Ironically, many of the reports include the information that the teacher under surveillance had served valiantly or had been wounded or gassed in the war.

32. Le Peuple, May 10, 1923. He was later acquitted.
33. AN, F7 13734.
34. AN, F7 13727.
35. AN, F7 13734.
36. Le Matin and Le Journal, November 12, 1922.

the government was very specific about the electoral campaign: "It is inadmissible that they [fonctionnaires] fight for their individual needs against the general interest, that they try to substitute their personal will for the national will, that they use the office they hold from the state and the influence their position gives them to throw themselves into an electoral battle." The reaction to this denial of the right to participate in electoral politics was immediate. An article in L'Ere Nouvelle, posing the question, "Is the fonctionnaire a citizen?" answered itself, "Yes, said Monsieur Millerand in 1897, No, instructs Monsieur Poincaré in 1923." The independent left-wing newspaper, one of whose frequent contributors was Painlevé, went on to analyze the Republic of the Bloc National: "If the Republic refuses freedom of thought, the citizen's right to a free opinion, this is no longer a Republic. But are we really in a Republic? Sad question, even more painful answer." In a series of articles on the liberties of fonctionnaires written for Le Peuple, Raymond Figeac decried "the regime of bullying." It was forbidden to read: douaniers had been denied the right to read or even to carry their syndicat newspaper L'Action Douanière or other corporative newspapers while in uniform. It was forbidden to attend meetings: the minister of education, Léon Bérard, had supported disciplinary action against teachers who spoke against their local deputies or attended syndicat meetings. And, of course, it was forbidden to be a syndicalist.[37] The droit syndical once again merged with the droit d'opinion. Fonctionnaires renewed their pledge to go into the elections against the Bloc National for freedom of opinion.[38]

As the election drew closer, it became obvious that the Bloc National was having difficulties. The occupation of the Ruhr, the reestablishment of relations with the Holy See, the worsening economic crisis—the wholesale price index went to 510 in March, 1924, and the head of the government was facetiously called "Poincaré la livre à 100 francs" (Poincaré the pound at 100 francs)—and the attacks on the syndicats all helped to pressure the Left into organizing a coalition of its disparate parties. In 1919, the Left had been in disarray, the Right able to maintain electoral unity. Now the situation was reversed. The Radical party ceased supporting the disappointing Bloc National and joined with the SFIO, despite some disapproval among the left-wing socialists, to form an electoral coalition, the Cartel des Gauches. The fonctionnaires, most of

37. L'Ere Nouvelle, May 17, 1923; Le Peuple, May 18, 22, 1923.
38. Bulletin Officiel des Contributions Indirectes, June, 1923.

whom were attached to the parties of the Left, rallied to the coalition. The CGT had already made its demands known. Of prime importance was the maintenance of the eight-hour day, the extension of social insurance, the implementation of levies against capital in lieu of the income tax on workers' salaries, and the creation of a Conseil Economique du Travail. Such an economic council had been proposed by the CGT in 1919 to include representatives from industry, government, and labor, as well as technical experts, economists, and lawyers, to help coordinate French industrial production. One purpose of the council was to begin studying the possibility of nationalizing some parts of French industry. But of equal importance to the CGT was the demand for the maintenance and extension of state monopolies and for the droit syndical for the fonctionnaires.[39] Electoral meetings and demonstrations were planned. Jouhaux warned: "If we do not win, if our efforts are in vain, it would mean the stifling of the syndical movement for a good number of years. If those in the Bloc National are returned to power, this time they will be able completely to institute their programs and use them against us. Let's oppose our will against their greed."[40]

The election of 1924 was the first time the fonctionnaires were effective as a group in an electoral campaign. Taking their lead from the Union des Intérêts Economiques, the Confédération Générale de la Production Française, the Union de la Propriété Batie de France, the Comité des Forges, and other capitalist pressure groups, the fonctionnaires claimed their right to influence the election on behalf of their corporative interests. The fonctionnaires did not want to get involved in politics, the confédéré cheminot Marcel Bidegarray told a meeting in Valenciennes, but politics was all around them: "The railroad worker is political when he demands the nationalization of the rail system. The fonctionnaire is political when he demands what is his due. It is also politics which creates the problems and raises the cost of living. Poincaré does politics when he says at Dunkirk that the occupation of the Ruhr doesn't cost a penny and that anyone who disagrees is a liar."[41]

39. Alfred Sauvy, *Histoire économique de la France entre les deux guerres* (4 vols.; Paris, 1965–75), I, 47, 54, 57.

40. AN, F7 13735.

41. AN, F7 13732; see introduction to electoral questionnaire of the Fédération des Fonctionnaires; *ibid.*, November 21, 1923.

Candidates received a questionnaire asking for an indication of support for the droit syndical, freedom of opinion, amnesty for fonctionnaires penalized for their opinions or for syndicalist activity, cost-of-living increases, and the collaboration of the state and fonctionnaires in effecting administrative reform.[42] Results of the poll were made known at meetings and in newspapers.

The disaffection of the fonctionnaires most certainly contributed to the defeat of the Bloc National. On May 11, the Cartel des Gauches won a surprising victory, which was to bring to power under the leadership of Edouard Herriot a host of Radicals who were to play an influential role in the remaining years of the Third Republic.[43] The fonctionnaires lost no time in making their demands known to the newly elected cartel. Even before the new government was formed, Laurent, Glay, and others issued their call for salary increases, the droit syndical, and administrative reform.[44]

Plagued with a hostile Senate and near economic disaster, various governments of the Cartel des Gauches eventually moved closer and closer to the center. Within two years Poincaré was called on once again to form a government of Union Nationale. But during the first year of its life, the Cartel des Gauches effected important changes in government policy with regard to fonctionnaire syndicats.

Almost as soon as the new cabinet was constituted, the Herriot government turned to the question of amnesty. Maginot told the Radicals, "Amnesty is the price of the cartel which you have been forced to form." With feelings about the amnesty of two former ministers, Malvy and Caillaux, running high, the Chamber debate was prolonged. Finally, at an unusual July 14 session, an amnesty bill was approved. Included in the pardon of wartime deserters and others condemned by the Courts was an amendment which ordered the "obligatory" reintegration of railroad workers who had been fired after the railroad strike of 1920. The Senate, unhappy that amnesty was granted to fonctionnaires who had been on strike, decided to delay action on the law. Neverthe-

42. Ibid., November 21, 1923.

43. The new cabinet included Camille Chautemps and Edouard Daladier and a carryover from previous cabinets, Henri Queuille. The 1925 Painlevé cabinets introduced Georges Bonnet and Pierre Laval to the government.

44. See most newspapers in May, 1924, for example, L'Eclair, May 19; Le Rappel, May 20; Le Quotidien, June 1.

less, in September, the government ordered the reintegration of seven hundred former railroad strikers and asked the owners of the private lines to follow suit. The reintegration of a number of instituteurs was also announced. For the political right and the railroad companies, this was too much; for the left-wing fonctionnaires, not enough. The Fédération de l'Enseignement Laïc (the Bouët group) complained about the limits of the amnesty. Five teachers, Marthe Bigot, Marie and François Mayoux, Claudius Buard, and Marie Guillot, had been amnestied, but dozens of others, including such important syndicat leaders as Julia Bertrand (fired in 1914), Hélène Brion (fired in 1918), Louis Bouët (fired in 1920), and Gabrielle Bouët (fired in 1921), remained condemned for their pacifist or syndicalist activities. The opposition at the Luxembourg eventually caused even the limited amnesty proposals to be weakened. The National Assembly now asked the government to use its discretionary powers of pardon to "demand of the railroad companies the largest possible number of reintegrations."[45] Few companies responded.

As the amnesty proposals were being discussed, the government moved toward legalization of the fonctionnaire syndicats. In a ministerial declaration read to the Chamber on June 17, Herriot affirmed the intention of the government to recognize the droit syndical of the fonctionnaires. In August, the syndicats were tacitly accepted when representatives of the Fédération des Fonctionnaires were officially received by the minister of the interior, Camille Chautemps, in the presence of other ministerial officials, and in September, an official circular urging cooperation between government and representatives of the fonctionnaires was sent to all ministers. It stated: "The government considers that it is good for the proper functioning of services and social peace that the heads of the administrations and the majority of their staff, instead of building a wall of ignorance and hostility between the two, maintain regular and trusting relations."[46]

But the law extending the droit syndical to fonctionnaires still did not come. In February, 1925, Chautemps, questioned in the Chamber as to why there was not yet such a law, answered that the government planned to offer, "in a short while, a projected law recognizing the droit

---

45. Bonnefous, Histoire politique, IV, 34, 39; see articles in L'Humanité, October 30, 1924.
46. Ferré, Instituteurs, 296.

syndical for the fonctionnaires."[47] Of course, the law would not provide the right to strike. But the Chabrun-Bertholet proposition of June, 1925, which would have extended the law of 1884 to fonctionnaires, was never seriously discussed. At any rate, it is not likely that any such legislation would have passed the Senate. Although de facto recognition of fonctionnaires was accepted by successive governments of the Third Republic, it was not until October 19, 1946, that the fonctionnaires would finally receive the benefits of the droit syndical.

Although the struggle for their organizational and political rights was the focus of much fonctionnaire activity, other issues were also of vital concern to them in the early 1920s. One issue that touched fonctionnaires and ordinary citizens alike was the apparent inefficiency of public service. Complaints about bureaucratic red tape, poor telephone service, unequal tax collection, and wasteful expenditures were heard in the press, at citizens' and businessmen's meetings, at market stalls. As always, the public frequently blamed the most obvious target, the state employees. This antagonism toward the fonctionnaires was intensified by the belief that the state payroll had grown enormously during the war. In actuality, at a time of great expansion of government service, fonctionnaires' positions had increased from 1914 to 1922 by only 18 percent, mostly to cover extension of financial services (income tax), telephone, social insurance, and services related to national defense and the war such as pensions for widows and war wounded and the administration and rehabilitation of the "liberated areas."[48] Although there was a good deal of "antifonctionnairisme," the fonctionnaires themselves agreed with the consumers. There was indeed inefficiency and waste. The fault, however, lay not with the poor petits fonctionnaires but with the indifferent hauts fonctionnaires, the hierarchical and archaic organization, and the government. The inefficiency and wastefulness of public service was nowhere more evident than in the PTT. The vast communications network of this service had been neglected during the war, and as the postwar financial crisis worsened the government attempted to save money by curtailing employment and appropriations.

47. *Le Quotidien,* February 27, 1925.
48. François Perroux, *Les Traitements des fonctionnaires* (Paris, 1933), 13.

The postal workers appealed to the public: a 1920 poster entitled "Are we Heading Toward the Paralysis of the PTT?" accused the government of promoting a "speed-up" and gross inefficiency.[49] By 1921, there was a new crisis. The government of the Bloc National had recently turned over the developing radio industry to a private monopoly, and it was feared that other state monopolies would be similarly sacrificed. The telephone service was particularly vulnerable.

To the CGT and the fonctionnaires who had been campaigning for the expansion of government control of public service, including the nationalization of the railroads and the municipalization of gas and electric utilities, the possibility that existing state monopolies might be lost to private enterprise was of great concern. The postal workers, their service immediately threatened, once again appealed to the public. Posters were circulated and put on walls of cities and towns all over France. One poster, titled "The Auctioning off of the PTT," warned against private ownership of the PTT: "The powerful financial interests who dominate France have chosen the PTT. They have just taken over the radio. They would now love to get their claws on the telephone service. Tomorrow, the telegraph service, then the mail will stimulate their lust and will be in danger of becoming their prey." The PTT must be reorganized and given a proper budget; the monopoly must not be turned over to private industry. Another poster entitled "A Catastrophe Awaits!!!" warned that the inadequate proposed PTT budget would mean the sacrifice of much needed repairs stemming from neglect during the war and the equally needed expansion of services.[50] The monopolies were defended at fonctionnaire meetings, which protested the ceding of the radio to groups of private capitalists by the secretary of state without the permission of the parliament.[51] More posters appeared. A 1922 poster of the Fédération Postale (confédérée) asked the public, "Must we yield the telephone to private industry?" The poster told the public that fonctionnaires agreed that telephone service in France was inefficient and expensive. But giving telephone service to private industry would encourage not competition but monopoly, and private monopoly was interested only in profit,

49. AN, F7 13804.
50. Le Travailleur des PTT, July 1, 1921.
51. AN, F7 13730, Nice, November 21, 1921. See also AN, F7 13732 and 13731, meetings at Lille, October, 1921, and Bordeaux, January, 1921.

which well might not be efficient. The state gave honest and efficient service; it had done well during the war. Telephone service was bad because money was not spent on it.[52]

The threat against the government monopolies continued. Private industry received permission to take over the manufacture of matches, and there were plans to do the same for tobacco. Digat, speaking at the March, 1924, congress of the Cartel Confédéré des Services Publics, attacked the "liberal" economists who viewed the state's role as that of a policeman who must not interfere in the "free play of economic forces." There was no "free play" under the regime of trusts and monopolies, which sacrificed the "general interest to profit their individual interests."[53]

With the defeat of the Bloc National, the danger of the suppression of state monopolies subsided somewhat, but the question of inefficiency did not. For the fonctionnaires, the solution to the problem did not lie in bringing in more private management. After all, the ongoing inflation and financial crisis only proved the failure of capitalism. The answer was administrative reform with the cooperation of the fonctionnaires. The PTT employees called not only for financial autonomy but for the PTT to be directed, not by an irresponsible bureaucracy but by an administrative council, which would be composed of elected representatives of consumer groups: chambers of commerce, blue-collar syndicats, agricultural groups, and workers' cooperatives, as well as government representatives and fonctionnaires themselves.[54] The Fédération des Fonctionnaires also called for the reorganization of services and cooperation between government and fonctionnaires.

The necessity for the fonctionnaires to cooperate in the reorganization of public service was the subject of a major discussion at the 1922 congress.[55] Aware of the public hostility to fonctionnaires, the federation distributed handbills to voters before the elections which blamed the administration rather than the fonctionnaires for bureaucratic inefficiencies.[56] These issues of the 1920s—administrative reform and fonc-

---

52. AN, F7 13805.
53. *Le Peuple,* March 10, 1924.
54. AN, F7 13805; see poster, "Il faut réorganiser les PTT," December, 1921.
55. AN, F7 13727.
56. AN, F7 13735.

tionnaire cooperation versus government monopoly—continued to be discussed throughout the 1930s and, indeed, are discussed in France today.

The political shift to the right that had brought about the election of the Bloc National and the resurgence of ultraconservative forces in the early 1920s raised other issues of prime importance to the thousands of teachers in the state school system. The renewal of official ties with the Vatican, the reluctance of largely Catholic Alsace and Lorraine, now returned to France, to accept the French secular school system, the rise in the number of church schools in the more conservative areas in the west of France, and the attempt to get state financial aid for private religious schools brought to the surface once again the old but still festering antagonism between defenders of the faith and defenders of the republican *école laïque*. The harassment and firings of prominent syndicalists further convinced the state teachers that the very existence of the école laïque was in danger. When the government in a 1922 economy measure announced that fifty thousand fonctionnaires would be dismissed from service, including sixteen hundred teachers, it was seen not as an economy move but as an attempt to weaken the école laïque. Teachers were to be fired, but there would be no troop reductions in the Ruhr occupation or in Syria.[57]

The defense of the école laïque was one issue on which both revolutionary and reformist teachers agreed, and the congresses and meetings of both syndicats in the early 1920s devoted much discussion to the danger of clerical resurgence. The 1922 congress of the Syndicat des Instituteurs was particularly concerned with the clerical domination of education in Alsace and Lorraine,[58] and congresses of both groups in 1923 passed resolutions in favor of the école laïque. Committees of Défense Laïque were established in many areas, and large meetings were called to protest religious infiltration into the educational system; seven thousand attended a meeting in just one city, the industrial center of Saint Etienne. At a meeting of the Cartel de l'Action Laïque in Lyons in June, 1923, the huge crowd of mostly teachers was told by Cazals of the Fédération Postale that they must defend the école laïque as the only place where

57. AN, F7 13745, meeting at Marseilles, November 11, 1922.
58. *L'Ere Nouvelle,* August 9, 1922, report on congress.

the social ideas of the Left could be developed.[59] The children were mobilized: fête days were inaugurated, marches were organized, and plans
were made for a Week for the Defense of the Secular Schools to counter
the very popular Catholic Weeks.[60]

Even after the election of the Cartel des Gauches, the fears for the
secular school system continued, as hundreds of thousands of practicing
Catholics rallied to such organizations as the Ligue des Catholiques,
Union Catholique, Association de la Jeunesse, Union des Hommes
Chrétiens, and Fédération Nationale Catholique. At the August, 1924,
congress of the Syndicat des Instituteurs, a resolution beginning with
the words "Considering that the assault on the secular schools is more
vigorous than ever . . . reaffirms that the teachers, by making the secular school active and attractive, thereby make it beloved," asked for,
among other things, the implementation of the same public school statute for Alsace and Lorraine as existed in the rest of France, that fonctionnaires be obliged to send their children to state schools, the elimination
of all remnants of teaching orders, the denial of any state funds to private schools, and the assurance that all teachers hired by the state were
indeed laïques.[61] Herriot's attempt to laicize Alsace and Lorraine and to
close the embassy at the Vatican only intensified the antagonisms between "the cartel of materialists and the cartel of believers."[62] In 1925, as
tensions mounted, street demonstrations ended in violent clashes between the two groups; in Marseilles, one such clash resulted in two
deaths and dozens wounded. The church-state controversy, which had
dominated the domestic politics of the early Third Republic, continued
to plague its twilight days as well.

The church-state controversy spilled over to yet another educational
concern of teachers and other fonctionnaires—the reform of the educa-

59. AN, F7 13746, March 13 and June 8, 1923.
60. AN, F7 13746, December, 1923, and AN, F7 13745. At Dieppe in March, 1922,
the Jeunesses Laïques were denied permission to have a choir rendition of "La Carmagnole,"
"La Marseillaise," "Ca Ira" and "Le Chant des Jeunesses Laïques" because the songs were
considered "too revolutionary." The meeting went on; the audience, told that the "Chant des
Jeunesses Laïques" had been sung in 1909 for the subprefect who had helped found their group,
erupted in shouts of "Vive la Liberté."
61. AN, F7 13746.
62. Bonnefous, *Histoire politique*, IV, 62, quoting words used by the Abbé Bergey at
Rennes, spring, 1925.

tional system to make it more utilitarian and accessible to children of workers, artisans, and peasants. The primary school system, with its *certificat des études primaires* awarded to those thirteen-year-olds who had passed an examination, had been, since the Ferry laws, the foundation of popular education. Open to all, these schools, taught by teachers devoted to republicanism and laicism, were instrumental in training millions of French children to an appreciation of French culture and devotion to the Republic. But if the primary schools were the cornerstones of democratic education, secondary education, particularly the lycées, which trained for the baccalaureate, remained the preserve of the bourgeoisie. Students destined for the lycée usually attended primary schools attached to the lycées. Regular primary school children desirous of continuing their education were channeled into *écoles primaires supérieures,* but the *brevet* awarded those who completed the curriculum did not permit them access to universities and Grandes Ecoles or to the more prestigious and well-paid positions in government and industry. Indeed, most instituteurs were themselves products of these poor relations of the more prestigious lycées. Only a handful of students were able to enter the lycées, which charged tuition, were located in larger urban areas, and required courses, such as Latin, not usually taught in primary schools. Lycées continued to be the training ground for the elite. John E. Talbott, in his study of the politics of educational reform, says that "it is not wholly an exaggeration to say that under the Third Republic, the 'sans-latin' was the social counterpart of the 'sans-culottes' of the Revolution."[63]

Despite the fear of some on the extreme Left that lycées would indoctrinate workers' children with the values of the bourgeoisie, the democratization of the school system and the equalization of opportunity for all children to receive a high-quality education, including free access to lycées, had long been urged by left-wing teachers and others interested in promoting the interests of working-class and peasant children. The periodical of the revolutionary teachers, *L'Ecole Emancipée,* had pushed for such reform even before the war. By 1919, the CGT, the SFIO, and a number of influential Radicals had become convinced that educational

63. John E. Talbott, *The Politics of Educational Reform, 1918–1940* (Princeton, 1969), 31–32. In 1913, only 2.5 percent of children between the ages of eleven and eighteen attended lycées.

reform was a critical issue. Under the rubric *l'école unique,* demands were made for reform of curriculum, abolition of lycée fees, and improvement of secondary education for those who did not attend lycées. Edouard Herriot, in his 1919 book *Créer,* envisaged the école unique as a means of social reconciliation, a way of tying the working class to the Republic and, perhaps, to the Radical party: "We will not have the right to invite the workers to consider themselves members of the common family as long as we have not put our children and their children side by side. . . . If the French people do not have the clairvoyance and the courage to assure regular social advancement by work and knowledge, we will lose any right to protest against revolutionary demands."[64] Indeed, in an effort to expand its electoral base, the Radicals made educational reform an important part of their postwar program.

As the Left continued to press for reform to democratize the schools, it met opposition from numerous Catholics, who viewed the école unique as another attempt to extend the state monopoly over the educational system, and from sections of the bourgeoisie anxious to maintain their control over positions of power in government and industry. From 1919 to 1924, the government of the Bloc National, representing these more conservative elements of French society, offered little hope for the realization of the école unique. Indeed, the reform legislation of the Bloc National was to deepen the elitism of the lycées. In 1922, at the same time the teachers' syndicats were being dissolved, the minister of education, Bérard, sought to make Latin a requirement for all lycée students. At once, the old argument that had raged in the seventeenth and eighteenth centuries, that of moderns versus ancients, was the subject of private and parliamentary discussion. But the discussion was more than philosophical; the implications of the Bérard decree were clear. Without other reforms opening access to the lycées, the Latin requirement would make it even more difficult for the children of workers and peasants to receive distinguished higher education; children from primary schools and from *écoles primaires supérieures,* not having studied Latin, would be unable to transfer to lycées. In that context, even those supporters of the école unique, who favored the latinized curriculum, could not accept

64. Edouard Herriot, *Créer* (2 vols.; 1919), II, 135–38, 157–58, quoted in Talbott, *Educational Reform,* 55.

Bérard's proposals, which were finally made official in the spring of 1923.

The instituteurs, of course, opposed the Bérard reforms, but the professors of the lycées and the universities would be the most vocal against the latinization of the lycée curriculum. Their support of the école unique had already been indicated by the enthusiastic response to the formation of the Compagnons de l'Université Nouvelle. Even before the war was over, a group of professors had been writing articles about proposed changes for what they hoped would be a new university system. Calling themselves les Compagnons de l'Université Nouvelle, the Fellowship of the New University, the group published in 1919 a two-volume critique of the system with proposals for a thorough reform of the entire school system and specifically of higher (including lycée) education. Condemning the heavy-handed centralism and orthodoxy of government control, which created teachers who were "an anarchic group of fonctionnaires, badly paid, without soul and without their own thoughts," the Compagnons recommended greater diversity and decentralization in higher education. But most critical in their reform plan was the establishment of equal education for all students and the opening of higher education to the most qualified students no matter what their class origins.[65]

A number of secondary school and university professors had belonged to the syndicat of instituteurs before the war, but they did not begin to form their own syndicats until the postwar period. Less proletarian than primary school teachers, the professors were slower in coming to syndicalism. Nevertheless, in the early 1920s, several syndicats were established. In 1924, under the leadership of Ludovic Zoretti of the University of Caen, Lucien Herr, the influential librarian of the Ecole Normale Supérieure, and several lycée professors, the Syndicat National des Membres de l'Enseignement Secondaire et de l'Enseignement Supérieur was established and brought into the CGT.[66] Although the secondary and university professors continued to maintain a separate syndicat, when the instituteurs and the Fédération des Fonctionnaires reentered the CGT in 1925 and 1927, Zoretti would be instrumental in

65. Paul Gerbod, "Associations et syndicalismes universitaires de 1828 à 1928," *Le Mouvement Social*, No. 55 (April–June, 1966), 34.
66. AN, F7 13746.

creating a federation of all the teachers' syndicats. It was these professors and others who led the fight for the école unique. At a meeting of the Compagnons de l'Université Nouvelle, the eminent Sorbonne professor Daniel Mornet told an audience of more than four hundred secondary and university professors, "One does not need four years of Latin to be intelligent and one can be an eminent man even without Latin." Another Sorbonne professor, Charles Guignebert, addressed the same meeting on the question of the école unique: "Governments have always made the mistake of failing to instruct people, and it is ignorance which is the best guarantee of tyranny. Democracy must begin by democratizing the mind. The democratic machine must be run by competent people and all the proletariat must have access to the leadership of the country."[67] On December 13, 1923, a huge meeting held "against the Bérard decrees and for equal educational opportunity for all children" featured dozens of speakers, including Herriot and Painlevé, both former professors, the syndicalist leaders Glay, Laurent, and Jouhaux, and a host of eminent professors, among them Henri Lévy-Bruhl, Paul Langevin, Emile Borel, and Daniel Mornet.[68]

The Cartel des Gauches made much of its support for the école unique in its election campaign, but even though the Bérard decree on Latin was rescinded, little else was accomplished by Herriot and succeeding ministers. Educational reform, like so much else, fell by the wayside in the face of the enormous financial crisis that destroyed the coalition. The teachers, however, never forgot the goal of free, open education for all. In the mid-1920s, a compromise between the ancients and the moderns was reached, allowing students to continue to choose modern languages as an alternative to the classics. And finally, in 1930, the process of eliminating lycée tuition was begun; in 1933, in the depths of the economic depression, lycées and collèges were made tuition-free.

The abhorrence of war and the desire to train students who would be rational, socially conscious adults led many teachers in the early 1920s to maintain another ideological position which in hindsight seems most unusual. Because the teaching of chauvinist devotion to la Patrie and the glorification of military exploits dominated much of the curriculum of

67. AN, F7 13745, June 23, 1922.
68. AN, F7 13746.

French history taught in the state school system, many syndicalist teachers, especially those who had been horrified by the war, came to the conclusion that history as a subject must not be taught to primary school children. The teaching of history, they argued, must be postponed until the children were old enough to reason; history must be limited to the secondary school curriculum. The issue was debated at the 1924 congresses of both syndicats, and it was finally decided that the content of the curriculum, not the subject itself, should be changed. Indeed, history prepared students to participate more fully in society.[69]

The increased class consciousness and political activity of fonctionnaires affected women employees as well. Compared to other industrial countries, France had always had a high proportion of working women, and increasingly, these women were entering public service.[70] The war had, of course, accelerated the process, and large numbers of women, many of them war widows or women whose marriage prospects had been diminished by the high casualties of the war, remained in government service. In 1921, approximately 27 percent of state workers were women, and as government services expanded in the interwar period, large numbers of women employees were hired in the Ministries of Hygiene, Commerce, Labor, Industry, and Public Works.[71] Despite the objections of some who wanted women dismissed so more war wounded would be employed, the women not only continued to work, they continued to press their demands for improved working conditions.[72] The nontenured auxiliaries, mostly women, had formed their own organizations during the war, and now they used these groups to fight for the regular appointments the government was so slow in granting, for housing indemnities and other benefits awarded to regular fonctionnaires, and against the preemptory firings of auxiliaries whenever the government decided to tighten its purse strings. During the financial

69. See discussion in newspapers, *L'Ecole Emancipée,* June, 1924, and AN, F7 13746.

70. See Evelyne Sullerot, *Histoire et sociologie du travail féminin* (Paris, 1968).

71. *Les Femmes dans la fonction publique,* Notes et Etudes Documentaires, La Documentation Française No. 4056–57 (January, 1976), 9. The figures cited come from A. Sauvy, *Bureaux et Bureaucraties* (Paris, 1967). M. A. Brimo, "La Femme dans la fonction publique," *Actualité Juridique* (1956), gives lower figures for 1921 but higher ones for 1931.

72. AN, F7 13804; see, for example, a June 18, 1920, meeting of postal workers which voted a resolution demanding "the dismissal of women as letter carriers and their replacement with war wounded."

crisis of the early 1920s, the auxiliary state employees and the "war victims" met frequently to voice these demands. Threatened with firings in
the spring of 1922, hundreds of auxiliaries organized a series of demonstrations at the Chamber of Deputies. At one such demonstration, several women were arrested. As the crisis deepened, the question of regular appointments became more critical. Receiving little real support
from the syndicats of "official" fonctionnaires, the auxiliaries took to the
street once again in the spring of 1925, this time bringing their case to
the Ministry of Labor.[73]

Among the "regular" fonctionnaires, the women employees were
most concerned with equal pay and equal advancement. Equal pay for
equal work had long been the aim of women fonctionnaires, and in
the 1920s, with prices rising, this demand took on added importance.
The Fédération des Fonctionnaires had voted at its 1919 congress for the
principle of equality of salaries, working conditions, recruitment, and
retirement, as well as maternity leave, but the issue of women's rights
was just one of many demands made by the fonctionnaires, and it did
not receive top priority.[74] Only the institutrices had achieved the principle of wage parity. The ministries of Education and the PTT had the
largest number of female employees, and it was in these two services
that the women were most active. Throughout the 1920s, dames téléphonistes and other women employees met to protest their working
conditions and unequal wages. Twelve hundred telephone operators,
meeting in June, 1923, complained that though telephone use had expanded, the economy-minded government had reduced the number
of operators. At a February, 1926, meeting of fifteen hundred PTT
women, concern was expressed that the government, by granting higher
salaries to institutrices, was trying to split the women fonctionnaires.
The women teachers responded that they had fought within their syndicats to receive the same wages as men; they advised the PTT women
to do the same. And in the spring of 1927, there came into existence the
Ligue des Dames des PTT. Committed to equal pay for equal work and
for equal access to all examinations and all jobs, the organization lasted

73. AP, BA provisoire 305, March 21, 1922. At one demonstration on April 2, 1925, a
wounded veteran was arrested but later released when it could not be proven that the veteran,
confined to a wheelchair, had actually kicked a policeman.

74. AN, F7 13727.

for just over one year, when it was reabsorbed by the regular confédéré Syndicat des Agents.[75]

For many women fonctionnaires, particularly those militants in the Syndicat de l'Enseignement Laïc, the corporative issues of equality of wages and advancement were part of a wider question, one which took into account the political and social position of all women in French society. Women teachers had always been active in their syndicat—Hélène Brion had been among the leaders of the syndicat when she was arrested during the war—and they had been equally active in the political struggles of the era. Marie Guillot, Marthe Bigot, Hélène Brion, and others, who had been the leaders of the pacifist movement during the war, were more than syndicalists, more than communists or socialists; they were also feminists. Their activity centered around their syndicat, but for these feminists, syndicalism was not enough. For Marie Guillot, for example, feminism was an integral part of the social revolution. Writing in *L'Ecole Emancipée* in 1921, she urged the women to meet separately to press for action.[76] At the same time, she chastised the male syndicalists: how could they expect women to join the syndicat, she asked, when they were given no power? Hélène Brion had earlier put a statement into the minutes of the 1919 teachers' congress which said that women attending the congress observed with regret that in the various discussions pertaining to ways to bring about the social revolution not one reference had been made to the emancipation of women.[77]

In early 1920, militant women of the federation decided to form feminist groups so that, "in a sympathetic and welcoming atmosphere," they could speak their minds more freely. The demands of the feminist teachers are perhaps best described by outlining the program of the Groupes Féministes de l'Enseignement Laïc.[78] The corporative program demanded longer maternity and nursing leaves and equality of wages on all levels of teaching. The pedagogic program called for the end of the separation of the sexes, that is, for coeducation on all levels, and for sex education in the schools, an important demand considering the wave of

75. AP, BA provisoire 307; Frischmann, *Histoire PTT,* 272–73, 295–96.
76. *L'Ecole Emancipée,* February 5, 1921.
77. From *L'Ecole de la Fédération,* August 30, 1919, cited in Ferré, *Instituteurs,* 287.
78. See Anne-Marie Sohn, "Féminisme et syndicalisme: Les institutrices de la fédération unitaire de l'enseignement de 1919 à 1935" (Thèse en doctorat de troisième cycle, Paris X, Nanterre, 1973).

pronatalism sweeping the country and the passage in 1920 of legislation that outlawed "provocation to abortion" and "contraceptional propaganda."[79] The group's social program called for taking part in the struggle for the rights of women—for reform of the Napoleonic Code, the right to vote, and a social transformation.[80]

The syndicat newspaper *L'Ecole Emancipée* continued to carry feminist articles throughout the 1920s. In a series of articles on women's suffrage, the readers were reminded that even in the Orient, where there were so many chains to be broken, advances had been registered. In Madras, in Bombay, and in Rangoon, women could now vote in municipal elections. In France, where feminist thought had been born, where women had been called on so often to do their duty for society, women could not vote. The Senate, in 1919 and again in 1922, had rejected the suffrage law passed by the lower chamber. Apparently, the venerable gentlemen of the upper chamber, who could create national and international boundaries with aplomb, would not break down the barriers between the sexes.[81] Suffrage was defeated largely because of the overwhelming antifeminism of the Radical party; 70 percent of the antisuffrage votes in 1922 came from the Radical senators.[82] Oddly enough, support for female suffrage was not universal even among left-wing males. Conservatives worried that suffrage would bring about the breakdown of traditional society, and some socialists and communists feared giving women the vote because they worried about the political strength of bourgeois women and felt that many women, "under the influence of priests," would be anti-Left.[83] Just as fonctionnaires had to wait until the end of World War II to get the droit syndical, so French women had to wait until the constitution of 1946 to receive the right to vote.

The fonctionnaires emerged from the war more conscious than ever of their political and social needs. In the postwar period these fonctionnaires participated fully in working-class organizations and political ac-

79. Steven C. Hause with Anne R. Kenney, *Women's Suffrage and Social Politics in the French Third Republic* (Princeton, 1984), 231.
80. AN, F7 13746.
81. *L'Ecole Emancipée,* April 8, 1922.
82. Hause, *Women's Suffrage,* 242.
83. AN, F7 13732; see, for example, a preelection meeting at Arras, May 4, 1924.

TABLE I

Mean Annual Index of Retail Prices, 1919–1928

Year	Mean Index	Month of December	
		Sauvy	SGF[a] 13-Item Index
1919	255	289	285
1920	366	398	424
1921	324	312	323
1922	301	309	305
1923	334	364	365
1924	378	399	404
1925	414	451	463
1926	532	574	599
1927	549	538	523
1928	550	572	596

SOURCE: Alfred Sauvy, *Histoire économique de France entre les deux guerres* (4 vols., Paris, 1965), I, 499, 501.

[a] Statistique générale de France.

tivity. But the multiple political and corporative interests of all state workers, from the highest echelon to the lowest, was dominated, in the early 1920s, by one overriding concern—the economic crisis and inflation that threatened to destroy the already weakened standard of living of French fonctionnaires. The complicated economic history of this period—the postwar deterioration of the franc, the economic crisis of 1921–1922, the monetary crisis that reappeared in 1923 and began to develop into a panic in 1924—cannot be fully analyzed here. For the workers and fonctionnaires of France, however, one aspect of the monetary crisis was of critical importance—the rise in the cost of living. Using a 1914 base of 100, Alfred Sauvy determined the mean annual index of retail prices as shown in Table 1. Prices rose rapidly in 1919 and 1920 (the inflation rate between these two years was 44 percent), tapered off with the business crisis of 1921–1922, began to climb again with the revival of the monetary crisis and the occupation of the Ruhr, and soared in 1925 and 1926 (between these two years the inflation rate was 29 percent). By 1925, there was talk of foreign speculators and plots, and it was feared that France would experience a catastrophic inflation similar to the one that had devastated Germany.[84]

Both blue-collar workers and fonctionnaires struggled to have their salaries keep pace with the spiraling prices, and apparently, in the immediate postwar period, blue-collar workers were more successful than fonctionnaires in approaching this goal. In their study of salaries and buying power between the wars, Sauvy and Pierre Depoid calculate that by 1928, based on an index of 100 for 1913, the *pouvoir d'achat* (buying power) was 144 for blue-collar workers and only 128 for state workers. But this was after the stabilization of the franc and the substantial salary increases of 1925, 1926, and 1928 for fonctionnaires. Until 1925, François Perroux concludes, fonctionnaires were grossly underpaid: "The fonctionnaire has been sacrificed." In 1923, when the cost-of-living index had gone over 330, the salary index for the lowest-paid fonctionnaires (3,000 to 6,000 francs per annum) was only 253, while the medium echelon (6,000 to 12,000) was at a still lower index of 202. For the highest-paid fonctionnaires (from 12,000 to 25,000 in 1913 and 30,000 in 1923), salaries increased only 54 percent, which caused many officials to worry that they might lose their higher and middling cadres to private industry and commerce. In 1926, when the cost-of-living index soared way above 500, fonctionnaires' salaries were still under 400. It was not until the stabilization of the franc and the salary increases of January, 1928, that fonctionnaires were able to regain and surpass their 1913 buying power. By 1938, the fonctionnaires were to pull ahead of blue-collar workers.[85] Fonctionnaires maintained their standard of living in the late 1920s and early 1930s largely because they made such a strong effort to present their case to the government.

At the end of the war, in addition to increased family allocations, a special indemnity of 720 francs had been awarded to those fonctionnaires earning under 6,000 francs per annum. The indemnity was meant as a

84. The economic and financial crisis is fully analyzed in Sauvy, *Histoire économique*, I, esp. 74–81.

85. Alfred Sauvy and Pierre Depoid, *Salaires et pouvoirs d'achats des ouvriers et des fonctionnaires entre les deux guerres* (Paris, 1940), 58, 30; Perroux, *Les Traitements*, xiii, 44, 142–43. Fonctionnaires' wages in 1938 were at 148 compared with 139 for blue-collar workers; agricultural wages fell to 80.

temporary measure, and in the spring of 1919 the first of numerous postwar commissions established to study fonctionnaires' salaries was convened under the chairmanship of the vice-president of the Conseil d'Etat, Henri Hébrard de Villeneuve. Within a few months, the commission recommended increases which raised starting salaries to 3,800 francs (they had been 1,200 to 1,500 in 1914) and maximum salaries to 30,000 (as opposed to 25,000). No sooner were the 1919 increases implemented than the soaring inflation rendered them insufficient. The legislature in 1920 had no choice but to vote the 720-franc indemnity.

Because of its assumed temporary nature, the indemnity was a doubtful award, and each year much agitation surrounded its renewal. Furious that war profiteers had gone unpunished—many workers and fonctionnaires were convinced that inflation could be blamed on war profiteers and postwar speculators—that the income tax affected workers more than capitalists, and that precious money was being spent fighting in Russia, fonctionnaires' meetings, leaflets, and posters argued "for the maintenance of the 720 francs." A leaflet headlined "Defend Our Bread," issued in the summer of 1921, indicated that the thirteen-item "market basket" index had, in the second trimester of 1921, reached 364, while salaries had remained at 250. The fonctionnaires further argued that this particular price index, including such items as bread and meat, which the government had made a special effort to control, did not accurately reflect the true situation. The maintenance of the indemnity was essential.[86]

It was a new phenomenon for the syndicats and others to use wage and price indexes to support wage demands, even though there was some disagreement over the accuracy of the government's statistics. Wage indexes for fonctionnaires, for example, sometimes included cheminots and sometimes did not. The Statistique Générale de France (SGF) calculated a wholesale price index which included a wide number of manufactured goods. Of far greater concern to the general public, of course, was the retail price index, which the government calculated on the basis of a meager thirteen items, refusing, as Sauvy laments, to issue a true index of the cost of living, which would include housing, clothing, and other expenses such as health care. As Sauvy says, "And it

86. AN, F7 13731, August, 1921.

was just this which interested, and rightly so, the syndicats and public opinion." The SGF apparently had a wider, more useful index, but, afraid of the misinterpretations already evident with the thirteen-item index, it released those figures only to "experts" and to international conferences. Even though a complete cost-of-living index was not available, there was no doubt that fonctionnaires' salaries were lagging behind prices.[87]

In the spring of 1922, with the inflation rate slowed—it had even decreased somewhat—and business in crisis, it was feared that the government would allow the indemnity to die its scheduled death in June. The government had already discussed the elimination of fifty thousand fonctionnaire positions to save money. Once again a campaign was launched for the indemnity; the fonctionnaires argued that despite recent price decreases, salaries had still not kept up with the inflation. An April, 1922, leaflet insisted that the indemnity should be kept as long as the index remained over 200. (It had slipped just below 300 in March and April.) Moreover, given the volatile nature of the economy, with prices rising and falling each month, there was no guarantee that the 1922 hiatus would last. And, indeed, the fonctionnaires were correct in this assumption.

The fonctionnaires had always argued that the answer to their cost-of-living problem lay not in temporary expedients like the 720-franc indemnity but in a wage structure that would reflect accurately the needs of state employees. Until wages were more responsive to the inflation rate, however, the indemnity was to remain critical. For the first time, there was talk of an *échelle mobile,* a sliding scale that would attach salaries (or indemnities) to fluctuations in the cost of living.

The slowdown in the inflation rate did not last. By spring, prices had begun to creep upward again; by fall, the price index was nearing 350 and still rising. The 720-franc indemnity could no longer bridge the gap between the 1919 salary scale and the actual cost of living. *Le Populaire* commented on June 7, 1923: "Salaries no longer correspond to what is needed to live. The fonctionnaire, like the worker in private industry, sees his buying power reduced every day." The fonctionnaires, con-

87. Sauvy, *Histoire économique,* III, 353. Sauvy discusses the problem of the SGF on pp. 344-64.

fédérés and unitaires alike, launched a campaign for salary increases (three times the 1914 scale was the goal in October, but this was to be raised as prices increased), for an échelle mobile, and, knowing how long such legislation would take, for an immediate indemnity of 1,800 francs. Throughout the fall of 1923, thousands of fonctionnaires rallied "to defend their bread."

One of the more interesting aspects of this campaign for the 1,800-franc indemnity was the strong support it gathered in the liberated provinces of Alsace and Lorraine. More than three thousand fonctionnaires came to a meeting in Mulhouse in October, and in November and December meetings in Strasbourg drew crowds of more than four thousand. The fonctionnaires of Alsace and Lorraine had been complaining since the end of the war that their reintegration into the French system had placed them in a disadvantageous position. The German system had afforded fonctionnaires higher salaries and better working conditions. Now they wanted from France what they had received from Germany—their *droits acquis,* vested rights. Coloring these corporative demands was the fear of many that the French educational system would destroy their culture; their maternal language, German, was being condemned by "metropolitan teachers" coming to Alsace-Lorraine from France. At a 1921 meeting, fonctionnaires of the Bas Rhin (old Alsace) agreed with a speaker who said that they had greeted *la Patrie* with open arms only to find themselves treated as foreigners, as *boches.* In the fall of 1923, the Alsatians, disgusted with the "hideous spectacle" of fonctionnaires remaining under the German system receiving pensions that enabled them to live better than those under the French system, enthusiastically declared that they would "march with their French comrades" for the 1,800-franc indemnity.[88]

As 1923 drew to a close, the campaign for the 1,800 francs intensified. On November 24, hundreds of fonctionnaires leaving a meeting called by the Cartel Unitaire, which had drawn an attendance of nearly five thousand, streamed onto the Grands Boulevards, shouting for "our 1,800 francs." The December issue of the *Bulletin Officiel des Contributions Indirectes* carried the banner headline, "Everyone out for the 1,800

88. AN, F7 13732; see meetings of February 27, 1921, December 9, 1923, and a Strasbourg meeting of January, 1921.

francs."[89] On December 10, a meeting organized by the Fédération des Fonctionnaires brought eight thousand fonctionnaires of all ideological persuasions to the largest meeting place in Paris, the gymnase Japy. Confédérés, unitaires, *autonomes*—all were united in their demand for the 1,800-franc indemnity. On December 17, Parisian fonctionnaires took to the streets. Thousands of state employees, responding to a call from the Cartel Unitaire to demonstrate at the Place de l'Opera, were met by a huge number of police, who had been instructed to prevent the demonstration from taking place. The fonctionnaires, attempting to reach the open square in front of the Opera, were attacked in the numerous side streets leading to the square by policemen on horseback. The demonstrators dispersed, regrouped, dispersed, and regrouped again. The next day *L'Humanité* wrote, "Last night, the center of Paris, the area of business and pleasure, was under police martial law." Seventy-seven were arrested.

The role played by the police in this demonstration illustrates a dichotomy that has continually troubled the fonctionnaire organizations. On December 17, the Paris police had attacked and arrested fonctionnaires demonstrating for their indemnity. The very next day, a delegation of police agents arrived at the Chamber of Deputies to ask their representatives to take a written statement to the minister of the interior demanding the implementation of the 1,800-franc indemnity.[90] Only a few weeks before, on November 19, seven thousand police had rallied for their bonus at the Salle Wagram in Paris, and on December 11, when another meeting scheduled for a hall on the Quai de Gevres proved too large for the room, thousands of policemen spilled out onto the plaza in front of the Hotel de Ville. On-duty policemen were sent by the prefect of police to attack the off-duty police. The cry went up, "The cops are fighting each other!" Several police officials were hurt, and sixty members of the police federation were arrested and subsequently suspended from their jobs.[91]

The policemen, so often used to break up demonstrations and strikes,

89. AP, BA provisoire 305; *Bulletin Officiel des Contributions Indirectes*, No. 181 (December, 1923).

90. *L'Ere Nouvelle*, December 19, 1923.

91. Frischmann, *Histoire PTT*, 248; *L'Humanité*, December 12, 1923. Frischmann also cites the memoirs of Piquemal of the Contributions Indirectes.

were, after all, fonctionnaires. Many were organized and affiliated with the Fédération des Fonctionnaires. The attitude of workers and fonctionnaires toward the police agents reflected this dual position. Many viewed the police as enemies; others saw them as comrades in misery. When the police were disparaged by a speaker at a preelection meeting in the spring of 1924, a PTT member rose to their defense: "The police are fonctionnaires and like any other employees of the government, they also want to improve their conditions."[92] The federal council of the Fédération des Fonctionnaires voted a gift of one thousand francs "to affirm sentiments of fraternal solidarity to the police personnel charged with having demanded the right to a decent living by demonstrating for the 1,800 francs."[93] But the question posed by a fonctionnaire at another meeting reached the heart of the matter. The question, Were the police "good men and comrades or were they brutes?" continued to be debated in working-class and fonctionnaire circles.[94]

One day after the December 17 demonstration, the Chamber began its discussion of the fonctionnaires' indemnity. For Poincaré and the Bloc National, it was to be another test of the coalition's policy of opposition to the fonctionnaires' syndicats. Salaries were scheduled to be revised in December, 1924; there was no need to do anything until then. Money was short; the indemnity was to be denied. When several left-wing deputies then tried to introduce an amendment to have the scheduled salary adjustment advanced a few months, that also was rejected. The Bloc National would not even tolerate an amendment that would have divided representation on the salary commission equally between administration appointees and elected delegates of the fonctionnaires. Poincaré accepted that fonctionnaires might make up one-third of the committee, but they would be appointed, not elected. There was an uproar on the Left. Poincaré was accused of being antidemocratic. The revered old Radical Ferdinand Buisson, barely audible above the din, rose to make an appeal for "republican principles." Poincaré responded: "According to republican principles, authority rests here and not in the fonctionnaire associations. We will not prepare the ground for sovi-

92. AN, F7 13733, meeting at Annemasse, Haute Savoie, April 14, 1924.
93. Le Populaire, January 9, 1924.
94. AN, F7 13733, meeting at Le Mans, December 2, 1923.

ets."[95] The fonctionnaires, both confédérés and unitaires, vowed to continue the struggle.

The rejection of the fonctionnaires' demands for more money, coupled with the refusal to recognize the legitimacy of their syndicats, made the removal of the Bloc National a prime objective of the fonctionnaires in 1924. As the spring election approached and the cost of living continued to rise, fonctionnaire meetings and newspapers campaigned vigorously for the droit syndical, amnesty for fired fonctionnaires, and salary increases. Confédérés and unitaires were united in these demands. A mass meeting "against the high cost of living" on February 8 was addressed by Lartigue of the Fédération Postale Unitaire, Laurent and Glay of the Fédération des Fonctionnaires, and Rigail of the Fédération de la Police.[96] By favoring the rich, the speculators, and the capitalists, the Bloc National had brought ruin to the country and to the workers. A large preelection meeting in Nice issued a condemnation of the Bloc National, determining that "the high cost of living has no other cause than the antidemocratic policies followed for these four years. . . . Men who by their negligence, their incapacity or their impartiality, have assured the victory of mercantilism and speculation." The fonctionnaires had been shamefully underpaid in 1914, and now their standard of living was deteriorating even further; the postwar inflation was eliminating whatever vestiges of middle-class life-style they had. Piquemal told a Rochefort audience: "The middle class has disappeared. Only the proletariat and an enriched bourgeoisie remain."[97]

The election of the Cartel des Gauches raised the hopes of many fonctionnaires. Throughout the summer, the cost of living, though high, had remained stable. In August, Herriot had officially received the delegates of the fonctionnaire syndicats, and the limited amnesty had been voted. In July, the new Villeneuve commission (with two-thirds administrators and one-third appointed fonctionnaires) began to discuss the salary adjustments scheduled for December. Although the 1,800-franc indemnity was not forgotten, particularly by the unitaires, interest now centered on making salary demands known to the Villeneuve commis-

95. *L'Humanité,* December 23, 1923.
96. *Bulletin Officiel des Contributions Indirectes,* March, 1924.
97. AN, F7 13730, meetings at Nice, April 28, 1924, and Rochefort, April 27, 1924.

sion. The Fédération des Fonctionnaires launched a campaign for a 6,000-franc minimum and an échelle mobile tied to the cost-of-living index. The demand for the 6,000-franc minimum received support from most of the fonctionnaires although the unitaires and Piquemal of the independent Contributions Indirectes insisted that with the cost of living index over 350, the scale should begin at 6,500. Nor did they relinquish their campaign for the 1,800-franc indemnity. Until the commission acted on the salary increases, the unitaires argued, fonctionnaires needed an immediate indemnity. The unitaires had never supported the Cartel des Gauches, and by September, when it seemed clear that the Villeneuve commission would reject even the more modest demands of the Fédération des Fonctionnaires, the unitaires talked more and more about "the treason of the Left." L'Humanité equated the politics of the Cartel des Gauches with those of the Bloc National.[98] At the end of September, the Villeneuve commission decided not to accept the 6,000-franc minimum; it would go no higher than 5,600. A special congress of fonctionnaires was called for early October. Clearly the honeymoon was over; the fonctionnaires were determined to fight for their money.

As disappointment with the Herriot government grew, so did the antagonism between confédérés (including the autonomous Fédération des Fonctionnaires) and unitaires. At a large Cartel Unitaire meeting held on the evening of October 4, not only was Herriot attacked but Laurent and Digat of the federation were accused of playing the government's game. Six thousand francs were not enough; the unitaires continued to press for 6,500. The crowd spilled out onto the streets shouting for the 1,800-franc indemnity, booing Herriot. L'Eclair headlined the event, "The beautiful electoral promises were not kept."[99]

On October 5, a special congress of the Fédération des Fonctionnaires convened to decide what would be done about the government's reluctance to grant the desired 6,000-franc minimum. Also present at the meeting was a delegation of unitaires and, representing the left wing of the federation, Piquemal of the Contributions Indirectes. The tone of the congress was set by one delegate who interrupted Laurent to cry

98. L'Humanité, September 4, 24, 1924.
99. AN, F7 13733; L'Eclair, October 5, 1924.

out, "This is the moment for fonctionnaires who gave their electoral support to the Cartel des Gauches to make them pay the price of their victory," and the position of the Fédération des Fonctionnaires was set by Laurent's answer: "Obviously we contributed heavily to the electoral battle. However, we are not demanding to be paid for our actions of May 11, but rather salaries that will enable us to live."[100] The congress voted overwhelmingly to continue the struggle for the 6,000-franc minimum and the échelle mobile. The question was, What tactics should be used? Piquemal offered a program of action that included the reconstitution of the Cartel des Services Publics, consisting of the Cartel Confédéré, the Cartel Unitaire, and the Fédération des Fonctionnaires; refusal to collaborate with the Villeneuve commission; and a leaflet, poster, and press campaign. Finally, instead of meetings where the convinced addressed the convinced, Piquemal suggested the organization of public demonstrations: fonctionnaires must go into the streets. Laurent expressed the hope that pressure put on the legislature would make Piquemal's plan unnecessary and eliminate the possibility of a strike, but he added that if the government failed them, fonctionnaires might consider such actions.[101] The congress voted to continue the federation's policy of collaboration, but there was a real possibility that the more extreme tactics of the unitaires might be used.

Even the hauts fonctionnaires were dissatisfied. The commission was offering them an insignificant increase. With the index approaching 400, they wanted increases of four times the 1914 wages, to cover every category of fonctionnaire. On October 9, more than one thousand hauts fonctionnaires at the Ministry of Finance met in the great hall of the ministry to express their dissatisfaction with the work of the salary commission. The newspapers made much of "a demonstration by the highest level of finance personnel."[102]

As winter approached and prices began to rise again, leaflets, articles, and speakers at meetings became more agitated. Six thousand francs had been the demand when the index was at 330; it was now at 390. Some unitaires were talking not of 6,500 francs but of 7,000. *L'Humanité*

100. AN, F7 13733; *L'Humanité,* October 6, 1924.
101. AN, F7 13733, October 7, 1924.
102. See, for example, *Le Journal,* October 10, 1924.

quoted Piquemal: "This struggle between the state personnel and high finance is in reality only an episode in the battle of wages and the class conflict. If we carry it off, the government will have to start down the path of recovering capital, the only way of getting out of the current situation." If the fonctionnaires succeeded in getting their desired minimum salary, it would be difficult for private industry to ignore the example set by the state. A victory for the fonctionnaires would be a victory for the entire working class.[103]

In 1925, the fonctionnaires received their salary increase with a minimum set at 5,600 francs. Once again, almost as soon as the new salary schedule was introduced, the increases were outpaced by a galloping inflation. In February, the price index went over 400, by December it had risen another 50 points, and by the middle of 1926 it was moving dangerously close to 600.[104] The Cartel des Gauches changed finance ministers and then cabinets. Herriot gave way to Painlevé, Painlevé to Briand, Briand to Herriot. Nothing could stop the inflationary spiral. Finally, at the end of July, 1926, what was left of the coalition of the Left gave way completely. Poincaré took over the reins of government, inaugurating a harsh financial program that would help stabilize France's troubled economy.

In the difficult period 1925–1926 fonctionnaires' discontent reached a fever pitch. Meetings and leaflets gave way to street demonstrations and work stoppages. The fonctionnaires, having joined the organizations of the blue-collar working class, moved closer and closer to accepting the tactics of the working class as well. The rising cost of living was driving respectable fonctionnaires into the streets. The heightened financial crisis also aggravated the ideological and tactical differences that continued to plague the fonctionnaire organizations. Fonctionnaires of all persuasions were most anxious to present a unified front to the government, and, indeed, during this period, there were frequent meetings and demonstrations which brought together unitaires, confédérés, and autonomes. But discussions of tactics and policies also brought to the surface the bitter antagonism that separated unitaires and confédérés. The uni-

103. AN, F7 13731, meetings at Bordeaux, November 16, December 2, 1924; *L'Humanité*, November 18, 1924.
104. Sauvy, *Histoire économique*, I, 498–500. In October, 1926, the thirteen-item index went over 620 and the forty-five-item wholesale index was at 768; it had been 854 in July.

taires were accused of being extremists, confédérés of having sold out. Laurent was increasingly criticized, even in Fédération des Fonctionnaires circles, for his reluctance to take stronger action on the salary question. The CGT disapproved of the fonctionnaires' growing opposition to the Cartel des Gauches. Finally, there were bitter feelings between fonctionnaires of different ministries. The Fédération Postale Confédérée, for example, felt that the salary commission had failed to put PTT salaries on a par with those in other ministries, particularly the Ministry of Finance. In April, the Fédération Postale Confédérée issued a leaflet entitled "Postmen, Be Watchful," which complained that the postiers had been placed in a disadvantageous position.[105] Agents of the Contributions Indirectes were concerned that the PTT employees might break ranks, opting for independent action for their own demands, instead of supporting the struggle for the salaries of all fonctionnaires.[106] Despite these difficulties, the fonctionnaires continued to wage an increasingly militant campaign for their dignity and their standard of living.

The militant tone of the period was set at the beginning of 1925 by the frightfully underpaid *jeunes* of the PTT. In March, these young workers, some under fourteen years of age, staged demonstrations and finally a strike, demanding a more equitable indemnity than the government was willing to grant. The very militant strike received sympathetic support from older postiers. The Fédération Postale Unitaire was particularly strong in its support of the youngsters of the PTT. Money was collected, and Gourdeaux, the secretary-general, sent a letter to the parents of the strikers asking them to support their children.[107] Finally, the government agreed to raise the indemnity award, and although it was not as high as the *jeunes* had demanded, it was considered a victory.

The strike of the *jeunes* illustrates also the ongoing antagonism between the unitaires and the confédérés. The latter recognized the validity of the demand for the indemnity—during the strike, a delegation of confédérés had asked the minister of commerce and PTT to award the money to the young workers—but they never supported the *jeunes* as

105. AN, F7 13806.

106. See May, June, and July issues of *La Vie Syndical des Contributions Indirectes*, formerly *Bulletin Officiel des Contributions Indirectes*.

107. Frischmann, *Histoire PTT*, 366.

strongly as did the unitaires. One can only speculate that the unitaires' support for the strike helped temper the enthusiasm of the confédérés. At a Tours meeting of the Fédération Postale Confédérée held two weeks after the end of the strike, the unitaires were reproached for sending fifteen-year-olds to make a strike: "When the Fédération Postale goes into battle, we put men in front, then the women and the children behind."[108]

The activity of the Fédération Postale Unitaire in the strike of the *jeunes* and in the campaign against the sending of troops to Morocco for the Rif war-led to difficulties with the government. On June 18, responding to articles in *Le Travailleur des PTT* and *L'Humanité* which referred to the government as "assassins" in Morocco, the minister of commerce and the PTT broke relations with the Fédération Postale Unitaire. The police report on these events sent to the minister of interior speculated that the rupture would cause the unitaires to lose strength; it was hard to be a syndicat if one could not reach the government.[109] In July, Henri Gourdeaux, the secretary-general, was fired, not to be reinstated until 1936. Also dismissed from their jobs were two young leaders of the strike of the *jeunes*.

In the meantime, the confédéré postal workers, under the leadership of Digat, continued to press for special increases, *péréquations,* which would bring certain categories of PTT agents, notably the commis, to wage parity with the *vérificateurs* of the Contributions Indirectes. Throughout the month of June, protest meetings multiplied and newspapers talked of an imminent PTT strike.[110] The confédérés, declaring that the Senate had made the budget at the expense of the postiers, vowed at their congress on June 10 to go as far as a general strike if necessary; they were determined to preserve their dignity and to get their parity. On June 26, there were reports of scattered work stoppages in several cities, but there was no real strike.[111] The agitation continued throughout the summer. In August, the PTT members of the new salary commission, the Trépont commission, resigned.[112]

108. AN, F7 13806.
109. *Ibid.*
110. See *L'Eclair, L'Avenir, La Liberté, Le Petit Parisien,* and *L'Oeuvre* of June 3, 1925.
111. AN, F7 13806.
112. *L'Humanité,* August 2, 1925.

Also in August, the bank employees went on strike. Most of the bank workers were members of the Catholic Confédération Française des Travailleurs Chrétiens (CFTC). Originally organized in the late 1880s, the CFTC repudiated both class struggle and economic liberalism, championing the independent worker and family values; it supported the eight-hour day and family allowances. By 1920, it had approximately 120,000 members (less than one-tenth of the CGT membership of that year). Its strength rested largely with clerks and with miners and textile workers in strong Catholic areas; only about 11,000 were fonctionnaires. The militancy of the striking bank workers in 1925 and the textile strikes of the late 1920s and early 1930s pushed the conservative CFTC into direct action, some of it in alliance with the CGT.[113] Calling themselves "proletarians in blue tunics," the bank workers asked for support from the working class and the fonctionnaires. Two thousand members of the Fédération Postale Unitaire joined the bank workers at a meeting at the Bourse du Travail, and the Contributions Indirectes issued a strong statement of support, calling on the Fédération des Fonctionnaires to aid the bank workers.[114]

By September, the situation in the battle for special increases had worsened, Digat declaring, "We are not in conflict with the government but with other fonctionnaires." The Contributions Indirectes threatened a *grève des yeux fermés,* a strike of "closed eyes," unless its demands were met. "We also have decided to defend our members' situation." The postal unitaires, however, felt that the confédérés, by demanding salary increases only for the commis, were hurting the campaign for salary increases for all. Anxious for unified action, the Fédération Postale Unitaire told the Contributions Indirectes, "We are returning to action but you should know that the struggle we are waging is against the government and not against our brothers in misery and that we are doing this not for the commis alone but for all." The Contributions Indirectes

113. Lefranc, *Mouvement syndical,* 241. For a short history of the CFTC before 1940 see T. B. Caldwell, "The Syndicat des Employés du Commerce et de l'Industrie, 1887–1919: A Pioneer French Catholic Trade Union of White Collar Workers," *International Review of Social History,* XI, (1966), 228–66; Emile Coornaert, "Le Mouvement ouvrier 'chrétien' en France de 1919 à 1939," in *Mouvements ouvriers et dépression économique de 1929 à 1939* (Assen, 1966), 144–51; and J. Sternheld, *Cinquante années de syndicalisme chrétien* (Paris, 1937).

114. AN, F7 13807, August 28, 1925; *La Vie Syndical,* September, 1925.

responded by reaffirming its solidarity with the Fédération Postale Unitaire.[115]

By September 21, much to the chagrin of the CGT and the Fédération des Fonctionnaires, which wanted to avoid particularist action on the part of one syndicat as well as open conflict with the Cartel des Gauches, the agents of the telephone and telegraph service, mostly women, led a two-hour work stoppage for higher pay. In Paris, Marseilles, Lyons, and several other cities, from 11 A.M. to 1 P.M., there was no telephone or telegraph service. Confédérés and unitaires all stopped work. Calling the strike a "revolutionary coup d'état,"[116] Charles Chaumet, the minister of commerce and the PTT, fired a number of strikers, including Jean Baylot of the Fédération Postale. "The postal service does not belong to the postmen, the telegraph does not belong to the telegraphers, and the telephone does not belong to the women clerks; they belong to the nation," Chaumet told the agents.[117] The fired strikers told a Paris meeting that the strike had achieved its goal; the affair had been opened to the public. Now the government would have to act on the salary increases. The Fédération Postale leadership urged calm as protest meetings were organized in the wake of the firings.[118]

The beginning of October brought another round of meetings protesting the firings and demanding the *péréquations*. On October 8, 9, 10, and 11 thousands came to PTT meetings. On October 12, the same day the Communist party, the CGTU, and other left groups had called for a general strike against the war in Morocco and the Caillaux laws, there were PTT meetings in dozens of cities, but the discussions all centered around the specific wage demands of the postal employees, and they did not join the strike. There was, however, considerable criticism of Laurent and the Fédération des Fonctionnaires for not doing enough for the PTT.[119]

On October 13, Chaumet decided to end the sanctions against the two-hour strikers. Apparently the failure of the PTT syndicalists to join

115. *La Vie Syndical*, August, September, 1925; AN, F7 13729; *L'Avenir*, September 12, 1925.
116. *L'Echo de Paris*, September 23, 1925.
117. *L'Avenir*, September 24, 1925.
118. AN, F7 13807.
119. *Ibid.*, meetings at Cherbourg and Nantes, October 12, 1925.

the Communist-called general strike influenced his decision. Chaumet explained: "Never would I give in to political pressure on this question of reintegration. But when I observed the flawless attitude of the entire PTT personnel on the question of the attempted general strike yesterday, I did not hesitate to propose steps to pardon the agents punished following the two-hour strike." The floundering Cartel des Gauches was not anxious to alienate the confédéré section of the working class; a good part of its electoral support had come from the CGT and the reformist fonctionnaires. L'Humanité took this opportunity to point out that "against the Fédération Postale Unitaire, repression increases, but the confédérés are pardoned, indeed they are congratulated."[120]

The rift between the postal workers and other fonctionnaires was particularly distressing at a time when the financial crisis was becoming more and more severe. As the cost of living continued its upward climb, the need for unity of all fonctionnaires became more critical. Throughout the winter of 1925–1926, there were numerous calls for a unified organization and unified action. Piquemal, speaking at a November, 1925, meeting, called on all syndicalists, confédérés, and unitaires to form a bloc "to defeat the common enemy: capitalism," and in December, both the Fédération Postale Unitaire and the Fédération de l'Enseignement Laïc called on the Fédération des Fonctionnaires to join them in a front unique.[121] The échelle mobile would never become a reality while unitaires and confédérés, postiers and instituteurs, fought each other.

The Fédération des Fonctionnaires, led by the moderate Laurent, had, until now, avoided direct action. But as the winter progressed and the discussions of the salary commission dragged on and pressure from the unitaires mounted, the autonomous Fédération des Fonctionnaires became more active in the campaign for higher salaries. At the end of December, an appeal to the public, which began with the words, "What! The Fonctionnaires are Making Demands Again?" explained in great detail how the degradation of fonctionnaires' salaries was causing a crisis in recruitment on all levels, which boded ill for the public service. The leaflet, which called for the raising of salaries and the implementation of the

120. L'Avenir, October 14, 1925; L'Humanité, October 15, 1925.
121. AN, F7 13729, Cherbourg; L'Humanité, December 19, 1925.

échelle mobile, closed with a veiled warning: "If they don't listen to the complaints about our distress, the justice of our demands, they will be shirking a social and moral duty, and if the standard of revolt is raised among us, they must be aware that this is a revolt for rights and they must assume responsibility for it."[122]

In January, the Fédération des Fonctionnaires joined the unitaires in the streets. The two organizations, the Cartel Unitaire and the federation, had planned a demonstration for the "raising of salaries and the sliding scale" to take place on January 17. On January 14, the government, claiming that despite Laurent's assurances of a peaceful demonstration, the involvement of the more militant Piquemal and the "communist" Cartel would make the demonstration political rather than corporative, forbade the demonstration. The government prohibition failed to stop the action. Glay, writing in Le Quotidien that the demonstration was for liberty was well as wages, asked why the police and the army were more worried about the fonctionnaires than the fascist processions of Georges Valois.[123] The federal committee of the Fédération des Fonctionnaires, pledging an orderly demonstration, announced its determination to participate in the action. Notices were posted, and the January 16 issue of the newspaper La Tribune des Fonctionnaires carried Laurent's call for all fonctionnaires to come into the streets to demonstrate for their salaries. "The fonctionnaires are impatient with the government," wrote L'Ere Nouvelle on January 16. That evening more than two thousand unitaires gathered at the Bourse du Travail to hear representatives of various syndicats present their wage demands and call for unity of fonctionnaires and workers. The animosity between "fonctionnaires in jackets" and "workers in caps" must be swept away; "all wage earners are victims of the same exploiters and we must congratulate the cartel for leading such an energetic action for achieving a wage increase."[124]

On the afternoon of the seventeenth, a crowd of fonctionnaires, unitaires, and reformists, gathered on the sidewalk near the Tuileries at the Pont de la Concorde and the Ministry of the Marine. Blocked by a police barricade, several thousand headed for the Louvre, where they

122. AN, F7 13731.
123. Le Quotidien, January 15, 1926.
124. AP, BA provisoire 305.

picked up more demonstrators who had come across the Pont de Solférino. At the Carrousel, they held a meeting, and Métayer of the Douanes and Piquemal of the Indirectes addressed the crowd. The rest of the Tuileries demonstrators, attempting to get to the Opera, were blocked by the police, who waded into the crowd with their clubs. Some participants were hurt and eight demonstrators were arrested.[125]

The tenuous agreement that had permitted the coordination of effort for the January demonstration never blossomed into complete unity, organization, or action. The government's assurances on wage parity had permitted the dispute between the postiers and the other fonctionnaires to subside somewhat, but the ideological and tactical rifts in the Fédération des Fonctionnaires deepened. Between Laurent and Piquemal, who, despite their differences, had worked together for the development of fonctionnaire organization, there now existed open hostility. Piquemal and the militants of the Contributions Indirectes, who had continued to hold meetings and demonstrations in the provinces despite the disapproval of the federal bureau, were attacked as troublemakers by the *Tribune des Fonctionnaires*. The newspaper of the Contributions Indirectes, *La Vie Syndical,* remarked in its spring issue that, "pitted against the administration, against the Fédération des Fonctionnaires, against the Fédération Postale Confédérée," it had been a difficult year for their syndicat.[126]

The inflation continued; the fonctionnaires grew more impatient and the government more desperate. In April, mass arrests prevented a demonstration called by the Cartel Unitaire from taking place at the Opera, but there were scattered work delays by postiers and cheminots demanding immediate salary revisions. In June, with the cost-of-living index over 500, fonctionnaires' discontent intensified. Both the Fédération des Fonctionnaires and the municipal workers (mostly unitaires) had called for demonstrations on June 14. The municipal workers were to

125. The January events are described in detail in AP, BA provisoire 305. Both syndicats complained about the police brutality, as did journalists who had been manhandled by the police. For their part, the police complained about the fonctionnaires who had their families with them at the demonstration; they had most certainly brought their babies to prevent the police from hitting them.

126. AP, BA provisoire 307. Digat held a press conference on April 16 at which he expressed his satisfaction with the government's promises. See also *La Vie Syndical,* No. 205.

hold their demonstration in front of the Hotel de Ville, the fonctionnaires at the Chamber of Deputies. Then, on June 13, Piquemal was
called before the council of discipline for having sent a circular to the
members of his syndicat calling for direct action. The Contributions Indirectes membership responded immediately by calling for yet another
demonstration on the fourteenth, this one in support of Piquemal, to
take place in front of the Ministry of Finance. Thus Paris was treated to
the unusual phenomenon of three fonctionnaire demonstrations on the
same day. Crowds of fonctionnaires came down the Boulevard St. Germain to the Chamber of Deputies, some going over the river to join the
finance workers at the Tuileries as thousands of municipal workers
moved from the Hotel de Ville toward the Concorde and the Opera.
The day ended with hundreds of fonctionnaires, including Piquemal, arrested. On July 27 yet another unitaire demonstration, this one protesting the government's slowness in taking action on salaries, ended with
more confrontations with the police and numerous arrests.[127]

During the month of July, after speculation had plunged the franc to
an all-time low and the retail price index for June was at 544 and climb-
ing, the government was in crisis. The minister of finance, Caillaux, had
proposed a new financial program which included a disputed provision
for government carte blanche on the question of taxes. On July 17, the
Briand-Caillaux government gave way to a government headed once
again by Edouard Herriot, but before the cabinet could be seated it, too,
was rejected by the Chamber. On July 23, Raymond Poincaré formed
the fourth government of his career. Although the socialists refused to
join this cabinet, other members of the Cartel des Gauches, including
Herriot and Painlevé, did join, and the Union Nationale government
took office. On August 1, the recommendations of the salary commission were implemented; fonctionnaires' salaries now ranged from 6,900
to 75,000 francs, an enormous increase for the upper-level fonctionnaires. Although the new minimum did not match the inflation rate, this
increase in 1926, coupled with yet another in January, 1928, helped
bridge the gap between prices and wages.

In the fall of 1926, the Fédération des Fonctionnaires, always ideologically sympathetic to Jouhaux's organization, asked to be readmitted to

127. AP, BA provisoire 305.

the CGT. In 1927, although a minority group under the leadership of Piquemal remained autonomous, the formal adhesion of the federation to the CGT was ratified by the annual congress. Through the rest of the 1920s and early 1930s there were agonizing recriminations and organizational splintering until the dangers of economic depression and fascism encouraged the warring organizations to unite once again.

9

Before the Storm, 1927–1932

The decision of the Fédération des Fonctionnaires to reenter the CGT brought to the stagnating and weakened blue-collar federation a highly organized and politically active bloc of workers, which until 1936, combined with the federations of teachers and postal workers, was to constitute over one-third of the CGT. The next two chapters will show how in less than a decade, from the official entrance of the Fédération des Fonctionnaires into the CGT in January, 1928, to the Popular Front victory of May, 1936, the fonctionnaires were to emerge not just numerically but politically as the most important bloc within the labor federation. That the fonctionnaires would play such an important role in the CGT could not have been envisioned in 1928. Despite their superior numbers, they were newcomers to the federation, mistrusted and largely ignored by the deeply entrenched blue-collar leadership under Jouhaux's direction. The fonctionnaires had not shared the history, the strikes, the struggles, or the ideology of the blue-collar working class. But their numerical strength, their powerful and well-organized syndicats and federations, their steady membership, which did not rise and fall with each strike and demonstration, and their articulate and seasoned leadership could not long be ignored. For a few years, the fonctionnaires, mired in their own concerns, worked alongside but not with the other federations in the CGT. But by the early 1930s the tide was turning. Gradually the fonctionnaire leadership began to play a stronger role at the federal level of the CGT. Most critical were the economic and political developments outside the syndicat. The severe economic depression, the attempt of the government to lower the employment and salaries of fonctionnaires, and the rising threat of fascism brought the fonctionnaires into the political mainstream. They would emerge as the crucial voice for unity and for political involvement within the CGT. The fonctionnaires, never fully accepting the schism, steered the unity talks so that the final victory would not only be a reunified CGT but a CGT that would continue as a bastion of reformism. And the fonctionnaires, drawing on their tradition of political involvement, firmly led the CGT into open and clear support of the Popular Front government.

The fonctionnaires' reentry into the CGT was not only a conscious choice of an official alliance with the organized working class, it was also a clear commitment to the reformist politics of the vieille maison headed by Léon Jouhaux. And the addition of the large and articulate bloc of fonctionnaires committed to reformism would reinforce that position in the CGT. Although the CGT did not abandon entirely its revolutionary rhetoric in the interwar period, it was clear that its tactics for implementing social change were more and more directed toward working with its political allies on the noncommunist Left to legislate reforms. Eschewing the mass demonstrations and strikes of the preschism period, the CGT began to advocate the rationalization and nationalization of industry with worker participation to ensure that the nation, not just the capitalists, would benefit from the streamlined efficiency of the French economy.[1] This approach to the economy was echoed by the CGT's political ally the Socialist party. Speaking to the National Council of the party in early 1928, Vincent Auriol told his colleagues that to realize social reform, "it would be appropriate to proceed with the immediate nationalization of the following de facto monopolies owned by a minority of the privileged: insurance, petroleum, sugar, mines, and in the interest of agriculturalists, fertilizers, to be managed by corporations of users, the personnel and representatives of the state."[2]

Most fonctionnaires were at home in the house of reformism. Except for the postal workers and some members of the Contributions Indirectes, most state employees did not perceive the strike, illegal as it was, as a useful tactic for them. The Fédération des Fonctionnaires, under the leadership of Laurent, and the Syndicat National des Instituteurs, under Glay and Roussel and later André Delmas, had always preferred working with electoral campaigns and with petitions and delegations to depu-

1. For a discussion of the CGT's economic program, see Richard F. Kuisel, Capitalism and the State in Modern France (Cambridge, Eng., 1981), chaps. 3 and 4.
2. AN, F7 13079, January 5, 1928.

ties and ministries to demonstrating or holding protest meetings. Laurent spoke often about collaborating with the ministries to improve the efficiency of the public service, and Delmas was proud of the monthly meetings of the Syndicat National des Instituteurs with the Ministry of Public Education. "We don't want to take over the direction of public service," Laurent wrote, "but we want to be represented on the committees of direction." "We need to control the direction of the economy. . . . If we don't take over the direction of the economy, if we don't discipline the economy, I think we will see a collapse of the working-class movement and we will experience, as other countries have, the fascist regime which none of us want."[3] In 1927, as the Fédération des Fonctionnaires was entering the CGT, Laurent declared, "Reformists we are and we boldly proclaim it."[4]

Unfortunately, the unstable economy, the ever-changing ministries, the deep divisions and numerical weakness of the organized working class, and the general reluctance of French employers to grant any concessions to their employees worked against any reform. Except for some social security legislation, nothing the CGT asked for was accomplished. The calls for more worker control of rationalized and nationalized industries and for a planned economy went unheeded, as did less ambitious demands such as paid vacations. In short, the CGT before the era of the Popular Front was not only reformist, it was ineffectual.

In opposition to the class-collaboration position of the CGT, its rival federation, the CGTU, advocated class conflict. After the schism of 1921–1922, the CGTU had retained within its ranks not only those individuals and syndicats who were allied with the French Communist party, the Third International, and the Trade Union Revolutionary International, it had as well a large minority membership of noncommunist revolutionaries—prewar revolutionary syndicalists, anarchists, and others on the extreme Left whom modern French political analysts group under the rubric les gauchistes. These gauchistes were ill at ease with the ideology, highly centralized organization, and tactics of the Communist party but were nonetheless committed to revolutionary social

3. André Delmas, Mémoires d'un instituteur syndicaliste (Paris, 1979), 122–24; Charles Laurent, Le Syndicalisme des fonctionnaires (Paris, n.d. [1938?]), 29, 31.
4. La Tribune des Fonctionnaires, October 29, 1927, quoted in René Bidouze, Les Fonctionnaires, sujets ou citoyens? (2 vols.; Paris, 1979), I, 158.

change and found the position of the CGTU in supporting strikes, demonstrations, and other forms of direct action closer to their own political
position than the inactivity and reformist ideology of the CGT. Among
that group was a large fraction of the old prewar instituteur syndicat in
the Fédération de l'Enseignement Laïc. But gradually the revolutionary
syndicalists and anarchists became disillusioned or were purged. Some
went reluctantly into the CGT, others chose to be autonomous. By the
late 1920s the CGTU was more than ever tied to the politics of the
French Communist party.

Following the party position that the syndicalist movement was a
"school" for building the class consciousness and tactical expertise necessary for the ultimate victory of the proletarian revolution led by the
Communist party, the CGTU continued throughout the 1920s and
early 1930s to organize demonstrations and strikes for political as well as
economic purposes. The CGTU, for example, had been instrumental in
the calling of a general strike against the war with the Rifs in Morocco
in June, 1925. The CGTU, in direct contrast to the CGT, opposed the
rationalization of French industry as useless under capitalism and condemned all efforts to collaborate with capitalists and the government.
Although the direct action policies of the CGTU were in sharp contrast
to the lethargy of the CGT, the results were the same. A few individual
strikes for higher wages were victorious, but on the whole French industry, abetted by cooperative governments, made few concessions to
the workers' demands. CGTU membership was maintained through
most of the 1920s and recorded a sharp increase in 1926, but, troubled
by internal strife and party sectarianism and harassed by frequent arrests
of its leadership, it fell below three hundred thousand in the early 1930s.
The CGT registered a small membership increase in the late 1920s but
also fell short of five hundred thousand in the early 1930s, and most
of these members were fonctionnaires and other salaried workers, not
blue-collar workers. In 1934, a mere three-quarters of a million workers, slightly less than at the time of the schism in 1921, belonged to the
two major federations. The problem of determining official membership in the major labor federations is discussed by Antoine Prost. Both
the CGT and CGTU were fairly vague about membership figures during the time of the schism and when they were unified in 1935 issued
figures that would put them at an advantage in the new federation. Most

THE PROLETARIANIZING OF THE FONCTIONNAIRES

TABLE 2

CGT and CGTU Membership, 1921–1934

Year	CGT	CGTU	Total
1921	488,777	349,283	838,060
1924	491,114	—	—
1926	524,960	431,240	956,200
1928	554,796	370,260	925,056
1930	577,280	322,545	899,825
1932	533,197	258,575	791,472
1934	490,984	264,085	755,069

SOURCE: Antoine Prost, *La CGT à l'époque du front populaire, 1934–1936* (Paris, 1964), 35.

labor historians have traditionally used the figures of Georges Lefranc, which are, as Prost explains, the figures of Jouhaux and hence advantageous to his position as head of the CGT. Lefranc himself, in the leadership of the CGT as director of its workers' school, the Centre Confédéral d'Education Ouvrière, would also be anxious to use figures that would inflate the CGT's strength. Lefranc says that by 1930, there were over eight hundred thousand members of the CGT.[5] The very careful statistical study of Prost arrives at the figures shown in Table 2.

The period of the schism, 1921–1935, is one of the saddest chapters in French working-class history. Both federations, unable to gain support from most of the working class, ineffectual in their tactics, and powerless to bring about reforms in a period of calm, continued to fight each other rather than unite to win better conditions for French workers. Reading the reports of the annual congresses and the syndicalist press, one is struck by the constant internecine agony of the divided organizations. Although there was much activity on behalf of wage increases, paid vacations, the eight-hour day, and other worker demands, too much effort was wasted on blaming the other federation for the obvious failures of the working-class organizations. Both federations declared their fervent desire for unity, but their animosities clearly belied their

5. Antoine Prost, *La CGT à l'époque du front populaire, 1934–36* (Paris, 1964), 1, 2, 34; Georges Lefranc, *Le Mouvement syndical sous la troisième république* (Paris, 1967), 280.

spoken intent. The CGTU attacked the CGT for its inactivity, its collaboration with the class enemy, and its failure to support strikes initiated by the unitaires.[6] The CGT, led by men who were deeply anticommunist, constantly vilified the unitaires as agents of Moscow, betrayers of syndical independence, agitators who led workers into reckless and fruitless strikes. When unitaire leaders were fired or arrested, the confédérés did nothing to protest these attacks on working-class militants. And, of course, the powerful employer federations and the government used the schism to advantage. The demands of a divided and ineffectual working class were ignored.

To the divided and languishing CGT of 1927, the fonctionnaire syndicats brought a well-disciplined, relatively stable, and large membership. The Fédération des Fonctionnaires wanted to enter the CGT as one large federation of all state workers, encompassing the Syndicat National des Instituteurs, which had entered the CGT in 1925, and Zoretti's syndicat of higher education, the Fédération de l'Enseignement Supérieure, which had entered in 1923, as well as the Fédération Postale. The leaders of the Fédération des Fonctionnaires, Laurent and Neumeyer, argued that since other federations were industrywide, encompassing, for example, metals, mining, and construction, it would appear logical for all state employees to enter as one group. But both the teachers, who were wary of losing their independence to Laurent and the federation, and the CGT leaders, who did not trust the "intellectuals" and did not wish to allow such a large number of members to be in one federation, perhaps to dominate the CGT itself, blocked this formula. So the fonctionnaires entered as two federations—first, the Fédération des Fonctionnaires: Fédération de l'Enseignement, and second, the Fédération des Fonctionnaires: Fédération des Services Administratif. The Fédération Postale was to remain an independent federation within the CGT.

But not all fonctionnaires entered the CGT. A minority of postal workers in the Fédération Postale Unitaire (strongest in the Paris area) and the Fédération de l'Enseignement Laïc, as well as other workers in the public sector, were attached to the CGTU. The Contributions Indi-

---

6. See the syndicalist press and the description of the Fédération des Fonctionnaires in Bidouze, *Les Fonctionnaires,* I, 173.

rectes, led by the ever-dissenting independent Michel Piquemal, made it clear that they were unwilling to enter a CGT that was so reformist and would deny them the independence to join in meetings and demonstrations with the unitaires. Since neither Jouhaux nor Laurent was anxious to let in thousands of members who might strengthen the existing left wing within the CGT, the Fédération des Fonctionnaires expelled the Contributions Indirectes as well as the Eaux et Forêts, Douanes Actives, Penitentiaires, Enregistrement, and the commis de la Marine. In 1928, these organizations formed an autonomous cartel of public workers (autonomes) under the leadership of Piquemal.[7]

From 1927 to 1935, the fonctionnaires shared not only the working-class organizations but their ideological division, internal dissensions, and tactics as well. Split into three organizations and facing dissent within each group—there was a left wing among the fonctionnaires in the CGT, a right wing in the autonomes, and a noncommunist left in the CGTU—the fonctionnaires in this period were the largest and most stable bloc of adherents in the working-class organizations, especially the CGT, in which fonctionnaires made up between one-third and one-half of the total membership. Except for the approximately five or six thousand teachers and twelve or thirteen thousand postal employees, very few fonctionnaires, perhaps no more than 10 percent of the total membership, were in the largely blue-collar CGTU. If one adds state and municipal blue-collar workers who were in the autonomous federation and who frequently joined the meetings and demonstrations of the unitaires, between fifty and sixty thousand state workers at most were allied to the ideology and tactics of the CGTU. Using the figures from CGTU congresses, Roger Dufraisse says that in 1929 the unitaires had 182,000 in public service as compared to 229,000 in private industry. The figures for 1931 are 153,000 and 141,000—more public than private.[8] These figures do not correspond to most other estimates and must involve a very broad definition of public service workers, including not only railroad workers but those in such positions as municipal road repairers as well.

7. On the fear of the left wing in the CGT, see police reports in AN, F7 13580.

8. Roger Dufraisse, "Le Mouvement ouvrier français 'rouge' devant la grande dépression économique de 1929 à 1933," in *Mouvements ouvrier et dépressions économiques de 1929 à 1939* (Assen, 1966), 184.

Most fonctionnaires who supported the reformism of the CGT entered that organization. Whether one uses the higher figures of Lefranc, which indicate that the fonctionnaires, teachers, PTT, and public service federations numbered approximately 300,000 of the 800,000 members of the CGT during this period, or the lower figures of Antoine Prost— approximately 200,000 of 550,000—it is clear that for most of the eight years before the unity congress of 1935, the fonctionnaires made up more than one-third of the CGT membership. If one adds other state workers such as railroad workers on state-owned lines and other transport workers employed by state or municipal governments, the number grows even larger. The police figures of 1935—perhaps too generous— indicate that there were 350,000 fonctionnaires out of 800,000 in the CGT.[9] The fonctionnaires were thus the largest segment of the CGT; indeed, without the fonctionnaires to make up for its lost blue-collar following, the CGT would truly have been a mere shadow of its former self.[10]

While the fonctionnaires were determining their organizational and ideological allegiances with the blue-collar working class, other issues were affecting the daily working conditions of fonctionnaires in all services. Gone was the springtime of the Cartel des Gauches. With the election of the Poincaré government in April, 1928, the quest for the droit syndical was once again frustrated. Just before the election, the question of a parliamentary debate on the droit syndical had been turned into a vote of confidence by the government, and the legislators obediently acquiesced, denying the proposed law a hearing in the Chamber of Deputies. On a speaking tour just after the election, Poincaré made his government's approach to the question of fonctionnaires' rights crystal clear. "We must restore the authority of the state," he declared, "we must stand the pyramid back on its base."[11]

With the droit syndical out of reach, bread-and-butter issues once again took center stage. The use of public services had expanded, and

9. AP, BA 300.
10. See D. Blum, R. Bourderon, et al., Histoire du réformisme en France depuis 1920 (2 vols.; Paris, 1976), I, 48–49.
11. Bidouze, Les Fonctionnaires, I, 172–73; Georges Frischmann, Histoire de la fédération CGT des PTT (Paris, 1967), 290.

while the right-wing press railed against the fonctionnaires, blaming them for the inefficiencies and heavy financial burden of the public services, the state began experiments in "rationalization," a reorganization of services which often meant reducing the number of fonctionnaires. A fight against raising the retirement age and maintaining the pension level was also begun, and most urgent of all, there was the continuing problem of inadequate wages.[12]

The first public service to be touched by the national enthusiasm for rationalization was the PTT. As the most public of all the government's services, its weaknesses and inefficiencies were most obvious to the entire nation. Who did not have a story or complaint about lost letters, delayed telegrams, inkless or penless post offices, and, most frustrating, wrong numbers or long waits for telephone service. The most factorylike of all the services, the PTT seemed an ideal candidate for the French government's version of American "fordism." But though there was an attempt to make some technological improvements in telephone service by slowly introducing the automatic telephone, little was done to mechanize other parts of the service. Rationalization of mail delivery revolved around saving money: changing pickup stations, reducing shifts, and using more auxiliary and hence lower-paid personnel. To the postal workers, rationalization translated as more work with less personnel, and confédérés and unitaires alike were angered by the changes.

The Fédération Postale Unitaire issued statistics on the growth of postal service. From 1913 to 1928, postal usage had increased 78 percent (not taking into account the increased weight of newspapers and periodicals), whereas the number of general service employees (agents) had been increased by 29 percent and the distributive forces by only 13 percent. Telephone subscriptions had increased by 200 percent and long distance calling by 211 percent, but the staff had been increased by only 156 percent. The unitaire newspaper La Bataille des PTT claimed that there was more inefficiency because of lost personnel and called for the end to the "sabotage" of rationalization.[13] The CGT, of course, officially supported the rationalization of French industry and government services, but the postal workers attached to the CGT quickly registered

12. François Perroux, Les Traitements des fonctionnaires (Paris, 1933), 134. Perroux ascertains that between 1914 and 1930, 220,000 more fonctionnaires had entered the retirement system.
13. La Bataille des PTT, October 18, 1928, February 21, 1929.

their disapproval of attempts at rationalization that meant the loss of jobs. A member of the board of the Fédération Postale Confédérée, Dutailly, told a meeting of postiers, "I am a partisan of rationalization but in the interest of the worker not of the exploiter."[14]

Wildcat strikes erupted in Nice, Marseilles, Nantes, and Paris during the winter of 1928–1929, and in some centers rationalization plans were abandoned. But the issue would not go away. The readers of the *Bataille des PTT* were told in 1930 that the syndicat must continue to struggle for higher base pay, equal pay for women, and the end of rationalization.[15]

The question of efficiency in the post office and telephone service would be a long-term problem for fonctionnaires and administrators; a much more immediate problem in the waning years of the 1920s was the effort to raise the standard of living of the petit fonctionnaires in the PTT. This struggle for higher wages was to epitomize the agonies of the divided syndicats and federations. At the same time that postal workers of disparate factions met together in an effort to unify their campaign for higher salaries, charges and countercharges of collaboration and sabotage were traded by the leaders of each faction. And each faction had internal divisions as well.

The crux of the salary dispute was the relationship of the minimum wage in each job category to the cost-of-living index. The stabilization of the franc had helped stem inflation, but fonctionnaires' salaries still lagged behind the cost of living. After much saber-rattling on the part of PTT employees, including a five-hour strike of Paris telephone and telegraph workers and numerous protest demonstrations in 1927, the government had, in January, 1928, raised the minimum wage to 8,000 francs.[16] But the fonctionnaires had demanded at least 9,000. By 1929, the situation had worsened. The retail price index, which had been just above 500 in 1927 (on a base of 100 for 1914), was now once again near 600.[17] *L'Humanité* of June 14, 1929, including items not in the national official market basket, said that the index was 500 in November, 1927,

---

14. AN, F7 13811, February 16, 1930.
15. *La Bataille des PTT,* February 6, 1930.
16. AN, F7 13809.
17. Alfred Sauvy, *Histoire économique de la France entre les deux guerres* (4 vols.; Paris, 1965–75), II, 501. Sauvy's index of retail prices puts the figure at 530 for November, 1927, and 588 for November, 1929.

and 615 in April, 1929, a rise of 23 percent in eighteen months. The government proposed a new salary base of 8,500 francs, but with the index at 600 many fonctionnaires, especially those on the unitaire side, demanded six times the 1914 minimum, or 10,500.[18]

Aggravating the salary dispute was the knowledge that the salaries of the highest fonctionnaires were being raised enough to maintain or increase the wage gap between the lowest and the highest employees. The salaries of high-level administrators had lagged behind those in private industry, and the government attempted to maintain its staff by granting substantial increases at the highest level. But ordinary fonctionnaires saw only the obvious—their bosses were receiving huge wage increases. In January, 1928, when the minimum was raised to 8,000 for most fonctionnaires, the maximum salary for hauts fonctionnaires was 75,000 francs. In January, 1929, with the minimum still at 8,000 (maximums had been raised 500 francs to 10,500 for the facteurs, and the dames-employées had received a 1,000-franc increase, putting their maximum at 15,000), the salary for directors had been raised by 25,000 francs to 100,000.[19]

Throughout 1929 there was much turbulence in the PTT, aggravated among the unitaires by the "preventive" arrest of thousands of CGTU activists before May 1. At the end of May, young Paris facteurs participated in a short work stoppage that resulted in dozens of suspensions, and on June 4 thousands of Paris postal workers, after attending a protest meeting addressed by both unitaires and confédérés, inaugurated a twenty-four-hour sit-down strike. Two days later, the government promised to raise the minimum to 9,000 francs in 1930—the directors' salaries were to be raised another 25,000 to 125,000—a partial victory for the postiers. Although the suspensions of May were lifted, a leader of the Fédération Postale Unitaire, Jean Grandel, was fired for leading the June 4 strike.[20]

Although there was much hostility between the two federations in the form of constant attacks by the unitaires on the Fédération des Fonctionnaires and the confédérés in general for accepting the 8,500-franc raise instead of holding out for the 10,800, and attacks on the unitaires

18. L'Humanité, October 28, 1929.
19. AN, F7 13811; Perroux, Les Traitements, 49.
20. Frischmann, Histoire PTT, 301–302.

as communist dupes, on the question of salaries, the postal workers showed encouraging signs of unity. A police observer reported in 1928 that the Fédération Postale Confédérée was clearly separating itself from the more timid demands of the Fédération des Fonctionnaires.[21] Throughout 1928 and 1929, unified meetings, frequently turbulent, were held in numerous cities. At a meeting in Mâcon in early 1930, attended by all factions, a speaker insisted on the "unanimous and profound discontent which enraged *all* postiers on the subject of salaries."[22]

The year 1930 opened with additional pressures on fonctionnaires' salaries. The starting salary of 9,000 was to be implemented, but by now the cost-of-living index was seven times the 1914 base. The discrepancy was hardest felt among the young, the women (dames-employées), and the commis (clerks of all categories), whose maximum salaries were only five times the 1914 figure. Throughout the spring, unitaires and confédérés held protest meetings, and the syndicalist press called the 9,000 francs an *aumone,* a pittance, and the 125,000 top salary a *prébende,* a gift. By the beginning of May, with the government holding the line, there was talk of a strike. *Le Figaro* called the state a poor and inefficient employer but condemned the notion of a strike, and Gustave Hervé's ultra-right-wing *Victoire* ran the sarcastic headline "Again the Postmen."[23] Unitaires and confédérés agreed; there must be action. Posters signed by Baylot and Paul Gibaud of the Fédération Postale Confédérée and Neumeyer and Robert Lacoste of the Fédération des Fonctionnaires called for a protest meeting in Paris with the warning, "Don't let them sacrifice you."[24] Gourdeaux, recently released from ten months in prison, addressed a joint meeting in Paris, and at the huge meeting on May 14, Jean Mathé of the Syndicat National des Agents told the audience of confédérés, unitaires and women: "The government is taunting us. We must take up the challenge the only way we have—with a strike."[25]

In Paris, Marseilles, Lyons, Lille, and numerous other cities, there were work stoppages, slowdowns, and protest meetings on May 15 and

---

21. See, for example, *La Bataille des PTT,* May 30, June 27, 1927, and speeches reported in AN, F7 13809; *ibid.,* October 29, 1929.
22. AN, F7 13811, January 13, 1930.
23. *La Bataille des PTT,* March 13, 1930. *Le Figaro,* May 13, 1930.
24. AN, F7 13811.
25. *La Bataille des PTT,* May 15, 1930; AN, F7 13811.

continuing throughout the week following. The government responded by firing syndicalist activists in both camps. Mathé, Emile Courrière, and René Belin, leaders of the confédérés, were also fired despite the brilliant defense of their lawyer, Paul-Boncour. Solidarity statements came from all sides. The unitaires issued a leaflet, "The Communist Party is with you in the struggle against the bourgeoisie." Neumeyer of the Fédération des Fonctionnaires told the annual congress of the agents on May 19, "If the government which gives in to speculators but holds the line with fonctionnaires wants a fight, OK, they'll have it." At the end of May, the CGT plastered numerous city walls with a support poster, "The Postmen Are Right." It read: "In 1930, two years after the legal stabilization of the franc, at a time when the cost-of-living index is in the neighborhood of 7, the government has decided to increase the salary that clerks get after 23 years of service by less than 400%, thus condemning dames-employees, telegraph operators, and all the lesser personnel to scandalous underpayment." [26]

The unitaires continued to call for a general strike, but the confédérés, sympathetic to Jouhaux's advice not to push the government too far, slowed down. Within a year, most of the fired leaders had been reinstated (but not the unitaire leaders) and the postiers faced new crises as France felt the first jolts of the worldwide economic crisis.

The struggle for salary increases and better working conditions frequently drew participants from all factions but was hindered by the mistrust and differing tactics of the two federations. Complicating this disunity were additional splits within the Fédération Postale Confédérée. In the late 1920s there were continuing difficulties between the syndicat of employés, led by Louis Digat, who did not always follow federation directives, and the other syndicats. The agents were divided between a right-wing faction led by Baylot and Gibaud and a left-wing faction led by Mathé that was more willing to work with the unitaires. Most serious for fonctionnaire unity was the continuing battle between the fonctionnaires of the PTT and the instituteurs and institutrices, a conflict that worried the CGT enough that it intervened in the salary dispute of 1927–1928. [27]

26. AN, F7 13811.
27. AN, F7 13580.

A continuing bone of contention between the two services was that teachers received higher salaries than commis in the PTT, positions the PTT considered equal in rank. Finally, the CGT's efforts to end the dispute between the Syndicat des Instituteurs and the Syndicat des Agents ended with an agreement with the government to equalize the salaries of teachers and commis. This agreement, however, only exacerbated the difficulties with another group of dissidents in the PTT, the dames-employées, whose pay was lower than that of both institutrices and male commis in the PTT.

Both unitaires and confédérés had long declared their support of equal pay for equal work, but more general salary demands in a difficult economic climate were given higher priority, and the women's demands were usually left to "next time." By the beginning of 1926, when the government's reclassification of salary schedules placed dames-employées below the commis, the patience of the twenty-six thousand women who worked in the post offices and telegraph and telephone offices came to an end. Disenchanted with the government and with the inactivity of both federations, but especially with the Syndicat National des Agents to which they belonged, three thousand women held a protest meeting in Paris at the beginning of February. When the Syndicat des Agents questioned the legality of their separate meeting, the furious women responded by founding the Ligue des Dames-Employées.

Although the women claimed that they did not want to separate from their syndicat and that their new organization was only a temporary measure to try, as the syndicat had not, to reach the government with their demands, it was nonetheless a serious threat to postier unity. Even the unitaires, who claimed to support the women's just demands and emphasized the confédérés' neglect of the women, argued that separation from the rival agent syndicat was not the answer, that the women must continue to work within the syndicat. The employer-state would be happy with the split, wrote *La Bataille des PTT*.[28]

But the sixteen thousand members of the Ligue des Dames-Employées continued to argue their own case. At a large "equality" meeting in early 1928, speaker after speaker criticized not only the government but Laurent of the Fédération des Fonctionnaires as well. When a con-

28. *La Bataille des PTT*, January 28, February 4, 1928.

fédéré rose to defend Laurent, he was hooted off the stage, as was Jean Grandel of the unitaires. The women issued their demands. Stating that they supported two major objectives—the emancipation of women and equal recruitment and equal pay for equal work—they outlined the problem. For years, dames-employées had received the same or higher salaries than institutrices. Now institutrices, having finally received pay equity with male teachers, were earning one thousand francs more than dames-employées. This, they claimed, was unjust. Even more unjust was the situation in the PTT, where dames-employées received less pay than the male commis who did work they considered equal to their own. Not only did they receive less pay for equal work, they could not advance to the higher positions, including that of commis, within the PTT. The women demanded that dames-employées be reclassified so they were equal to commis and that female supervisors be in the same pay classification as male supervisors.[29]

Finally, a commitment was made by the government. Women could be classified as commis, but they would have to take the commis examination, a move which many women, especially those who had many years of seniority, considered an insult. Exacerbating the relations between male and female employees was the knowledge that many of the female commis would be replacing men. The Chamber then voted to allow nineteen hundred women to become dames-commis, hardly a victory for the majority of the twenty-six thousand dames-employées who would not receive equality.[30]

At the end of 1928, the dames-employées reentered the Syndicat des Agents, and both federations declared their support for equal pay and a living wage for female employees. In 1930 demonstrations by the women against the examination led to numerous arrests. The battle for equal pay was far from over.

The deep commitment of the French instituteurs and institutrices to syndicalism maintained the strength and morale of the teacher organizations during this trying period for fonctionnaire syndicalism. While a mere 10 percent of blue-collar workers were paying dues to a syndicat, it was

29. AN, F7 13809, January 20, 1928, leaflet of October 27, 1927, and article in L'Intransigeant, January 20, 1928.
30. La Bataille des PTT, December 13, 1928.

estimated in 1928 that in both the CGT and CGTU over 70 percent of teachers were organized. On the international scene only one in five teachers was organized so the strength of unionism among French teachers was striking. The only other European country with a large fraction of organized teachers was the Soviet Union; in England, Germany, and Austria, teacher unions were just beginning, and in the rest of the world only the United States had any organization at all.[31]

The Syndicat National des Instituteurs (SNI) had entered the CGT in 1925, a full two years before the Fédération des Fonctionnaires, and when that organization sought to unify all fonctionnaires under its aegis, the instituteurs, anxious to maintain their independence, refused. At first they remained separate from Ludovic Zoretti's syndicat of higher education as well, but in 1928 an agreement was made and teachers on all levels, from primary schools to the universities, became part of the Fédération Générale de l'Enseignement. The unified teachers with a membership of nearly one hundred thousand became one of the three largest federations in the CGT; only the mining and railroad federations were larger.[32] With blue-collar membership varying so dramatically, the stability of the teachers' federation made the role of the teachers in the CGT even more significant. André Delmas, who became secretary-general of the Fédération Générale de l'Enseignement in 1932, was to play a major role in the CGT until the final days of the Third Republic.

The teachers, of course, were not immune to the ideological struggles that rent the labor movement. The SNI had a right wing and a left wing, and in the Fédération des Syndicats de l'Enseignement Laïc, affiliated to the CGTU, there were three distinct tendencies that will be discussed below. Yet, as with the postiers, despite intense political animosities, teachers of all tendencies agreed on most issues affecting education and frequently worked together for higher salaries, antiwar and antichauvinist teaching, and, most critically, the maintenance of the école laïque.

31. AN, F7 13748, Vernochet speech at Toulouse, June 18, 1928, to Groupe des Jeunes de l'Enseignement Laïc. The figures are verified in police estimates as well; see AP, BA 304.

32. François Bernard et al., Le Syndicalisme dans l'enseignement (Avignon, 1953), 61. Again, figures differ. Prost, La CGT du front populaire, 183, estimates teacher strength at just below 70,000 in 1929–1931. Lefranc, Mouvement syndical, 280, says that there were 90,000 in 1930, and the police estimated that there were 80,000 in the SNI in 1931, but this may not count those in higher education (AP, BA 304). Estimates for the unitaires vary from 3,500 in 1932 (police estimate) to 5,500 in 1931 (Bernard et al., Le Syndicalisme, 61).

The teachers were as anxious as other fonctionnaires to have a decent standard of living, and they frequently demanded higher salaries at syndicat meetings and in conferences with the Ministry of Public Education.[33] The leaders of the SNI were also understandably upset with the postiers' attack on their "superior" salaries.[34] And for a brief period in the late 1920s, the unitaire teachers demanded not only higher salaries but, in an apparently politically motivated appeal to the younger and more worker-oriented teachers, advocated the end of salary differentials for seniority and school level, the *traitement unique,* the single salary.[35] But unlike other fonctionnaires such as the postiers, to whom salary issues were of prime importance, teacher syndicats continued to devote their greatest effort to issues affecting the education of children in the republican school system.

One issue that continued to interest those who were concerned with this republican school system was the reform that would make the lycées free and available to all, the école unique. Although the teacher organizations and the CGT supported the école unique in principle, most instituteurs and institutrices were content to leave that struggle to the political parties of the Left and to Zoretti and the higher education syndicalists, advocating instead a vague plan for nationalization.[36] The instituteurs were much more concerned with the teaching of children in the primary schools, and they continued to hope for reform of the curriculum, especially in the teaching of chauvinistic and militaristic history. The minister of education of the Cartel des Gauches, Anatole de Monzie, had issued a circular in late 1925 against the teaching of antiwar propaganda, but the agitation for curriculum reform continued.[37]

Unitaires and confédérés alike felt it their duty to educate children away from chauvinism and the glorification of war.[38] In his memoirs,

33. AN, F7 13747, meetings in 1925–1926.

34. Article by L. Roussel in *Revue de l'enseignement primaire,* November 4, 1928.

35. *Bulletin des Groupes des Jeunes de l'Ecole Laïque,* supplement to *Bulletin Syndical* of February 19, 1927. See also article in *L'Humanité,* January 10, 1929.

36. John E. Talbott, *The Politics of Educational Reform, 1918–1940* (Princeton, 1969), 136–37.

37. *L'Humanité,* September 16, 1925. De Monzie also declared himself against the use of patois in the schools, a policy that greatly upset the Alsatians (*L'Eclair,* September 20, 1925).

38. AN, F7 13749; see, for example, the meeting of the Seine section of the SNI, February 25, 1929, addressed by Marthe Pichorel and Georges Clemendot.

André Delmas, the head of the confédéré teachers after 1932, discussing the conflict over the interpretation of World War I and other events, says the aim was not just to reinterpret history but to inculcate the spirit of peace in students. The unitaire periodical of the Finistère in its issue of November 28, 1929, explained that war preparation destroyed government budgets as well as lives: "Our duties as educators and syndicalists, in a word, our duty as men, is to constantly denounce militarism and preparation for war. We haven't the right to fall asleep because the enemy is always stalking the earth."[39]

In 1927, the Fédération de l'Enseignement Laïc finally issued its long-awaited textbook for the "children of the people." The new textbook for ten- to twelve-year-olds, written by a committee of professors and instituteurs and institutrices, would be objective and teach the "true" history of France, the syndicat explained in a publication announcement. True history would show that diplomacy was only one aspect of the history of war and that war had economic causes as well. The announcement also promised that the new textbook would study materialist history, the history of work, workers, tools, and everyday life. The history of war and of political events would take its rightful place as one aspect of the history of civilization. Indeed, the section of the text on the contemporary era began not with the Napoleonic Wars but with a part entitled "The Rise of Industry, 1815–1870," and its first chapter, "Work," began with a description of the poverty of the peasants after the French Revolution.[40] The antiwar attitudes of many teachers would continue to be an important issue within the syndicat, especially as the menace of fascism intensified in the 1930s.

But the issue that most united teachers of all persuasions was the continued need for the defense of the école laïque. In a December, 1925, encyclical, Pius XI had identified laicism as "the plague of our era which has corrupted human society." The French Catholic church and the right-wing organizations, strengthened by the political shift to the right in the late 1920s, sustained a constant attack on the public school system. "Look how many youthful criminals there are," wrote the parish paper of Villeneuve–St. Georges. "No wonder," it continued, "children are

39. Delmas, *Mémoires*, 217; AN, F7 13749.

40. AN, F7 13747, leaflet announcing publication, specimen from *Nouvelle Histoire de France*.

brought up in Freemason schools, with no word of God, what chance do they have?"[41] A royalist paper in the conservative west called the instituteurs nonbelievers, the institutrices, fallen women. The école laïque taught the children only four things: to spit on the flag, to walk on the cross, to say "Quack Quack" to the priest, and to say "le mot de Cambronne" to their parents.[42]

Most distressing to the syndicalist teachers was the situation in the areas of France which were traditionally strongly Catholic and had resisted the establishment of the secular schools. In the west of France, in the Massif Central, and in Alsace, the continued strength of confessional schools was alarming. In 1926, in all of France, there were still approximately 1 million schoolchildren in private schools as opposed to 2.5 million in public schools. In Morbihan, Maine-et-Loire, and Loire-Inférieure, private school pupils were in the majority. In the Loire Inférieure, for example, in 1914 there had been 576 public schools serving 51,406 pupils and 370 private schools serving 44,655. In 1924, even considering declining enrollments, the balance had shifted. Public schools now numbered 556 with 30,968 pupils and 398 private schools taught 31,698. Teachers, deputies, and various fonctionnaires, attending a special congress at Nantes organized by the confédéré teachers, reacted to these figures with the cry from the early days of the Third Republic— "The Republic in danger."[43] Reports from western France also told of numerous institutrices joining the sororitylike religious organization the Davidées. Marie Guillot did two special reports on the Davidées for the Groupes Féministes, one in 1927–1928 and another in 1931–1932, warning the syndicats of the danger of having practicing Catholics as teachers in secular schools.[44]

The teachers responded with huge meetings in defense of the école laïque. A leaflet announcing a meeting at Auray in June, 1927, declared that the teachers of Morbihan belonging to the CGT and the CGTU

41. *Ibid.*, Pius XI quoted in a leaflet of the FSEL, October, 1926; *L'Echo de Villeneuve–St. Georges*, June 1, 1927.

42. AN, F7 13747, discussed at a meeting at St. Etienne, October 31, 1926. "Le mot de Cambronne" is a euphemism for excrement.

43. *Ibid.*, from speeches at a large meeting at St. Etienne, October 31, 1926; *ibid.*, April 25, 1927.

44. Bernard *et al.*, *Le Syndicalisme*, 78, 159.

were "totally united for the defense of their material interests, their dignity and for the defense of the école laïque." Léon Jouhaux was the main speaker.[45] Confédéré teachers, Radical and Socialist deputies, communist professors, and ordinary republicans came to mass meetings held by the Association pour la Défense de l'Ecole Laïque. At one such meeting in December, 1929, twelve hundred met at Lille to hear the university professor (Ecole des Hautes Etudes) Albert Bayet, the deputies Alexandre Bracke-Desrousseaux and Pierre Renaudel, Emile Glay of the SNI, and the former minister of education, François Albert. The meeting was chaired by the deputy mayor, Roger Salengro, later to be an important member of the Popular Front government.[46] In 1931, the fiftieth anniversary of the école laïque was an occasion for the government and the syndicalist teachers to affirm once again their commitment to free secular republican schools.[47]

The right-wing attacks on the public school teachers went beyond the issue of secular schools; for many, the CGT was still anathema and the CGTU, of course, was the bolshevik devil. A leaflet addressed to fathers and mothers of Valenciennes asked the parents to consider the import that eighty thousand of one hundred thousand teachers belonged to the CGT, a socialist and revolutionary organization, and that unitaire teachers had been asked to give a day's pay for the revolutionary action committees. "Do we pay teachers to teach, to raise children in a decent, respectable way, or do we pay them to prepare revolution?" the leaflet asked.[48] The government did not worry about the CGT instituteurs, who had always worked well with the ministry; it was the unitaire teachers whom it harassed. The Cartel des Gauches had reintegrated many of the teachers fired during and just after the war—Marthe Bigot, the Mayoux, and Marie Guillot, for example—but many teachers and other fonctionnaires such as Gourdeaux and Piquemal remained re-

45. AN, F7 13747.
46. AN, F7 13749.
47. Institut Français d'Histoire Social, Fonds Dommanguet, 14AS 372. The revolutionary syndicalists in the CGTU, despite their preference for "proletarian" schools rather than the bourgeois-dominated école laïque and their antagonism to the glorification of le tonkinois Jules Ferry, nevertheless supported the anniversary, defending the école laïque against private confessional schools.
48. AN, F7 13747, July, 1927.

moved from their occupations. In the late 1920s, unitaire teachers, including the Bouëts, continued to be harassed, fired, and in the case of one teacher, jailed for spreading antimilitarist propaganda. One of the most celebrated cases of the period was the indictment of the feminist teacher Henriette Alquier.

The Groupes Féministes de l'Enseignement Laïc (GFEL), attached to the unitaires but including in its membership feminist institutrices of all tendencies, had, since its rebirth in 1919, studied and supported issues of concern to women that went far beyond the strictly professional interests of institutrices. The Groupes Féministes worked actively against war and militarism, for improved working conditions for all women, and for female suffrage. In addition to these larger political issues, the feminist teachers had also taken positions on issues affecting the personal lives of women and their children. Throughout the 1920s, the feminist groups issued reports and statements on alcoholism, prostitution—Hélène Brion wrote the report on prostitution in 1921—health care for children, child labor legislation, mechanization of housework, and single motherhood and the illegitimate child. In keeping with this general feminist orientation, the GFEL, at its 1925 congress, had asked a young teacher from the Hérault, Henriette Alquier, to do a study entitled "Maternité, Fonction Sociale" (Maternity, a social function). [49] The report, accepted by the 1926 congress, was published in the Bulletin des Groupes Féministes in February, 1927.

Alquier's report examined the health and life of mothers and children in working-class families. Many children of the working class, she indicated, deprived of proper nourishment, fresh air, and proper health care, were sickly and weak. Using the statistics on infant mortality of a noted physician, she indicated that because of these poor living conditions, more than one hundred thousand children died each year. To remedy this situation, Alquier recommended special allowances for pregnant women and for large families, maternity leaves, milk stations, and day care centers and crèches for infants and children of working mothers. In addition, she suggested that maternity should not be based on chance but on the state of the mother's health and on the possibility of raising a

49. Anne-Marie Sohn, "Féminisme et syndicalisme, les institutrices de la fédération unitaire de l'enseignement de 1919 à 1935" (Thèse en doctorat de troisième cycle, Paris X Nanterre, 1973), 256. Alquier's father had been an activist railroad worker fired for striking in 1910.

healthy child. In other words, Alquier recommended for working-class women what bourgeois women had been doing for over a century in France—limiting their births to conform to the requirements of the entire family.

The report was immediately condemned by the Catholic press and, most critically, by General Edouard de Castelnau, president of the Fédération Nationale Catholique. Pushed by these right-wing organizations and in the Chamber by Poincaré and Barthou, the government under Herriot's direction charged Henriette Alquier with violation of the law of July, 1920, the law for the repression of anticonceptional propaganda. The penalty for this violation was a prison term of from six months to three years and a fine of up to three thousand francs. As editor of the *Bulletin Féministe,* which had published the offending material, Marie Guillot was charged as well. The syndicalist women and their male supporters correctly saw this as an attack on the école laïque, on the syndicat, and, most obviously, on the feminist movement. Dozens of books had been written on women's issues and birth control. At the moment Alquier was charged, thousands of copies of Michel Corday's book *Suzanne ou la maternité consentie* (Suzanne or maternity by consent) and Victor Marguerite's *Ton Corps est à toi* (Your body belongs to you) were being read and circulated. Why was Alquier singled out?

Gabrielle Bouët, addressing the 1927 congress of the unitaire teachers on the question of Alquier and feminism, said, "The government fears the emancipation of women because it knows that is what is necessary to bring about a revolution." There was a trial, and Alquier and Guillot were acquitted.[50]

Though theoretically united in defense of the école laïque and for better wages, the teachers' organizations remained hopelessly split on the ideological and tactical level into reformists and revolutionaries. It is difficult to determine the numerical strength of each faction from membership figures alone. In many provincial areas, it was difficult to maintain two distinct syndicats, and, just as before 1914, when there were syndicat supporters in the amicales, so in the 1920s and 1930s numerous teachers who may have been more sympathetic to the ideology of the unitaires belonged to the only organization available to them, the reform-

---

50. AN, F7 13749. The material on Alquier comes from the supplement to the *Bulletin* of the GFEL, 1927, and from Sohn, "Féminisme et syndicalisme," 79–82.

ist SNI. Official membership figures give the SNI an overwhelming advantage over the unitaires—perhaps fifteen times the membership—elections of departmental councils tell a different story. The unitaires were very active. Proud of the role they had played in the teachers' movement, they reminded all instituteurs and institutrices through leaflets, speeches, and articles that when the amicales had cowered before the prewar governments, they alone had organized a syndicat. In the dark days of the war, they alone had suffered repression and prison in the struggle to end the slaughter, and it was thanks to them, they reminded the institutrices, that equal pay for men and women in public education had finally been won.[51] In addition, the *Ecole Emancipée* still enjoyed a substantial readership, and the unitaires were active in organizing young teachers and students. There was an active Groupes des Jeunes de l'Ecole Laïque, and the Union Générale des Etudiants pour l'Enseignement worked with future teachers in the écoles normales.[52]

In the 1926 elections for council seats in twenty-eight departments, the unitaires received over one-third of the votes, and in a few departments such as Basses Alpes and Côtes-du-Nord, they had made agreements with the confédérés to support one unified slate. The report on the election sent by the Sûreté Générale (police intelligence service) to the Ministry of the Interior remarked on the significance of these votes. The first point made was that almost all the teachers were either CGT or CGTU (only one hundred of fifty-five thousand votes went to independents). It was then noted that there was a significant growth in communist strength. Finally, the Sûreté noted that the voting pattern of institutrices was similar to that of instituteurs: "Those who think that they will find among the women a more moderate point of view, a greater tendency to avoid political extremes, see by this example, their theory disproven."[53]

The confédéré federation, the Fédération Générale de l'Enseignement, having united teachers and professors in 1928, could count on approximately one hundred thousand members, but this numerical strength did not guarantee unity. Aside from the obvious unitaire sym-

51. AN, F7 13747, leaflet of 1927; Institut Français d'Histoire Sociale, Fonds Dommanguet, 14AS 371, speech of Bouët in 1933, "La Fédération de l'enseignement dans les assises syndicales."
52. AP, BA 304.
53. AN, F7 13747.

pathizers in the SNI, there were also the professors, who, under Zoretti's leadership, often took an independent left-wing position. And in
the reformist mainstream of the SNI, there was an internal struggle between younger, more militant teachers such as André Delmas, who had
come to the syndicat after the war, and the old prewar, conservative
amicalist leadership of Roussel and Glay. Many in the SNI believed that
the syndicat would remain ineffective unless the leadership was changed,
and there were constant maneuvers on the federal council to oust the old
war-horses. Finally, in 1932, Glay and Roussel retired and the leadership
went to the ambitious and energetic André Delmas.[54]

Within the smaller Fédération de l'Enseignement Laïc (with a membership of about five thousand in 1928–1929), the divisions were even
more intense. The unitaires rejected the reformism of the CGT and
identified themselves as revolutionaries. The question was in what way
they were revolutionary and what connection they would have with the
Communist party (PCF). By the time of the 1929 congress, when the
question of Communist party membership was the dominant issue,
the unitaires had developed three distinct positions. The majority position, represented by Jean Aulas and the history professor Maurice Dommanget, who was president of the Federation, was communist—"We
consider that the French Communist party, despite its faults and weaknesses, is the only revolutionary political group of the working class"—
but it did not want to see the Communist party dominate either the
federation or the CGTU. The second group, led by Jean and Josette
Cornec, the Bouëts, and Marie Guillot, was the old minority of revolutionary syndicalists who had connections to the independent Ligue Syndicaliste. They considered all Communists too committed to Moscow
and to the politics of the party and wanted complete independence from
all political parties. The independent syndicalists also rejected participation in national politics. They condemned the teachers who had run for
office in 1928 as candidates of the Socialist party (CGT) and the Communist party (CGTU). The third group, the Minorité Oppositionnelle
Révolutionnaire (MOR) led by the professor Gustave Vernochet and the
historian Georges Cogniot, argued for the leadership of the Communist
party.[55]

54. This internal struggle is described by Delmas, *Mémoires*, 158–62.
55. Bernard et al., *Le Syndicalisme*, 100, 62–63. Many of the unitaire leaders were historians.

Eventually, the Communists who refused to follow the party line in the syndicat resigned or were forced out of the party, but they retained the leadership of the federation, carrying their fight for syndicalist independence into the CGTU as part of the *opposition unitaire*. Gilbert Serret, Bouët, and Salducci spoke at the 1933 CGTU congress, arguing that the policies of the PCF had lost the support of the masses but vowing that the minority teachers would continue the fight within the CGTU for the revolutionary syndicalism of the masses, for world socialism, for the dictatorship of the proletariat, and, of course, for the political independence of the syndicalist movement.[56]

By 1932, with the SNI and the Fédération de l'Enseignement a powerful and influential force in the CGT, the unitaire teachers, except for a few individuals, were largely isolated from the mainstream. But by 1932 as well, international events would force the fonctionnaires to shift from their campaigns to raise salaries and improve working conditions to a defense of their livelihood, their jobs, and the government of which they were both employees and citizens, the Third Republic.

56. Fonds Dommanguet 14AS 371, "Les Assises."

IO

The Republic in Danger, 1932–1936

The worldwide economic depression had come late to France, but by 1932 falling markets, falling production, and massive unemployment had plunged the economy into a deep crisis that would not bottom out until 1935 and would not really improve until 1938. In his study of the depression, Julian Jackson states that though the Radicals saw themselves as a party of the Left, in economic and fiscal matters they were conservative. For Radicals and conservatives, the main issue was financial stability.[1] Hence the government, faced with insufficient income and mounting deficits, adhered to its classical liberal economic tradition; it would balance the budget with a policy of deflation. For the fonctionnaires, the handwriting was already on the wall. All over Europe, governments had reacted to budgetary deficits by lowering fonctionnaire employment and salaries. It was only a matter of time before French fonctionnaires would face the same threats. In May, 1932, legislative elections took place, and this time the Cartel des Gauches was victorious. For the twenty months between June, 1932, and February, 1934, six ministries led by Radicals and supported by Socialists attempted to solve the economic crisis.

On June 8, after issuing an official declaration opposing any change in salary scales, the leadership of the Fédération des Fonctionnaires met with the head of the new government, Herriot, who told them, "I can make neither threats nor promises." If it should become necessary to lower the income of the fonctionnaires, Herriot assured them, he would "ask the same sacrifices from all categories of citizens."[2] The Cartel des Services Publics Confédérés, consisting of all the fonctionnaire federa-

1. Julian Jackson, *The Politics of Depression in France* (Cambridge, Eng., 1985), 18–19, 49.
2. *La Tribune des Fonctionnaires,* June 11, 1932.

tions attached to the CGT, gathered its considerable forces—estimated at over four hundred thousand members by the police—to face the impending crisis.[3]

The Fédération des Fonctionnaires issued a comparative study of fonctionnaires' wages in major European cities. Emphasizing that France was still suffering from a high cost of living, the federation showed that Parisian fonctionnaires were the lowest paid of all European state workers. A facteur in Paris received less than one-half the salary earned by a postal worker in Berne, Switzerland, 60 percent of what his Dutch counterpart earned in Amsterdam, and slightly less than the notoriously low-paid London postman. Similar comparisons were made for other public employees.[4] Lobbying among its Radical and Socialist friends in the Chamber, the confédérés managed to achieve a compromise. The law of July 16, 1932, avoided references to specific salary and employment cuts but contained the dangerous Article Six, which provided that as of October 1, 1932, all government expenses would be reduced by the reorganization of working conditions and the "cutting of employment by slowing down recruitment."[5] The confédérés were thus victorious in the fight to save their salaries, but the 5 percent reduction permitted by Article Six allowed the government to cut recruitment and to fire auxiliary and other nonpermanent employees. These cuts were felt most severely in education.[6]

Fearing that the 1933 budget would be even more devastating than the vague phraseology of Article Six, the confédérés continued to pressure the government and the legislature, holding numerous protest meetings against any reduction in fonctionnaires' salaries. The unitaires, castigating the confédérés for cooperating with the government on Article Six, took to the streets. In June and July and again in November and December, the Cartel Unitaire staged demonstrations in Paris which resulted in numerous arrests.[7] Throughout the fall, thousands of fonction-

---

3. AP, BA 306. The police reports of 1932 estimated the cartel strength as follows: Fonctionnaires, 250,000; PTT, 68,000; Tabac, 15,000; Allumettes, 1,000; Services Publics, 47,000; Eclairage (lighting), 25,000; and the rapidly growing Santé (Health), 17,000.

4. *Ibid.*

5. Georges Frischmann, *Histoire de la fédération CGT des PTT* (Paris, 1967), 327.

6. François Bernard et al., *Le Syndicalisme dans l'enseignement* (Avignon, 1953), 217.

7. AP, BA 1646; 1,320 were arrested on December 15. Paris was the stronghold of unitaire support among fonctionnaires.

naires of all factions, often in demonstrations of unity, met in cities all over France—1,300 at La Rochelle, 2,000 at Nantes, 700 at Brest, 1,300 at Perpignon. Frequently the meetings ended with fonctionnaires pouring out into the provincial streets to continue their protest with a march to the city hall or the office of the prefect.[8] André Delmas, addressing a meeting in July, warned the audience that if the government was allowed to lower the salaries of fonctionnaires, the door would be open "to attacks on the wages of workers in the private sector with whom we are one."[9] And, of course, he added, fonctionnaires would inevitably be attacked again and again. The Morbihan teachers, urging their members to join a meeting in Vannes which would eventually draw over one thousand fonctionnaires of all factions, wrote in its monthly bulletin, "One thing is certain, this time, if the government seems to exclude the lowest wages, the wages of beginners in general, it is certain that when there is a second decrease—which will surely follow the first if we let it happen—the salaries of beginners will also be attacked." Joining the fonctionnaires in protest were numerous veterans' groups whose pensions were also placed in jeopardy by the government's plans for reducing expenditures. On November 11, members of organizations representing hundreds of thousands of veterans and "victims of war" used the anniversary of the Armistice to protest plans for reducing pensions, reminding the politicians that they had "paid their taxes in blood."[10]

In October, the Fédération des Fonctionnaires sent a nine-page report to all its national and provincial leaders. The report began with a warning of the dangers that threatened them: a deflationary budget and the reduction of salaries of all fonctionnaires were being discussed by all the major newspapers and numerous politicians, "not all of whom are on the right." The federation's position was clear: "We will accept no salary reductions no matter in what form they are presented." The report then analyzed the current situation. The budget crisis was not the fault of the fonctionnaires. The government had inflated the figures indicating the growth of civil service employment since 1914 by including fonctionnaires from the liberated provinces of Alsace-Lorraine and departmental workers now under state jurisdiction. The increases had been not among

8. AN, F7 13318.
9. AP, BA provisoire 306, July 4, 1932.
10. AN, F7 13318, call for the meeting of November 17; meeting at Tulle.

civilian workers but in the military. The reasons for the crisis were the economic problems that had reduced tax revenues, especially from business; the scandalous growth of military expenditures, which had doubled between 1926 and 1931–1932; the antidemocratic and anti-economic fiscal policies of the government since 1926; and the widespread tax fraud. Salaried fonctionnaires and workers dutifully paid their taxes, but thousands of self-employed professionals, businessmen, and industrial firms were avoiding their proper payment. In addition, the government was spending millions in aid to foreign governments and to shore up the failing fortunes of numerous large business enterprises, including the Banque de France and the railroads.

From an economic point of view, the report continued, reducing fonctionnaires' salaries and employment made no sense. In Italy, Poland, and England, wherever deflationary policies had been used against fonctionnaires, unemployment had risen and deficits had deepened. The budget must be balanced by reducing the arms expenditures, by nationalizing key industries, and by eliminating tax loopholes. The cost of living was still high. Blue-collar workers and fonctionnaires had suffered while "fat cats" had gotten rich from the inflation. Let those who had made millions pay. Fonctionnaires had made sacrifices; they must not continue to be the ones who paid. The report ended with a warning that if these initial measures were not stopped, there were sure to be even more serious attacks on state employees.[11]

In December, 1932, before the 1933 budget could be discussed, the Herriot government fell and was replaced by one headed by a longtime defender of fonctionnaires' rights in the courts and in the legislature, Paul-Boncour. Louis Germain-Martin relinquished his portfolio as minister of finance to Henri Chéron.

Any hope that the government of Paul-Boncour would rescue the fonctionnaires from the budgetary ax were quickly dashed. At the beginning of January, Chéron, who, as Paul-Boncour quipped, ran public finance "like a good father runs his household," unveiled a new financial proposal designed to alleviate some of the government's fiscal woes.[12] Revenue was to be raised by levying some new taxes, but the main thrust of the Chéron proposal was to trim government expenditures.

11. *Ibid.*
12. Jackson, *Depression,* 63.

Some cuts would be made in the military, but most savings would come from cuts in hiring, a 5 percent reduction in fonctionnaires' salaries (those earning under twelve thousand francs would be exempt), and a 650-million franc cut in special benefits such as housing and clothing allowances. In addition, veterans' pensions would be "rolled back" five years and remarried war widows would lose all their benefits.[13]

The Cartel Confédéré, joined by Jouhaux, rushed to plead the fonctionnaires' case with the parliamentary delegation of the SFIO. The Socialist party, undergoing an ideological split between those who would collaborate with the government's military budget and those who would not (part of a deeper controversy within the party) agreed to have Vincent Auriol sponsor a crisis surtax on incomes over thirty thousand francs. But before the Auriol amendment could be proposed, the government, abandoned by the Socialists, fell, and on February 1, Edouard Daladier took office. On February 7, a new budget was proposed which called for a reduction of all fonctionnaire salaries over twenty thousand francs by 5 percent and all allowances by 10 percent.

The confédérés, who had eschewed the demonstrations and strike tactics used by the unitaires, now felt that it was important to show their strength to the government by taking direct action. They felt betrayed by some of the Socialist deputies in whom they had placed so much trust and who, though advocating exemptions for the largest number of petit fonctionnaires, who were paid less than twenty thousand francs, now accepted the principle of salary cuts for fonctionnaires. Even though the SFIO continued to support fonctionnaires' interests in the Chamber, many socialists felt that the fonctionnaires were being intransigent by refusing to accept any salary reductions.[14] On February 17 and 18, dozens of meetings of fonctionnaires of all services took place. Unitaires, autonomes, confédérés, all called for a work stoppage of at least one hour on February 20. Even the teachers would join, starting classes half an hour late after the midday break. André Delmas, who had always maintained that teachers must not strike, told his members: "We accept the challenge which has been flung at us, not by the Senate which has no importance, not by the politicians who are merely puppets, but by the

13. AP, BA 305.
14. AP, BA provisoire 306. This failure of mutual confidence is discussed in a police report to the government, February 24, 1933.

employer organizations and by the Comité des Forges who pull the strings in the corridors. If this is a social struggle which is beginning, then we are ready, with all the fonctionnaires, to face without fear all the risks involved."[15]

On February 20, 1933, in response to the threat to their salaries, the fonctionnaires of France staged their first general strike. The strike, though limited, was effective, especially in Paris.[16] Even the busses and trams stopped for ten minutes in a show of solidarity. *Le Quotidien,* reporting on the effectiveness of the strike, commented on the order and discipline of the work stoppage, which they said astonished even the syndicat leadership. Nonunion workers had joined the strike as well.[17] Only the police did not take part in the strike, but at their general assembly on February 27, five thousand Paris police passed a resolution condemning the threat to their salaries and pensions, which they pledged to defend "with all the energy they possessed."[18] Most significant for the political future of the syndicats was that confédérés and unitaires, as Gourdeaux of the Fédération Postale Unitaire told a crowd of cheering fonctionnaires gathered on the evening of the twentieth, had joined hands to fight against capitalism and the politics of the "lesser evil" to stop the proposals of "misery" put forth by the corrupt government.[19] As if to emphasize the unified strength of the fonctionnaires, the February 20 strike was followed on February 27 with a joint meeting of unitaires and confédérés which was so huge (estimated at ten thousand) that it overflowed into the streets in front of the Bourse du Travail.

Finally, the government agreed to a progressive tax on salaries of from 2 to 8 percent with an exemption for those with salaries below fifteen thousand francs, but the battle over the allowances continued. Throughout the spring and summer, fonctionnaire delegates to a special finance committee battled to save the most important allowances, and finally the government retracted some of its demands. The worst had been avoided, but with hiring halted and even the lower salary losses,

15. AP, BA 306. In his memoirs, written thirty years later, André Delmas downplays the import of the February 20 strike (*Mémoires d'un instituteur syndicaliste* [Paris, 1979], 174–75).
16. AP, BA 306.
17. *Le Quotidien,* February 21, 1933.
18. *Le Journal,* February 28, 1933.
19. AP, BA 305.

fonctionnaires' standard of living was declining. Even these small victories could not survive the government's preoccupation with the ever-deepening deficit. The 1934 budget, released at the beginning of October, 1933, proposed another special levy of from 6 to 9 percent on fonctionnaires' salaries and on all pensions. Once again the fonctionnaires sprang into action. Throughout the month of October, thousands of fonctionnaires came to protest meetings in every department in France—in Mazières (Ardennes), Moulins (Allier), St. Quentin (Aisne), Bourges (Cher), and Besançon (Doubs). In Marseilles, four senators and ten deputies, representing all the parties of the Left—SFIO, Radicals, Socialists, and Communists—came to show their support.[20] In Paris, thousands attended dozens of meetings held night after night.[21] Courrière of the Fédération Postale Confédérée spoke at Toulouse, Delmas of the teachers spoke at Bordeaux, Lacoste and Laurent of the Fédération des Fonctionnaires at Nancy, Belin and Piquemal at Le Havre. At Lille, where three thousand fonctionnaires formed a huge line of march, the deputy mayor, Salengro, addressed the crowd. Everywhere the message was the same.

The government was making fonctionnaires pay to balance a budget that had been destroyed by tax frauds and excessive military expenditures. Fonctionnaires opposed the ruinous policy of deflation. They did not want to be treated differently from other citizens; everyone should pay a fair share. At some meetings, veterans and blue-collar workers joined the crowds, and from all over there came the call for unity. They must present a united front. At a meeting of all three cartels held in Toulon, thousands cheered a motion that saluted the first unity talks of confédérés, unitaires, and autonomes: "Long live the common action of all the exploited workers of the state's public services and of private industry. Down with the proposals of famine and deprivation."[22]

On October 24, the Daladier government fell, to be replaced by the ministry of Albert Sarraut. Abel Gardey took over the budget. The fonctionnaires continued to agitate. On November 18 and 19 there was another round of protest meetings all over France—Grenoble, Nar-

20. AN, F7 13736.
21. AN, F7 13737.
22. AN, F7 13736, meetings at Toulon, October 17; Bellegarde, October 21; St. Quentin, November 19; Toulouse, October 17.

bonne, Poitiers, Clermont-Ferrand, Albi.[23] Gardey now proposed to replace the special salary levy by raising workers' contributions to the pension system, an increase of about 4 percent on all salaries. The fonctionnaires were not taken in by Gardey's numbers game; 4 percent was still 4 percent. A Cartel Unitaire leaflet entitled "Another Alert" attacked the new plan. There would be strong resistance: "By struggle, by a united front, we have already crushed the plans of Herriot, Boncour and Daladier."[24] And indeed, the finance committee abandoned the 4 percent pension levy, substituting a levy of from 1.5 percent for salaries between ten thousand and twelve thousand to 6 percent for those earning over forty thousand francs. But when the Socialists, supporting the fonctionnaires, proposed a new tax plan to raise revenues, the government fell once again. This time the problem of balancing the budget and dealing with the fonctionnaires fell to Camille Chautemps.

On December 2, the minister of finance, Paul Marchandeau, introduced a new budget which again threatened veterans' pensions (a substantial amount of the pension fund would now depend on revenues from the national lottery) and, under the authority of Article Six, called for a special levy on fonctionnaires' salaries ranging from 2 to 8 percent for those paid over twelve thousand francs. This time the Chamber, aided by votes from a now divided Socialist party, acquiesced. Once again there was a round of meetings, talk of a strike, calls for a united front. The autonomes printed a leaflet addressed to "Public Opinion," which asked the causes of the budget deficit and then answered: the military, the tax frauds, and the untouched profiteers. An appeal was made to shopkeepers, who, not wanting their own taxes raised, were often hostile to the fonctionnaires' demands for the maintenance of their salaries. Shopkeepers were told that the lower pay and higher unemployment engendered by the deflationary policies would mean fewer and fewer purchases. Posters appeared on walls: "Workers and Fonctionnaires: Come to Our Rescue. . . . For Christmas: No Buying. . . . For New Year's: No Buying. . . . Shopkeepers: For you, it will mean ruin."[25] At a meeting in Lille on December 4, fonctionnaires, taxpayers, and veterans joined in passing a resolution declaring, that they would

23. *Ibid.*
24. AN, F7 13737, November 21.
25. AN, F7 13735; poster example is from Montpelier.

"refuse to be dupes in the divisive maneuvers which attempt to pit one against the other—veterans and taxpayers, victims both of the same governmental errors."[26]

On December 14, a demonstration at the Opera called by the Cartel Unitaire resulted in over three hundred arrests, and when the finance committee of the Senate supported the proposed budget, confédérés demonstrated on December 18 in front of the Senate itself. More people were arrested, among them André Delmas of the instituteurs and Neumeyer of the Fédération des Fonctionnaires. City workers demonstrated their anger on December 29 at the Hotel de Ville, where another 220 were arrested.[27] In the midst of all this agitation, there was the terrible Christmas Eve railroad disaster at Lagny which took 200 lives. Could the government do nothing right?

With the beginning of the new year 1934, there came the news of the arrest on December 24 of the director of the Crédit Municipal of Bayonne and of his "patron" the deputy mayor, for criminal financial manipulations involving approximately 200 million francs. On January 8, Alexandre Stavisky, the notorious swindler and confidant of politicians, including the accused of Bayonne, committed suicide. Before long, stories of connections and cover-ups emerged, and numerous government officials, including Colonial Minister Albert Dalimier, Paul-Boncour, and the head of the government, Chautemps, were tainted with the mud of the Stavisky affair. The right-wing organizations and newspapers and the growing fascistlike leagues attacked not only the government but the parliamentary system. The fonctionnaires, of course, were quick to raise for public scrutiny the complicity of the Chautemps government in the attempted Stavisky cover-up at the same time that it attacked the standard of living of petit fonctionnaires. "Will the salary reductions go to pay for Stavisky's swindles?" asked the *Tribune des Fonctionnaires*.[28]

With the new year there came as well the first attempts to implement the budgetary decisions made at the end of 1933. The first reductions would be on allowances, most critically those for housing. To show their discontent with this decision and the reaction of the fonctionnaires,

26. *L'Ami de Peuple* and other newspapers of December 15, 1933.
27. AP, BA 306, contains information on all the 1933 demonstrations.
28. *La Tribune des Fonctionnaires,* January 6, 1934.

"who are fed up with sustaining alone with their coworkers in private industry the consequences of a crisis for which they are not responsible," the Cartel Confédéré called for a mass demonstration at the Hotel de Ville on January 22.[29] The unitaires, who had been planning to meet at the Bourse du Travail, quickly announced that they would join the confédérés, as did the autonomes. Shouting "Our Wages" and "Down with Chautemps," thousands of fonctionnaires—socialists, communists, autonomes—streamed into the square in front of the Hotel de Ville. The leaders of the CGTU, Julien Racamond and Pierre Semard, were there. The Garde Républicain mounted a charge, demonstrators and police were hurt, and more than three hundred were arrested. The police estimated the crowd at four thousand, but the CGT paper Le Peuple said twenty thousand were there, and the Communist party newspaper L'Humanité ventured a figure of fifty thousand. Its editor, Paul Vaillant-Couturier, compared the January 22 demonstration of the fonctionnaires to the Commune. The conservative Le Temps was less enthusiastic: "For seven years, thanks to an organization which has not broken down, Paris has hardly known anything but ritualistic demonstrations which took place in peace and followed strict directions. Yesterday, disorderly elements tried once again to gain possession of the street."[30]

Battered by the Stavisky affair, pilloried by the right-wing leagues, attacked by the fonctionnaires, the Chautemps government fell, and on January 30 Daladier was back as chief of a new government. It would last only one week.

Thus in the crucial years 1932–1934, with the nation suffering a severe economic crisis, the fonctionnaires of France were suddenly thrust into the center of the political stage. In the course of twenty months, the struggle of the fonctionnaires in the streets, in the press, and in the corridors of the National Assembly to halt the implementation of the budget proposals had contributed to the downfall of six ministries. In addition, the debate within the Socialist party over support for the fonctionnaires had exacerbated the ideological and tactical splits of the SFIO, contributing to the division that led to the expulsion from the party of the twenty-eight "neosocialist" deputies, led by Pierre Renaudel, Marcel

29. AP, BA 306.
30. AP, BA 1648; January 23, 1934, for all newspapers; Le Temps, January 24, 1934.

Déat, and Adrien Marquet, who had voted with the Albert Sarraut government in October, 1933. The "neos" formed a new party, leaving Léon Blum as undisputed leader of the SFIO and eventually paving the way for Socialist participation in the Rassemblement Populaire, the Popular Front. In the course of twenty months as well, the usually cautious and largely reformist fonctionnaires, driven by the government's attack on their standard of living, had resorted to previously rejected tactics of mass direct action. The general strike of January 22, 1933, and the demonstration of January 22, 1934, indicated that fonctionnaires, including those who belonged to the reformist CGT, were ready to use the weapons of the working class to defend their interests. The leader of the Fédération des Fonctionnaires, Charles Laurent, had declared in the course of the 1933 struggles that "collective work stoppages must become a part of our normal means of action."[31]

In light of the political consequences of the decisions of 1933, the question naturally arises as to why the government decided to cut fonctionnaires' income and why the fonctionnaires reacted so strongly. For the Radical leaders of 1932 and 1933, ideologically committed to classical liberal economics, there appeared to be only two choices in the effort to counter plummeting prices and productivity and rising deficits—deflation or devaluation. Anxious to avoid devaluation as long as possible and fearful of alienating their bourgeois supporters by raising taxes more than minimally, the various governments opted to cut government expenditures. Because of the threatening situation in Germany and the commitments to the colonial empire, especially in the wake of the war in Morocco, it was felt that the military budget could stand only limited reductions without endangering national security. Decreases in expenditures would have to come primarily from salaries and pensions paid by the state to employees and veterans.

Sagging prices, the government argued, had raised the purchasing power of these two segments of the population; they would not suffer. And, indeed, using the new base year 1930 as 100, the cost of living in Paris had fallen to about 90 in 1933 (89.3 in May and 91.2 in November); the real wages of employed fonctionnaires and workers had risen by 10 percent. But the fonctionnaires argued that they had never fully recuper-

31. René Bidouze, *Les Fonctionnaires, sujets ou citoyens?* (2 vols.; Paris, 1979), I, 209.

ated from the lagging salaries of the great inflation, and just as they were about to catch up the government was reducing their income. Moreover, every housewife knew that although agricultural prices were disastrously low and some prices had fallen sharply, for example, beef, the cost of other necessities of life was being maintained at high levels by unscrupulous merchant profiteers.[32] It was not just the proposed salary reductions, which were heaviest for the highest-paid government employees, that were onerous to the fonctionnaires. The decreases in the special allowances affected all fonctionnaires, hitting the lowest paid hardest of all. For the low-paid teacher, douanier, or postman and for families with children, decreases in family allowances and housing bonuses represented a serious attack on their standard of living.

In addition to the economic arguments revolving around the cost of living, there were political and psychological aspects to the resistance movement. The fonctionnaires were loath to relinquish their *droits acquis,* benefits they had worked years to achieve. Once these benefits were taken away, it would be a difficult struggle to get them back. Even more distressing was the feeling among fonctionnaires that only they were being asked to give up their rights. The writings and speeches of syndicalist leaders of the period indicate the depth of the chagrin of the fonctionnaires at being singled out, separated from the rest of the population, forced to sacrifice more than the ordinary citizen for the good of the nation. Over and over, they stated their desire to aid the troubled budget, but they insisted that others, wealthier than they, should pay their fair share. Reformists and revolutionaries alike were incensed that so many of the "fat cats" who had benefited from the inflation, "these tax evaders, these cowards who shift onto the people the weight of the burdens they should be carrying," were not being asked to make the same sacrifices as the fonctionnaires. The budget crisis was not their fault; why must they pay?[33]

Even though the fonctionnaires had managed, through their political maneuverings in the Chamber and their protests at meetings and demonstrations, to avoid the worst of the proposed cuts, the government's

---

32. Alfred Sauvy, *Histoire économique de la France entre les deux guerres* (4 vols.; Paris, 1965–67), II, 503, 522. For another complicated price story, see *ibid.,* 66, for an analysis of the government's maintenance of high bread prices when wheat prices were at a nadir.

33. AN, F7 13736, poster from Angoulême, October, 1933.

determination to continue the policy of deflation at the fonctionnaires' expense drove the syndicats to increased direct action and to deeper political alliances with the left-wing opposition in the legislature. Events in 1934–1935 would push them even further along this path and lead eventually to their strong commitment to syndicalist unity and the Popular Front.

As ministry after ministry toppled, unable to solve the problems of the deepening economic crisis, there arose yet another, potentially more dangerous, threat to the life of the Third Republic. Adolf Hitler and the National Socialists had come to power in Germany, and all over Europe fascistlike parties and organizations, often paramilitary, were gaining adherents and strength. In France, numerous leagues of diverse ideologies but united in their support of authoritarian governments and in their desire to destroy communism, socialism, and "decadent" liberalism had by 1934 become a major political force. Right-wing, ultranationalist leagues had a long history in Third Republic France, emanating from organizations founded at the end of the nineteenth century and active as the most vehement of the anti-Dreyfusards. But now these older organizations and new ones founded in the 1920s and early 1930s had adopted tactics and ideology more suited to the politics of the interwar period.

Among the more violent of these leagues were the small but well-disciplined shock troops of the Action Française, the Camelots du Roi, and the powerful Association des Jeunesses Patriotes, led by Pierre Taittinger, which had several hundred thousand youthful members, including a small group of well-trained and uniformed *groupes mobiles* (flying squads). Newer and more closely allied to modern fascist ideology were Solidarité Française and Francisme. One of the most influential leagues was the Croix de Feu, founded in 1928 by veterans who had been decorated for heroism under fire in World War I. Under the leadership of Colonel François de la Rocque, the Croix de Feu had opened its membership to the general public and moved closer in ideology and tactics to the fascist leagues. By 1934, it was holding large mobilizations in the Paris area. Numerous other organizations such as Henri Dorgères' Front Paysan and some sections of the veterans' organization Union National des Anciens Combattants, though not as politically oriented as the leagues, were nonetheless potential allies of the more fascist organizations. Newspapers such as *Action Française, Gringoire,* and *Je Suis Partout,* aided by the regular extremist right-wing press, railed against the floundering and ineffectual legislature and its ministries.

Throughout 1932 and 1933, the leagues grew stronger. It is difficult precisely to determine their membership figures, but even without the veterans' organizations, the leagues could count on hundreds of thousands of sympathizers. They held rallies, marches with bright young men in uniformlike garb, and weekend military training sessions. Strong-arm squads broke up left-wing meetings and harassed communists, syndicalists, socialists, and even middle-of-the-road supporters of the government. The Stavisky affair intensified their attack on the government, now tainted with verifiable corruption. Throughout the early days of February, there were street incidents, rock throwing, car burnings, and skirmishes with the police and with left-wing groups. When Daladier decided to dispose of the troublesome right-wing prefect of the Paris police, Jean Chiappe, by appointing him to a position in Morocco, the stage was set for the incidents of February 6.

In the late afternoon of February 6, thousands of members of the various leagues massed on the Place de la Concorde, broke through police barriers, and attempted to cross the Seine to storm the Palais Bourbon, where the Chamber of Deputies was holding a chaotic session. Gardes mobiles, attacked with various missiles, knives, and razor blades by the crowd forcing its way closer to the Assembly, fired on the demonstrators, killing and wounding several of them. Other demonstrators massed in various locations took up the battle, and veterans, who were holding a forbidden march, joined the chaos. Busses were burned, horses were slashed, clubs were swung, shots were fired. By the evening there were approximately twenty dead and at least six hundred wounded. The police suffered hundreds of casualties as well.

The nation was in shock. The leagues claimed that they were not attempting a coup d'état; they merely wanted to invade the Assembly, to toss the corrupt politicians into the street, to "give them a spanking." Certainly the poor tactics and general disarray of the leagues diminished any chance of a successful coup. But to many observers, particularly on the Left, aware of what was happening in Germany and Italy and of the leagues' military training, the attempted storming of the Assembly was a clear effort by the fascists to destroy the republican government. The next day, Daladier resigned, and as crowds continued to surge up the Grandes Boulevards, breaking windows and attacking passersby, Gaston Doumergue was asked to form a new cabinet. Doumergue proclaimed that this government of National Union would rescue the Republic in its darkest hour, but to the left-wing politicians, the new government seemed like a return to the Bloc National, which had been defeated in 1932. Léon Blum said, "I say the Bloc National and not Union National because there is no nation united without the workers."[34]

The fascist leagues had been stopped on February 6, but they remained an enormous danger. With the image of Germany close at hand, syndicats and political parties of the Left knew that they must make a strong show of resistance to the supporters of fascism. The Communist party called for a demonstration against the fascists to take place on February 9 at the Place de la République. Thousands of communists, joined by CGTU members and some left-wing socialists, finding the République blocked off by the police, surged into the neighboring streets, and near the Gare de l'Est shots were fired and a number of demonstrators killed.

In the meantime, meeting in an all-day session on the seventh, the national council of the CGT had urged Jouhaux to declare a general strike on February 12. Jouhaux and other CGT leaders were rightfully worried about the success of such a strike, which, contrary to CGT tradition, was political. Could it be organized in five days, and would the workers respond? If it was a failure, might not the weakness of the CGT be exposed? Most crucial to the success of the strike was the response of the workers in the public sector. When workers in a suburban factory strike, the public barely notices, but when the mail is not delivered, when teachers are not in the classroom, the public knows there is a strike. The teachers and the postal workers assured the national council that their members would strike, as did Laurent, who, declaring his deep attachment to the Republic, gave the strike order to members of the Fédération des Fonctionnaires.[35] The CGTU decided to join, and both the

---

34. Edouard Bonnefous, *Histoire politique de la troisième république* (7 vols.; Paris, 1959), V, 219.

35. For an account of this meeting, see Delmas, *Mémoires,* 228–29.

SFIO and the Communist party called for demonstrations in support of the strike on the twelfth. The messages went out by telephone and telegraph. Opposition to the budget cuts and to fascism were seen as two parts of the same struggle. The postal federations launched a joint appeal: "All together. For the defense of your threatened freedoms. . . . For the safeguard of your salaries, allowances and pensions."[36] The teachers issued the following call: "The Fédération de l'Enseignement, the Syndicat des Instituteurs, in solidarity with the working class, will participate with all its strength in the general action." Classes would be closed on February 12. When the minister of public education asked administrators to turn in the names of striking teachers, the syndicat replied that it would not be intimidated, that its members "put their devotion to the Republic above their obedience to any government whatever it is."[37]

The strike of February 12 proved to be an enormous success, a victory for the CGT and for the Left. Between 4 and 5 million French workers participated. In Paris several hundred thousand marchers, first in two separate contingents—one of socialists and the CGT and one of communists and the CGTU—joined to form one massive line of march. In the provinces there were numerous demonstrations and in some cities—Marseilles, Roubaix, Villeurbanne—violence and deaths.[38] But most impressive was the response of the public sector. In Paris there were no newspapers or public transportation. The PTT, with 90 percent of its workers on strike, ceased to function. In the schools, 80 percent of the classrooms were empty of teachers; 70 percent of other fonctionnaires answered the strike call. The headline of the *Tribune des Fonctionnaires* declared, "On the twelfth of February, the fonctionnaires of France demonstrated with dignity their faith in public and syndicalist freedoms."[39] For the first time, fonctionnaires and blue-collar workers participated in the same strike. And everywhere there was the call: Unity, Unity! The working class had shown its resistance to fascism.

36. Frischmann, *Histoire PTT*, 344.
37. Delmas, *Mémoires*, 231–33.
38. For an analysis of the success of the strike in the provinces, see Antoine Prost, "Les Manifestations du 12 février 1934 en province," *Le Mouvement Social*, No. 54 (January–March, 1966).
39. *La Tribune des Fonctionnaires*, February 12, 1934.

But neither the fascist menace nor the attack on fonctionnaires' salaries would be subdued. The new Doumergue government was determined to alleviate the budget crisis, and to avoid the pitfalls of political shifts and bitter debates that had caused other ministries to fall. Except for a large minority on the Left, the legislature, frightened by the events of February 6, was also more amenable to maintaining the life of the Doumergue government. Responding to pressures to reform the government, the National Assembly was in the process of creating a committee to study proposals for reorganizing the state. But even before the committee was given its full charge, on February 22 the government received full power from the legislature to deal with the budget through executive order, that is, government by decree, décrets-lois. On February 28, the budget was passed, and on March 15 the legislature, clearing the way for the décrets-lois, adjourned itself until May 15.

Throughout February and March, the fonctionnaires held protest meetings against fascism and the threat of the décrets-lois. Delmas, Lacoste, and other leaders traveled from city to city to urge the fonctionnaires to organize the defense against these two dangers in their syndicats.[40] Although the exact contents of the décrets-lois were still officially unknown, it was leaked to the press that the government would make the fonctionnaires its first priority. L'Humanité published the expected legislation—there would be large numbers of dismissals, salary reductions of from 5 to 10 percent (without exemptions for low-paid personnel), and reductions of retirement pensions and health benefits.[41] A second series of laws was planned to decrease veterans' benefits.

The meetings became larger and angrier. The walls were plastered with unitaire posters: "Under the Régime of Exceptional Powers—With the Scandals, the Poverty. . . . The Stavisky-Chiappe Gang. . . . Now it's time to pay." On March 29 and 30, thousands of unitaires and confédérés flocked to the Bourse du Travail in Paris. There were meetings at Lille, Bordeaux, Clermont-Ferrand, Brest, Bourges, and Toulon. A police report sent to the Ministry of the Interior on March 29 analyzed the situation, warning that notably the postiers but also teachers and finance workers were waiting for the word to launch a general strike. Expecting

40. AN, F7 13953.
41. L'Humanité, March 20, 1934.

the décrets-lois to be issued on April 4, the Cartel Confédéré, under the signature of the CGT, called for mass meetings on that day. The CGT poster was addressed "To the working class, to confederated manual workers and intellectuals," whom it called on to protest the government's planned reduction of salaries, pensions, and employment. News of protest meetings came from all over. The Fédération Postale Confédérée called a special congress.[42]

On April 4, Doumergue returned from his Easter vacation and immediately asked the cabinet and the minister of finance, Germain-Martin, to authorize the first series of décrets-lois. As expected, most of the decrees concerned the fonctionnaires. Citing employment figures of 837,000 in comparison to 619,000 in 1914, the government decreed that in addition to a regular budget reduction of 10 percent to encourage reforms and consolidation of services, the number of employees would be reduced by 10 percent; eighty thousand public service workers would be asked to "retire early." Pensions would be reduced to 50 percent of the last active pay period, and, most critically, there would be a *prélèvement*, a special reduction of fonctionnaires' salaries. In earlier plans lower-paid fonctionnaires had been exempt from the salary reductions. Under the décrets-lois of April 4, there would be a levy of 5 percent on all fonctionnaires' salaries and an additional levy of from 6 to 10 percent on salaries over twenty thousand francs.

It was reported that the Comité National d'Entente Economique was pleased with the budget, as were the Union de Commerce et de l'Industrie and Fédération des Commerçants et Industriels Mobilisés, but the fonctionnaires, the syndicats, and the left-wing parties were up in arms. The April 5 issue of *L'Humanité* called for immediate action: "It's an all-out attack on the laboring masses." Writing in *Le Populaire*, Léon Blum called the décrets-lois "a brutal attack." Regarding the proposed layoffs of eighty thousand state workers, Laurent declared: "It is not possible to put such a measure into effect. That's gall." At an April 6 meeting of the Syndicat des Instituteurs, Delmas told the teachers, "The decrees emanate from a fascist government." The postiers called for a strike.[43]

The fonctionnaire confédérés and the CGT were placed in a difficult

---

42. All these meetings are covered in AN, F7 13953.
43. AP, BA 305; *Le Populaire*, April 6, 16, 1934; Bonnefous, *Histoire politique*, V, 232.

position. Committed to tactics that involved political lobbying and the pressuring of legislators and government officials, they were quite willing to use mass protest meetings as a way of exerting political pressure. But now there were calls for stronger action—for a strike—and the unitaires were in the vanguard of this agitation. Despite the calls for unity and the honest attempts at unity of individual fonctionnaires and syndicats, there was still a good deal of hostility between the confédérés and the unitaires, and it was clear that neither side wanted to yield the leadership of the movement. The unitaires castigated the confédérés for dragging their feet, and at a special meeting of the council of the Fédération des Fonctionnaires, which declared itself ready to join with the Cartel Confédéré in "any action it decided to take," many members of the council reproached the leadership for "lacking courage." They complained that they would find it embarrassing to return to their organizations to explain the "inertia" of the federation. It was necessary to make some gesture to show the anger of the fonctionnaires.[44] The CGT indicated that it might be willing to support a short and well-disciplined work stoppage rather than yield the battlefield to the CGTU, which might gain support from some angry confédérés by calling a more serious strike. Jouhaux asked for an audience with Doumergue. It was clear that there was no hope that the government would back down without indications of massive public resistance. An Interior Ministry report of April 7 says that Doumergue was being pressured to "close his eyes" to a short strike called by the CGT rather than permit the CGTU to gain control of the protest movement.[45]

The wave of protest meetings continued. There were spontaneous demonstrations at the telegraph offices in Paris.[46] Finally, the Cartel Unitaire issued a strike call for April 13. The Cartel Confédéré countered with a call for a day of meetings for Sunday, April 15, and for demonstrations at the workplace, a "national day of protest" for Monday, April 16. The unitaires responded by asking their members to join both protest movements.

All over the nation, plans were made by the confédérés and the uni-

44. AP, BA 247, police report of April 8.
45. AN, F7 13953.
46. AP, BA 247.

taires for the days of protest. Posters went up: "Alarm! Alarm! . . . . We paid for their great war, will we pay for their bankruptcy. . . . NO." "Fonctionnaires, Workers, You will be reduced to the miserable prewar standard of living." The autonomes declared their support of the "national day" of April 16: "We must answer the attack vigorously and victoriously."[47]

On April 13, in Paris and in various provincial centers where the Fédération Postale Unitaire was strong, there were scattered work stoppages and meetings, but most of the fonctionnaires were waiting for the fifteenth and sixteenth. Twenty-nine postal workers were suspended for urging their colleagues to strike.[48] On April 14, Le Peuple printed a call from the Fédération des Fonctionnaires signed by Laurent, Neumeyer, Lacoste, Delmas, and others: "Your demonstrations on the fifteenth and sixteenth will bear witness to your cohesiveness and discipline. It will clearly show your willingness to carry out with patience and courage activities in coming months which will break the steady sequence of salary and wage decreases." In working-class centers such as Le Havre, appeals were made to dockers, factory workers, and veterans to come to the meetings on the fifteenth to fight the "program of poverty." The unity of the working class would "crush fascism."[49]

On Sunday, April 15, in almost all the towns and cities of France, there were meetings and street parades. In Chartres, fifteen hundred fonctionnaires carried signs saying, "We Want to Live." "Down with Fascism."[50]

On April 15, the fonctionnaires had responded en masse to the call of the cartels. Less impressive was the national day of protest of April 16. There were some work stoppages and slowdown strikes, notably among PTT workers, finance workers (Contributions Indirectes and Douaniers), and employees of the tobacco monopoly and the mint. The instituteurs demonstrated in Paris and signed petitions against the décrets-lois in their towns and villages. There was a demonstration in front of the Finance Ministry in Paris. Other fonctionnaires held noontime meet-

47. AN, F7 13954.
48. AP, BA 247.
49. AN, F7 13954.
50. Ibid.

ings or distributed leaflets. The left-wing press cheered the successes of the sixteenth, but they were not as impressive as a real general strike. At any rate, meetings and work stoppages could not stop the government. On April 15, a second series of décrets-lois lowered the pensions and medical benefits of war veterans, and on April 20 the pensions of railroad workers were reduced. On April 20, forty thousand fonctionnaires, railroad and other workers, forbidden to hold a demonstration, jammed the streets of Paris and massed in the square of the Hotel de Ville, shouting slogans against fascism and the décrets-lois. The government, in an obvious show of strength, arrested almost one thousand demonstrators.

The fonctionnaires' response to the policy of deflation was necessarily largely defensive; they held meetings, demonstrations, and strikes demanding the abrogation of the décrets-lois and the restoration of their *droits acquis* (vested rights). Among a group of influential fonctionnaire syndicalists, however, a longer-range response to the failure of the French government to deal with its severe economic problems, *le planisme* (planning), was presented for public study and discussion in 1934 and 1935. The failure of the numerous patchwork solutions to the crisis—artificial price supports, deflation, financial subsidies to ailing industries—had convinced many economists and politicians that a more basic structural reform of the French economy, under the direction of the state, was necessary. In the mid-1930s numerous plans were presented, among them a program for economic reorganization proposed by the CGT.

The CGT had indicated as early as 1919 its desire to restructure the French economy. The depression and the influence of the economic theories of the Belgian integral socialist (later to be a National Socialist) Henri de Man gave new impetus to the desire of the CGT to change the economic life of the nation. The crux of the CGT plan was the development of a mixed economy of nationalized and private industry with both sectors using government credit and with more government involvement in the direction of the economy. For the immediate future, concentration on developing internal markets, the promulgation of a forty-hour workweek, and the institution of public works programs would aid workers in overcoming the disaster of the depression.

Although many CGT leaders, notably Jouhaux, were enthusiastic about the plan, it was among the fonctionnaires of the CGT that the *planistes* were most influential. René Belin of the Fédération Postale Confédérée, now sitting on the national council of the CGT and considered by many to be the "dauphin" of Jouhaux, was a strong supporter of the plan, as was André Delmas of the teachers.[51] But the most active supporters of the plan were Robert Lacoste of the Fédération des Fonctionnaires and one of the leading intellectuals of the CGT, Georges Lefranc. Through the pages of the *Tribune des Fonctionnaires,* Lacoste publicized and analyzed de Man's philosophy and the CGT plan.[52] And Lacoste lobbied successfully to have the CGT organize a meeting of the Etats Généraux de Travail (the Estates General of Work) on April 7, 1934, at which three thousand delegates voted unanimously for "the reorganization of the country."[53] Considering that the meeting took place just as the CGT was preparing for the protest movement against the décrets-lois, the size of the Etats Généraux indicates the strength of the *planiste* movement. During the winter of 1934–1935, Georges Lefranc used his CGT school, the Institut Supérieur Ouvrier (Workers' Institute of Higher Education), to present a series of lectures on the plan. The lectures were published in the spring of 1935. Lefranc and Delmas were active in the SFIO and pushed the plan among the less than enthusiastic socialists. The revolutionary wing of the fonctionnaire syndicats was, not surprisingly, even less enthusiastic. The CGTU described the plan as "getting the capitalist machine moving at the expense of the working masses." On June 23, 1935, the CGT sponsored a "day for the plan," and in September the CGT officially adopted the plan of "economic and social renovation." Its success was evidence of the growing influence of the fonctionnaire leaders in the CGT.[54]

For most fonctionnaires, however, the plan did not solve their immediate problems. By the spring of 1934, in the wake of February 6 and the

51. In his memoirs, Belin says that Jouhaux, who considered himself the CGT, had no "dauphin" (*Du Secrétariat de la CGT au gouvernement de Vichy* [Paris, 1978], 12).

52. *La Tribune des Fonctionnaires,* December 9, 30, 1933; January 13, and throughout the month of March, 1934.

53. Bidouze, *Les Fonctionnaires,* I, 231.

54. For a summary of the *planiste* movement, see Richard F. Kuisel, *Capitalism and the State in Modern France* (Cambridge, Eng., 1981), 98–119, and Georges Lefranc, *Le Mouvement syndical sous la troisième république* (Paris, 1967), 308–13 (quote on 313).

April décrets-lois, it was becoming increasingly clear that to combat the double menace of deflation and fascism not only syndicalist unity but a real change in government was necessary. Even as the path toward unity was being prepared in the spring and summer of 1934, the Doumergue government continued its policy of battling the crisis by curtailing public expenditures. In a radio address to the public, Doumergue said the dissenting fonctionnaires had been influenced by a "turbulent and undisciplined minority," who had little attachment to state service and used "threats and even violence" to influence the majority of fonctionnaires "not to serve the state but to do it disservice."[55] In November, when "reform" propositions aimed at strengthening the authority of the Council of Ministers at the expense of the legislature were introduced by Doumergue, Radicals withdrew from the cabinet and the government fell. On November 8, the Flandin government was formed.

Pierre-Etienne Flandin's rejection of the reform project, his willingness to lessen the government's reliance on deflationary policies, and the nation's preoccupation with foreign affairs marked a slight easing of the government's relations with the fonctionnaires. In the spring of 1935, when a legislative committee recommended nonratification of the décrets-lois on pensions, the issue came to the floor of the Chamber for open debate. The Fédération des Fonctionnaires pushed for an abrogation of the April 4 décrets-lois and a full return to the 1924 law on pensions, but the legislature temporarily avoided the issue by appointing another committee to study revisions to the pension law. When the committee reported in May, it agreed to the principle of the 1924 law, but it also allowed a temporary tax on retirement pensions.[56]

For the teachers and the postal workers there was no easing of relations with the government; rather, there was a continuing deterioration. The education minister, André Mallarmé, zealously carried out the reduction of personnel, especially at the secondary level, at the same time that he harassed active syndicalists with the time-honored use of administrative rebuke and sanctions. For the postal workers, their nemesis was to appear in the person of the new minister of the PTT, Georges Mandel. Determined to raise the level of service and to increase efficiency,

55. La Bataille des PTT, September 27, 1934.
56. Bidouze, Les Fonctionnaires, I, 233.

Mandel proceeded to open complaint bureaus and reintroduce Sunday post office service (considered an abrogation of the hard-won semaine anglaise by the syndicalists), firing fonctionnaires of all ranks who did not perform with the required zeal. His much publicized determination to serve the public and his awareness of future developments, which led him, despite the extra expense, to expand air-mail service and government radio programs, made Mandel popular with the press and many ordinary French men and women in the street. To the fonctionnaires, faced with increased work loads and decreased personnel and threatened with basing all advancement on merit, Mandel was an authoritarian right-winger, reminiscent of the 1909 minister, the hated Simyan.

This negative view of Mandel was reinforced in April, 1935, when the facteurs of Nice, protesting a planned speedup, initiated a strike. Mandel immediately mobilized Parisian postiers, sending them by airplane to replace the workers at Nice. The press reported with pleasure that the mail was only a few hours late. The suspension of 190 Niçois strikers further fueled the fires of outrage; the syndicat was still smarting from the prison sentences recently given to four syndicat activists who had been convicted of having urged postal workers to strike the previous April.

The antipathy to Mandel was so strong that in 1936 the Syndicat National des Agents took the unusual step of publishing a pamphlet, *Mandel, Ministre de la IIIème République et des PTT,* which detailed his "crimes" against the PTT, its workers, and the nation. Included in the list of grievances was the accusation that Mandel was planning to hand over to private industry the development of a new phenomenon, television. The forward-looking Mandel was apparently also one of the first politicians to use the technique of tapping telephones. The pamphlet ended by accusing Mandel of causing the "disorganization and demoralization" of the PTT for political ends.[57]

The financial crisis deepened, and after the first victories of the Popular Front in the municipal elections of May, 1935, an upsurge in the flight of capital aggravated an already grave situation. The Flandin gov-

57. The pamphlet is located in the Institut Français d'Histoire Sociale, Fonds Monatte 14AS 172. For an analysis of the life of Mandel, see Georges Wormser, *Georges Mandel, l'homme politique* (Paris, 1967).

ernment asked for more power to deal with the financial crisis. When the legislature refused to extend executive privileges, the Flandin government fell, as did the four-day ministry of Buisson, which followed it. On June 7, 1935, Pierre Laval formed a new government and immediately got from the legislature the full powers that had been denied to the previous ministries; "to avoid the worst," said the Radical Yvon Delbos. On June 30, the legislature "went on vacation," and on July 16, two days after an enormous display of Rassemblement Populaire unity, Laval introduced the first of a series of far-reaching décrets-lois. There would be a 10 percent reduction in all treasury payments, including those to holders of government bonds, a move that terrorized numerous petit-bourgeois *rentiers*. (There were some exceptions for national defense and unemployment insurance.) To sweeten this cut, some taxes would be raised on income from stocks and bonds and on general income over eighty thousand francs. But once again, it was the fonctionnaires who were hardest hit. Those earning under ten thousand francs would have a 5 percent pay cut and those under eight thousand, 3 percent, but the salaries of the majority of fonctionnaires would be reduced by 10 percent. The *Tribune des Fonctionnaires* made the comparison: "The décrets-lois appropriates more than three billion from the pay of the state workers and those in the contracted services, and only three million from capital."[58]

The Cartel Confédéré published a manifesto which declared that the only way to defeat the décrets-lois was to "substitute for the policies of economic and social regression the politics of economic renovation and social progress," and efforts toward the election of a Popular Front continued.[59] The fonctionnaires, however, knew that they could not wait for new elections. On July 19, responding to a call from all the syndicats in the public sector, more than fifty thousand fonctionnaires demonstrated in and around the Place de l'Opera; more than fifteen hundred demonstrators were arrested.[60]

58. Bonnefous, *Histoire politique*, V, 341; *La Tribune des Fonctionnaires*, July 20, 1935.
59. Bidouze, *Les Fonctionnaires*, I, 236.
60. AP, BA provisoire 305. An interesting aspect to this demonstration can be seen in the *états-civils* of those arrested. The *états-civils* record names, occupations, dates, and places of birth. They show that the Parisian fonctionnaires of 1935, born mostly at the turn of the century, originated from the towns and villages of the provinces.

The two cartels planned to hold a protest meeting on July 30 at the Gymnasium Japy. The crowd was so enormous that other meeting halls had to be opened, and to the strains of the "International," thousands of fonctionnaires, confédérés, unitaires, and autonomes marched to CGTU headquarters at the Grange aux Belles or simply held meetings in the street.[61] There were numerous demonstrations in provincial towns and cities, and on August 6 a strike of arsenal workers at Brest turned into a riotous confrontation between police and workers; iron grills were ripped down and the red flag was flown. Two days later, there were two deaths and many injuries in a bloody confrontation with arsenal workers at Toulon. In November, there were more mass meetings in Paris and dozens of other cities.[62]

Among the hardest hit by all the décrets-lois were the women fonctionnaires. The feminization of the public services had continued throughout the 1920s and 1930s, and by 1936 approximately 30 percent of state workers were female. The reductions in salaries had affected all fonctionnaires, but the reduction of personnel had been particularly hard on women, many of them auxiliary workers, who were not protected by contracts of permanent appointment. Among the Laval décrets-lois there were several decrees specifically aimed at reducing the income of married women and widows. One decree eliminated the housing allowance for women fonctionnaires married to fonctionnaires, which meant a loss of over two thousand francs a year for Parisian women. Another eliminated the "reversibility pension" of widows of fonctionnaires so that women receiving their own pensions would no longer get the extra money from their widows' benefits.[63] On October 15, women fonctionnaires responded by holding a huge meeting at the Bourse du Travail. The meeting was chaired by Marthe Pichorel of the Syndicat National des Instituteurs, who told the audience: "The concept of a family wage is unacceptable. It leads to the consideration of a married woman's salary as pin money. Work must be paid for itself without consideration of who earns it." Syndicalists have only one rule, declared another speaker, "Equal pay for equal work."[64]

61. *Ibid.*
62. Bidouze, *Les Fonctionnaires*, I, 237.
63. Frischmann, *Histoire PTT*, 381.
64. Bidouze, *Les Fonctionnaires*, I, 248.

By the end of 1935, the mass of fonctionnaires knew that Mathé of the Fédération Postale Confédérée was correct when he had told the Japy crowd on July 30 that the fight against the décrets-lois was only a prelude to a change of regime.[65]

The desire for working-class unity and for ending the debilitating schism of CGT and CGTU had been voiced frequently by syndicat leaders in both factions. For most of the interwar period, these calls for unity were largely rhetoric. For the CGT, the concept of unity was simple: the unitaires must abandon their organizations and their political affiliations and return *au bercail,* back to the fold, to be submerged by the numerically stronger confédérés. But even this demand rang hollow because it was clear that the CGT leaders were worried about admitting such a militant and well-organized minority into their rather undisciplined and weak organization. Speaking in 1925 on the question of syndicat unity, Louis Digat, then secretary of the Fédération Postale, claimed that the CGT was for unity "with independence" but then vilified both Marxism and bolshevism and declared himself against a "front unique," which he characterized as a plot to discredit the syndicalist movement.[66]

For their part, the unitaires, while voicing loud demands for unity, continued to condemn the CGT's tactics of class collaboration. Clearly, the unitaires could not accept an arrangement wherein they would have neither a separate organizational base nor a voice in the leadership at the confederal level. Nor were they anxious to enter a unified CGT while their numbers were so small. That both organizations were unwilling and unready for unified action is evident from the failure of the appeal of twenty-two syndicalist leaders for unity in 1930–1931. This appeal, made by mainly leftover revolutionary syndicalist members of all three factions (confédérés, unitaires, autonomes), was condemned by the leadership of both federations. The unitaires saw it as another attempt to have them reenter the CGT without proper guarantees for political independence, and the CGT rejected any unity proposal that did not entail an unconditional surrender on the part of the unitaires. André

65. AP, BA 305.
66. *L'Unité Syndical,* conference of July 6, 1925. Pamphlet in the Institut d'Histoire Sociale, Fonds Dommanguet, 14AS 373.

Delmas's resolution calling for the "return to the CGT, to the 'vielle maison,'" was passed almost unanimously. The appeal of the "twenty-two" and its failure not only highlights the unwillingness to compromise on the question of unity but indicates the growing importance of fonctionnaires within the unity movement and the CGT. Among the prime movers of the appeal were the fonctionnaires Pichorel and Lucie Colliard of the teachers, Digat of the postal workers, Piquemal and Robert Laplagne of the autonomous Contributions Indirectes, and Métayer of the state workers. And, of course, it was Delmas of the teachers' syndicat who firmly closed the door to the appeal in the CGT.[67]

But the door could not stay closed. The enmity between the unitaires and the confédérés remained strong, but the political situation had changed rapidly. The deteriorating economic conditions, the disastrous décrets-lois, and the menace of fascism made working-class unity a necessity. And beyond the need for syndicat unity, there was a growing desire of workers, intellectuals, and others on the Left for unified political action to bring about a change in government. The events of February, 1934, and the decrees of 1934 and 1935 made these goals even more urgent.

The building of the Popular Front coalition has been analyzed by numerous scholars and politicians. The first steps were taken in 1932 with the formation of the Amsterdam-Pleyel peace movement under the leadership of the left-wing antiwar writers Henri Barbusse and Romain Rolland. In March, 1934, the manifesto of the Comité d'Action des Intellectuels Antifascistes et de Vigilance, commonly known as the Comité de Vigilance des Intellectuels Antifascistes, issued under the signatures of three leading intellectuals of the Left—the scientist Paul Langevin (procommunist), the ethnologist Paul Rivet (prosocialist), and the writer Alain (proradical)—helped to link the antifascist Left into a broad coalition. Within a few weeks, twenty-three hundred intellectuals had signed the manifesto. It is amusing that this success was hailed by the postal workers in their newspaper with the headline, "The intellectuals stand with the postmen."[68] By July, 1934, the Communist and So-

---

67. Bernard et al., Le Syndicalisme, 170–80. For a personal analysis of the "twenty-two," see Daniel Guérin, "Une tentative de réunification syndicale: Les 22, 1930–31," Revue d'Histoire économique et sociale, XLIV, No. 1 (1966), 107–21.

68. La Bataille des PTT, May 24, 1934.

cialist parties had forged an electoral alliance, pledging "unity of action" against the décrets-lois and against fascism. And in the fall of 1934 the two labor federations took the first positive steps toward a reunification of the CGT. The fonctionnaires' political consciousness and influence had been intensified by the protest meetings, demonstrations, and strikes against the decrees, and they were to play a crucial role in the unification process and in the eventual victory of the Popular Front.

The pressure for unity had been building for months among rank-and-file fonctionnaires. For many of these syndicalists, the deep animosities of the decade-old schism, felt so strongly by the CGT and CGTU leadership, were ancient history. The global implications of the struggle between revolutionaries and reformists appeared less critical than the immediate threats to their jobs and security and the danger of fascism. Having avoided the early, most bitter days of the schism, having reentered the CGT well organized and numerically strong, and having been politically conditioned by the struggles against the décrets-lois, the fonctionnaires were able to play a leading role in the rank and file and in the leadership of the CGT in reunifying the two labor federations.

The CGTU took the first steps toward reunification. The threat of fascism had forced a change in international communist ideology and tactics. If revolutionaries and reformists in the Socialist and Communist parties and in the CGT and CGTU continued to battle each other, the only victor would be the fascists; unity of the Left must be achieved at all costs.

In July, the two left political parties had signed their agreement; there remained the question of the labor federations. On June 8, a few days after the Communist party had made its approach to the Socialist party, the CGTU issued an appeal for unity to the CGT. The CGT gave the usual response: the unitaires must dissolve and reenter the CGT. In a second appeal on June 13, the CGTU, arguing for "fusion" rather than reentrance, called for assemblies of syndicats of all tendencies to create one union of all workers who would fight for the "forty-hour week, against war preparations and for the dissolution of the fascist leagues."[69] Within a few days, the fonctionnaire federations began the drive for the

69. *La Tribune des Fonctionnaires*, June, 1934.

unification of their organizations. Letters asking for a fusion congress were sent from the autonomes to the Fédération des Fonctionnaires, and Henri Gourdeaux brought the appeal of the postal unitaires to the June congress of the confédérés. The confédérés, always worried about communist influence in the CGTU, hesitated. But the pressure for unity was mounting.

Building on the rank-and-file desire for unification, the unitaires had been preparing the ground for the policy of fusion for several months before the unity appeal was made. Calling for unity "at the base," the CGTU had encouraged unity meetings on the local and regional levels. Although only a few syndicats, notably the railroad workers and some postal and municipal workers, actually fused, joint meetings of confédérés and unitaires, especially among the fonctionnaires, began to mushroom all over France. By mid-July, with pressure building on the local level and with the threat of more décrets-lois, the leaders of the two postal federations were holding meetings to discuss reunification, and the numerically powerful Fédération des Fonctionnaires agreed to join with the autonomes to plan a unity congress. In September, the Cartel des Services Publics Confédéré, echoing the demands of the central CGT for a democratic and politically independent union, also called for the fusion of the two federations. This groundswell for unity, emanating from many sections of the organized working class and especially from the fonctionnaires, could no longer be contained. On October 9, 1934, representatives of the two federations met officially for the first time to discuss the conditions under which unity could be achieved.

The composition of the two delegations sent to this first meeting is a clear indication of the growing influence of the fonctionnaires in the CGT and in the movement for unification. Among the main spokesmen of the unitaire delegation were their leaders Benoît Frachon, Racamond, and Gaston Monmousseau, as well as Léon Mauvais (electricity), Pierre Semard of the railroad workers, and, representing the only substantial fonctionnaire organization in the CGTU, Henri Gourdeaux of the Fédération Postale Unitaire. They were pledged to winning as much ground as they could for the unitaire position, and all were strongly committed to unity. The main part of the CGT delegation, with Léon Jouhaux conspicuously absent, consisted of Francis Million, known to be against unity, and three fonctionnaires, Charles Laurent of the Fédération des

Fonctionnaires, Albert Perrot of the Fédération Postale, and André Delmas of the teachers' federation. The fonctionnaire delegates, though deeply suspicious of communist policies and committed to holding the line on the CGT's position of absorption and political independence, were nonetheless openly committed to unification.[70] The leaders of the two postal federations had held their first joint meetings, and Delmas had spoken and written with increasing frequency on the question of unity.

Despite the obvious desire for unity, this meeting was little more than an airing of the demands of both sides. The unitaires pushed for fusion, the confédérés for return. The confédérés insisted that the union be politically independent without political factions; the unitaires responded that their politics were their own personal business—they were independent. The two delegations parted, promising to discuss their respective positions with their federations. But three and one-half months would pass before they would meet again.[71]

In the waning months of 1934, the tactical and verbal duel continued. Editorials in L'Humanité and the unitaire newspapers accused Jouhaux of dragging his feet; they reminded their members of his collaborative role in the Union Sacrée of 1914–1918. In an article published in the Bataille des PTT, Gaston Monmousseau told the confédérés that Jouhaux had his political ties and so did the British Trades Unions to the British Labour party; why attack the communists?[72] On the CGT side, Jouhaux was still very hesitant about unity with the communists and wrote and spoke of his misgivings, but most antagonistic was one of the most influential members of the federal board of the CGT, the former PTT leader René Belin, who categorically rejected unity with the CGTU.[73] The CGT issued a special pamphlet, La CGT et l'Unité Syndical to explain its position. The CGT, the pamphlet began, wanted unity; it was

70. Belin, Du Secrétariat, 57–58, 55. Belin says that Jouhaux sent Million because he was against unity. In fact, Million retired from activity when it became obvious that unity would occur. Belin strongly opposed unity but agrees that all the delegates favored unity.

71. A brief account of this meeting appears in Delmas, A Gauche de la barricade (Paris, 1950), 55–57, and in Mémoires, 262–63. The minutes of the meeting are in the archives of the Fédération des PTT (current CGT), lent to me by the former secretary-general of the federation and a labor historian, Georges Frischmann.

72. La Bataille des PTT, January 3, 1935.

73. Article in La Tribune des Fonctionnaires, March 2, 1935.

imperative to stop Hitler and Mussolini. But the CGT wanted "unity that was loyal, sound and durable, and which must be in line with the aspirations of the working class of this country." The syndicalists must remember the history of the schism so mistakes would not be repeated. The unitaires wanted guarantees that they would not be destroyed, the pamphlet continued, and the CGT wanted guarantees of the independence of syndicalism. The demands of the CGT were repeated: why push for a new union? What was wrong with the old CGT? The unitaires must enter the CGT and agree to political independence, and the CGT must maintain membership in the Amsterdam Labor International, not the Labor International run by Moscow.[74]

While both federations continued to argue the proper path to the salvation of the French working class, the fonctionnaires were continuing to move toward unification. In a letter of December 14, Perrot of the Fédération Postale Confédérée told Gourdeaux that they were almost in agreement; the only obstacle was the question of political factionalism, and they must be assured of the political independence of the unitaires. But, added Perrot, even with these difficulties, they must press on. Gourdeaux responded in the affirmative. Yes, he agreed, unity was necessary.[75] And every week brought reports of fonctionnaire locals forming *syndicats uniques*.

Finally, on January 25, 1935, the two delegations met again. Once more the question of political independence, of rejection of political factionalism, dominated the meetings, and once again, the fonctionnaires were the main defenders of the CGT position. Laurent attacked the assertion of Benoît Frachon that the CGT was attached to the Socialist party the way the CGTU was attached to the Communist party. "Yes," he argued, "we do adopt certain programs, but your leadership is the party leadership. We do not want internal disagreement."[76] Frachon responded that he believed in independence, and his opinions as a communist were his personal business. Laurent, after all, attended international socialist meetings.

But it was André Delmas who dropped the bombshell. Delmas re-

74. Institut Français d'Histoire Sociale, Fonds Monatte, 14AS 172.
75. These letters are in the archives of the Fédération des PTT (CGT) and were published in the December 20, 1934, *La Bataille des PTT*.
76. Archives of the Fédération des PTT, minutes of meeting of January 25, 1935.

jected the declarations of political independence of the unitaires, citing an article in the November 1, 1934, issue of *Les Cahiers du Bolshevisme* in which the author, Ossip Piatnisky, the secretary of the Communist International, explained how unity would enable the French Communist party to influence the masses. Although the CGTU disavowed the inopportune article, whose author had no connection to the CGTU, the CGT viewed it as an indication that the communists would work to undermine the policies of the CGT.

Most distressing to the CGT were two sentences in the article: "The French communists, wanting to take a truly decisive step in the direction of syndicalist unity, have accepted the formula of independence. But that does not at all mean that they are renouncing their task of influencing the actions of the unified syndicalists through their factions."[77]

Frachon discounted an article written by a nonsyndicalist: "We don't take orders from nonsyndicalists. We are here as the CGTU, not as the Communist party." The meeting ended in angry debate between the CGTU leader Frachon and Delmas. Both were committed to unity, but once again the reformist-revolutionary split had emerged triumphant. At a meeting on February 1 the debate was repeated, again centering on the Piatnisky article, which Frachon once more rejected. He pledged political independence, adding, however, that even though the syndicat was independent, "it would be impossible to oppose the parties who support the working class in its struggle." Each member had the right to be in the party of his choice and to be active in it.[78]

For the fonctionnaires, the spring of 1935 brought a renewed threat of fifty-five thousand firings, the anniversary of February 6 brought a reminder of the growing strength of the fascist leagues. On May 12, the "unity of action" of the Socialist and Communist parties in the municipal elections brought the first important victories for the developing Popular Front; Paul Rivet was elected for the fifth arrondissement in Paris. A week later, more than two hundred thousand people made the annual pilgrimage to the Mur des Fédérées to honor the dead of the Paris Commune.

77. Quoted in the minutes of the meeting (*ibid.*), as well as in Antoine Prost, *La CGT à l'époque du front populaire, 1934–36* (Paris, 1964), 133, and Lefranc, *Mouvement syndical,* 324–25.
78. Archives of the Fédération des PTT, minutes of the meetings of January 25 and February 1, 1935.

Finally, the CGTU acquiesced to the CGT's demands. On June 5, the executive committee issued a new statement of principles on syndicalist independence and democracy. Most critical was declaration number seven: "The freedom of opinion and the free play of syndicalist democracy must not lead to the establishment of groups that behave like factions. Each syndicalist, being completely free to belong to and agitate in the political and philosophical organizations of his choice, cannot use the name of the syndicat except in his capacity as a member of that syndicat." The statement ended with the hope that, "by making this new concession, it will put an end to the discussions which make us lose precious time, that the merger of the syndicats will continue without delay and that in accord with the CGT the details and the date of the unity congress can be determined."[79]

The dam was broken. All the federations made plans for unification. On June 25 the public service workers became one union, and on July 24 the CGT and the CGTU agreed on the essentials of unification. At the August 3 session of the annual congress of the Syndicat des Instituteurs, Delmas called for unity "without victors, without vanquished," and for the formation of a Popular Front. Delegates from the unitaires were welcomed, and the congress passed a motion calling on the two syndicats to make the final arrangements for a unity congress.[80] On July 12 a huge unity meeting of Parisian postal workers was held, on July 14 the massive meeting of the Rassemblement Populaire, and at the end of July a huge demonstration at the Stade Buffalo, followed by large rallies in Marseilles and other cities.

At the end of September, the two great federations met simultaneously at their annual congresses, the CGT in Paris, the CGTU in the nearby suburb of Issy-les-Moulineaux. Delegations were exchanged and finally there was a joint session. When Racamond of the CGTU arrived at the CGT congress, all stood to sing the "International." A delegate described the meeting: "Joy filled our hearts. It was the end of the deadly split." Between December 10 and 14 the postal federations became one. The secretary-general would be the CGT Perrot, the vice-secretary general, Gourdeaux of the CGTU. The syndicat newspaper joyfully announced: "The postmen who were the pioneers of syndicalism are also

79. *La Bataille des PTT,* June 13, 1935; Frischmann, *Histoire PTT,* 379.
80. AN, F7 13949.

the pioneers of unity."[81] And on December 28, the Fédération des Fonctionnaires, including the nearly one hundred thousand members of the teachers' federation, unified. Even the dissidents in the Fédération de l'Enseignement Laïc joined the unity movement. Caught between two orientations they rejected—the class collaboration of the CGT and the communist domination of the CGTU—they had continued to argue for unity based on class struggle, union democracy, and liberty of opinion, that is, the right to remain a faction.[82] The *gauchistes* of the Fédération de l'Enseignement Laïc were particularly worried about losing their identity in a reformist-dominated Fédération des Fonctionnaires and CGT. In 1935, for example, the Fédération Laïc denounced the Franco-Soviet Pact, stating that its members would not fight a war for either France or the Soviet Union. Nonetheless, they knew the importance of unity at this crucial moment. Maurice Dommanget, speaking at the congress of the autonomes at the end of 1933, had called for a congress of fusion.[83] And, of course, the "twenty-two" had asked for such a fusion three years earlier. At the unity congress of December 28, 1935, Neumeyer of the Fédération des Fonctionnaires reassured the left-wing teachers with a special welcome "to our comrades of the unitaire federation who only yesterday unquestionably were a small minority compared to the mass of other organized fonctionnaires . . . friends who were animated by a faith and an activity which we always sincerely acknowledged even while wishing them to be more practical."[84]

On January 26, 1936, a unified congress of the Cartel des Employés Publics, now representing six hundred thousand state and municipal workers, met. One of its first resolutions was in support of the Comité du Rassemblement Populaire, the Popular Front. Finally, on March 2 to 5, 1936, at Toulouse, the CGT ended the fourteen-year schism of the organized working class.

The unification of the CGT, a vital necessity for defense of working-class interests, was only one step in the development of a larger political movement that would result in the election of a Popular Front govern-

81. *La Bataille des PTT*, September 26–October 3, December 19, 1935.

82. Institut Français d'Histoire Sociale, Fonds Monatte, 14AS 172, from a speech by Bouët at the unitaire congress of September 1, reprinted in a pamphlet, *La Fédération de l'enseignement dans les assises syndicales*.

83. Bernard *et al.*, *Le Syndicalisme*, 284.

84. *La Tribune des Fonctionnaires*, December, 1935.

ment. Even though they recognized the need for a change of regime, the CGT's support of the Popular Front was by no means automatic. Most syndicalists eagerly supported the efforts to bring about the political union of the Left and its electoral campaigns. But for many of the militants of the old CGT, even though some were active in the Socialist party and most looked to the left-wing members of the Chamber of Deputies to support their legislation, the independence of the CGT from any political party stated in the venerated Charte d'Amiens, remained, at least theoretically, a basic tenet of syndicalism. The fonctionnaires, however, employed by a government based on political allegiances, whose salaries and working conditions were determined by politicians, saw participation in party and electoral politics as an important part of their syndicalist activity. Throughout their history as syndicalists, fonctionnaires had fought for their political rights as citizens, the droit d'opinion—the right to speak, to campaign, and to support political positions. And they had used that right. Fonctionnaire syndicats had campaigned vigorously over the years for left-wing parties and coalitions such as the Cartel des Gauches. Fonctionnaires had run for office, and many syndicalist leaders such as André Delmas and Robert Lacoste were important figures in the Socialist party.[85]

This tradition of political involvement was intensified in the fight against the décrets-lois. During their three-year battle with government after government, with deputies only too willing to give free rein to budget-cutting ministers, it had become crystal clear to the fonctionnaires that their working conditions would not improve and their jobs would not be safe until they elected a government sympathetic to their needs and to the needs of other workers. "The syndicat can no longer be above the struggle; it is no longer apolitical," wrote the Bataille des PTT.[86] The fonctionnaires were thus almost unanimous in their support of the developing Rassemblement Populaire. After the May, 1935, municipal elections, they voiced their support for a new government with meetings and leaflets. In June, the Cartel des Employés Publics issued a huge wall poster addressed to "Our Fellow Citizens," which blamed the deflationary policies of the government in power for the misery of state

85. Delmas, representing the SFIO, ran for a Chamber seat in 1924, and Lacoste became a member of the government in 1939.
86. La Bataille des PTT, November 14, 1935.

workers, farmers, and consumers. It asked for work for the unemployed, a minimum wage, decent prices for farmers, and protection for the small saver. Finally, it called for a new government: "Let us put into power a government which as the vehicle for the popular will, will substitute for the murderous policies of economic and social repression, a bold policy of economic renewal and human progress."[87]

At each fonctionnaire unity congress, support of the Popular Front was among the major resolutions. The postal congress "asks the reunified CGT. . . . to use all its forces to institute a new regime which will achieve the equal participation of all in the rights and responsibilities that arise from the necessary relations among men."[88] Neumeyer, addressing the unity congress of the Fédération des Fonctionnaires, condemned the deflationary policies of the government and declared that the fonctionnaires were "determined more than ever to bar, by all means, the road to fascism." He said they welcomed the Popular Front: "It [the congress] is convinced that the working, peasant and democratic masses, badly battered by the crisis, will enthusiastically welcome the announcement of the creation of a popular front."[89]

The unity congress of the CGT debated whether to give formal support to the Popular Front. Jouhaux, among others, still worried about the political independence of the syndicats. Yet the congress clearly wanted to support the movement. Finally, Robert Lacoste of the Fédération des Fonctionnaires introduced a motion, which was passed unanimously, pledging support for the program of the Popular Front, which would include, of course, the program of the CGT:

> The congress continues the support given by the syndicalist representatives to the program of the Rassemblement Populaire, with the aim of mobilizing the mass of the French people toward the improvement of their conditions and for the defense and triumph of liberty and peace.
> The CGT and all its constituents with unceasing struggle will support the demands of the program. . . . It supports the structural reforms enunciated in the CGT plan: national unemployment insurance, the forty-hour week, minimum wages, public works, collective bargaining and workers control.[90]

87. AN, F7 13735.
88. Frischmann, *Histoire PTT,* 394.
89. *La Tribune des Fonctionnaires,* December, 1935.
90. Lefranc, *Mouvement syndical,* 332.

In May the Popular Front was victorious. Writing in 1938, Charles Laurent of the Fédération des Fonctionnaires took pride in the role played by the fonctionnaires in that victory: "We have led an enormous effort throughout the country: distributed millions of tracts, asking all our members to engage in a fervent campaign on the electoral front, and we have thus been happy to be among the artisans of the victory of the Popular Front."[91]

The emergence of the fonctionnaires as a powerful voice in the CGT and in national politics was based on more than their numerical strength, their well-organized, well-supported syndicats and federations, and their articulate, politically astute leadership. It was based to a large extent on their response to the economic and political developments of the 1930s. In the struggles over the décrets-lois, the fonctionnaires had entered the political mainstream, proving their syndicalist determination through a combination of their traditional legislative tactics and the tactics of the blue-collar working class—the demonstration and the strike. On February 12, 1934, the fonctionnaires had proven themselves good organizers, strong antifascists, and devoted syndicalists. Finally, they were active in the campaign for labor unity and the Popular Front.

It would be incorrect to overemphasize the role of the fonctionnaires in these two momentous events. The blue-collar federations on both sides recognized the need for labor unity. The left-wing political parties, numerous intellectuals, and the majority of the working class wanted and worked for a Popular Front government. But it was the fonctionnaires who emerged as the crucial voice for unity and for political involvement within the CGT. It was the fonctionnaires who, never fully accepting the schism, steered the unity talks so that the final victory would be not only a reunified CGT but a CGT that would continue to be a bastion of reformism. And it was the fonctionnaires who, using their tradition of political involvement, firmly led the CGT into open and clear support of a Popular Front government. The fonctionnaires' syndicalist and political consciousness had been deeply affected by the twin specters of economic depression and rising fascism. Highly organized, politically astute, and now firmly in the mainstream of syndicalist and political activity, the fonctionnaires were able to play a determining role in the labor movement and in national politics.

91. Charles Laurent, *Le Syndicalisme des fonctionnaires* (Paris, n.d. [1938?]), 27.

In considering the French fonctionnaires' identification with left-wing politics and their role in the forging of labor unity and in the political struggle against fascism, one cannot but think of comparisons with the state workers of Germany, who mostly allied themselves with the more conservative elements in German political life. While French fonctionnaires were demonstrating and striking against economic impoverishment and right-wing policies, most German civil service workers either openly supported or quietly acquiesced to fascism. The differences in the behavior of teachers such as the French teachers' devotion to positivism and pacifism is most obvious.

The experiences of the 1930s were, of course, not identical in each country. German workers, white collar and blue, suffered more severely than French workers from both the depression of the 1930s and the inflation of the 1920s. Nor did fascism in France attract the same large numbers of supporters as it did in Germany; no French fascist league or party ever had anything near the electoral strength of the Nazi party in Germany. Even considering these variables, however, the response of German and French state workers to fascism was very different. Until there is a thorough study of German state workers, no accurate comparison can be made. Nevertheless, using the material on France from this study and Jürgen Kocka's excellent comparison of American and German white-collar workers (though he studied white-collar workers in the private sector), a comparison can be attempted.[92]

The first obvious differences between the two groups of state workers emanate from the educational system and the civil service structure. In contrast to the majority of German civil service workers, who had been trained in the authoritarian schools of the Wilhelmine tradition to learn devotion to kaiser and state, French civil service workers had been since the 1880s the products of secular, rational, and, most critically, republican schools. These schools not only trained ordinary citizens to republican devotion, they supplied the civil service with workers who tended to be free thinkers and fervent republicans. The civil service, though highly centralized and bureaucratic, was nonetheless the product of the French Revolution, infused with the democratic ideology of *liberté* and *égalité*. Although the French fonctionnaires complained bitterly about

---

92. Jürgen Kocka, *White Collar Workers in America, 1890–1940: A Social-Political History in International Perspective* (London, 1980).

authoritarianism and favoritism, there was a good deal of egalitarianism in the French system. Free education, an open examination system, and the democratic ideals of republicanism all contributed to a recruitment and advancement system that allowed open access to the children of the "nonpossessors." The early feminization of teaching and of the PTT contributed to this egalitarian tradition by exposing male fonctionnaires to concepts of equal pay and even feminism. In German schools more men than women taught in boys' schools, even at the primary level, until after 1945.[93]

Most critical in the analysis of education and recruitment is the French fonctionnaires' devotion to republicanism. Educated as republicans, recruited for their republican beliefs, French fonctionnaires automatically entered state service on the left of the political spectrum. They battled various ministers and governments, but they never attacked the Republic. Like so many of their blue-collar counterparts, state workers responded with vigor and force when called upon to "save the Republic." Although many German civil service workers welcomed the Weimar Republic, the republican tradition had neither the deep roots nor the devotion it had in France. German civil service workers served the state; French civil service workers served the Republic.

A last major difference was the class identification of state workers. As this study has shown, French fonctionnaires organized early, and even though they recognized the differences in status and security between white collar and blue, they allied themselves with the blue-collar working-class organizations. German white-collar workers were also well organized, but they thought of themselves more as a *stand* (social echelon) than a class and avoided identification with the blue-collar working class. When battered by economic crisis, they railed against "those up there," but they also wanted to keep their distance from "those down there."[94] As German state workers became more proletarianized, they perceived this condition as a threat to their existence as a *stand* and turned to fascism. As French state workers became more proletarianized, they joined the proletarian movement.

93. Unpublished data from Katherine Stodolsky's study of women teachers in Germany.
94. Kocka, *White Collar Workers*, 4.

I I

The End of the Republic, 1937–1940

How satisfying it would have been to end this history of fonctionnaire syndicalism with the grand speeches of the unity congresses, with the cheers of the euphoric crowds, and with the great electoral victory of May, 1936. This, of course, was not to be. Although the spirit of the movement was not forgotten, becoming a glorious legend for the Left and a frightening and bitter memory for the Right, and though some of its limited social and economic programs were maintained or reintroduced after the war, the Popular Front government had a short and beleaguered life. The Popular Front committee continued to meet until late 1938, but by the spring of 1937, with all its innovative legislation and plans halted—the "pause" of February—and with the resignation of Léon Blum as chief minister in June, the Popular Front government was moribund, finished in all but name. In November, 1938, the Popular Front ended officially.

The failures of the Popular Front have been analyzed by numerous historians and political commentators.[1] Attempts to end the depression by raising buying power and public works programs, as was done under the New Deal in the United States, were thwarted by the flight of capital, by the declining value of the franc, and by the deepening depression. Attacks on Blum and his cabinet from the Right and especially from the proto-fascist parties created in the wake of the dissolution of the leagues—the Parti Social Français of Colonel de la Rocque and Jacques Doriot's Parti Populaire Français—filled the press and made an appear-

---

1. See Joel Colton, *Léon Blum* (New York, 1966); Daniel R. Brower, *The New Jacobins: The French Communist Party and Popular Front* (New York, 1966); "Front Populaire," *Le Mouvement social*, No. 54 (January–March, 1966); Georges Lefranc, *Histoire du front populaire* (Paris, 1965); Henry Ehrmann, *French Labor from the Popular Front to the Liberation* (New York, 1946); and Julian Jackson, *The Popular Front in France* (Cambridge, Eng., 1988).

ance in every political oration. The Popular Front, wrote the rightist Henri de Kerillis, "hideous bandits, scoundrels, emanating from the dregs of society, will make the entire country feel the weight of the dictatorship of crime." An intense personal campaign of vilification by the extreme rightist newspaper *Gringoire* drove the minister of the interior, Roger Salengro, to suicide. Léon Blum, a socialist and a Jew, brought to the surface the anti-Semitism that had been festering since the days of the Dreyfus affair. At the opening session of the new Chamber, the rightist deputy Xavier Vallat voiced his dissatisfaction that "France, an ancient Gallo-Roman country, will be governed for the first time by a Jew."[2]

Battered from the Right, Blum and the Popular Front government alienated support from the Left and from among the anti-fascists in general by the decision not to aid the Popular Front government of Republican Spain in its civil war but to follow the British policy of nonintervention even in the face of fascist aid to the rebels of Francisco Franco. The March, 1937, shooting by the police of Popular Front supporters protesting a meeting of de la Rocque's Parti Social Français at Clichy further weakened Blum's support from the Left, some of whom compared him to "bloody Noske," the villain of German socialism. Finally, after a year of increasingly conservative policy, there was Munich and the failed general strike of November, 1938. The Popular Front was dead and with it any hope for the maintenance of the democratic Third Republic.

One of the most important events during the Popular Front was the spectacular growth of the CGT. The addition of millions of new members was to change the nature of the organization and mark its emergence as an important voice in national politics. And fonctionnaires, now a vital part of the CGT, were to be deeply involved in these developments.

The enormous growth in membership, the *ruée syndicale* (the syndicalist drive or rush), began with the wave of strikes in May and June, 1936.[3] The harsh economic realities of the depression and the weakness of the CGT had kept strike activity at a low level through most of the

2. Claude Fohlen, *La France de l'entre-deux-guerres* (Paris, 1966), 132; Colton, *Léon Blum*, 144.
3. Antoine Prost, *La CGT à l'époque du front populaire, 1934–36* (Paris, 1964), 37. The term is Léon Jouhaux's.

months preceding the victory of the Popular Front. In April, 1936, in all of France there were only thirty-two strikes involving a few thousand workers. Then on May 11, 1936, five hundred aircraft workers at the Bréguet plant in Le Havre, demanding the forty-hour week and the reinstatement of two fired militants, took over their factory. The Bréguet workers were victorious, and within a few days the strike movement spread to other aircraft factories, to Toulouse, and to the industrial suburbs of Paris.[4]

Suddenly, a new type of strike, the *grève sur le tas,* the sit-down strike, emerged as a powerful weapon of the working class. From the aircraft industry the movement spread to the automobile plants, then to construction, chemical plants, textiles, clothing, food, and retail stores. Factories, shops, department stores, and hotels were occupied, demands were issued. Pictures of smiling men and women, sitting at their machines or waving from their shop windows, filled the newspapers and the newsreels of movie theaters. The month of June brought more than twelve thousand strikes and involved 2 million workers.

Despite charges that the massive strike movement was the result of a syndicalist or communist plot, it seems clear that the sit-down strikes of 1936 were spontaneous. Years of frustration with conservative and backward employers who refused to recognize unions and to bargain collectively, combined with the hope that the Popular Front government would move quickly to initiate social and economic programs to benefit workers, sparked the flames that spread almost literally like wildfire. Most analysts agree that the political parties and the syndicats were completely surprised by the magnitude of the movement. Indeed, most CGT leaders were at first worried that the strike movement might jeopardize the newly elected Popular Front government and its programs. This concern caused the leaders of the fonctionnaire syndicats to move quickly to separate the fonctionnaires from a strike movement that was meant to be only against private employers. Fonctionnaires, as employees of the state rather than private enterprise, were asked not to strike against their employer, which was, of course, the government of the Popular Front. The *Tribune des Fonctionnaires* of June 6, 1936, stated the position of the Fédération des Fonctionnaires: "Despite all the mas-

---

4. See Herrick Chapman's forthcoming book on aircraft workers.

terly provocations of the powerful employers and their press, the public service employees will not allow themselves to catch the contagion. They will remain at the government's side, in agreement with the CGT." René Belin, speaking for the central bureau of the CGT, told the fonctionnaires: "A public service strike, that's a strike against the government. We have nothing about which to reproach the government which has only been in power for a few days, which is in constant contact with the CGT, and which is studying and preparing with the CGT new social laws." Hopeful that the new government would rescind the worst of the décrets-lois and respond favorably to other workplace demands, the fonctionnaires did not join the strike movement. Within two months, the fonctionnaires' loyalty to the Popular Front government was rewarded with amnesties for fired militants and the abrogation of many of the décrets-lois.[5] In the aftermath of the Matignon accords, the workweek was shortened, vacations were extended, and postal workers finally attained the much desired Sunday off.

For millions of strikers in the private sector, their victory would begin with the Matignon accords, the agreement signed on the night of June 7–8 by French employers, represented by the Confédération Générale de la Production Française (CGPF—*Production* was changed to *Patronat* in August), and French workers, represented by the CGT. Sometimes called the Magna Charta of French labor, the Matignon agreements allowed official recognition of the syndicalist movement and its right to organize, as well as making provisions for legal collective bargaining. A shop steward system was established, and wages were increased from 7 to 15 percent. Within a few days, legislation was passed legalizing the agreement, and further advances were made with the introduction of required paid vacations and, finally, after many years of struggle, the reduction of the workweek to forty hours without a reduction in pay.

But the new legislation did not immediately put an end to the strikes. The momentum carried through much of June as workers continued to strike recalcitrant industries. On June 12, the head of the Communist party, Maurice Thorez, told the workers, "one must know when to end

5. René Belin, *Du Secrétariat de la CGT au gouvernement de Vichy* (Paris, 1978), 93; Georges Frischmann, *Histoire de la fédération CGT des PTT* (Paris, 1967), 420–21.

a strike," and finally, when legislation was passed and demands were met, by July the strike movement began to wind down.[6]

The occupiers of the factories and shops danced, played cards, cooked their meals, and, most critical for the future of the organized working-class movement, they talked about politics and about syndicalism. Leaflets and newspapers were read and discussed, speakers were heard. Those workers who were striking, those who had finished their strikes, those who hoped to benefit from the strikes—all flocked to the syndicat offices or to the syndicat activists who had brought literature and membership cards to the factory or shop, eagerly signing their names and paying for the "stamp" that made them members of their occupational federation and the CGT.

Historians of the *ruée syndicale* disagree on exact figures, but all agree on the magnitude of the phenomenon. There is no doubt that within the few months of the spring and summer of 1936, workers joined the CGT in what Antoine Prost calls a "veritable tidal wave." Most students of the strike movement use the CGT figures popularized by Georges Lefranc, which claim that the CGT grew from just over 1 million members in the spring of 1936 to over 5 million by the spring of 1937. But even if one uses the more modest but carefully analyzed figures of Antoine Prost—785,000 at unification to nearly 4 million in 1937—the growth is just as phenomenal. In just one month, from May 15 to June 15, 1936, the CGT grew to 2.5 million members. Even after the strikes subsided, memberships continued to flow in. The metalworkers' syndicat (including aircraft and automobile workers), which had approximately fifty thousand members at unification, had grown to six hundred thousand in September, 1936 and to eight hundred thousand by the spring of 1937. All sectors were affected by the growth—chemical workers, glass workers, metalworkers, textile workers—all registered phenomenal spurts in membership. Even agriculture quintupled its membership in fifteen days by receiving twenty thousand new members during that short period.[7]

Throughout the year 1937, the CGT maintained between 4 and 5 mil-

6. Ehrmann, *French Labor*, 40.
7. Prost, *La CGT du front populaire*, 38, 34n.3, 35, 38, 40, 53; see also Georges Lefranc, *Le Mouvement syndical sous la troisième république* (Paris, 1967), 410–11.

lion members, the largest membership it had ever known. Even though it lost members in textiles and metallurgy in late 1937, other syndicats held their strength. The failure of the Popular Front and the agony over Munich reduced membership to 2.5 million, but, except for the wartime period, the CGT never again returned to the low levels of the membership and influence it had experienced in the pre–Popular Front era.[8]

The enormous new membership could not but change the CGT. The pre-1936 CGT had its largest membership among state workers—cheminots and fonctionnaires. The fonctionnaires were already highly organized and could add only a limited number of members. Although fonctionnaire syndicats also registered a doubling of membership, they could not compete with the growth figures of the other federations. For blue-collar workers, who had been largely unorganized in the interwar period—some federations had only 1 or 2 percent in their syndicat—the growth potential was enormous. Suddenly, once again blue-collar workers numerically dominated the new CGT.

The Catholic trade union federation, the Confédération Française des Travailleurs Chrétiens, also grew significantly during this period, from approximately 150,000 to 500,000. Most of its pre-1936 strength came from employés (office workers in the private sector) and from industrial workers in Catholic areas—textile workers and miners in the Nord and Alsace-Lorraine. It was not until the postwar period, when some banks and other financial institutions were nationalized and then when a more left-wing faction developed, becoming in 1964 the Confédération Française Démocratique du Travail (CFDT), that fonctionnaires joined in significant numbers. Before 1940, except for a small group of fonctionnaires in the CFTC and a handful of teachers connected with the remnants of the revolutionary syndicalists in the CGT Syndicaliste Révolutionnaire, almost all fonctionnaires were in the CGT.

Antoine Prost in his thorough and penetrating analysis of CGT membership recognizes multicausal factors, including the political milieu in which the growth took place, but nevertheless stresses a sociological explanation of the CGT's expansion of 1936–1937. Separating syndicats into two categories—the blue-collar production, or secondary sector, and the private and government services, or tertiary sector—Prost con-

8. Prost, La CGT du front populaire, 48.

firms my view that because of the security of employment and the strong organizational and occupational identification and discipline, the tertiary sector, mainly fonctionnaires, was able to maintain syndicat membership when blue-collar syndicalism declined in the 1920s and 1930s. He also views the fonctionnaires' reformist tendencies as an important aspect of their strength in the CGT. Prost sees the growth of blue-collar syndicalism during the period of the Popular Front as a combination of historical tradition and industrial geography; the new syndicalism arose first in older cities with a history of syndicalism and industries characterized by larger plants. Workers organized because of specific conditions in their plants, in their industry, and in their geographic area. Although Prost recognizes the importance of political ideology and organization on the development of the CGT and its members, his analysis does not sufficiently stress the conjunction of membership decline in the 1920s and the subsequent growth in 1936–1937 with the political events and developments of the period. The *ruée syndicale*, whatever its sociological, historical, and economic roots, was initiated only after the victory of the Popular Front.[9] Indeed, a recognition of the importance of the political consciousness and activities of the fonctionnaires helps explain much of their influence in the CGT during this period, their strength in the pre-1936 CGT, and, even as their numerical strength declined in proportion to that of blue-collar workers, their continued influence in the newly unified federation. The decision not to join the strike movement of 1936, though influenced by the fonctionnaires' general reluctance, particularly among teachers, to use the long-honored tactic of the blue-collar workers, was nevertheless a political decision to support the new government. Certainly fonctionnaires supported the strikers in the private sector and welcomed the resulting reduction in the workweek, but as they had demonstrated so often in the early 1930s, political decisions and activity were for them an important part of the struggle for economic justice.

9. Michael Seidman sees even less political influence in the strikes of 1936. He maintains that workers, particularly in the newer industries such as automobile and aircraft, were not political. They were rejecting work discipline and in many cases rejecting work itself, interested primarily in a shorter workweek and paid vacations ("The Birth of the Weekend and the Revolts Against Work: The Workers of the Paris Region During the Popular Front," *French Historical Studies*, XII [Fall, 1981], 249–76).

The increased number of blue-collar workers in the CGT challenged the old ideologies and the old leadership as well. Although some former unitaires sat on the federal bureau and were important in local organizations, the leadership of the newly unified organization remained primarily in the hands of Jouhaux and, except for the younger fonctionnaires, a coterie of aging reformists. For the new members, more familiar with February, 1934, and the Popular Front than with the bitter struggles of the 1920s, the appeal of the highly organized, younger, and more fervent communists in the syndicalist movement was undeniable. Communist influence in the CGT, though later weakened by the Nazi-Soviet Pact and the outlawing of the Communist party in 1939, was firmly established. Opposition to communist activities in the CGT was also firmly established. Although unity held until late 1939, almost from the moment of unification the ideological lines were drawn.

Although the former unitaires never controlled the reunified CGT in the years before the war, there is no doubt that their influence among the new members was increasing. Circulating the old unitaire weekly publication *La Vie Ouvrière* on the shop floor and at syndicat meetings, the former unitaires were able to present their position to hundreds of thousands of members of the CGT. Starting with printings of only 16,000 copies in early 1936, *La Vie Ouvrière* jumped to over 170,000 copies in January, 1937, and by June of that year it was printing 260,000 copies.[10] Some CGT leaders, centered around René Belin, the former postal leader and one of the secretaries of the CGT, worried about this growth in communist influence and began in the fall of 1936 to publish a rival paper, *Syndicats*. Though ostensibly dedicated to syndicat "independence" and pacifism, and though it did attract some old-time revolutionary syndicalists, the primary impetus of the *Syndicats* movement was anticommunism.

Marie-France Rogliano, in her study of *Syndicats,* agrees. Noting that *Syndicats* drew its support from syndicalists devoted to the political independence of the CGT and from traditional antiwar militants, Rogliano concludes that the main purpose of the *Syndicats* group was anticommunism, which was exacerbated by the admittance of the uni-

10. Prost, *La CGT du front populaire,* 155.

taires into the CGT and by the growing strength of the communists among the new members flocking to the reunified CGT.[11]

The first issue of *Syndicats* emphasized this group's basic aim, "to bar the route to the growing influence of the communists." Belin and many of the other *Syndicats* supporters never accepted the reunification of the CGT with the communists of the CGTU. In his memoirs, Belin castigates Jouhaux for not supporting *Syndicats,* and though he goes on to say that one of its aims was to prevent another war, he states clearly that in the last analysis, "at bottom, the creation of *Syndicats* had only one object: to bring Jouhaux back to the camp of the ex-confédérés, to restore the spirit, to organize a decisive mass battle which would bring about a break with the communists. The break was inevitable. It would occur ten years later. The *Syndicats* team was ten years ahead of its time. They'll never forgive us for that."[12]

Although the periodical *Syndicats* was never as widely read as *La Vie Ouvrière,* it did attract a substantial number of followers, perhaps as much as one-fifth of the membership of the CGT, and a not insignificant number of these were fonctionnaires.[13] Belin, of course, came from the postal federation, as did Courrière and Perrot. More important to *Syndicats* was the support of Ludovic Zoretti and especially of André Delmas of the teachers' federation, both of whom represented a strong current of anticommunism and pacifism among teachers. Other syndicalist leaders in the *Syndicats* movement were Raymond Froideval of the Seine ironworkers, Pierre Vigne of the miners, Henri Cordier of construction, Marcel Roy of the metalworkers, and Georges Dumoulin, the secretary of the northern syndicats. Although they forswore party connections, Nathaniel Green has noted that many of the *Syndicats* leaders—Belin, Dumoulin, Roy, and Delmas—were active socialists, and their later vehement stand for Munich and against war with Germany at all costs par-

11. Marie-France Rogliano, "L'Anticommunisme dans la CGT: Syndicats," *Le Mouvement social,* No. 87 (April–June, 1974), 63–84.

12. René Bidouze, *Les Fonctionnaires, sujets ou citoyens?* (2 vols.; Paris, 1979), I, 258; Belin, *Du Secrétariat,* 72.

13. Belin says that *Syndicats* reached a printing level of 150,000 (*Du Secrétariat,* 69). Prost says it was less popular; he does not accept the official figure of 130,000 (*La CGT du front populaire,* 155n.31). Lefranc, who contributed articles for *Syndicats,* says it published 60,000 copies in 1936 (*Mouvement syndical,* 374).

alleled the views of the right-wing segment of the Socialist party led by Paul Faure.[14]

The bulk of the fonctionnaires, however, supported neither the communists nor the *Syndicats* faction. Following their traditional allegiance to the CGT of Léon Jouhaux, the powerful Fédération des Fonctionnaires and its leaders, Charles Laurent, Neumeyer, and Robert Lacoste, refused Belin's overtures to join *Syndicats,* opting instead to support the sorely beleaguered middle position and maintaining the agreements of the unity congress. In 1938, this group attempted to replace both *La Vie Ouvrière* and *Syndicats* with its own official CGT weekly, *Messidor.* It did not survive the summer of 1939.

While debate raged among the CGT factions on the questions of communist influence and the political independence of the syndicalist movement, events were unfolding in the world of European politics which would soon make foreign policy a primary concern of the CGT and its members. The Spanish civil war had severely wounded the Popular Front, Austria had been swallowed up by Hitler's Germany, and in the summer of 1938 war seemed imminent as Hitler threatened to abrogate Czechoslovakia's territorial integrity by claiming the Sudetenland. The sudden danger of war with Germany brought to the fore the differences in attitudes toward the question of peace which had long been festering within the ranks of the CGT. No one wanted war, everybody wanted peace, but the debate over the way to achieve peace pitted worker against worker, fonctionnaire against fonctionnaire. It was an ideological and tactical struggle complicated by considerations other than war and peace—patriotism, pro- and anticommunism, pro- and antifascism, and the historical devotion to pacifism.

Since the turn of the century, the left-wing political parties and the CGT had been staunchly antiwar. Although the antimilitarism championed by Jean Jaurès had collapsed under the pressure of World War I and the Union Sacrée, the horrors of that war had reaffirmed the commitment of the Left to resist capitalist wars, which took as their victims workers and peasants. The monuments in every town and village, the *gueules cassées* (disabled veterans) on the street corners, and the popula-

14. Nathaniel Green, *Crisis and Decline: The French Socialist Party in the Popular Front Era* (Ithaca, 1969), 237n.32.

tion declines in the schools constantly reminded all Frenchmen and Frenchwomen of the grim toll of modern warfare. Throughout the 1920s and early 1930s, while the right-wing parties glorified the military and waved the flag of patriotism, communists and socialists, revolutionary syndicalists and ordinary syndicalists voted against military appropriations, joined peace organizations, and spoke, wrote, and rallied against war.

But the militarism of Germany and its stated territorial ambitions were to muddy the waters that had previously separated the traditional Right from the Left on the question of war and peace. For many on the Left, the way to peace became identified with military preparedness and strong resistance to Hitler's policies, while the previously bellicose rightists now urged the government to show caution and conciliation in its dealings with Hitler. In 1935, Pierre Laval had signed a pact with the Soviet Union, and the Communist party in France rallied to the side of strong resistance to Hitler. Fascism is war, antifascism is the way to peace, became the slogan of the communists. Although many who identified with the Right continued to support a strong military and a forceful foreign policy toward Germany, numerous anticommunists viewed this turnabout as ominous proof of their worst fears—that republican France would spill French blood to defend Stalin and Soviet communism. For others on the extreme Right, distressed with the weaknesses of the parliamentary system, their distrust of republican democracy exacerbated with the victory of the Popular Front, the lure of fascism and fascistlike leagues became more appealing. Better Hitler than Blum.

Within the CGT, the anticommunism of the *Syndicats* group led most of its supporters to advocate appeasement of Adolf Hitler. Anticommunism was not the only determining factor in the debate over foreign policy. There were in 1938, as Antoine Prost notes, two pacifisms: one historic and traditional, strong in the areas of old syndicalism, and the other a new pacifism, the root of which was anticommunism.[15] Within and without the *Syndicats* group there were numerous pacifists, old revolutionary syndicalists and ordinary CGT members, who, underestimating the nature of the fascist threat as just another capitalist dispute and

15. Prost, *La CGT du front populaire*, 152.

faithful to the antiwar tradition, advocated peace at any price. Among the devotees of both groups of pacifists were numerous fonctionnaires, especially teachers and agents of the PTT. At the unity congress of 1936, during a speech on the subject of peace, Mathé of the PTT concluded his remarks with the words, "I do not hesitate: sooner slavery than war, because from war, there is no return. You can survive slavery." [16]

The notion that servitude was better than war, though openly rejected by the leaders of the *Syndicats* movement and other pacifist leaders—Belin says their position was closer to "neither wolf nor sheep"—nevertheless reflected an underlying sentiment that grew stronger as the danger of war intensified. [17] Whether through the vehemence of their anticommunism or through the naïveté of the old syndicalist devotion to pacifism, numerous assumedly well-meaning CGT militants followed René Belin, later minister of labor under the Vichy government, into open collaboration with the Nazi occupation. For the Right it was "rather Hitler than Blum"; for the anticommunist Left centered around *Syndicats*, it was "rather Petain than Thorez" or "rather servitude than war."

All these ideological conflicts came to a head in the summer and fall of 1938 with the crisis over Czechoslovakia. In September, as Neville Chamberlain traveled to Berchtesgaden and Gotesberg, trying desperately to avoid conflict, and as mobilization was ordered, the political lines were being drawn in the CGT. A new CGT group, the *centre syndical d'action contre la guerre*, had been formed by revolutionary supporters of *Révolution Proletarienne* and joined by members of *Syndicats*. While the communist-led Parisian regional CGT assured the Czechs of the opposition of the Parisian proletariat to the dismemberment of Czechoslovakia, the central board of the Syndicat National des Instituteurs asked the government "to pursue as far as possible negotiations which would see a peaceful settlement to the conflict." [18]

In late September, under the leadership of André Delmas, who had consulted with Foreign Minister Georges Bonnet and the reactionary, proappeasement deputy Pierre-Etienne Flandin, an appeal was launched asking for the signatures of labor leaders, socialists, and antifascist intel-

16. Apparently because of his later activity on behalf of appeasement policies, André Delmas was accused of uttering these words. It was indeed Mathé.
17. Belin, *Du Secrétariat,* 73.
18. Lefranc, *Mouvement syndical,* 378.

lectuals. Within a few weeks, 150,000 signatures were gathered. Under the title "We don't want war," the appeal asked the government to take to the negotiations table the ardent desire of the French people for peace and to pursue the negotiations vigorously.[19] It carried the signatures of two syndicalist organizations—the Syndicat National des Instituteurs and the Syndicat National des Agents des PTT (Mathé was a sponsor). The leaders of the Fédération des Fonctionnaires refused to sign. Laurent, Lacoste, and other leaders of the federation had earlier expressed their opposition to appeasement. Writing in the *Tribune des Fonctionnaires* in January, 1938, Charles Laurent called on his country to "awake," to create a committee of public salvation during this time of crisis. In the *Tribune des Fonctionnaires* of October 8, approximately ten days after the Delmas appeal was issued, the federation leaders explained why they did not sign the appeal. Rejecting the emotionalism of the title—there were no syndicalists who wanted war—they saw the appeal as a denial of official CGT policy that "peace at any price" would permit the crushing of the Czech people.[20] Robert Lacoste also worried about the ideological split the *Syndicats* group was fostering in the CGT: "I will not accept that one can claim that there are partisans of war here. I refuse to howl with the wolves. And I state, I who am not a communist, that when I see the violent anticommunist campaign being spread in this country, I will not forget that anticommunism serves to pave the way for fascism . . . we are neither for war nor surrender."[21] Once again the fonctionnaires were in the thick of the political and ideological struggles in the CGT. While Delmas, Zoretti, Belin, Mathé, Courrière, and others defended the politics of anticommunism and appeasement, the Fédération des Fonctionnaires was the main supporter of the middle-of-the-road position of Jouhaux.

If Delmas's petition was perhaps motivated by genuine feelings against war and was signed by many sincere individuals who feared another disaster such as the one of 1914-1918, the motives of others were not so high. Ludovic Zoretti, a longtime militant of higher education syndicalism and one of the leading members of the Socialist party, who or-

19. The text is in André Delmas, *Mémoires d'un instituteur syndicaliste* (Paris, 1979), 351.
20. Bidouze, *Les Fonctionnaires*, 279–80.
21. *Le Populaire*, October 12, 1938, report of federation central committee meeting of October 10–12.

ganized within the party the isolationist *redressement* faction, was already expressing some of the sentiments that would later allow him to work under the Vichy regime. Writing in *Le Petit Normand* in the last critical days of September, Zoretti accused Blum of having provoked war. "The French people," he wrote, "do not want to see millions of human beings killed and see a civilization destroyed in order to render life more agreeable to the one hundred thousand Jews of the Sudetenland." [22]

On the night of September 29–30, the Munich accord was signed and war was temporarily averted. The world, the country, and the CGT, immediately divided into those who viewed the destruction of Czechoslovakia as a step toward war and those who saw the Munich accords as the herald of peace. The CGT was thus divided into *munichois* and *anti-munichois,* and the bitter debates continued to rage. The *Syndicats* group led the defense of Munich: Belin wrote strongly pacifist articles, and Delmas, writing in the socialist paper *Le Peuple* stated that "most of the Sudeten residents went joyfully into the Reich." [23] A *Syndicats* banquet in early October had as one of its honored guests Marcel Déat, the right-wing neosocialist and professor of philosophy, who was already giving evidence of his drift toward support of fascism.

The debate over Munich came to a head at the CGT congress held at Nantes in mid-November. With the Popular Front a failure and its legislation, including the forty-hour week, under attack from the Daladier government's recently issued décrets-lois, there was much on the domestic scene to discuss. But the debate over Munich could not be put aside. The discussions about foreign policy, about syndicalist independence, and about the décrets-lois were merely the political and economic manifestations of a deeper ideological struggle between the *Syndicats* faction and the rest of the CGT. Jouhaux tried to act as conciliator. "The CGT is not made up of pacifists and warmongers. We all want peace," he said, but he added significantly, "peace with honor and dignity." The fierce anticommunism and intransigent pacifism of the *Syndicats* group galvanized the communists and the Jouhaux supporters, including the leaders of the Fédération des Fonctionnaires, to join forces to make con-

22. *La Lumière,* September 30, 1938, quoted in Ehrmann, *French Labor,* 106. My colleague Werner T. Angress tells me that this statement is not only morally repugnant but demographically inaccurate.

23. *Le Peuple,* October 11, 1938, quoted in Green, *Crisis and Decline,* 237n.32.

cessions so as to forge a unified position that could defeat the supporters of *Syndicats*. At Nantes, Delmas introduced a "peace" resolution; it was defeated, 16,784 to 6,419, in favor of a motion put forth by a middle-of-the-road delegate. Motions on syndicalist independence received approximately the same votes.[24]

Although René Belin, who had not spoken at the congress, later told a *Syndicats* meeting that the faction would again win the majority in the CGT and "liberate the syndicalist movement from unbearable communist oppression," the *Syndicats* position had been clearly rejected by the former unitaires and confédérés in the CGT. This show of unity and strength was unfortunately to be short-lived.[25]

On November 30, 1938, in response to a series of décrets-lois which retracted several economic policies of the Popular Front including the forty-hour week, the CGT called a general strike lasting twenty-four hours. It was crushed by the government, and the period of syndicalist expansion and hope came to an end. The background of this strike is the story of the failure of the economic policies of the Popular Front and of the Popular Front as a political force. The legislation that was passed so rapidly in the summer of 1936 had given hope to all workers in France in both the public and private sectors that conditions of work and daily life would be vastly improved. In June collective bargaining, paid vacations, and the forty-hour week were legislated. In July the proposals for public works programs were passed, and in August the war industries were nationalized, bringing yet more workers into the public sector. In August as well, the legislation to extend compulsory public education by raising the school leaving age to fourteen was passed as the first part of what Jean Zay, the dynamic young minister of education, and most teachers hoped would be a program to expand and democratize the French educational system.

Although the pre–Popular Front décrets-lois lowering fonctionnaires' salaries had been somewhat eased in June and some services in the public sector had begun to initiate the forty-hour week, there was still much to be done to meet the stated needs of the fonctionnaires. At their December, 1936, congress, the Fédération des Fonctionnaires made its de-

24. Lefranc, *Mouvement syndical,* 381; Delmas, *Mémoires,* 368. Vivier-Merle, 16,582; Delmas, 7,221; Serret, 121; abstentions, 1,280.
25. Delmas, *Mémoires,* 370.

mands strongly and clearly—they wanted salaries, especially those of auxiliaries and young workers, and pensions of retired fonctionnaires to be linked with the cost-of-living index and a revision of salary scales with an annual minimum of twelve thousand francs. The congress also passed resolutions calling for amnesty, for the droit syndical, for collaboration between the syndicats and the administration, and, most strongly, for the forty-hour week in all the services. At the end of December, the government abrogated still more of the décrets-lois on salaries and gave two thousand auxiliaries permanent appointments. The problem of implementing the forty-hour week in government service was given to a study commission.

But on February 13, 1937, Léon Blum, citing the serious economic problems France was facing, asked the fonctionnaires for a pause in the application of economic and social measures. Although some cost-of-living adjustments and housing allowances were raised in early 1937 and, symbolically, the first of May was made a national holiday, by the time the Blum government fell in June, 1937, fonctionnaires had still to attain the droit syndical and the forty-hour week. Most serious for the fonctionnaires was the rising cost of living. Rising prices had eaten away some of the benefits of higher salaries. Alfred Sauvy and Pierre Depoid have determined that fonctionnaires' buying power had increased between 1936 and 1937 but add that it is difficult to ascertain the cost-of-living index for fonctionnaires because of the wide differences in the salary structure as compared to blue-collar workers.[26] The fonctionnaires' main concern was rising prices, and they felt themselves losing ground, which by the end of 1937 was true.

Although the fonctionnaires continued to assure the Chautemps government of their devotion to the Popular Front, syndicalist agitation and mass action again began to surface. Prices for government services—railroads and metro fares, postal and telegraph fees—had risen. Why wasn't this money available for fonctionnaires? Postal workers were once again bitter that the notoriously low-paid teachers had gotten a special bonus. On October 6, in answer to a call from the Cartel des Fonctionnaires et Services Publics, fifty thousand government employees rallied at the Velodrome d'Hiver in Paris, and by the end of the year strikes

26. Alfred Sauvy and Pierre Depoid, *Salaires et pouvoirs d'achats des ouvriers et des fonctionnaires entre les deux guerres* (Paris, 1940), 36–47.

were erupting in the PTT. On January 10, 1938, thousands of postal workers marched through Paris asking for more money and for "our forty hours." In the spring of 1938, the PTT finally achieved the forty-hour week. It was to be a Pyrrhic victory; the Popular Front was nearing its end.

Economic problems continued to plague the various Popular Front governments. The ministries of Blum, Chautemps, and, finally, the more right-wing Daladier could do little to get the economy moving. Devaluation, nationalization, and increasing buying power through public works programs and higher salaries—nothing worked. In 1938, despite the hopes that increased armament production would benefit the entire economy, industrial production was lower than in 1937, falling back to just about the 1934 level. Most critical for the working class was the steady rise in the cost of living and the continuing high level of unemployment.[27] Two new devaluations of the franc, in June, 1937, and May, 1938, did not alleviate the price situation, and the expectation that the forty-hour week would reduce unemployment proved to be false.

In 1938, hopes for inaugurating an economic upswing began to hinge more and more on the forty-hour week. The industrialists claimed, and the government came to agree, that production could only be stimulated and increased if the workweek was lengthened. Blum had already released the aircraft industry from this restriction. In many industries, the forty-hour workweek had never been fully implemented, and even where it was in effect workers frequently worked overtime, happy for the extra pay in a period of rising prices. It is difficult to ascertain the real effect of the forty-hour week on production. Clearly, the average workweek and production had fallen, but whether the forty-hour week was the main hindrance to recovery is problematic. For workers and bosses alike, however, the forty-hour week had become a symbol. For the employers it was the root cause of the continuing business doldrums; for the workers it was the one great achievement of the Popular Front.[28] Yet given the dangers of the international situation and the grave economic

27. Unemployment is not included in Sauvy's figures, an important omission when talking about the working class in general. See J. Lhomme, "L'Evaluation du revenue global de la classe ouvrière en France de 1929 à 1939," in *Mouvements ouvriers et depression économique de 1929 à 1939* (Assen, 1966), 220–28.

28. René Belin disagrees. He says the forty-hour week as it was implemented was a mistake from the beginning (*Du Secrétariat*, 103–106).

crisis, there remained hope for compromise. The CGT did not want to be a danger to France. During the Czechoslovakian crisis the CGT had stated that to strengthen national defense, the syndicats were willing to allow temporary extension of the forty-hour week in certain industries. They insisted, however, that the syndicats be consulted on all such questions. The government ignored the attempts at compromise—1938 was not 1936.

On November 2, Paul Reynaud became minister of finance, and ten days later, a day before the opening of the CGT congress at Nantes, the Daladier government issued a series of décrets-lois which in essence abolished the forty-hour week (forty hours remained only as the point at which overtime would be paid), lowered overtime pay (from time and one-quarter to 10 percent), and reestablished piecework in many industries. Severe penalties were outlined for workers who refused to work overtime in the interest of national defense and for those who counseled against overtime. The syndicats would not be consulted. The CGT protested; many employers were not even using the full forty hours, and because of their unwillingness to pay extra wages, many were not allowing overtime. Even before the exact implications of the decrees were known, many syndicalist leaders, especially in the communist-dominated industries, were demanding that the CGT respond more vigorously to what they considered an attempt to take away the social and economic gains of 1936. At the Nantes congress, the decrees were attacked; a motion to have a national day of protest on November 26 was passed, and there were calls for a general strike. The anticommunist bloc demurred, and Jouhaux hesitated; conditions were not ripe for a strike. A series of wildcat strikes had been put down violently by the government with tear gas and truncheons.[29] Jouhaux hoped for compromise; he hoped the government would call for the collaboration of the CGT. The government was silent.

Pressure for a strike was building; numerous moderates in the CGT agreed with the communists that the government was intent on destroying the gains made by the CGT and even the CGT itself. Moreover, talk about increasing totalitarian rule and the penalties established for anyone who acted against the longer workweek made many CGT members see

29. Tear gas had been used during a night attack on strikers at the Renault plant. *Le Populaire* (November 25) ran a banner headline, "Tear gas against workers!"

these decrees not only as an attack on syndicat liberties but as a significant loss of civil liberties for all, a step on the path to fascism.[30] And in the background there was the lingering resentment over Munich. It was becoming evident that appeasement would not stop the Nazis. In late November, an announcement was made that a Franco-German pact was near agreement and German Foreign Minister Joachim von Ribbentrop would come to Paris.

Finally, on November 25, with Renault workers already on strike, the CGT announced a twenty-four-hour general strike against the décrets-lois to take place on November 30. The militants of the CGT had five days to spread the word and organize their forces. Daladier also had five days to prepare the government's response. In light of the subsequent failure of the November 30 strike, much has been made of that five-day grace period allowed the government. André Delmas defends the decision to wait five days. Practical difficulties of sending signed letters to all the provincial syndicat leaders made it necessary to have enough time to organize a successful strike. Other observers cite Jouhaux's hope for reconciliation with the government as the reason for the five-day wait. René Belin says that when he tried on behalf of the CGT to make contact with the government through the minister of public works, Anatole de Monzie, he was told that in essence, Paul Reynaud had stated, "Let the strike go on. We must put an end to a CGT dominated by the communists. They want to fight? OK, we'll fight. We'll make them eat their words. The opportunity is too beautiful, I can't let it pass."[31]

The five-day grace period gave the government enough time to prepare its response. The CGT tried to emphasize the nonpolitical nature of the strike; it was against the economic policies of the décrets-lois. But clearly for many, the high emotions over Munich were involved. And, of course, a strike against the government could hardly be separated from politics. The government made much of the political nature of the strike. Daladier was to save the nation from "disorder and anarchy."[32]

Since this strike was indeed to be against government policies and not specifically against private industry as the 1936 strikes had been, the

30. Ehrmann, French Labor, 94n.34, citing statements of Jean Mistler in Ere Nouvelle, October 4 and 12, 1938, where the chair of the Foreign Affairs Committee in the Chamber thought it possible that France would have to establish concentration camps.

31. Delmas, Mémoires, 373; Ehrmann, French Labor, 116; Belin, Du Secrétariat, 116.

32. Radio reports and press of November 30, 1938.

strong participation of government workers was again necessary as in February, 1934. Transportation and utilities would be key to the success of the strike. The postiers declared themselves unanimous for a strike, and Delmas told the CGT that it could count on the teachers.[33] The usually militant railroad workers, carrying the bitter memory of their failed strike of 1920, had participated minimally in the 1936 events. Now their cooperation was vital, and Semard, the communist leader of the syndicat, promised that support. But Daladier moved quickly and firmly. On November 25, the railroads were requisitioned, and on the twenty-eighth, all personnel of the state, departments, and communes, that is, all fonctionnaires—from the highest ministerial officers, to the local road pavers, teachers, nurses, and telephone operators—were placed under military authority. A government circular declared that all fonctionnaires who refused to work would be liable to the penalties of the law. The circular continued in a tone reminiscent of Clemenceau in 1909:

> By his acceptance of the office which is bestowed upon him, the fonctionnaire places himself under the obligations which stem from the needs of public service and has given up all rights which are incompatible with the continuity essential to national life. . . . By going on strike, public servants are committing not only an individual offense, but by their collective acts, they put themselves outside the sphere of applicability of the laws and rules that had been promulgated to guarantee them the rights due them with respect to public authority: hence, any strike action would result in dismissal.[34]

The requisitioning and threats of arrest caused some transport syndicats to make a serious tactical error. Because of the government's requisition, they told their members to report to the work site but not to work. The drivers and conductors arrived to find a host of police and soldiers. Those who refused to work were arrested and taken away in army trucks. When a few fearful workers put some trams and busses into service, the others eventually followed. From the very beginning of the twenty-four-hour period, newspapers and radio announced the failure of the strike. Many workers in private industry, seeing the public services functioning, were in a state of confusion. Numerous teachers and agents of the PTT, unwilling to follow "communist-inspired" actions, did not strike. There was strong participation in private industry,

33. *Le Populaire,* November 28, 1938.
34. Delmas, *Mémoires,* 377.

especially among textile and clothing workers, metalworkers, leather, chemical, and construction workers, printers, and longshoremen. Although the left-wing press commended the public service workers, who struck "despite the governmental pressure," the strike was a near disaster in the requisitioned public services.[35]

The repression was brutal. In the wake of the strike, employers in private industry, with the consent of the government, fired, either temporarily or permanently, almost eight hundred thousand workers, nearly 10 percent of the working population, perhaps a good indication of the strength of the strike.[36] There were thousands of suspensions in public service, including André Delmas of the teachers. Over three thousand were fired from the PTT.[37] Some regained their jobs in the course of the next few months, but others had to wait until 1944.

About 2 million workers had participated in the November 30 strike, fewer than had struck on February 12, 1934, but still a good showing. But the atmosphere surrounding the two strikes was very different. In 1934, at a time of great CGT weakness, the strong show of syndicat discipline and political unity made that strike a huge success. In November, 1938, the confusion, the internecine struggles, the hesitation of many to go along with a strike so desired by the communists, the absence of huge public demonstrations, and the swift government requisitions and effective propaganda turned this strike, though large compared to most strikes, into a major failure.

November 30 marks another crucial turning point in the history of the labor movement and the political Left in France. The CGT was demoralized. Although the fonctionnaires, as might be expected, maintained most of their membership, the blue-collar syndicats lost between one-fourth and one-half of their members. The organized labor move-

35. *Le Populaire*, December 1, 1938. Delmas says that twenty thousand teachers struck but the postiers did not strike (*Mémoires*, 379). Frischmann says many postal workers struck but the teachers were "less successful" (*Histoire PTT*, 446). *Le Populaire* says 50 percent of Parisian teachers did not work. For an analysis of the strike, see Guy Bourdé, "La Grève de 30 novembre 1938," *Le Mouvement Social*, No. 55 (April–June, 1966).

36. *Le Populaire*, December 2, 3, 1938, says that nearly 500,000 metalworkers were fired, among them 40,000 aircraft workers. Belin's estimate of the number of fired metalworkers is 280,000 (*Du Secrétariat*, 116).

37. Frischmann, *Histoire PTT*, 447. Frischmann notes that the ministry reported on November 30 that 126 workers were on strike. He comments that 3,392 suspensions was a high price to pay for 126 strikers.

ment was no longer an important influence in the political arena—
Jouhaux's removal from the governing board of the Banque de France
was just one indication of the decision of the government to end its collaboration with the syndicalists. November 30 also marks the official
end of the Popular Front. The Third Republic would soon follow.

Torn with dissension, weakened by defections, excluded from public
power, the CGT could do nothing to stop the continuing erosion of the
benefits that had been won from the Popular Front government. Nor
could it stop the continuing erosion of civil liberties and the steady advance toward war. In February, 1939, the government refused amnesty
to those fonctionnaires who had been suspended or fired for taking part
in the November 30 strike, and in May and August another series of
décrets-lois permitted a workweek of up to sixty hours and cut yet more
fonctionnaire benefits. Within the CGT, the ideological and tactical
battle between the communists and the anticommunists of the *Syndicats*
group frequently erupted into shouting matches and even street brawls.
And the pacifists, in a desperate effort to halt the drift toward war, continued to support a policy of appeasement. In May, when Marcel Déat
asked, "To die for Danzig?" this position was supported by André Delmas in an editorial in *L'Ecole Emancipatrice.* In his memoirs, Delmas defends his support of Déat's position, saying that it would have been
foolish to go to war over the independence of one city.[38]

On August 23, 1939, the Nazi-Soviet Pact was signed and the dissension in the CGT reached a fever pitch. On August 26, the Communist
party dailies were suspended, but *La Vie Ouvrière,* technically an organ
of the CGT, was allowed to continue for a few more weeks, much to the
consternation of the *Syndicats* followers. Then on September 1, Germany invaded Poland, and on September 3, Great Britain and France
declared war. On September 17, Soviet troops entered Poland, and one
day later the administrative committee of the CGT passed a motion to
exclude from membership in the syndicalist organizations all federations, all syndicats, and all militants who did not publicly disavow the
Nazi-Soviet Pact. On September 26, the government dissolved the
Communist party. Without waiting for formal disavowals, all over
France militants were purged from syndicats, syndicats from federations
and the CGT. In the communist-dominated industries, whole syndicats
disappeared. Unlike the 1921–1922 schism, this time there was no op-

38. *L'Oeuvre,* May 4, 1939; Delmas, *Mémoires,* 387.

portunity to form unitairelike syndicats; the procommunist syndicalists went underground. The government aided the massive purge by arresting leading communist militants, including those who had issued a special call for syndicat unity. By March, 1940, 620 syndicats had been dissolved, 3,400 syndicalists had been arrested, and 10,000 fonctionnaires had received disciplinary punishment.[39] Under new laws, numerous "suspects" were interned in concentration camps; the government dragnet frequently caught noncommunists or even anticommunists who were considered too militant. For Belin and the *Syndicats* group, their time had come. The asserted belief in the political independence of the syndicalist movement gave way to the joy of ending communist influence in the CGT.

Although the leaders of the Fédération des Fonctionnaires eventually went along with the exclusion decision, they were deeply disturbed by the political nature of the purge, by the threat to civil liberties, and especially by what it would mean to the CGT—another schism, one they could ill afford in this time of crisis. The Fédération des Fonctionnaires never had many communist members, and its leaders, except for the recent defections of Delmas and others to *Syndicats,* had always fought hard for the reformism of Léon Jouhaux. Neumeyer, Laurent, and Lacoste were strongly anticommunist but nevertheless saw the purge as the work of a "defeatist clique" whose aim was to split the CGT. And the CGT was indeed split and severely weakened as the days of the *drôle de guerre* gave way to Nazi conquest.

If the anticommunists of the *Syndicats* group were victorious in ousting the communists from the CGT, the pacifists were less successful in stopping the war. In late August, Delmas and two other socialists made a futile trip to Belgium to see the intellectual leader of *planisme* and a leading socialist, Henri de Man, hoping he would help them launch an antiwar appeal in France, Belgium, and Great Britain. De Man, a future collaborator, told them their cause was hopeless—the German workers and the entire German people supported Hitler, and war was inevitable—but he would try to get the Belgian Socialist party to agree to support the appeal. The Belgians, anxious to maintain neutrality, answered in the negative.[40] In early September, with France already at war and Poland under bombardment, numerous syndicalists and other pub-

---

39. Bidouze, *Les Fonctionnaires,* 296.
40. Delmas, *Mémoires,* 389–91.

lic figures circulated a public declaration calling for immediate peace. Signed by revolutionary syndicalists and *Syndicats* supporters—Dumoulin, Vigne, and a number of fonctionnaires, mostly postal workers and teachers (Delmas did not sign; he was in the army)—as well as the writers Alain, Victor Marguerite, and Jean Giono, and by Marcel Déat, the tract began with the words, "Despite all the efforts of genuine pacifists, blood is flowing," and ended with the plea, "Let us demand peace." The critical message was that "the price of peace will never be as ruinous as the price of war." Several weeks later, after the conquest of Poland, Ludovic Zoretti, acting in his capacity as leader of Redressement, the pacifist group in the Socialist party, wanting perhaps, says Georges Lefranc, to begin a new Zimmerwald—an outrageous statement—again made contact with de Man and with Senator Pierre Laval, the future chief minister of Vichy.[41] Zoretti was later tried and acquitted for this action. France remained at war.

By the spring of 1940, with many of its militants in the army and the communists underground or in prison, the CGT was reduced to under 1 million members. Once more the balance had shifted and the Fédération des Fonctionnaires with its more than three hundred thousand members again became the backbone of the confederation. But within a few months, invasion and occupation would end the life of the Third Republic and the CGT. On May 9, complaining of Jouhaux's monolithic leadership, René Belin resigned from the central board of the CGT. On May 10, the Germans invaded Belgium, Holland, and the Netherlands and on the fourteenth they crossed the French border. Within one month the battle was deemed hopeless; on June 10 the government fled Paris, and on the sixteenth, two days after the Germans occupied Paris, Philippe Pétain became head of the government. An armistice was signed. On July 10, the legislature, meeting at Vichy, gave full powers to Pétain, who became head of *l'Etat Français*. The Third Republic was at an end.

Decrees were issued in rapid succession: fonctionnaires who did not collaborate with the government would be fired; no Jews could enter public service. A law of August 16 permitted the dissolution of professional organizations. In October, the fonctionnaire syndicats were dissolved and their property confiscated, and on November 9 the CGT and

41. Georges Lefranc, *Les Expériences syndicales en France de 1939 à 1950* (Paris, 1950), 25–27.

the CFTC were dissolved. The order was signed by the new minister of labor and industrial production, René Belin.

During the four-year occupation, French fonctionnaires behaved like numerous other Frenchmen and Frenchwomen. Most went about their business—their most urgent need was to survive. Others became resisters, performing acts of sabotage and heroism which sometimes led to prison, torture, and death. Still others collaborated openly with the Vichy government and with the Nazi occupiers. Sadly, although few had prewar connections to fascism, many of the collaborators came from the ultrapacifists and anticommunists who were attached to *Syndicats* as their political beliefs led them more and more to an acceptance of totalitarianism.

René Belin, who evaluated Vichy as "neither better nor worse than the regimes which preceded and succeeded it, but what it lacked the most was political experience," became minister of labor and industrial production. Even before the Nazi victory, Belin had come over to a defense of "constructive syndicalism," a revision of the economy based on class collaboration.[42] He took onto his staff Emile Courrière and Albert Perrot of the PTT, F. Medori, the former secretary of the Fédération des Fonctionnaires, and Emilie Lefranc, the wife of Georges Lefranc.[43] Francis Million, opponent of unity in 1935, and Raymond Froideval, the editor of *Syndicats,* also served on his staff.

Among those collaborating with Vigne and Dumoulin on the publication *L'Atelier,* which recruited French workers to go to Germany, was Ludovic Zoretti. It is indeed ironic that those who claimed to defend the independence of syndicalism were to yield the syndicats to the authority of the Vichy state. André Delmas, who had gone to Vichy to plead the case for syndicalist teachers with Marshal Pétain, found the new government hostile to those who had educated children to put rationalism and republicanism above "Work, Family, and Country," and retired from the political scene.

Fonctionnaire syndicalists were also active in the resistance. The cheminots destroyed trains and tracks, the postal workers cut telephone and telegraph lines, and numerous syndicalist leaders became the vanguard of the resistance organizations. Among the signers of the Manifesto of

42. *Syndicats* editorials, November 30, 1939–June 6, 1940, cited by Rogliano, "L'Anticommunisme," 78.

43. See Belin, *Du Secrétariat,* 15n.11.

the Twelve, the November 12, 1940, declaration denouncing the dissolution of the CGT and stating that syndicalists would never tolerate anti-Semitism and limitations of freedom, were Lacoste and Neumeyer. Lacoste went on to be a leader of the resistance organization Liberation in the south, and Laurent and Neumeyer helped to establish Liberation-Nord. Laurent and Neumeyer joined with René Bontems, a former unitaire of the CGT, to help unify the two factions of the underground CGT. Many others were active in fighting units: Colonel André (Ouzoulias) was a member of the PTT, and among the twenty-seven executed at Chateaubriant on October 27, 1941, was Jean Grandel, a former unitaire member of the PTT. Fonctionnaires, including the police, were active in the uprisings that helped bring about the liberation of Paris.

In 1946, fonctionnaires were granted the droit syndical.

Conclusion

One of the most significant developments in twentieth-century French working-class history was the emergence of the state as the largest employer in the nation. In little less than half a century, the fonctionnaires of France grew not only in number but in organizational and political importance. From the disparate offices and schoolrooms of the Belle Epoque, French fonctionnaires were to become, by the end of the Third Republic, the most highly organized sector of the French working class, playing a crucial role in union and national politics.

This study has traced the unionization of the fonctionnaires and their organizational and ideological attachment to the working class. It has stressed the growing consciousness of fonctionnaires as the hired workers of a powerful employer-state, a consciousness that was intensified by the failure of the Third Republic to meet the fonctionnaires' demands for the right to unionize, for improved working conditions, for a decent salary structure, and for general social reform. Although fonctionnaires still differed from blue-collar workers, especially in the security of their employment, similarity in social origins engendered by the democratic recruitment of state workers from the republican school system, the proletarianization of the fonctionnaires through changing working conditions and lowered wages, and the changing political situation all pushed fonctionnaires closer to the blue-collar working class. The shift in the organized working class toward reformism and political involvement allowed the fonctionnaires to unite with the blue-collar working class under the aegis of the major labor federation, the CGT.

But this history of fonctionnaire unionism shows us much more than the development of union consciousness and organization. It is also the story of the political maturation of the fonctionnaires and how that development influenced and was influenced by political events in Third Republic France. Although many blue-collar workers, following the principles of political independence established by the Charte d'Amiens, moved slowly and hesitantly toward involvement with political parties and alignments, the fonctionnaire organizations, almost from the beginning, understood the importance of electoral politics. Fonctionnaires, employed as they were by a government based on political allegiances, whose salaries and working conditions were determined by politicians, saw participation in party and electoral politics as an important part of their syndicalist activity. Throughout their history as syndicalists, fonctionnaires fought for their political rights as citizens: the right to speak, to campaign, and to support political positions. And they used that right. Fonctionnaire syndicats campaigned vigorously for parties and candidates who supported both fonctionnaire and CGT demands. Fonctionnaires ran for office, and numerous syndicalist leaders were important figures in the leading left-wing parties and coalitions. The political involvement of the fonctionnaires was deeply affected by the political and economic events of the period. The Great War, the Russian Revolution, the inflation of the 1920s, the depression of the 1930s, the battles over the décrets-lois, and, finally, the threat of fascism not only influenced their consciousness as state workers but intensified their political involvement. The culmination of this political involvement was the tremendous support given by fonctionnaires to CGT unity and the Popular Front. This evolution emphasizes the important connections between experience at the workplace and the wider political and economic developments in determining working-class consciousness and activity.

Moreover, this history of developing fonctionnaire consciousness and political activity tells us a good deal about the political shifts of the French working class and about Third Republic politics. Hired as republicans, trained in republican schools, the fonctionnaires entered state service on the left of the political spectrum. At the beginning of the century, this commitment to left republicanism made most fonctionnaires supporters of the Radical party and its allies. But as the Radical party became less and less responsive to the demands of the fonctionnaires and failed to create the social republic they had hoped for, fonctionnaires began to turn more and more to the Socialist party, the SFIO. The defection of the fonctionnaires from the Radicals to the Socialists was one more indication of how the Socialist party replaced the Radical party as the champion of the republican Left in the interwar years. It also indicates the continued commitment of the fonctionnaires to the left wing of Third Republic politics. It helps explain why French fonctionnaires, despite some disaffections fostered by anticommunism and pacifism, were by and large antifascist. Today, state workers in France remain the stalwarts of the moderate Left.

This history ends with the fall of the Third Republic. State service, however, has continued to grow at a phenomenal pace. The traditional postal services now include all telecommunications; state education now takes its students from the école maternelle to the university; fiscal services have gone beyond taxation to include such social services as housing, health care, and retirement; and the nationalization of banks and insurance companies has turned even more clerical workers into fonctionnaires. And significantly, many of these fonctionnaires are women. Because of the power of the state to control legislation, police forces, and fiscal policy, the employer-state is not only numerically the largest employer in France, it is much more powerful than any employer in the private sector.

A similar story is being repeated all over the world. This study of France suggests questions for further scholarly exploration, which should expand our understanding of the political importance of state workers and their organizations as well as the relationship of state power not only to state workers but to blue-collar, white-collar, and technical workers in the private sector as well.

The unionization of state workers needs further study. State workers in France were unionized early compared to other countries, but now civil service workers in all industrialized nations are either organized or organizing. Aside from organizational histories of the various unions, important questions to be examined would include the strength of the identification with the blue-collar movement, how the strength and activity of the blue-collar unions affects the organization of state workers, and how influential the state unions are within the larger labor movement. Since the antipathy of the French state to fonctionnaire unionism was so critical in the development of fonctionnaire consciousness, it would also be important to examine the attitude of the state toward unionization and union militancy.

Studies of the social origins of state workers would necessarily have to discuss the impact of free public education on the development of technical and clerical skills among rural and working-class youth. The commitment of the Third and subsequent republics to public education is crucial to the understanding of the development of a cadre of state workers as well as to the understanding of a modern blue-collar work force. For the fonctionnaires, free and widespread education brought into the state system thousands of teachers, many of them women, who were recruited from the very classes they were supposed to teach. In an effort to recruit a loyal republican corps of teachers willing to live and work in small towns and isolated villages, the state recruited the sons and daughters of poor farmers, small-town artisans, and shopkeepers, young people whose economic opportunities were continually narrowing. But more critical than this recruitment of new teachers was the creation of a mass of literate children who were taught not only the skills needed for clerical work but devotion to the Republic as well. They were ideal material for state employment. The recruitment of most fonctionnaires from the newly educated "have-nots" rather than from the wealthier middle class was one factor in the fonctionnaires' identification with the blue-collar working class.

Further study along this line might also deepen our understanding of the attraction of fascism to certain social classes. In the advanced societies that have experienced significant fascist movements in the twentieth century, large numbers of peasants, shopkeepers, and artisans expressed their discontent in antidemocratic right-radical movements. But in France, since the late nineteenth century, many of the most active and talented members of these social groups, already recruited to republican philosophy, were drawn into, and rewarded with, service to the Republic. Thus the Republic served those with diminishing economic resources not only as a pedagogue but also possibly as a safety valve. Although the democratic culture of the fonctionnaires could not prevent the creation of l'Etat Français under the extraordinary conditions of 1940, the majority of fonctionnaires remained loyal to republican values.

Historians of the working class have studied the deskilling of the blue-collar work force, but only sociologists have paid much attention to this question as it affected white-collar workers, and most such studies have concentrated on the private sector. The workplace has changed for those in state service (and in other white-collar occupations as well).

Small independent offices have given way to huge enterprises in which there is little decision making and little worker control. Except for cleanliness, there appears to be little difference for hundreds of women sitting in large offices tapping away at typewriters or computers and women who run the looms in textile mills. This deskilling has also forged connections between fonctionnaires and blue-collar workers.

The culture has been homogenized so that there are fewer differences between white- and blue-collar workers in family size, education, entertainment, and so on. In the nineteenth century, there was a real separation between the culture of blue-collar workers and that of fonctionnaires, of which education was only one aspect. Fonctionnaires, of course, were better educated, but they also wore different clothing, a "white collar" and a suit jacket rather than overalls or a *bleu de travail*. Fonctionnaires were also pioneers among the lower paid in restricting family size. Before World War I, when many blue-collar workers continued to have four or five children, fonctionnaires, anxious to provide the best housing and education for their children, were restricting themselves to one or two. Now the spread of mass consumption and mass culture have lessened these differences. Fonctionnaires and blue-collar workers go to the same schools, wear the same clothing, see the same movies, listen to the same songs, and have the same number of children. There are still cultural differences, and they should be analyzed, but the gap is smaller than it was.

The feminization of state employment, the impact of campaigns for equal pay and for advancement, and the impact on family life need further study. In France the postal and educational services began to feminize in the nineteenth century, but now every ministry office is filled with women. Even the universities have succumbed. And in the summer of 1988, the largest postal federation (CGT) for the first time elected a woman as its chief officer. At first, there was some antagonism between male and female employees—men feared the loss of jobs and the lowering of wages. In actuality, women were usually moved into newly created positions, that is, jobs men never held. For example, women became the telephone operators and the postal savings clerks rather than the letter carriers. But the antagonism, that Proudhonist view that women belong "in the home," was never as strong as among blue-collar workers. Teachers were the first to achieve equal pay for men and women, and other services followed. The examination system permitted women to enter jobs that were closed to them in the private sector. Difficulties, of course, remain. Women still generally hold lower-level positions. But the feminization of state service was a boon to both men and women. It opened up professions to women when little was available in the private sector, but it also accustomed men to working with women as equals. Feminist sympathies and organization were strong among women fonctionnaires, and men were exposed to the campaigns for female equality in the workplace. I would postulate that the experiences of state service encouraged better relationships between the sexes and made male fonctionnaires more sympathetic to women's rights and feminism. I would also postulate that since fonctionnaires usually married fonctionnaires and both continued to work, state workers were and are more likely to share family responsibilities. We need more work on the feminized work force and its impact on family life.

Study of the relationship of state workers to the employer-state would include an examination of how the state treats its employees in such matters as wages and decision sharing. Most studies of the state and its apparatus fail to include an analysis of the state as an employer of millions of workers, most of whom are now highly organized. Fiscal policy, political ideology, and political alignments both influence and are influenced by the vast army of state workers, and this must be part of any analysis of state power.

Finally, there is the question of the influence of political events and of the political activity of state workers. Too often studies of state bureaucracies have focused on internal organization, on the study of hierarchical decision making, or on the nature of the workplace. It is clear from this study of France that the consciousness and activity of state workers is influenced by more than the structure of the workplace. National and international events—deflation, military spending, electoral politics, blue-collar activity, the policies of the state they work for—all influence the behavior of state workers. Moreover, as has been indicated in this study, because of their direct involvement in government activity, civil service workers are frequently very politically active. There must be an examination of how fonctionnaires' political activity is determined and how this affects the policies of the state. Because of their position as state employees, as the conveyers of state services and policies, organized fonctionnaires frequently went beyond the bread-and-butter issues of blue-collar unionism and became involved in issues affecting state policy. The efficiency of state service and the defense and expansion of nationalization, particularly after World War I, were crucial issues for fonctionnaire unions. Although their primary concern was the maintenance of their jobs and improved working conditions for state employees, the fonctionnaires' defense of state services also helped to expand egalitarianism in state employment and in French society as a whole, and, most critically, their campaigns greatly influenced national policy. The workers of the PTT fought to prevent the privatization of the telephone service and urged the nationalization of other telecommunications such as radio. Teachers were concerned with the development of a secular republican curriculum and with the expansion of educational opportunity for children of all classes. And all fonctionnaire syndicats, throughout the entire history of the Third Republic, continued to demand the egalitarianism and social justice envisioned in the promise of the social republic.

Bibliographical Essay

There is a great deal of satisfaction and excitement in doing research in a relatively untouched field, but an obvious difficulty in such a venture is the scarcity of secondary literature. How reassuring it is to have some other work for reference and comparison, even if those other efforts serve only as a foil for argument. Though sociologists have studied and continue to study modern-day fonctionnaires and other white-collar workers in great detail, they give only the merest hint that these workers have a historical past. Michel Crozier speaks briefly of the history of fonctionnaire syndicats in *The World of the Office Worker* (Chicago, 1971) and has contributed an essay to Adolph Sturmthal (ed.), *White Collar Trade Unions* (Urbana, 1966), but until recently only one of the sociological studies that carefully weighed historical factors was the analysis of white-collar class consciousness among English office workers by David Lockwood, *The Blackcoated Worker* (London, 1966). Alan Clinton's impressive history of British postal worker unionism, *Post Office Workers: A Trade Union and Social History* (London, 1984), includes much useful information on unions (and the development of public communications) and is the most thorough study of public employee unionism to date but does not have much political analysis beyond the unions and their relationship with parliamentary parties. Happily, a book by Jürgen Kocka, *White Collar Workers in America, 1890–1940* (London, 1980), offers much valuable political and historical analysis, though it does not include state workers.

I am happy to report that a carefully researched history of fonctionnaire unionism has finally appeared in France, Jeanne Siwek-Pouydesseau, *Le Syndicalisme des fonctionnaires* (2 vols.; Paris and Lille, 1989). It was published after this book was in press. In general, historians of French labor have largely ignored the fonctionnaire organizations and activities in their histories. Edouard Dolléans in his very thorough *Histoire du mouvement ouvrier* (3 vols., Paris, 1968) describes the 1909 postal strikes, but the important connections to the blue-collar movement receive only cursory treatment. The important role played by the fonctionnaire syndicats in the last decade of the Third Republic has been recognized by several historians. Georges Lefranc, an interwar CGT activist, has discussed the role of the fonctionnaires in the CGT in his *Le Mouvement syndical sous la troisième république* (Paris, 1967), and Antoine Prost's superb analysis, *La CGT à l'époque du front populaire, 1934–36* (Paris, 1964), includes an excellent discussion of the growth and influence of fonctionnaire syndicats during this period. One of the first scholars to recognize the significance of the fonctionnaire syndicats in the Popular Front era was a political scientist, Henry Ehrmann. It was his study, *French Labor from the Popular Front to the Liberation* (New York, 1947), that first kindled my interest in fonctionnaire unionism.

Both the PTT workers and the instituteurs have benefited from the publication of histories of their organizations. Max Ferré, *Histoire du mouvement syndicaliste révolutionnaire chez les instituteurs* (Paris, 1955), and François Bernard, Louis Bouët, Maurice Dommanget, and Gilbert Serret, *Le Syndicalisme dans l'enseignement* (Avignon, 1953), trace the history of teacher unionism; the latter book was written by activists in the revolutionary faction. Other union leaders who have written histories of their respective organizations are René Bidouze of the Fédération des Fonctionnaires, *Les Fonctionnaires, sujets ou citoyens?* (Paris, 1979), and Georges Frischmann, *Histoire de la fédération CGT des PTT* (Paris, 1967). Both of these books are based almost directly on their unions' respective newspaper files and are useful as such. Another interwar leader of the Fédération des Fonctionnaires, Charles Laurent, published a brief history, *Le Syndicalisme des fonctionnaires* (Paris, n.d. [1938]), which, though interesting, is little more than a summary. Paul Gerbod continues to study higher education unionism, and his work is very useful. I used "Associations et syndicalismes universitaires de 1828 à 1928," *Mouvement Social*, 55 (April–June, 1966). For those interested in cheminots, there are Joseph Jacquet (ed.), *Les Cheminots dans l'histoire sociale de la France* (Paris, 1967), and Guy Chaumeil, *Histoire des cheminots et leurs syndicats* (Paris, 1948).

The burgeoning interest in women's history has led to a number of excellent dissertations on fonctionnaire unionism among women: Anne-Marie Sohn, "Féminisme et syndicalisme, les institutrices de la fédération unitaire de l'enseignement de 1919 à 1935" (Thèse en doctorat de troisième cycle, Paris X, Nanterre, 1973); Persis Charles Hunt, "Revolutionary Syndicalism and Feminism Among Teachers in France" (Ph.D. dissertation, Tufts University, 1975); and Susan Dimlich Bachrach, "The Feminization of the French Postal Service, 1750–1914" (Ph.D. dissertation, University of Wisconsin, 1981). Bachrach's dissertation was published by the New York Institute for Research in History as "Dames Employees: The Feminization of Postal Work in Nineteenth Century France," *Women and History*, No. 8 (Winter, 1983). Scholars may look forward to more work on women fonctionnaires. Another excellent thesis concentrates on the 1909 postal strikes, Danielle Tartakowsky, "La Grève des postiers de 1909" (Master's thesis, University of Paris, 1969).

Although I have used the above studies extensively, most of my data necessarily had to come from archival sources. Another major difficulty faced by all students of pre–World War I labor history is that syndicats did not always keep minutes of meetings, and letters and papers of labor militants are not easy to find. Except for those who had a sense of historical importance (and there were some), revolutionary syndicalists did not expect to donate their papers to the Archives Nationales. My efforts to find such material at various union headquarters were further complicated when I was told that to prevent information about the identity and activity of militant syndicalists from falling into the hands of the Nazis, archival files had been systematically (and wisely) destroyed in 1940. The lack of these usual sources did not prevent me from finding a good deal of material elsewhere. Still, one cannot help but wish that those minutes and letters were still available; the finding of one such forgotten volume on the top shelf of a cabinet at the syndicat of the Contributions Indirectes (finance workers)—minutes of pre-1914 executive committee meetings—only confirmed the value of such sources.

The most useful source of information on fonctionnaire organizations is the F7 series of the Ministry of Interior, the series called Police Générale, housed in the Archives Nationales. Despite the tendency of the normal citizen to be somewhat outraged by the extent of police surveillance of union activity, the historian cannot but be grateful for the enormous body of material in this collection. The boxes I used most heavily are cited in the footnotes, but I would like to summarize some of the holdings so that other scholars may learn what is available. General fonctionnaire activity from 1901 to 1936 is covered by boxes F7 13724 to 13738. Several boxes cover the provinces (13730 to 13733), rather cursorily but enough to give the researcher a good idea of what was happening outside of Paris without having to journey to all the provincial archives. Naturally, anyone contemplating a deeper analysis of provincial activity would be wise to use the provincial sources. Instituteurs (1917 to 1936) are covered by boxes 13743 to 13749, and the PTT information can be found under the numbers 13802 to 13811. The 1909 strike is covered separately, in boxes 12712, 12792, and 12918. Information about douaniers (1906 to 1930) is in boxes 13712 and 13713. Some information about police organization can be found in 13043, but it appears to be the sparsest file of the lot. Various fonctionnaire demonstrations of 1932–1933 are in 13318, and detailed information about the fonctionnaires and their struggle against the décrets-lois are in 13953 and 13954. There also exist some data on municipal workers, communal workers, and blue-collar employees, especially arsenal workers. And, of course, there is a wealth of material on the CGT, strikes of blue-collar workers, and the various political parties, especially those of the extreme Left or Right. (For the pre–World War II Ministry of Interior, that included the Socialist party.) A word of caution: although there is a certain amount of flexibility, depending on current ministerial policy, scholars may have to get permission from the Ministry of the Interior to use this series. Material dating from the last fifty years is not yet officially open to the public.

The thoroughness of the French police is legendary. All general meetings, many committee meetings, and all demonstrations were covered most carefully by the Ministry of the Interior. All the important speeches and many of the minor ones are summarized, with frequent long quotations. Motions are duly quoted as are the major sessions of all the annual congresses. In addition, every once in a while, a summary of the general situation and its history was written so that busy members of the administration could see what was going on without plowing through hundreds of papers. These reports often reflect the subjective analysis of individuals, but they do help the scholar understand just what information was reaching the makers of policy. There are letters and orders from the minister to the prefects and information on provincial activities sent by the prefects to Paris. These latter reports are generally less useful to the scholar because it appears that many prefects, wanting very much to convince their superiors that they were successful in keeping things running smoothly, often wrote that there was no syndicalist activity in the provinces, when, in fact, there was.

Are the reports of the Ministry of Interior accurate? In general, I would say they are. If one compares the information gathered from the F7 series with descriptions of the same events appearing in articles, books, or syndicat reports, there appears to be little discrepancy. Most of the daily newspapers carried news of the meetings or demonstrations covered by the police (many of these clippings are in the Archives Nationales), and again there is an amazing similarity between police and newspaper reports. The extensive coverage of the 1909 strikes by both the police and the press offers a good opportunity to compare reports, and once again, the police seem to be accurate. One can be sure that many opinions or even incorrect information made their way into the police reports, and one must be wary, but I would expect that the government was most anxious to know what was really going on. This information, after all, was not meant for the general public.

Less complete but still valuable as a complement to the F7 series in the Archives Nationales are the archives of the Préfecture de la Police of Paris, now housed at the police headquarters in the fifth arrondissement. Since the Paris police were mainly interested in keeping order rather than surveillance, the material available, mostly in series BA, covers mainly strikes, demonstrations, and the meetings leading up to these events. The police interest in preventing possible trouble, however, sometimes makes these reports less accurate than those of the Ministry of the Interior. The police were anxious to find hints of impending demonstrations or other worker unrest, and their reports in this series often overemphasize the revolutionary aspect of speeches or activity. Occasionally, the report is slanted in the other direction, ignoring trouble, emphasizing the ability of the police to maintain order. Still, there is much useful material here, including the identification papers of all those arrested and detailed descriptions of the demonstrations of 1926 (box 1646) and 1933, 1934, 1935, and 1936. For the 1930s, the most useful boxes are BA 1648, 1638 and provisoire 305 and 306, but there is also material on the early PTT, the 1906 and 1909 PTT strikes (boxes 1390–1392), and reports of the final days of the syndicalist organizations and their dissolution under Vichy (provisoire 514 and 1687).

Other useful archival material can be found at the Institut Français d'Histoire Sociale, where in addition to books and newspapers of all the left-wing organizations, one can find the papers of such figures as Pierre Monatte, Maurice Dommanget, Gabrielle and Louis Bouët, and Hélène Brion (series 14AS). The Bibliothèque Marguerite Durand has the papers and printed matter of feminists and feminist organizations, including syndicat activists such as Marie Guillot, Marthe Pichorel, and Hélène Brion. The library of the Centre de Recherches d'Histoire des Mouvements Sociaux et du Syndicalisme has some books and newspapers as well as many dissertations on syndicalism. I was able to use the Quilici Papers there. Finally, there is the library of the Musée Social, which has few personal papers but many newspapers, journals, and hard-to-find books. It was there that I found a rare 1926 pamphlet of the briefly independent women's syndicat of the PTT, *Le Syndicat professionel féminin des PTT*. All of these places have extremely helpful staffs and pleasant surroundings—a far cry from the bedlam of the Bibliothèque Nationale.

Newspapers are, of course, a gold mine of information. Most of the daily press, particularly the left-of-center newspapers, the prewar *La Petite République, L'Humanité,* and for the 1920s, *Le Peuple* and *L'Ere Nouvelle,* covered meetings and demonstrations as well as printing articles about fonctionnaires' demands and problems. Most useful are the newspapers of the syndicats themselves—the *Bataille Syndicaliste* of the CGT (starting in 1911) and the papers of the fonctionnaire syndicats, *La Tribune des Fonctionnaires* (starting in 1913) and prewar 1914 *Bulletins* of the PTT and the Contributions Indirectes. The PTT archives also yielded *Le Cri Postal* and the postwar *Bataille des PTT* as well as shorter-lived papers such as *La Pile* of the sous-agents. For the activity of the police union, I used *La Voix des Police,* housed at the Fédération Autonome des Syndicats de Police. Most useful is the newspaper-cum-periodical of the revolutionary teachers' syndicat, *L'Ecole Emancipée,* a gold mine of information not only for union activity but for other political developments as well, especially those relating to education and l'école laïque. For those who do not wish to go through the entire run of newspapers (available on microfilm), there is now a summary volume available, Thierry Flamant, *L'Ecole Emancipée* (Les Monédières, Trei-gnac, 1982). One can also find material about fonctionnaires in *La Vie Ouvrière* and *La Vie Syndicale*.

One periodical of the pre-1914 era is also a superb source of articles about syndicalism, fonctionnaires, and general left-wing politics. Hubert Lagardelle's *Le Mouvement Socialiste* published dozens of articles by such people as Gabriel Beaubois, "Les Employés de l'etat et le socialisme ouvrier" (April 1, 1905), "L'Etat, les partis et le syndicalisme" (August 15–September 15, 1907), and Victor Monbruneau, "La Grève des postes et télégraphes" (May–June, 1906), as well as the numerous articles on teacher unionism by M. T. Laurin, among them "Les Idées socialistes des instituteurs et les amicales" (March, 1905) and "Le Syndicalisme et les instituteurs" (April, 1907). *Le Socialisme* also published numerous articles on fonctionnaire syndicalism. For a more middle-of-the-road view, one should see *Revue de Paris,* which published articles by Maxime Leroy, "L'Organisation ouvrière" (March, 1905), and Louis Barthou, "Les Syndicats des instituteurs" (March, 1906).

The debate over the droit syndical in the decade before World War I led to rash of publishing in the field of fonctionnaires' rights and theories of state authority by legal theorists, politicians, hauts fonctionnaires, and professors. Some were very informative—Jules Jeanneney, *Associations et syndicats des fonctionnaires* (Paris, 1908), Maxime Leroy, *Syndicats et services publics* (Paris, 1909), Leroy, *Les Transformations de la puissance publique* (Paris, 1907), Georges Cahen, *Les Fonctionnaires* (Paris, 1911), and Paul Louis, *Le Syndicalisme contre l'état* (Paris, 1910), for example. The rest deal primarily with theories and analyses which are mainly academic or judicial, but reading them does deepen one's understanding of the debate. See, for example, Pierre Harmignie, *L'Etat et ses agents: Etude sur le syndicalisme administratif* (Louvin, 1911), Alexandre Lefas, *L'Etat et les fonctionnaires* (Paris, 1913), and Henri Chardon, *Le Pouvoir administratif* (Paris, 1912). There are also pamphlets on the fonctionnaires' conflict with the state published during this period, and three were especially useful: M. T. Laurin, *Les Instituteurs et le syndicalisme* (Paris, 1908), Karl Oegel (pseud. for Le Gléo, syndicalist fonctionnaire), *Les Agents de la poste et le syndicalisme* (Paris, 1907), and Gabriel Beaubois, *La Crise postale et les monopoles d'état* (Paris, 1909). The most informative work published in the pre-1914 period was issued by the Musée Social in 1912,

Le Droit d'association des fonctionnaires, rapports et documents. A most careful analysis, it essentially tells the early history of fonctionnaire organizations and analyzes the problems they present for the state.

There are several secondary studies of fonctionnaires' rights and duties, among them Robert Catherine, *Le Fonctionnaire français* (Paris, 1961), Charles Fourrier, *La Liberté d'opinion des fonctionnaires* (Paris, 1967), Pierre Dietsch, *De la Légalité des syndicats des fonctionnaires* (Paris, 1934), and numerous books by Marcel Piquemal, among which *Le Droit syndical en France* (Paris, 1962) and *Le Fonctionnaire: Devoirs et obligations* (Paris, 1973) are just two titles. The fourth section of the Ecole Pratique des Hautes Etudes is publishing a series on the history of government administration; see *Histoire de l'administration française depuis 1800* (Geneva, 1975).

Although there are few books on fonctionnaire syndicalism, there are a host of publications on general Third Republic and working-class history which I used to deepen my understanding of the political milieu in which fonctionnaire syndicalism developed. To learn what happened in the legislature and executive branches of government—though with a conservative bias—the two old standbys are the multivolume histories of the Third Republic by Edouard Bonnefous (*Histoire politique de la Troisième République*) and Jacques Chastenet (*Histoire de la Troisième République*). Both series were published in the 1950s and 1960s. Otherwise I would recommend the more sophisticated and scholarly analysis by Madeleine Rebérioux, *La République radicale? 1899–1914* (Paris, 1975). Three excellent books on social reform are Sanford Elwitt, *The Third Republic Defended* (Baton Rouge, 1985), Henri Hatzfeld, *Du Paupérisme à la securité sociale, 1850–1914* (Paris, 1971), and Judith Stone, *The Search for Social Peace: Reform Legislation in France, 1890–1914* (Albany, 1985). Other books that cover important political developments and positions are Peter J. Larmour, *The French Radical Party in the Thirties* (Stanford, 1964); Robert Wohl, *French Communism in the Making, 1914–1924* (Stanford, 1966); Herman Lebovics, *The Alliance of Iron and Wheat in the Third French Republic, 1860–1914* (Baton Rouge, 1988); D. Blum, R. Bourderon, J. Burles, J. Charles, J. Gacon, R. Lagache, M. Margairaz, R. Martelli, J. P. Scot, and S. Wolikow, *Histoire du réformisme en France depuis 1920* (2 vols.; Paris, 1976); Joel Colton, *Léon Blum* (New York, 1966);

Daniel R. Bower, *The New Jacobins: The French Communist Party and the Popular Front* (New York, 1966); Nathaniel Green, *Crisis and Decline: The French Socialist Party in the Popular Front Era* (Ithaca, 1969); and even though I do not agree with his conclusions, the very enjoyable Eugen Weber, *Peasants into Frenchmen: The Modernization of Rural France, 1870–1914* (Stanford, 1976).

For the general history of French labor, I relied most heavily on Prost, Dolléans, Lefranc, and a study by Roger Picard, *Le Mouvement syndical durant la guerre* (Paris, 1927). It is always good to read Michelle Perrot, *Les Ouvriers en grève: France, 1871–1890* (2 vols.; Paris, 1973). There is, however, no outstanding overall history of revolutionary syndicalism. My favorite in English remains Val Lorwin, *The French Labor Movement* (Cambridge, Mass., 1954). One can get a good introduction from Henri Dubief, *Le Syndicalisme révolutionnaire* (Paris, 1969), but this book is meant more for the layperson than for the scholar, and there is always Peter Stearns, *Revolutionary Syndicalism and French Labor* (New Brunswick, 1971). Jean Maitron and Colette Chambelland have culled Pierre Monatte's papers for *Syndicalisme révolutionnaire et le mouvement ouvrier français* (Paris, 1967), and Jean Bron's *Histoire du mouvement ouvrier français* (2 vols.; Paris, 1968–70) outlines a procommunist but informative history. Finally, on the schism, there is the groundbreaking work of Annie Kriegel, *La Croissance de la CGT, 1918–1920* (Paris, 1966). I read Jean-Louis Robert, *La Scission syndicale de 1921* (Paris, 1980), but I got lost in the statistics. More useful to the general reader is the synopsis of this work, Jean-Louis Robert and Michel Chavance, "L'Evolution de la syndicalisation en France de 1914 à 1921," *Annales: Économies Sociétés Civilisations*, XXIX (September–October, 1974).

Women syndicalists get excellent treatment from Madeleine Guilbert, *Les Femmes dans l'organisation syndicale avant 1914* (Paris, 1966), and Marie-Hélène Zylberberg-Hocquard, *Féminisme et syndicalisme en France* (Paris, 1978). Jeanne Bouvier wrote *Histoire des dames employées dans les postes, télégraphes et téléphones de 1714 à 1929* (Paris, 1930), but it is interesting more as a piece written by a female syndicalist than as history. Three more generally political books on women are also very informative. I highly recommend Steven C. Hause with Anne R. Kenney, *Women's Suffrage and Social Politics in the French Third Republic* (Princeton,

1984), James McMillan, *Housewife or Harlot: The Place of Women in French Society, 1870–1940* (New York, 1981), and Charles Sowerwine, *Les Femmes et le socialisme* (Paris, 1978).

An excellent general analysis of modern French economic history is Richard F. Kuisel, *Capitalism and the State in Modern France* (Cambridge, Eng., 1981), and the classic book for the interwar years is the four-volume study by Albert Sauvy, *Histoire économique de la France entre les deux guerres* (Paris, 1965–75). There are also numerous excellent articles in the collection *Mouvements ouvriers et dépression économique de 1929 à 1939* (Assen, 1966). A good summary of the depression years can be found in Julian Jackson, *The Politics of Depression in France* (Cambridge, Eng., 1985). Fonctionnaire salaries are treated in François Perroux, *Les Traitements des fonctionnaires* (Paris, 1933), and by Alfred Sauvy and Pierre Depoid, *Salaires et pouvoirs d'achats des ouvriers et des fonctionnaires entre les deux guerres* (Paris, 1940). For two groundbreaking books on the modern state and workers (including state workers), read Harry Braverman, *Labor and Monopoly Capital* (New York, 1974), and James O'Connor, *The Fiscal Crisis of the State* (New York, 1973).

Two excellent books on education are Antoine Prost, *Histoire de l'enseignement en France, 1800–1967* (Paris, 1968), and John E. Talbott, *The Politics of Educational Reform, 1918–1940* (Princeton, 1969). The antiwar activities of blue-collar syndicalists and teachers can be found in Huguette Bouchardeau, *Hélène Brion, la voie féministe* (Paris, 1978), in Jean-Jacques Becker, *Le Carnet B* (Paris, 1973), and in sections of Becker's *The Great War and the French People* (New York, 1986). Judith Wishnia, "Feminism and Pacifism: The French Connection," in Ruth Roach Pierson (ed.), *Women and Peace* (London, 1987), explores the connections between syndicalism, pacifism, and feminism in World War I.

Historians of French labor should always make use of the excellent periodical *Le Mouvement Social*. I have used it extensively, especially for articles such as Marie-France Rogliano, "L'Anticommunisme dans la CGT: Syndicats," and Guy Bourdé, "La Grève du 30 novembre 1938," both of which are in the same issue: 55 (April–June, 1966).

Finally, when using memoirs, personal reminiscences, and oral history, one must be careful to understand the particular political ax each writer has to grind, but if that is kept in mind, memoirs are incredibly valuable. I used those of André Delmas, *A Gauche de la barricade* (Paris,

1950) and *Mémoires d'un instituteur syndicaliste* (Paris, 1979), as well as René Belin, *Du Secrétariat de la CGT au gouvernement de Vichy* (Paris, 1978). Both were extremely anticommunist, and Belin was a minister of Vichy and tries to explain that sin away, but what they have to say is fascinating. From the extreme left wing of the revolutionary syndicalists, one can get a good flavor of the ardor of this group of teachers by reading Jean Cornec, *Josette et Jean Cornec, instituteurs (1886–1980): De la hutte à la lutte* (Paris, 1981), and Louis Bouët, *Trente ans de combat syndicaliste et pacifiste* (Blainville, 1969). One wishes there were more studies like Jacques Ozouf, *Nous les maîtres d'école* (Paris, 1967), with its numerous testimonies and the marvelous Danielle Delhomme, Nicole Gault, and Josiane Gonthier, *Les Premières institutrices laïques* (Paris, 1980), but until there is a substantial increase in this branch of history, it is important to do as much oral history as possible. I interviewed several fonctionnaire activists (some of the interviews are on tape in my possession) and found their reminiscences a most valuable aid to understanding syndicalist politics and fonctionnaire consciousness.

Index

Action Française, 114n, 116, 121, 140n, 182, 309
Addams, Jane, 194
Alain, 324, 360
Albert, François, 291
Allard, Maurice, 88
Allemane, Jean, 88, 152n
Alquier, Henriette, 292–93
Amalric, 78, 79
Amicales, 3, 19–21, 46–47, 57, 63, 66, 89, 98, 100, 146, 147, 151
Anti-Semitism, 140n, 338, 360, 362
Antiwar movement, 138, 148, 174–78, 183–86, 192–97, 250, 324, 346–51, 359–60
Association Amicale de la Magistrature, 62
Association Amicale des Cours et Tribunaux, 62
Association Amicale des PTT, 19
Association des Abonnés, 70
Association des Dames Employées, 35
Association des Employés Supérieurs, 60
Association des Jeunesses Patriotes, 309
Association Générale des Agents des PTT: during early 1900s, 31–39, 41, 44, 66, 75, 78, 79; formation of, 31–39; and 1909 postal strikes, 107–11, 116, 117, 120, 125, 127, 132; during 1910s, 141, 145, 150, 153, 156, 159, 164, 170; transformation into syndicat, 170, 173, 198, 199, 205; during World War I, 181, 188, 191, 199, 200
Association Générale des Préposés, 62
Association Générale des Répetiteurs, 19
Association Générale des Sous-Agents, 31, 39, 132n, 143, 151n, 156, 169, 170

Association Professionnel de la Préfecture de Police, 142
Association Professionnelle du Personnel Civil des Administrations Centrales, 141
Associations, 3, 20, 23, 24, 28, 66, 89, 214. *See also* names of specific associations
Aulas, Jean, 295
Auriol, Vincent, 273, 301
Aurore, L', 64, 108
Austria, 287, 346

Bank employees, 265
Barbut, 115, 123, 127
Barthélemy, Henri, 104
Barthou, Louis, 41, 81, 83, 85, 108n, 112–13, 116, 119–23, 127–29, 157n, 160, 293
Bataille, La, 195, 198, 206
Bataille des PTT, La, 280, 281, 285, 327, 332
Bataille Syndicaliste, La, 26–27, 138, 149–50, 152, 157, 170, 171–72, 177, 178, 195
Bayet, Albert, 291
Baylot, Jean, 266, 283, 284
Belgium, 119, 359, 360
Belin, René, 284, 303, 318, 327, 327n, 340, 344, 345, 345n, 346, 348–51, 353n, 355, 359, 360, 361
Bérard, Léon, 233, 235, 245–46, 247
Berteaux, Maurice, 86, 121
Bertrand, Julia, 183, 184, 238
Bidegarray, Marcel, 236
Bigot, Marthe, 190, 193, 194, 233, 238, 250, 291
Binet, Henri, 88
Blanc, Alexandre, 83, 84
Blanc, Louis, 68